An Epidemic among My People

In the series

Religious Engagement in Democratic Politics,

edited by Paul A. Djupe

ALSO IN THIS SERIES:

Sabri Ciftci, *Islam, Justice, and Democracy*

Luis Felipe Mantilla, *How Political Parties Mobilize Religion: Lessons from Mexico and Turkey*

Jeremiah J. Castle, *Rock of Ages: Subcultural Religious Identity and Public Opinion among Young Evangelicals*

Brian R. Calfano and Nazita Lajevardi, ed., *Understanding Muslim Political Life in America: Contested Citizenship in the Twenty-First Century*

Jeanine Kraybill, *One Faith, Two Authorities: Tension between Female Religious and Male Clergy in the American Catholic Church*

Paul A. Djupe and Ryan L. Claassen, ed., *The Evangelical Crackup? The Future of the Evangelical-Republican Coalition*

An Epidemic among My People

RELIGION, POLITICS, AND COVID-19
IN THE UNITED STATES

Edited by Paul A. Djupe
and Amanda Friesen

With a foreword by Robert P. Jones

TEMPLE UNIVERSITY PRESS
Philadelphia • Rome • Tokyo

TEMPLE UNIVERSITY PRESS
Philadelphia, Pennsylvania 19122
tupress.temple.edu

Copyright © 2023 by Temple University—Of The Commonwealth System
of Higher Education
All rights reserved
Published 2023

Library of Congress Cataloging-in-Publication Data

Names: Djupe, Paul A., editor. | Friesen, Amanda, 1978– editor. | Jones, Robert P. (Robert Patrick), writer of foreword.
Title: An epidemic among my people : religion, politics, and COVID-19 in the United States / edited by Paul A. Djupe and Amanda Friesen ; with a foreword by Robert P. Jones.
Other titles: Religious engagement in democratic politics.
Description: Philadelphia : Temple University Press, 2023. | Series: Religious engagement in democratic politics | Includes bibliographical references and index. | Summary: "A social science examination of the role of religion in American society in the context of the COVID-19 pandemic, including its effects on attitudes and behaviors related to the state, experts, health policy, the First Amendment, cooperation, race, gender, generational differences, institutions, and legal issues"— Provided by publisher.
Identifiers: LCCN 2022029433 (print) | LCCN 2022029434 (ebook) | ISBN 9781439923399 (cloth) | ISBN 9781439923405 (paperback) | ISBN 9781439923412 (pdf)
Subjects: LCSH: COVID-19 Pandemic, 2020—Religious aspects—Christianity. | COVID-19 Pandemic, 2020—Political aspects—United States. | Christians—United States—Attitudes. | United States—Religion—21st century.
Classification: LCC BR526 .E65 2023 (print) | LCC BR526 (ebook) | DDC 362.1962/4144—dc23/eng/20221013
LC record available at https://lccn.loc.gov/2022029433
LC ebook record available at https://lccn.loc.gov/2022029434

Printed in the United States of America

9 8 7 6 5 4 3 2 1

To all the helpers.
You are the best of us
and may we all strive to be on the side of care.

Contents

Foreword, Robert P. Jones, PRRI — *xi*

Acknowledgments — *xiii*

Introduction | Paul A. Djupe and Amanda Friesen — *1*

PART I RELIGIOUS GROUPS CONFRONT THE PANDEMIC

1 Satan and a Virus Won't Stop Us: The Prosperity Gospel of Coronavirus Response | Paul A. Djupe and Ryan P. Burge — *13*

2 Are Religious Adherents More Likely to Buy Into COVID-19 Conspiracy Theories? | Diana Orcés, Ian Huff, and Natalie Jackson — *28*

3 Religion and Gun Purchasing amid a Pandemic, Civil Unrest, and an Election | Abigail Vegter and Donald Haider-Markel — *41*

4 Christian Nationalism and the COVID-19 Pandemic | Andrew L. Whitehead, Samuel L. Perry, and Joshua B. Grubbs — *54*

5 Syndemics during a Pandemic: Racial Inequity, Poverty, and COVID-19 | Dilara K. Üsküp and Ryon J. Cobb — *69*

6   Is the Effect of Religion "Raced" on Pandemic Attitudes
    and Behaviors? | Angel Saavedra Cisneros, Natasha Altema
    McNeely, and Paul A. Djupe   83

           PART II   ELITE ACTIONS AND MESSAGING

7   Precedent, Performance, and Polarization: The Christian
    Legal Movement and Religious Freedom Politics during the
    Coronavirus Pandemic | Andrew R. Lewis and Daniel Bennett   99

8   A Tale of Two Burdens: COVID-19 and the Question
    of Religious Free Exercise | Jenna Reinbold   111

9   High Stakes: Christian Right Politics in 2020
    | Angelia R. Wilson   122

10 Faith, Source Credibility, and Trust in Pandemic Information
    | Jianing Li, Amanda Friesen, and Michael W. Wagner   140

       PART III   PANDEMIC EFFECTS ON RELIGIOUS
                  GROUPS AND INDIVIDUALS

11 Women as Religious Leaders: The Gendered Politics
    of Shutting Down | Cammie Jo Bolin and Kelly Rolfes-Haase   159

12 Racialized Responses to COVID-19 | Shayla F. Olson   171

13 In God "Z" Trusts? Generation Z's Attitudes about Religion
    and COVID-19 | Melissa Deckman and Stella M. Rouse   184

14 Who's Allowed in Your Lifeboat? How Religious Identity
    Altered Life-Saving Priorities in Response to COVID-19
    | Matthew R. Miles and Justin A. Tucker   197

15 How the Early Stages of the COVID-19 Pandemic Affected
    Religious Practices in the United States | Kraig Beyerlein
    and Jason Klocek   210

16 Patterns of In-Person Worship Service Attendance during
    the COVID-19 Pandemic: The Importance of Political
    and Religious Context | Benjamin R. Knoll   226

    Conclusion | Amanda Friesen and Paul A. Djupe   239

Notes	*247*
References	*255*
Contributors	*295*
Index	*301*

Online appendix can be found at https://dataverse.harvard.edu /dataverse/epidemic_among_my_people

Foreword

ROBERT P. JONES

This unique volume brings together a diverse, interdisciplinary group of scholars to reflect on the religious, cultural, and political landscape at an inflection point in our nation's history. As the editors point out, the crisis of the COVID-19 pandemic has served as a rare, universally felt stimulus for Americans of all walks of life. At the time of this writing, the virus has claimed over 833,000 American lives—a number far higher than the estimated 675,000 from last century's 1918–1919 influenza pandemic and exceeding the 651,000 combined American battle deaths from every war conducted from the American Revolution to Desert Storm in 1991.[1]

Prior to the pandemic, the American religious landscape has experienced high levels of change and churn. Religious adherence has been on the decline, with approximately one-quarter of Americans—and about four in ten adults under the age of thirty—now claiming no religious affiliation, according to the Public Religion Research Institute's (PRRI's) 2020 Census of American Religion. Political partisanship has polarized denominations and churches, sorting the religious landscape along ethnoreligious lines; white Christian groups generally lean Republican, while nonwhite Christians, non-Christian religious groups, and the religiously unaffiliated each consistently leans Democrat.[2] In addition to the highly divisive 2020 presidential election accentuating these fault lines, the summer of 2020 also saw some of the largest and most widespread protests for racial justice in American history. Like an X-ray, the COVID-19 pandemic sent a current into this highly volatile cocktail, fluorescing to reveal the inner workings of religion and culture in America.

This volume is unprecedented in its breadth, gathering into a single volume the analysis and insights of more than thirty social scientists with expertise in political science, sociology, religious studies, public health, journalism and communications, psychology, and women's studies. Written in real time during the pandemic and grounded in public opinion survey data from early and late 2020, this volume promises to be the benchmark against which future analyses of religion, culture, and politics in this critical time in our nation's history are measured.

Acknowledgments

The COVID-19 pandemic hijacked our lives for the past two years and left many of us with serious burdens caring for littles, long illnesses, lost loved ones, and newfound voids to fill with much-reduced outlets for our anxieties and interests. Partly due to happenstance, it also left us awash in data. Ryan Burge, Andy Lewis, and Paul had dithered with a survey all winter and stumbled into a data collection two weeks into lockdowns as the first wave hit in March 2020. They wrote as much as they could but had way too much data for our bandwidth to handle. It was clear there were important stories to be told, and they needed help in telling them. Their data are the foundation for many of the contributions in this volume. Amanda and Paul have been fortunate to have recruited a group of excellent scholars from many social science disciplines to tell a rather complete story about religion, politics, and the pandemic. We thank our contributors for their contributions but also for being responsive and just good people to work with. Research was not easy for everyone to do during the pandemic, so we are extra appreciative that they used what energy they had to write for this project.

If you read the contributors list at the end of the volume, you'll see some common threads. One thick strand connecting many of us is PRRI, where Paul is a board member and has long been an affiliated scholar. PRRI is an outstanding organization for the insights it offers the nation about American religion and public life but should also be recognized for the diverse ways that they help academics amplify their voices through training, support, and data. PRRI has contributed to the volume in a direct way as well—Robby Jones was generous to offer to write a foreword and the research team contributed a chapter as well. We remain grateful for the connection and their generous support of the academic community.

Aaron Javsicas is a great editor to work with, and his continued belief in this project and the series means a lot to us. Temple remains the hardest working press out there and punches way above its weight.

The authors thank Harriet Finlayson for her research assistance and Nkemjika Kalu for the cover art design.

Paul would like to thank his coeditor, Amanda. It will be no surprise to any who know her that when she came on board, she took charge of a number of things, had sensible and thoughtful ideas for directions the collection should go, and remained reliable and timely—traits to be treasured. Doing books can make or break academic relationships, and Paul can say without hesitation that he'd work with her again and remains grateful for their productive and long academic friendship. Paul would also thank his pandemic people—Kate, Bear, and Gust—for weathering the storm with him, sending him off on rides, finding new adventures, and for remaining COVID-free. Amanda also thanks the Djupes for making Paul somewhat less cranky.

Amanda would like to thank Paul for having coffee with her in Seattle in 2011. Then an ABD on the job market, little did she know this new mentor would become a long-time coauthor, a coeditor of her first book, and one of her favorite people in the oft-strange world of academia. Though Paul could have just written or edited this book entirely on his own, his MO of always making room for others in the tent seems particularly inspiring for a book about collective action problems and our obligations to one another. Amanda also thanks Jen Guiliano for her friendship, writing accountability, and help in navigating her first book project. And finally, Amanda thanks her partner, Sean Murphy, for his unwavering humor and support spending every minute of this pandemic working from home under one roof, tolerating her loud Zoom voice, and up and moving to another country for her career. Paul also thanks Sean for telling Amanda when to chill out.

An Epidemic among My People

Introduction

Paul A. Djupe and Amanda Friesen

> If I shut up heaven that there be no rain, or if I command the locusts to devour the land, or if I send pestilence among my people; If my people, which are called by my name, shall humble themselves, and pray, and seek my face, and turn from their wicked ways; then will I hear from heaven, and will forgive their sin, and will heal their land.
>
> —II Chronicles 7:13–14 (King James Version)

A pandemic, unprecedented in nearly all of living human lifetimes, swept across continents starting in late 2019. By February 2021, total cases topped 100 million worldwide, with deaths numbering over 1.3 million. The United States' delayed shutdown and varied response across states and localities have resulted in hot spots, surges, uneven health care, and high mortality rates. The third wave of cases centered in deep-red Republican states dispelled early notions that this was a Democratic pandemic only spreading in coastal cities. The remarkable rise in Great Plains states in the fall and winter only then started to change their laissez-faire response.

COVID-19 (CO = corona, VI = virus, D = disease, 19 = 2019 the year the virus was identified) is a mild to severe respiratory illness that is caused by a coronavirus (severe acute respiratory syndrome coronavirus 2 of the genus *Betacoronavirus*), according to the U.S. Centers for Disease Control (CDC). The virus is primarily transmitted by contact with infectious material (including respiratory droplets—droplets of saliva or discharge from the nose) or contaminated objects or surfaces. The illness, at least those caused by the early variants, is characterized by fever, dry cough, fatigue, and shortness of breath and may progress to pneumonia, respiratory failure, and neurological symptoms that may be of short duration or turn into "long haul" cases. The novel coronavirus is clearly much more dangerous than the flu, both in how quickly it spreads and the severity of the illnesses that result. Moreover, it continues to mutate, with strains first identified throughout the world posing new threats and raising questions about the efficacy of vaccines created to work against prior strains.

Understanding, explaining, and responding to this (preventable?) catastrophe have pitted science against ideology, pushed tensions among people of faith, and drawn sharp lines between people and their governments struggling to respond in reasonable ways with lives on the line. Since it affected every aspect of our lives, there are so many ways to approach the pandemic and consider its implications. As social scientists interested in studying religion and society, we've been thinking and gathering data about the implications of the pandemic for our social institutions and individual behaviors as well as the reverse—how our social institutions shape the response to the pandemic.

We see the pandemic response as a massive collective action problem—individuals need to cooperate with others and their governments at a time when the individual costs appear high in terms of restricted behavior, and the benefits are distant and collective. Consider that the individual incidence of contracting COVID-19 is fairly low. So far in the pandemic, 45 million cases have been reported for the United States, which translates to 13.8 percent of the population as of late October 2021 via CDC data. But only slightly higher than normal population incidences overwhelm the health care system, and the fear of contagion deterred many from venturing into public.

Thinking about the pandemic in terms of collective action highlights core concerns in the social sciences regarding trust in others and in government, compliance with laws that are otherwise difficult to enforce, the availability and spread of accurate information, and the civil society forces that make or break effective governance. The questions almost ask themselves: Did religion promote public health measures and safe individual health behaviors? Was religion a force promoting cooperation with government or a divisive one? Did conspiracy theories flourish in religious circles? Did religion rise to the occasion and address problems facing their communities? That is to say, we believe that religion is a centrally important force in American society, which means we need to ask whether religion made the pandemic worse or helped keep it contained.

Considering some of the big stories about religion, society, and the pandemic will help give some shape to our inquiries. Ohio, like many states, locked down in mid-March leading to voluntary closures of houses of worship—Ohio remained one of the states that did not mandate closures of religious organizations. In hindsight, given what was to come, the decision to reopen in late May was a terrible one. Many churches reopened on Pentecost Sunday but in new ways. At one Catholic church in Columbus, "every parishioner wore a mask and 'Love your neighbor' signs encouraged physical distancing for safety" (King 2020). Other houses of worship limited gathering sizes through online registration; leaders excused members from attending if they felt sick and took temperatures of those wishing to attend. According to one pastor of a large congregation, "In my mind, the worst thing churches can do for the community is be a source of infection" (King 2020).

At the same time, a wide variety of incidents early in the pandemic made clear the risks generated by worshipping in person—a choir in Washington decided to meet for practice, which led to the infection of dozens and the deaths of two (Read 2020). This also applied to gatherings of church leaders. The historically Black Church of God in Christ (COGIC) denomination suffered heavy losses after church leaders gathered for conferences and continued in-person worship (Boorstein 2020)—dozens of clergy died of COVID-19. The Associated Press assembled a long tally of major religious figures who died during the pandemic (Crary 2020). Ultra-Orthodox Jews in New York continued to gather face-to-face and generated very high rates of transmission (Sales 2020).

During the pandemic, we learned that everything was going to be more complicated, with all new protocols designed to minimize the likelihood of virus transmission. Of course, this was true for houses of worship and perhaps in no ceremony was it more complicated than funerals, which could bring together diverse groups (e.g., coworkers, church members, family, neighbors) to grieve with little social distancing. To reduce the potential for the high number of funerals to become super-spreader events, guidelines from the Massachusetts Council of Churches encouraged moving funerals online, prioritizing ten people who should attend in person, avoiding hugs, and even delaying the ceremonies for the foreseeable future (Jenkins and Giangravé 2020).

The director of the National Institutes of Health and evangelical Christian Francis Collins went public at the end of 2020, looking to convince clergy to encourage the faithful to get vaccinated. His interview with the *Washington Post* revealed the stark realities in many American congregations. At a time when QAnon conspiracy beliefs had been raging like wildfire through conservative Christian circles (Djupe and Burge 2020), Collins pushed back: "The church, in this time of confusion, ought to be a beacon, a light on the hill, an entity that believes in truth. This is a great moment for the church to say, no matter how well intentioned someone's opinions may be, if they're not based upon the facts, the church should not endorse them" (Bailey 2020). Others agreed, arguing that religion would have to bridge the gap with science to defeat the pandemic, as it had with other epidemics (Marshall 2020).

Our Approach—Religion and Civil Society

The stories above highlight how much religion continues to be woven into American society. Of course, this is a descriptor of all nonsegregated societies—social ties are diverse and help spread ideas, information, norms, and even viruses throughout society rather quickly. As a result, the pandemic clearly could not be handled by disconnected individuals. It calls for a collective, institutional response to even know what the scope of the problem is, let alone how to treat it and deal with its lingering effects on every facet of society. In fact, it has required a level of cooperation that is perhaps unprecedented in world history, at least in some sectors. According to one investigation, "Never before, researchers say, have so many experts in so many countries focused simultaneously on a single topic and with such urgency. Nearly all other research has ground to a halt" (Apuzzo and Kirkpatrick 2020). Leaving pockets of unvaccinated people simply creates the conditions for the virus to mutate and spread yet again across any country with a porous border (see the emergence and spread of the omicron variant in late 2021). However, many nations have continued to take a nation-first approach, though world powers are engaging in varying levels of "vaccine diplomacy" (Safi and Pantovic 2021)—gaining influence by sharing surplus doses of vaccine.

From some perspectives, problems of cooperation in the interests of society are just the sorts that religion solves. As Justice Black wrote in *Engel v. Vitale* (1962), "The history of man is inseparable from the history of religion." That is, religion grew up alongside human civilization, in part because it systematizes responses to fundamental concerns that confront societies: "self-protection from humans and nature, disease avoidance, coalition formation, status seeking, mate acquisition and retention, and offspring care" (Johnson, Li, and Cohen 2015, 197; Kenrick et al. 2010). Since the pandemic has touched every part of our lives, it is easy to read that list with the pandemic in mind and recognize just how much has been disrupted but also how much may reflect on aspects of religious life and instruction.

In his travels around the United States in 1831, ostensibly to study American prisons, Alexis de Tocqueville (1835) observed all facets of American life, especially religion. While he believed in the value of free societies, he also anticipated great danger from the lack of restraints on individual actions. In the absence of governmental limitations, religion generated "habits of the heart" that "powerfully contributes to the maintenance of a democratic republic among the Americans" (Tocqueville 1835, ch. 17). Religion contributes answers to life's questions that are "clear, precise, intelligible, and lasting, to the mass of mankind," without which would lead people to "abandon all their actions to chance and would condemn them in some way to disorder and impotence" (Tocqueville 1840, ch. 5). This is no moderate, inclusive religion but a "dogmatic" one with "fixed ideas of God, of the soul, and of their general duties to their Creator and their fellow men" (1840, ch. 5). Put succinctly, religion circumscribes the limits of human and governmental action through its enduring influence on popular mores.

In modern terms, religion may help provide structure to society and rules helpful for human survival. For example, religious teachings and communities can denote what things are impure and disgusting and must be avoided (e.g., Graham and Haidt 2010; Djupe and Friesen 2018). Religions often have rules about food, clothing, and hygiene and cleansing rituals. But concerns about purity do not stop with pathogens and are often mapped onto traits of other people. That is, those outside the ingroup can be considered impure, even disgusting (Djupe et al. 2021), which can limit the radius of concern for others, increase blame of others for social problems, and decrease support for even equal citizenship for those outside the group (Bloom and Courtemanche 2015).

A particularly forthright example of this came from a woman interviewed by CNN (2020) as she came to worship at Solid Rock Church near Cincinnati, Ohio, in early April 2020—a time when upward of 90 percent of houses of worship had closed to in-person worship. She evinced no concern for the pandemic because she was "covered in Jesus's blood." And so were her fellow worshippers—they believed they were protected by the power of their piety, while others outside the group were clearly not.

The pervasiveness of the pandemic could not be better suited to stoking fears of threats from outside. And there was no shortage of elites doing just that. In 2020, there was a huge increase of prejudice and violence toward Asians in the United States, which can be linked to the anti-Asian, anti-Chinese rhetoric from former president Trump and others. They referred to the novel coronavirus as the "Chinese flu" and worse, claiming at times that the Chinese manufactured the virus as a weapon against the United States and the world (Singh, Davidson, and Borger 2020). But that's not all. A year later found Texas Governor Abbott blaming immigrants for the spread of COVID-19 in his state, not his orders to rescind public health measures (Higgins-Dunn 2021).

This is not to say that the threats to us all were not real. They were. And they hit particular communities harder than some. Some states have had worse waves of infections, hospitalizations, and fatalities. But poor and racial minority communities were beset by greater problems—both health and economic—than whites. Many things are potentially to blame for the health disparities, including discrimination, access to health care, preexisting health problems, occupations that increase exposure, and housing arrangements (e.g., CDC 2021). Until the research in this volume, we did not know in a systematic way what pandemic role religion had to play in racial minority communities, attuned to the particular blend of religious beliefs and the special organizational role that houses of worship have often occupied.

The pandemic presented religion with a paradox. From the discussion above, it is easy to see how religion may provide the beliefs, practices, and social connections that are crucial to helping people weather life's troubles and make difficult decisions. But how can religion continue to deliver these benefits when it is prevented from meeting? Put a bit differently, would religion continue to give structure to society without the same level of socialization pressures? Of course, religious groups did not stop meeting, but shifted online in a majority of cases. But as many of us found, meeting online isn't quite the same as meeting in person. That may mean that some people decreased their religiosity during the pandemic. This might be the thesis advanced by a "religious markets" approach, where religious organizations compete for members with variable benefit packages meant to meet consumer demand. If people are not engaging the rich, small-group infrastructure of most houses of worship and are only hearing the music through tinny computer speakers, then they may drift away. However, there are reasons to think that people would turn toward religion in a crisis, even if socially distanced in most cases.

Data and Our Research Designs

The coronavirus pandemic has imposed a set of conditions rarely available to study—where everyone is thinking about and reacting to the same thing (though obviously perceptions of it vary widely). And that thing—the coronavirus—is quite literally "novel." These conditions are important because they give us greater confidence in the statistical associations we find. The pandemic is not like abortion policy, where the same questions have been debated for fifty years. Conspiracy beliefs, such as that a lab in Wuhan, China, manufactured the virus, are brand new and therefore help us trace their causal pathways through the population. Moreover, state reactions to the pandemic have changed whether and how people worship, have incentivized some elites to mobilize resistance, and mostly have gained widespread support from religious (and nonreligious) Americans. The stark realities of the pandemic have exposed the fault lines between those willing to work with society and those who truly stand apart, self-sufficient in their belief systems.

One aspect of our collective investigations that helps enable comparison is that many are based on survey data gathered by Paul Djupe, Ryan Burge,

Andy Lewis, and colleagues in the last weeks of March and October 2020. Both surveys included responses of American adults acquired through Qualtrics Panels—with minimal statistical weights, the data are representative of the nation's demographics in age, gender, race, region, and education. They asked many of the same questions in the two surveys and attempted to include a very wide range of religious and political measures. Of course, the surveys are not conclusive efforts since they are both snapshots and do not follow individuals through time. But they are helpful given that March was really the beginning of U.S. federal and state efforts to confront the pandemic, and the third wave was in full swing in October. There are other data sets employed, not to mention different methodologies, which serve to provide more complete and diverse accounts of religion in pandemic society. We'd also like to point out that, throughout many chapters, authors point to further discussion and results made available in an online appendix.*

In This Volume

One of the values of this collection is the breadth and scope of how social scientists approach questions about religion and the COVID-19 pandemic. To keep the individual chapters in conversation with one another, we organized the chapters around themes. In the first part, we investigate the reaction of religious communities to pandemic public policies. Numerous churches, well covered in the media, defied state government public health orders, but how common was defiance?

In particular, Djupe and Burge in Chapter 1 argue that the prosperity gospel is a powerful force that maximizes perceptions of the pandemic threat, decreases social trust, and augments defiance of state closure orders. Diana Orcés, Ian Huff, and Natalie Jackson (Chapter 2) piggyback on Chapter 1 to examine the link between the prosperity gospel and conspiracy theories—prosperity-believing individuals are more likely than the nonreligious to believe that COVID-19 was created in a lab.[1] Both prosperity gospel views and magical thinking predict pandemic beliefs beyond partisanship and other group identities, highlighting the importance of analyzing orientations beyond typical religion and politics measures.

The perceived pandemic threat to personal health and safety and the increase in state-level restrictions could explain the major uptick in firearm sales, as Abigail Vegter and Donald Haider-Markel explore in Chapter 3. They find

---

* The online appendix is available here: https://dataverse.harvard.edu/dataverse/epidemic_among_my_people.

that evangelicals were more likely than all others to purchase firearms between March and August 2020, but they attribute these purchases to concerns over civil unrest in the wake of Black Lives Matter protests and the impending election.

If it feels difficult to disentangle the politics of the events of 2020, it may be because one worldview appears to underpin much of the politics on the Right. Andrew Whitehead, Samuel Perry, and Joshua Grubbs in Chapter 4 further unpack defiance to demonstrate that Christian nationalist beliefs are related to individual pandemic precautions, attitudes about how government should respond, and explanations for the spread of the virus.

Minority communities were hit the hardest by the pandemic for many reasons—access to health care, jobs that did not allow social distancing, and other reasons. Was religion one of them? We also have strong expectations that minority religious groups will be leaders of the community, begging a constant comparison to houses of worship and clergy in the Civil Rights movement. Multiple chapters focus on minority religious groups. Dilara Üsküp and Ryon Cobb (Chapter 5) focus on health, looking to see if houses of worship in minority communities were taking the threat to their congregants seriously. If so, then frequent attenders should show greater trust in clergy and medical professionals.

Then, Chapter 6 steps back to inquire about a broader concern. We often see upticks in religiosity during crises as religious institutions attempt to meet the needs of the congregation, though that would be complicated by distancing orders in the pandemic. Angel Saavedra Cisneros, Natasha Altema McNeely, and Paul Djupe follow this tack, wondering if clergy messaging was proportionate to the pandemic's impact as well as whether it affected pandemic behaviors, especially within the African American and Latino communities that were so hard hit by the pandemic. Surprisingly, they find few differences across racial groups.

Part II shifts gears to the courts and court of public opinion. In some cases, religious defiance went further as Christian conservative advocacy organizations rushed to defend it in court. None of them prevailed until the final Trump contribution to the court's composition (Amy Coney Barrett) took the bench, but the dynamics are valuable to examine. Andrew Lewis and Daniel Bennett in Chapter 7 take up the politics of challenging public health orders as religious freedom claims, describing the actions of the Christian legal movement and using original data to show that Republicans are far more supportive than Democrats in preserving the religious freedom of holding in-person services during the pandemic. Building on these questions of religious liberty, in Chapter 8, Jenna Reinbold explores whether COVID-19 restriction protocols were actual burdens or mere inconveniences to clergy and religious institutions. That is, because sincerity of belief is necessary for religious freedom claims, should we consider worship attendance essential for these believers? Similar to Lewis and Bennett's chapter, she highlights the court's use of a political narrative of burden.

Angelia Wilson in Chapter 9 draws on her vast collection of up-to-date email communication from Christian Right interest groups to describe how they reacted to 2020: the summer's George Floyd protests and COVID-19. Of course, they were framed as threats, a culmination of the many years of warning followers of the growing menace domestically and internationally posed by the Left. This is the job of any organized interest—to frame events in ways that will activate their base to maintain support and push for desired policy ends. Therefore, it is tremendously valuable to see the messaging that underpins the reactionary politics on the Right during the pandemic.

Of course, good conspiracy theories involve distrust of the media; in the case of the coronavirus, Republicans and other Far Right commentators peddled the notion that the media artificially inflated numbers to hurt Trump. In Chapter 10, Jianing Li, Amanda Friesen, and Michael Wagner show that this response was contextualized, with trust in Trump, news media, and the CDC varying by religious tradition and belief. There were consequences to this trust as evangelical Christians and those looking to former president Trump for pandemic information were more likely to underestimate the number of U.S. cases.

Part III reverses the causal arrow to examine how the pandemic (and pandemic politics) affected group and individual religious choices, behavior, and beliefs. The part starts with the effect on specific groups before opening up to track religious behavior across the pandemic.

For a variety of reasons, we would expect women clergy to respond differently to state public health orders—Cammie Jo Bolin and Kelly Rolfes-Haase use our late-March survey data in Chapter 11 to assess whether clergy responses are gendered. Indeed, in congregations where women leaders are present, individuals report more religious service cancellations and are more "likely to trust clergy to have their best health interests at heart," as compared to those in congregations without women leaders. Then, in Chapter 12, Shayla Olson explores how religious affiliation and race/ethnicity jointly affect religious behaviors like holding in-person services, attitudes about the pandemic itself, and how the pandemic has in turn affected religious faith.

Generation Z is the least religious generation yet in the modern United States and appears to think about the implications of religion differently than their grandparents. Melissa Deckman and Stella Rouse (Chapter 13) draw on data from a survey of just younger Americans to investigate how their religious attachments are linked to personal pandemic behaviors and how this compares across racial and ethnic groups within this cohort.

It is easy to see how the pandemic could further divide society with threats in the pandemic lingering everywhere in the air. Using a creative experimental design, Matthew Miles and Justin Tucker in Chapter 14 test what demographic groups their participants are more willing to "save." The results were surprisingly united but also predictably divided. Participants elected to save older Americans, regardless of religion, gender, or partisan leanings. Taking a closer look, however, reveals that participants with strong religious identities are more likely to save evangelical Protestants over Muslims.

With all of the discussions of religious liberty and reported rates of service cancellations, we close with two chapters that address the most obvious question that has not seen data analysis to this point—what actually happened to religious service attendance throughout the pandemic? Kraig Beyerlein and Jason Klocek (Chapter 15) focus on early in the pandemic to showcase the variety of effects of the pandemic on religious practice. And, as Benjamin Knoll shows in Chapter 16, though the majority of regular attenders were not present at in-person services after the COVID-19 shutdowns in March, those who continued to attend were younger, more likely to be encouraged to attend by their congregations, and believe in higher levels of perceived persecution by the Democratic Party.

We hope you learn as much as we did from these chapters. This one overwhelming, extended event, the pandemic, has touched every part of our lives and allows us to provide an unusually comprehensive portrait of religion in American public life. Religion promotes defiance and cooperation; it is weakened and strengthened; it is responsive and quiescent. Of course, there are forces that help explain how religion falls on either side of those coins, but you will need to read the chapters to discover them.

PART I

Religious Groups Confront the Pandemic

1

Satan and a Virus Won't Stop Us

The Prosperity Gospel of Coronavirus Response

PAUL A. DJUPE AND RYAN P. BURGE

> Satan and a virus will not stop us.
> —REV. TONY SPELL (qtd. in Seipel 2020)

At the time of writing, the coronavirus is sweeping the world with over 72 million cases and millions dead; the United States leads the world in both counts (more than 16 million cases and more than 300,000 dead).[1] In the face of the pandemic, some congregations are still meeting in person (or think they should be) with an apparent devil-may-care attitude. In this chapter, we ask what drives reactions to the coronavirus, with a focus on one rapidly growing religious belief system—the Prosperity Gospel. This belief system is particularly well tuned to trigger a strong reaction to the societal response to the spread of the coronavirus. With roots in the "power of positive thinking," Prosperity Gospelers believe that God controls access to earthly comforts and thus vest power in their beliefs and in the church to achieve earthly goals like health and wealth. As such, Prosperity Gospelers react negatively to collective action encouraged by secular authorities and express a desire for the instrumentality of their well-being—the church—to remain open, despite the likely consequences (Burke 2020).

An Overview of the Prosperity Gospel

This chapter is part of a broad set of work in the social sciences about religious belief (e.g., Bloom and Arikan 2013; Froese and Bader 2010; Jelen and Wilcox

---

Material referencing an appendix in this chapter can be found online available here: https://dataverse.harvard.edu/dataverse/epidemic_among_my_people.

1991).² Beliefs are understandings of how the world is and how it works—they are effectively perceived facts. This definition helps to categorize and distinguish religious beliefs, which include answers to questions about whether there is evil in the world, what behaviors are sinful, what is the nature of God, what happens after death, and what returns practitioners get for investing in worship. Beliefs pair well with values, which are commandments about how the world should be and how people should act. Together, beliefs and values in conversation constitute worldviews.

One of the most popular strains of Protestant theology in recent years is the Prosperity Gospel. This belief system rests on the assumption that those who are faithful to God and God's church will not just reap benefits in the afterlife but will gain health and wealth during this life as well. This is succinctly summarized in the title of Joel Osteen's best-selling book, *Your Best Life Now*, which sold over eight million copies in the decade after its release (Johnson 2014). Osteen, along with other such internationally known pastors as Kenneth Copeland, Creflo Dollar, and T. D. Jakes, reaches tens of millions of followers per week through television broadcasts and a social media presence with a message that is tinged with various levels of prosperity theology (Dougherty et al. 2019). In fact, there are some data that indicate that half of the largest churches in the United States (over 10,000 attendees) teach a theology that is rooted in the Prosperity Gospel (Bowler 2018).

Despite the apparently pervasive nature of Prosperity Gospel theology among American Christians, it has been dramatically understudied in the United States (though see, e.g., Harris 2010; McDaniel 2016). However, there has been a good amount of research in Africa, Asia, and Latin America that indicates that prosperity beliefs serve as a catalyst for entrepreneurial attitudes and social mobility (Marsh and Tonoyan 2009; Woodberry 2006) as well as political participation (McClendon and Riedl 2019). However, there are mixed findings about the link between prosperity beliefs and income across countries (Beck and Gundersen 2016; Koch 2009), with a strong negative cross-sectional relationship between prosperity beliefs, income, and education (Burge 2017; Schieman and Jung 2012).

However, the full implications of the Prosperity Gospel and how it orients individuals to the social world are not well understood. For instance, does the Prosperity Gospel act to comfort people or to elevate perceived threats? Do believers act individually as if the belief itself is sufficient, or do they react to threats to the collective set of believers?

Prosperity theology teaches that illness is a sign of sinful behavior (Bowler 2018) and that healing can be achieved through faith alone (Brouwer, Gifford, and Rose 1996). Thus, when confronted with the possibility of a global pandemic, such as COVID-19, a faithful believer should have nothing to fear. For instance, R. R. Reno, the editor of the influential Christian magazine *First Things*, argued that churches should defy government orders and continue gathering. He wrote, "When we worship, we join the Christian rebellion against the false lordship of the principalities and powers that claim to rule our lives, including sickness and death" (Reno 2020). While Reno is no prosperity theologian, this is one piece of the argument made when many churches remained open in the early weeks of the virus spread in the United States. For instance, Rev. Tony Spell of Life Tabernacle Church in Louisiana told a Baton Rouge newspaper, "When the paramedics can't get there, when the law enforcement can't get there, the Holy Ghost can get there and it will make a difference in someone's life" (Rocha 2020).

This sort of thinking has been characterized as bearing the hallmarks of individualism—that individual agency to believe or not is the critical choice to leading a successful life. In many ways, such individualism is at the heart of American evangelicalism (e.g., Guth et al. 1997, 59), where it is commonly thought that bringing the population to Jesus is the key to alleviating the world's various problems (Guth et al. 1997, 58) rather than building institutions and jump-starting collective action. One evangelical pastor argued, "Our problems are not drugs, divorce, abortion, greed, etc. These are but the symptoms of a much larger problem, that of alienation from God" (qtd. in Guth et al. 1997, 59).

However, a crucial aspect of prosperity theology is the belief that the church becomes the instrumentality of defense. The church enables followers to demonstrate their belief through giving and attendance, serving as a support network to overcome setbacks. Solid Rock Church in Ohio, one of the megachurches that gained considerable attention for remaining open at the beginning of the pandemic in March (Kaleem 2020), prominently displayed the passage from Hebrews 10:25 on their website, "Let us not give up the habit of meeting together, as some are doing. Instead, let us encourage one another all the more, since you see that the Day of the Lord is coming nearer." As, again, Rev. Spell argued, if a parishioner became sick, pastors serve as first responders: "If that is our command, they shall lay hands on the sick and they shall recover" (Rocha 2020). That is, it is not just the healing power of individual belief that matters but the physical connection to the church and its pastorate that will bring the blessings of belief (and a stunning reversal of the Protestant Reformation). On that basis, we would hypothesize that strong adherents to the Prosperity Gospel profess lower levels of concern about COVID-19.

However, where there is smoke, there is likely to be fire. One reason why prosperity preachers make claims about dominion over death is because of the profound fears that their followers have. The other reason is that such claims are a priming exercise that elevate those concerns—if you are told you have power over it, you understand it is to be feared—which serves to maintain reliance on the pastor's services. From this perspective, we hypothesize a greater sense of threat from COVID-19 among Prosperity Gospel believers as well as greater defiance against social-distancing / gathering-size orders.

A central thread to Prosperity Gospel belief systems is not just that belief can cure life's deficiencies but that unbelief can harm. Put another way, poverty and sickness are signs of sin, a lack of belief, and perhaps even the work of the devil. The latter is what Paula White was talking about when she called for all "Satanic pregnancies to miscarry right now" (Zaveri and Diaz 2020). Other Prosperity Gospel preachers make the link to the social dimensions of sin. For instance, Joel Osteen explicitly tells followers to avoid the sick and the poor: "You need to be careful about whom you surround yourself with, especially in difficult times. Misery loves company" (Osteen 2018). One implication is the belief that individuals are responsible for social problems, which has a natural affinity with American conservatism (McDaniel 2016).

It's hard not to see this as a direct attack on the fundamentals of collective action (see also Harris-Lacewell 2007). Others in similar circumstances are to be avoided—they are untrustworthy by dint of sharing your same circumstances and concerns. The solution to those problems is not working with others but increasing reliance on belief and the church. Such Prosperity Gospel solutions are vertical, individual, and antisocial rather than horizontal, organizational, and social. In particular, we hypothesize that Prosperity Gospelers are more distrustful of others. They seem to take seriously the admonition of St. James, who implored Christians "to keep oneself from being polluted by the world" (James 1:27 NIV).

The same logic can be applied on a societal scale, as well. If individual people who are sick and poor are not to be trusted because of their sin, then the widespread existence of poverty and health problems signifies an active, working presence of evil to promote so much sin. As such, we would expect that Prosperity Gospelers would be especially prone to conspiracy theories. We don't quite have the data to test that, except that early in the U.S. outbreak, right-wing commentators, including the president, were arguing that the hysteria over the coronavirus was politically motivated. We hypothesize that Prosperity Gospel followers would be more likely to believe that notion as an analog to the working presence of evil in the world—since good and bad things happen for a reason.

But this also suggests a potential causal problem—are attitudes and beliefs that we find linked to the Prosperity Gospel just a function of being a

Republican and being exposed to right-wing ideas? We grant it is possible that conservative commentators are driving these relationships, which is why we test interaction terms between party identification and Prosperity Gospel beliefs. That is, we hypothesize that prosperity beliefs will have less of an effect on Republicans, who are more frequently exposed to arguments consistent with the Prosperity Gospel. That means that prosperity beliefs should be linked to greater attitudinal shifts among Democrats and, to a lesser extent, independents, who are hearing messaging in church that differs from what Democratic elites are communicating.

Data and Measurement

We draw on data collected from March 23 to 27, 2020, which was well before the coronavirus spread peaked in the United States, as well as survey data from October, two weeks before the U.S. presidential election. In late March, many, but not all, states had issued "stay-at-home" orders. Some states, such as Michigan, had exempted religious organizations from gathering limits (often ten people), though they encouraged houses of worship to close voluntarily (as in Ohio), which most had done (RNS 2020). Only five states in the Great Plains remained holdouts with no statewide policy by mid-April. By October, the spread of the virus was in its third wave with cases soaring toward 150,000 new infections per day. North Dakota, ironically the hottest of hot spots in the nation, only imposed a mask mandate on November 14 to run through January.

In the March data, we found that only 12 percent of respondents reported their congregations to still be worshipping in person. Some high-profile congregations stayed open and, in some cases, defied orders to close—that was the case in Florida (Mazzei 2020) and Louisiana (Rocha 2020; see also Reuters 2020). This is to say that at the time of our spring data collection, there was still a national debate about whether houses of worship should close. By October, much of that had been resolved in favor of state power, though a recent Supreme Court decision pushed back against New York's orders (see chapter 7). However, most of the states reopened in the summer and had not locked down again in response to the rampaging pandemic. By the time of our October survey, two-thirds of respondents who attend worship services report that in-person worship had been canceled because of the virus. Thus, many had opened back up by the fall.

The roughly 3,100 respondents to our survey in March and 1,740 in October were supplied by Qualtrics Panels, filled according to quotas that matched current U.S. Census distributions on age, region, and gender.[3] The data are not generated by a probability sample but instead from a set of panelists whose responses were screened for speed (those who took the survey too quickly were kicked out of the sample) and accuracy (we included several attention check questions).

Social science has just begun to operationalize the Prosperity Gospel into survey questions in recent years. As such, there is no widely accepted battery that can be drawn upon. However, the questions that were employed in our survey closely mirror those used by Dougherty et al. (2019) and McDaniel (2016), as well as by McClendon and Riedl (2019) in their research situated in Africa.

We used a three-question battery refined across several survey efforts (α = 0.90 in March, α = 0.92 in October).[4] Shown in Figure 1.1, we see substantial agreement with these core Prosperity Gospel beliefs and little rejection of them. Near majorities believe that followers will be rewarded with health and wealth and will be "richly rewarded in this life." The least agreement is with the belief that God will give you the material things you want—"name it and

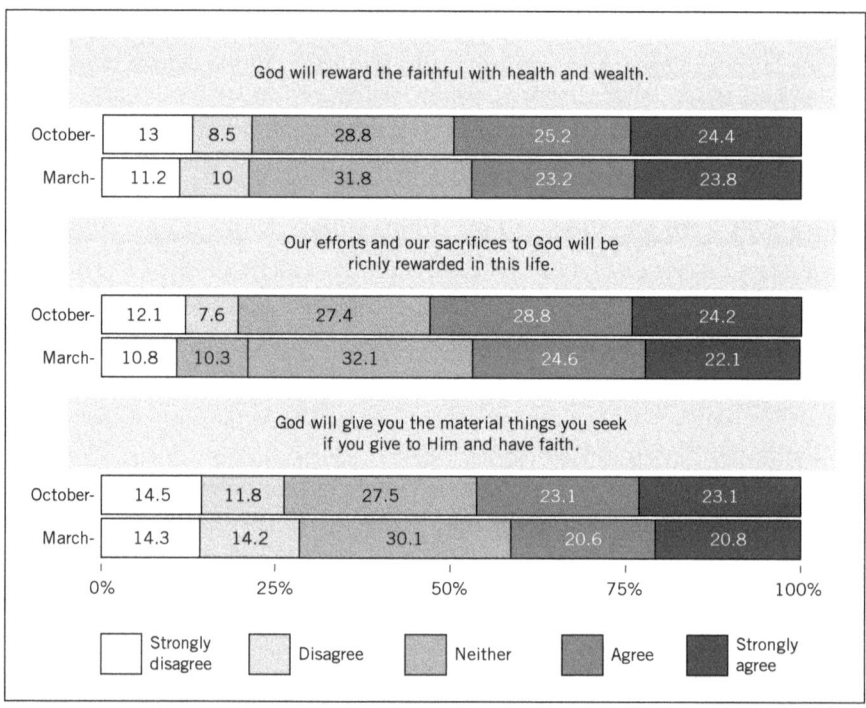

Figure 1.1 Distribution of Prosperity Gospel Beliefs (Source: March 2020 survey.)

claim it"—but the notion is still favored by 41 percent of the sample. Less than 30 percent of the sample rejects these beliefs. Simply put, the Prosperity Gospel is incredibly popular according to these data.

As Bowler (2018, 5) has argued, "The Prosperity Gospel cannot be conflated with fundamentalism, Pentecostalism, evangelicalism, the religious Right, the so-called black church, or any of the usual suspects (though it certainly overlaps with each)." While it would be easy to assume that the Prosperity Gospel has no place in mainline Protestantism, it is important to note that the gospel of wealth had its roots there (Bowler 2018, 31–32). Norman Vincent Peale, the author of *The Power of Positive Thinking*, was himself a pastor of a mainline congregation in the Reformed Church of America (George 2019). We likewise find that Prosperity Gospel beliefs are spread across American religious traditions in relatively high and not terribly distinctive concentrations. It is notable, though, that almost every group shows higher concentrations in October compared to March. The only religious group with demonstrably low values is the religious nones (see the appendix, Figure A1.1).

Moreover, the Prosperity Gospel is spread across American politics as well. As we show in appendix Figures A1.2 and A1.3, Republicans do have a stronger concentration of Prosperity Gospel views (hovering around 0.65 on a 0–1 scale), but Democrats are not far behind (at 0.59) and are indistinguishable from the sample mean. Only independents show less commitment to prosperity, which is partly a function of the high rate of religious nones among their ranks. Even when we control for religious tradition, though, independents still score lower on the Prosperity Gospel scale. The differences intensified by October as Republicans shifted markedly toward stronger prosperity beliefs, while Democrats split (some higher and some lower).

One key strategy of ours is to assess whether relationships with the Prosperity Gospel are simply masking partisan reactions by interacting partisanship (3-point scale; partisans include leaners) with the Prosperity Gospel scale. We do this for two reasons. First, partisanship appears to be the eight-hundred-pound gorilla in American politics, driving everything from economic beliefs (Enns et al. 2012) to religious behavior (e.g., Djupe et al. 2018; Hout and Fischer 2002; Margolis 2018). The default expectation is that reactions to the coronavirus will simply warp to fit the interests of the parties. Second, public officials and commentators, such as the president and Fox News, have been explicitly claiming that the coronavirus response is the Democrat's "new hoax" and the hysteria is a Democratic ploy to hurt Trump (e.g., Harvey 2020). This view has been widely repeated, including by a Virginia pastor who eventually succumbed to the virus (Palmer 2020).

Results

Our dependent variables are depicted in Figure 1.2. Though there is some variation, most respondents (86 percent) agreed that the coronavirus is a major threat. Even so, many (43 percent) believe that the hysteria over the pandemic is politically motivated. Given the widespread elite rhetoric making this point, especially early in the spread across the United States, it is no surprise to find it heavily tilted to the right.

Coronavirus protection measures clashed with First Amendment liberties, with some congregations remaining open because, in the words of one megachurch pastor in Louisiana, "The church is the last force resisting the Antichrist" (Reuters 2020). If evil lurks and people rely on the church as the instrument of their protection, we would expect Prosperity Gospelers to favor staying open and to urge defiance of government orders to close. Figure 1.2 shows that 28 percent agree that houses of worship should stay open; by October that number swelled to 45 percent. A random half of the March sample was given the additional words "even if more people die as a result." While support did drop overall as a result of this treatment, the difference was small and not signifi-

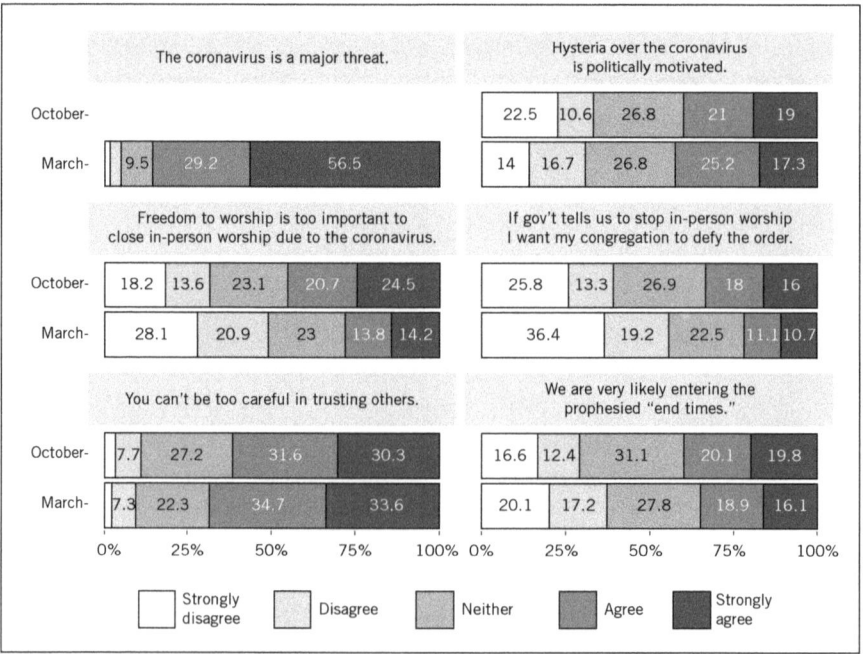

Figure 1.2 Distribution of Perceptions of the Coronavirus and Its Potential Response (Source: March and October 2020 surveys.)

cant—people were well aware of the consequences of houses of worship remaining open.

We went one step further and anticipated the current skirmishes, asking: "If the government tells us to stop gathering in person for worship, I would want my congregation to defy the order." A defiant stance is not common, but neither is it absent—22 percent agreed/strongly agreed in March, but it jumped to 34 percent in October. We also embedded an experiment here, substituting "the Trump administration" for "the government" in half the March cases, though again it made no difference to support overall (or among partisans who might react strongly to Trump).

We also include two measures that we believe are linked closely to pandemic politics—social trust and belief that we are entering the "prophesied 'end times.'" In many ways, pandemic politics are massive collective action games. The selfish course of action is to continue on as normal, even though, in the aggregate, selfish behavior will greatly help spread the virus through the population. Clearly, government action is a necessity for "flattening the curve," which could be hampered if there is little trust in government and each other (e.g., see Coyne 2020 on Idaho). It comes as little surprise that many (69 percent in March, 62 percent in October) agreed that "You can't be too careful in trusting others." Though asked differently in the General Social Survey, 59 percent in 2018 said that people usually or always can't be trusted, so our results are in the ballpark, but it is no surprise that caution increased as the pandemic got underway. Regardless, we expect that Prosperity Gospelers will be less trusting of others given that people's problems are the result of their own sin and unbelief.

Lastly, we asked about a specific aspect of Christian theology regarding the end of the world. Some previous work has found that such beliefs affect how people think about time-dependent policy options, such as environmental protection (Barker and Bearce 2012; Guth et al. 1995). We investigate it here as a way to index how Prosperity Gospelers think about the virus as an existential threat—a mechanism that helps to tie together the other findings. In March, 35 percent of respondents agreed that we are entering the "prophesied 'end times,'" which had grown to 40 percent in October. Given the concrete frame of the question, this is much higher than previous reports,[5] suggesting just how context-dependent this belief is.

Model Results

In what follows, we estimate each of the first four dependent variables using the same statistical model, and Figure 1.3 contains these results.[6] The figure

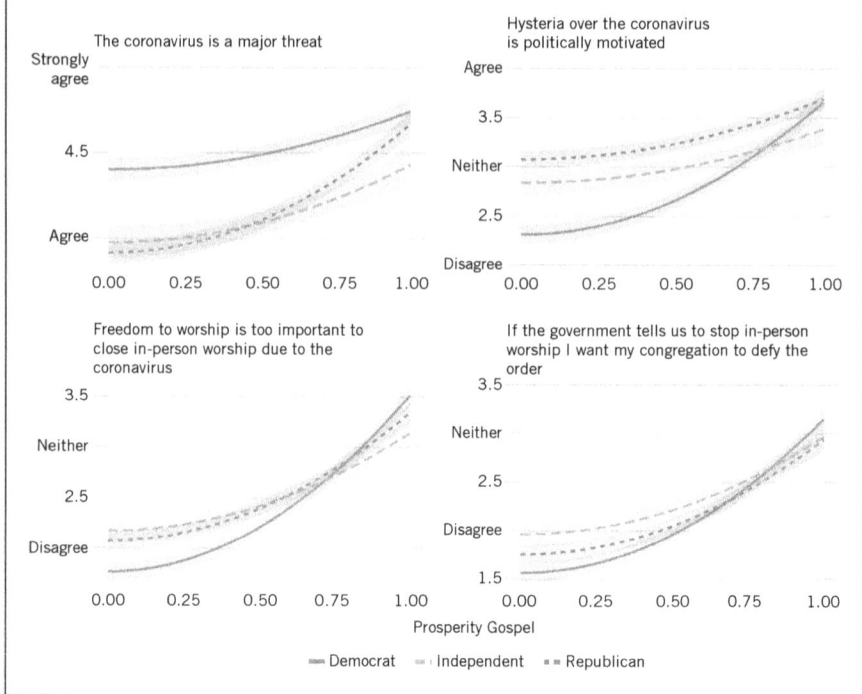

Figure 1.3 The Interactive Effect of Prosperity Gospel Beliefs by Partisanship on Coronavirus Threat and Response. Note: Comparison of any two confidence intervals is equivalent to a 90 percent test of significance at the point of overlap. (Source: March 2020 survey.)

shows the estimates (lines) with confidence intervals (lighter area around the line), which is a way of demonstrating the range in which we have confidence that the true estimate is likely to lie. They allow us to assess statistical significance visually—if the intervals do not overlap, we can say that the estimates are statistically distinguishable.

Coronavirus Threat

Given the messaging from conservatives and inaction from many Republican governors in the early months of the outbreak, it is no surprise that independents and Republicans are less likely to agree that the virus is a threat. Regardless, belief in the Prosperity Gospel boosts a sense of threat from the virus for each partisan group, backing our "where there's smoke, there's fire" thesis. And our expectation of an accelerating effect with higher prosperity belief finds support. There is no growth in agreement that the virus is a threat until roughly the midpoint of the scale. Moreover, the effect is greatest among Republicans, whose sense of threat climbs to equal that held by Democratic Prosperity Gospel believers. In this case, Republican elites have been downplaying the seriousness of the pandemic, which means that Republicans had more room to change their opinions due to their Prosperity Gospel beliefs.

Politicized Hysteria

The threat relationships just discussed do not mean that the threat is viewed in the same way. We expect that Prosperity Gospelers will view threats in an agentic way—that is, they see problems as the result of supernatural forces working through human action and inaction, sins of commission and omission. In this case, we expect that they will see the coronavirus hysteria as politically motivated, which is what Figure 1.3 shows. Surely as a result of elite communication, Republicans are more likely than Democrats to believe this, but all three partisan groups shift their views higher based on their Prosperity Gospel beliefs. And, again, the effects gain in strength with greater Prosperity Gospel beliefs. It is astounding to see that Democratic Prosperity Gospelers are more likely to agree that the hysteria was politically motivated than many Republicans. Prosperity Gospelers truly stand alone in their degree of agreement with this conspiracy theory.

By October (appendix Figure A1.4 compares the results from the two surveys), the relationship patterns look about the same, except that Republican belief in political motivation had grown by half a point—Republican Prosperity Gospelers now average just over "agree." Moreover, the shift driven by prosperity beliefs among Democrats is just enormous. Those who reject the Prosperity Gospel average "disagree," but those who affirm prosperity beliefs average "agree." After a year of the terrible spread of the pandemic throughout the United States, the parties polarized on the coronavirus response, exacerbated by belief in the Prosperity Gospel.

Keep the Churches Open

The bottom panels of Figure 1.3 highlight the positive effect that prosperity beliefs have on support for keeping the churches open despite public health threats that may pose. The left panel shows the priority of freedom of worship despite the coronavirus, while the right panel gauges support for defying (potential) government orders to close. Neither of these positions occasions considerable support, but, in both cases, the Prosperity Gospel serves to move people from opposition to support (even if very slim in the case of government defiance). There are minor differences by partisanship. Democrats who completely reject the Prosperity Gospel are more opposed to the idea of keeping churches open, but prosperity Democrats show the most support for keeping them open. The Democratic Party is quite ideologically diverse, and that heterogeneity may reach its peak over the role of religion in society.

The rhetoric of the Prosperity Gospel suggests that only belief is necessary to attain the desired benefits. But, instead, it is remarkable how believers have come to rely so heavily on intercessory agents in the Prosperity Gospel sector, a link we explore with our own data below. If the church is the instrumentality of health and wealth, then it is easy to imagine supporters wanting to keep them open at almost any price. There are a number of potential explanations for this that rely on the experiential nature of Prosperity Gospel services, since many are Pentecostal and believe in the necessity of laying on of hands in order to faith-heal believers (for a minority). But perhaps the simplest is that the church serves as a marker of the ingroup where "we" believers stand united against "they" unbelievers who have chosen to be poor and unhealthy by their sin and unbelief.

Likely Mechanisms

We can find evidence for our view of the effects of the Prosperity Gospel in a variety of other relationships that signal high barriers to those outside the group (full model results are available in appendix Table A1.2). For as sunny as are some proponents of the Prosperity Gospel, such as Joel Osteen, the worldviews of adherents shade considerably darker. We included a standard trust question that captures the perceived risk of relying on others, asking whether respondents agree or disagree that "You can't be too careful in trusting others." The results indicate the dramatic rise in distrust that accompanies prosperity beliefs, moving respondents almost 40 percent of the scale. Only among those who reject the Prosperity Gospel are there partisan differences—Democrats are more trusting. Among full-throated supporters of the Prosperity Gospel, partisanship is immaterial.

It is no surprise that the same distrusting orientation finds expression in how to organize social relations with respect to the church. That is, Prosperity Gospelers have much stronger exclusive orientations, which encompass social and economic cloistering with fellow religious identifiers. Among Democrats, exclusivity climbs almost the same amount as distrust, though the effect is a bit weaker among the other partisans. Together this helps to make sense of the CNN (2020) interview with a woman attending in-person worship at a Prosperity Gospel megachurch outside of Cincinnati. She felt protected not just because she was "covered in Jesus's blood" but because she was attending with other "covered" believers.

Generalized distrust and religious exclusivity go hand in hand with a belief that evil exists, that it is embodied, and that it is active in the world. A belief that evil exists is common (index mean = 0.7 on a 0–1 scale), and the only item in the scale that truly shows variation across religious traditions is whether the devil exists. In any event, Prosperity Gospelers occupy the highest end of the scale without distinction among partisans. Only among those who reject the Prosperity Gospel do partisans differentiate, with Democrats less likely to believe that evil exists.

Lastly, we examine the eschatological belief that the "end times" are near. There are many shades to beliefs about the end times, also known as judgment day, last things, and the apocalypse. In perhaps the most common form, the end times involve a battle between good and evil at Armageddon. Under this interpretation, it is no surprise to find Prosperity Gospelers 25 percent more likely to agree that "We are very likely entering the prophesied 'end times.'" As noted above, levels of this belief appear to be very high in the population at the moment, surely driven by the spread of the coronavirus. This is critical because it suggests believers expect evil to be on the loose and are on the lookout for battles between good and evil.[7]

Discussion—The Special Role of Race?

While race features prominently in the literature on the Prosperity Gospel, up until now we have only included a control in our models for racial identity differences. But race is essential to consider at a deeper level in the public expression of religion. Despite considerable religious similarities with white evangelicals, Black Protestants have diametrically opposed politics, at least in terms of partisanship (Burge and Djupe 2019), if not necessarily on some social issues, such as same-sex marriage (e.g., Sherkat, de Vries, and Creek 2010). As Shelton and Cobb (2018) put it, "Differences across Protestant affiliations pale in comparison to structural and cultural similarities resulting from the legacy of racial discrimination and inequality" (see also Shelton and Emerson 2012).

Does race similarly condition the effects of Prosperity Gospel beliefs? We took the same models used above for two dependent variables—government defiance and freedom to worship is too important to close—and interacted Prosperity Gospel, race, and partisanship. With some minor variation, the effects are *no different*. That is, nonwhite Prosperity Gospel believers have the same reaction to stay-at-home orders as white Prosperity Gospelers. Put another way, in this policy area, Prosperity Gospel beliefs function independently of race and partisanship, the two dominant sources of variation in American politics.[8]

It is also notable that the effects of the Prosperity Gospel are consistently lower for Republicans than Democrats. For nonwhites this variation in effect is insignificant. For whites, the effect of Prosperity Gospel beliefs is significantly lower for Republicans than it is for Democrats when predicting "freedom to worship is too important to close." The difference is reasonably close to significant in the government defiance model as well. While still very large effects, these differences are telling about the communication environment of the parties. Democratic messaging does not loop in arguments that are consistent with the Prosperity Gospel, while Republican "boot straps" economic policy aligns with the individualist prosperity approach. Moreover, Republicans have clearly joined forces with the COVID-rules resistance movement, reinforcing what Prosperity Gospelers are hearing from religious elites and what they are likely to think by dint of their beliefs.

Conclusion

Given its rampant spread around the world (Brouwer, Gifford, and Rose 1996), including throughout the United States (Bowler 2018), it is surprising that there is not more research on the Prosperity Gospel. We have attempted to show that the social effects of Prosperity Gospel beliefs are encompassing and deserve more of our attention. Using the coronavirus pandemic as the context, the results suggest that Prosperity Gospel believers have particularly high barriers to working with others that may translate into dangerous behavior when coordinated social distancing is the public policy of the day. Prosperity Gospelers are no more likely to report their congregations are open but were much more likely to indicate that they were still worshipping in person.

It is surprising to find a social force that is not limited by party or race. We did not determine this by simply controlling for racial and party identification differences but instead looked to compare effect sizes among these groups and found them to be largely invariant. There are differences in how much each group believes the Prosperity Gospel, but when they believe, their worldview dictates a very similar reaction to the coronavirus response.

Personal behavior during the pandemic is tremendously important, given that lives are at stake and simply attending worship in person can mean dozens, even hundreds of new infections as "Patient 31" in South Korea taught us (Shin, Berkowitz, and Kim 2020). But the relationships seen here suggest the Prosperity Gospel has much broader implications. Given that Prosperity Gospelers have such high rates of distrust, have a high belief in evil, feel religious commands to be rightly exclusionary, and appear to be imminent endtimes believers, we see little that is encouraging of collective action. Indeed, the explicit rhetoric parallels the pandemic—remain socially distant from those who may share the same problems. Misery loves company, and you sin by working in concert with the poor and those with health problems.

2

Are Religious Adherents More Likely to Buy Into COVID-19 Conspiracy Theories?

DIANA ORCÉS, IAN HUFF, AND NATALIE JACKSON

With the ongoing spread of COVID-19 in the United States and the world, global misinformation about the pandemic is also spreading. Since the start of the pandemic, a number of conspiracy theories have surfaced, including beliefs about the nonexistence of the new virus, its creation at a Chinese lab or as a biological weapon, and blaming 5G networks or Bill Gates for the spread. Unfortunately, belief in conspiracy theories can prevent people from taking appropriate health-related behaviors (Islam et al. 2020; Jolley and Douglas 2014). Previous research has found that willingness to believe in unseen, intentional forces is associated with support for conspiracy theories (Oliver and Wood 2014), a cognitive style of thinking—better known as magical thinking—more likely to be present among certain religious believers (Oliver and Wood 2018; Dyrendal, Roberston, and Asprem 2019). Both religion and conspiracy theory are usually understood as "involving specific patterns of thought and ideas" that are related in intricate ways to social power (Dyrendal, Roberston, and Asprem 2019), making it imperative to evaluate systematically how beliefs of particular religious groups are ideologically in line with conspiracy beliefs.

Are religious adherents more likely to buy into COVID-19 conspiracy theories, and if they are, why? To answer this question, we use the 2020 American Values Survey data collected by the Public Religion Research Institute

---

Material referencing an appendix in this chapter can be found online available here: https://dataverse.harvard.edu/dataverse/epidemic_among_my_people.

(PRRI) to investigate the relationship between religious adherence and support for the belief that COVID-19 is lab made, while accounting for key several sociodemographic and political factors.

This chapter hopes to illuminate, through a quantitative approach, whether religious adherence accounts for belief in COVID-19 conspiracy theories alongside political factors. With the current polarized nature of U.S. politics, increasing distrust in government and other institutions, and a growing skepticism of mainstream media outlets, better understanding of who is more likely to believe in COVID-19 conspiracy theories during the pandemic is vital given its health-related implications (Islam et al. 2020).

Why Do People Believe in COVID-19 Conspiracy Theories?

People are drawn to conspiracy theories due to many factors. The literature suggests that partisanship, ideology, distrust in political leaders, scientists, or other authorities, as well as individuals' predispositions and general views about the world, have an impact on how people think about conspiracy theories (e.g., Douglas and Sutton 2011; Oliver and Wood 2014; Uscinski and Olivella 2017).

President Donald Trump's administration was an era of conspiracy theories, which complicated the ability to accurately communicate about the spread of the coronavirus (Hellinger 2019). Recent research finds that the belief in COVID-19 conspiracy theories is tied to support for Donald Trump and the rejection of information from experts and other authorities, in addition to conspiracy thinking, party affiliation, and political ideology (Uscinski et al. 2020). Belief in COVID-19 conspiracy theories is also associated with lower levels of education, more negative attitudes toward government responses, and broader beliefs in conspiracy theories (Georgiou, Delfabbro, and Balzan 2020). In fact, Miller (2020a) shows that support for COVID-19 conspiracy theories is a form of monological belief system better understood as a "mutually supportive network of beliefs," adding evidence to a growing body of research that suggests that if people believe in one conspiracy theory, they tend to believe in other conspiracy theories too (e.g., Goertzel 1994; Lewandowsky, Oberauer, and Gignac 2013; Swami et al. 2011; Wood, Douglas, and Sutton 2012).

There has also been a problem with denial of science related to COVID-19. Lewandowsky, Oberauer, and Gignac (2013) find that believers of conspiracy theories are more likely to reject scientific propositions. The literature on the sources of science denialism argues that individuals who deny science lack scientific knowledge (Landrum and Olshansky 2019). However, science denialism is complex. Beliefs in science depend on individuals' prior attitudes and values.[1] Studies on the relationship between religion and science suggest that individuals see both religion and science as in conflict or that religion exists to answer questions about meaning and morality, whereas science answers questions about how the natural world works, or that both religion and science completement, influence, and guide each other (Ecklund 2010). In essence, most religious belief systems encapsulate a set of beliefs about perceptions of how a society works and a set of values of how society *should* work. In this study, we explore how religion is associated with belief in COVID-19 conspiracy theories, especially as religion has come to the forefront of American politics (Jones 2020).

The Role of Religion in the Belief of Conspiracy Theories

Religion and conspiracy theory are usually understood as "involving specific patterns of thought and ideas" that are related in intricate ways to social power (Dyrendal, Roberston, and Asprem 2019). In this section, we specifically seek to understand how conspiracy beliefs are connected to the beliefs of religious adherents.

Leveraging previous research, Oliver and Wood (2014) argue that belief in conspiracy theories is the function of two psychological predispositions. The first, "magical thinking," relates to "an unconscious cognitive bias to draw causal connections between seemingly related phenomena." This way of thinking is associated with religious beliefs because they project feelings of control when in situations of uncertainty. Beliefs in conspiracy theories are positively related to intuitive rather than analytic thinking (Swami et al. 2014; Oliver and Wood 2018), and religion reinforces intuitionist thinking through beliefs of magical thinking understood as "thinking that relies on omnipotent fantasy to create a psychic reality that the individual experiences as 'more real' than external reality" (Ogden 2010, 318). Religious concepts present in most religions, such as miracles, healing powers, and supernatural manifestations, are easily remembered because they are uncommon and challenge the way things happen typically. For example, magical thinking is present among evangelical Christians who believe in the Prosperity Gospel, a belief system that suggests that individuals who are faithful to God and God's church will be blessed with health and wealth (Burge 2017).

Belief in religious concepts often helps to make sense of nonsensical occurrences or offers comfort from a perceived higher power. In the same way, conspiracy theories are easily remembered because they involve concepts that are uncommon but can offer explanations for what might seem inexplicable

(Andrade 2020).[2] Both religion and conspiracy theories provide structure to uncertainty due to their reliance on magical thinking. In this sense, we expect the following hypotheses:

> H1: Religious adherents will be more likely to believe in COVID-19 conspiracy theories than religiously unaffiliated individuals.
>
> H2: Individuals who exhibit magical thinking will be more likely to believe in COVID-19 conspiracy theories than those who do not exhibit magical thinking.

Oliver and Wood's (2014) second predisposition to conspiracy theories relates to Manichean thinking, specifically the belief in a clash between good and evil, which is common in religious rhetoric and "comports with how some people process political information" and how they explain ambiguous events. Most religions subscribe to the idea that good things happen to good people and bad things to bad people (Furnham 2003), thus making them more receptive to messaging that benefits "good" people and punishes "bad" people. For example, evangelical Christians who believe in the Prosperity Gospel may think that those who are faithful will be blessed with health and wealth, while those who are unfaithful will be punished.

Dualistic-Manichean views in which human beings are believed to be composed of a body and a soul are closely related to religious dogmatic views (Del Rio and White 2012), and dogmatism is associated with lower critical reasoning skills. While confirmation bias is a universal human trait (Nickerson 1998), we suspect that religious individuals marked by Manichean worldviews tend to cling to specific beliefs that resonate with their moral views and affirm their thinking at greater rates. In short, high levels of dogmatism make individuals less likely to look at issues from others' perspectives and more receptive to messaging that strengthens their own views (Friedman and Jack 2018). Conspiracy theories also typically utilize Manichean thinking by creating an enemy—someone or something is doing something bad—that good people must contend with. Thus, we expect the following hypothesis:

> H3: Individuals who exhibit Manichean thinking will be more likely to believe in COVID-19 conspiracy theories than those who do not exhibit Manichean thinking.

Moreover, when experiencing anxiety-provoking events, individuals tend to resort more to magical or Manichean thinking as a way to control their surroundings, and religious thinking also operates this way, finding explanations for incomprehensible phenomena (Malinoswki 1992). In fact, conspiracy theories become especially attractive under societal crises, such as natural disasters, because they help reduce anxiety, uncertainty, or feelings of lack of control (Van Prooijen and Douglas 2017; Abalakina-Paap et al. 1999; Green and Douglas 2018). Thus, during the pandemic, we expect to see the following hypothesis corroborated:

> H4: The effects of both magical and Manichean thinking on the belief in COVID-19 conspiracy theories will be stronger among religious adherents than religiously unaffiliated individuals.

COVID-19 in the United States

The case of the United States and the Trump administration serve as a good test case for an analysis of the relationship between religious adherents and the belief in COVID-19 conspiracy theories. The Trump administration's response to the first year of the pandemic was incoherent and left plenty of space for conspiracy theories to take hold. Trump made his first public comment on January 22, 2020, downplaying the impact of the virus and suggesting that the United States had it under control. On January 30, 2020, the World Health Organization (WHO) declared the coronavirus a global health emergency, and a day later Trump prohibited entry to the United States for select individuals coming from China (Peters 2020). Recent studies suggest the coronavirus was already in the United States at that point and came from Europe (Zimmer 2020).

On February 25, 2020, Trump appointed then vice president Mike Pence to lead the coronavirus task force and a few days later suggested that the virus would miraculously disappear. On March 19, Trump alleged that the Food and Drug Administration (FDA) approved the drug hydroxychloroquine for treating COVID-19 and continued to support its use as a COVID-19 treatment after it was demonstrated to be less helpful than initially thought (Gittleson, Phelps, and Cathey 2020). On April 30, Trump said that he had reason to believe that the virus had originated in a laboratory in Wuhan, China (Mangan and Lovelace 2020). Trump himself was diagnosed with COVID-19 on October 2, and despite spending three days in the hospital, he continued downplaying the threat of the virus and its spread, even though COVID-19 cases were increasing everywhere and worsened throughout the fall of 2020 (Burns 2020).

Misinformation appears to influence people's response to the virus (Islam et al. 2020). Many religious groups, especially evangelical Christians, remain firmly supportive of and receptive to Trump's message (Strang 2020). When party leaders and other government officials misinform the public and promote conspiracy theories, likeminded individuals who perceive these leaders as credible and are exposed to this type of rhetoric are more likely to accept these ideas (Swire et al. 2017).

Data and Method

To test our hypotheses, we use the 2020 American Values Survey by PRRI, a random sample of 2,538 adults (age eighteen and up) living in the United States, including all fifty states and the District of Columbia. Interviews were mostly conducted online using a self-administered design in both Spanish and English between September 9 and September 22, 2020.[3]

This survey provides a few items that allow for the systematic assessment of the relation between religion and a belief in conspiracy theories. The survey includes one COVID-19 conspiracy theory question applied to half of the sample (1,285 cases) and serves as our dependent variable: "Which of these two statements do you think is most likely to be true? (1) The coronavirus was developed intentionally by scientists in a lab (2) The coronavirus developed naturally."[4] Americans are evenly divided on this question (50 percent vs. 49 percent, respectively). Because of the binary nature of our dependent variable, we use logit regression models and control for political variables as well as personal demographic and socioeconomic characteristics.[5]

Our key independent variable is religious affiliation. PRRI uses an identity measure to distinguish among Protestants, asking if they are born-again or evangelical Protestants or not. This is not the same as classifying their denominational affiliation, but analyses using either measure tend to return quite similar results (Burge and Lewis 2018). PRRI data show that the largest shares of religiously affiliated Americans are Christians, with 22 percent evangelical Protestants (13 percent white, 9 percent of color), 25 percent nonevangelical Protestants (17 percent white, 8 percent of color), 17 percent Catholics (10 percent white, 6 percent Hispanic, 1 percent all other of color), and 1 percent other Christians, including Latter-day Saints and Orthodox Christians. The rest of religiously affiliated Americans belong to non-Christian groups, which make up 9 percent of all religious groups, including Jewish, Muslim, Buddhist, and Hindu Americans as well as Americans who identify with other religions. One in four (25 percent) Americans identify as religiously unaffiliated. The survey also asks for religious service attendance. About one in four (27 percent) Americans reported they attend religious services either at least once a week or more, 21 percent indicated once or twice a month or a few times a year, and 52 percent said seldom or never.

Luckily, the survey includes a measure of magical thinking, asking if Americans completely agree, mostly agree, mostly disagree, or completely disagree with the following statement: "God always rewards those who have faith with good health and will protect them from being infected by the coronavirus." This measure allows us to capture one of the ways magical thinking is associated with religious beliefs, that of divine intervention and protection, which projects feelings of control when in an uncontrollable situation—the pandemic (Ogden 2010).[6] The belief that God will protect individuals from the coronavirus (magical thinking) could help them make sense of illogical occurrences, such as the possibility that a virus was manufactured in a lab. We also incorporate a proxy of Manichean thinking: "It is necessary to believe in God in order to be moral and have good values." Manichean thinking is closely related to dogmatic thinking, particularly regarding what is good and what is not, and this measure captures the belief in a dogmatic view of requiring a specific belief to qualify as good. Those who agree with this statement will suggest black-and-white thinking. The more moral correctness religious individuals see in something, the more likely this affirms their thinking of God rewarding those who have faith and punishing those who do not (Friedman and Jack 2018). We acknowledge the limits of both measures of magical and Manichean thinking as they capture part of multidimensional concepts. About one in four (23 percent) Americans either completely or somewhat agree that God always rewards those who have faith and will protect them from the virus, and 39 percent completely or somewhat agree that it is necessary to believe in God in order to be moral and have good values.

In addition, we add variables to assess how support for Trump impacts conspiracy beliefs. The survey asks, "Do you strongly approve, somewhat approve, somewhat disapprove, or strongly disapprove of the job Donald Trump is doing as president?" Since most of Trump's COVID-19 messaging to his supporters has been through Fox News, we add another variable that captures Americans who trust Fox News the most among television news sources to provide accurate information about politics and current events.

We also include an index of mistrust based on "not at all" responses to how much Americans trust various government officials and institutions to provide accurate information and advice regarding the ongoing coronavirus pandemic, including university research centers, Dr. Anthony Fauci, and then senator Joe Biden. We exclude trust in Donald Trump as this variable is highly correlated with Trump's job approval ($r = 0.80$).

We control for political ideology, partisanship, racial/ethnic identity, education, income, gender, age, and region. Following the literature on the sources of belief in conspiracy theories, we expect that those with lower levels of education and income will be more likely to believe that the virus was developed in a lab. Less educated individuals tend to attribute agency and intentionality where it is not present (Van Prooijen 2016).

Results

The first step in the analysis confirms (H1) that religious adherents are more likely to believe that COVID-19 is lab made than those who are religiously unaffiliated.[7] With respect to our second hypothesis (H2), we find support for the idea that individuals who exhibit magical thinking will be more likely to believe that COVID-19 is lab made (models 2 and 4 in Table A2.1 in the appendix). We find the degree of agreement with the statement "God always rewards those who have faith with good health and will protect them from being infected by the coronavirus" increases the mean predicted probability of believing the virus is lab made by *22 percentage points* as one moves from completely disagreeing (49 percent) to completely agreeing (71 percent) with this statement (Figure 2.1).

Moving on to our third hypothesis (H3), we also find evidence that individuals who exhibit Manichean thinking are more likely to believe that COVID-19 is lab made (model 3 and 4 in Table A2.1 in the appendix). The mean predicted probability increases by *29 percentage points* as one moves from completely disagreeing (38 percent) to completely agreeing (66 percent) with the statement "It is necessary to believe in God in order to be moral and have good values" (Figure 2.1).

Our last step in the analysis partially confirms our fourth hypothesis (H4). We find evidence in support of the *joint* impact between magical thinking and religious affiliation on the belief that COVID-19 is lab made, even after controlling for everything else.

Figure 2.2 (model 5 in Table A2.1 in the appendix) shows that among evangelical Protestants, the mean predicted probability of believing COVID-19 is lab made increases by *43 percentage points* ($p < 0.05$), moving from completely disagreeing (51 percent) to completely agreeing (94 percent) with the statement "God always rewards those who have faith with good health and will protect them from being infected by the coronavirus." Because of the

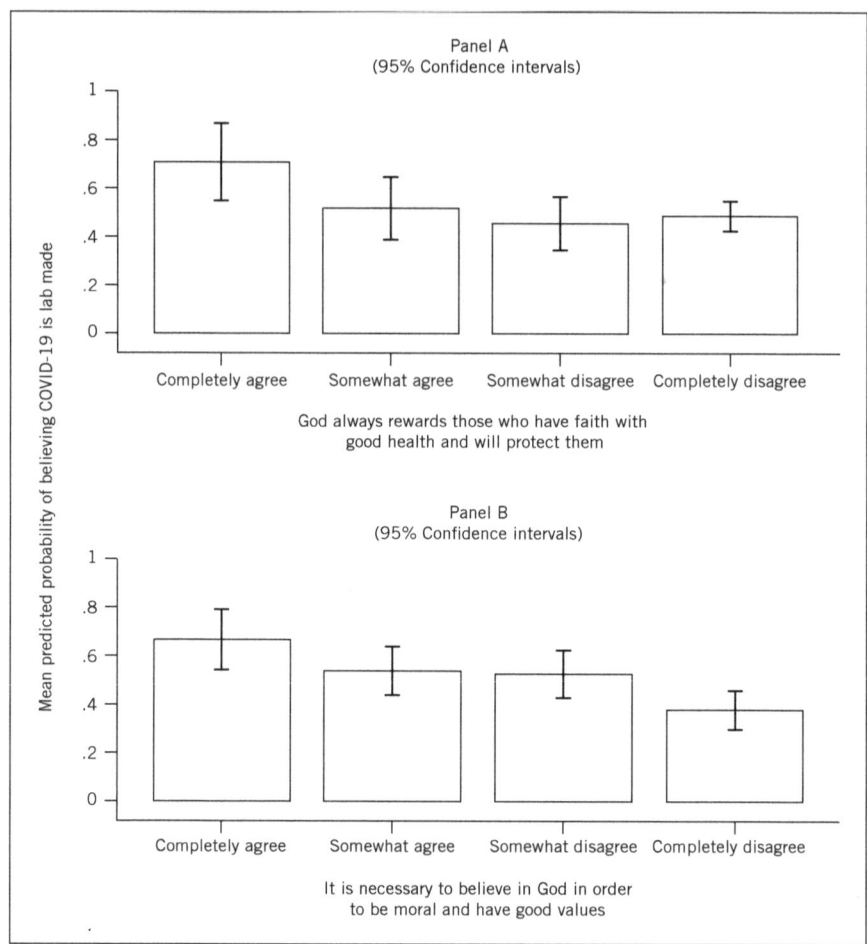

Figure 2.1 Predicted Probability of Believing COVID-19 by Magical Thinking and by Manichean Thinking. Note: Results based on model 4 in the online appendix. Differences in mean predicted probabilities for magical thinking between completely agree and completely disagree as well as for Manichean thinking between all categories and completely disagree are statistically significant at $p < 0.05$. (Source: 2020 American Values Survey.)

growing political significance of evangelical Protestants under the Trump administration (Jones 2020), these results add additional evidence to the corrosive impact of misinformation.

Further, while there are no significant differences in COVID-19 beliefs between nonevangelical Protestants who completely agree and completely disagree with the magical thinking statement, we do find that the mean

Are Religious Adherents More Likely to Buy Into COVID-19 Conspiracy Theories? | 37

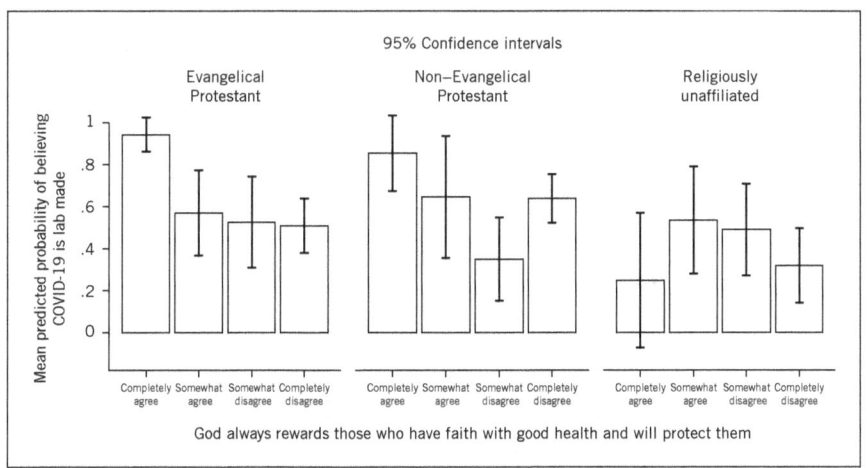

Figure 2.2 Predicted Probability of Believing COVID-19 Is Lab Made by Religious Tradition and Magical Thinking. Note: Results based on model 5 in the online appendix. Differences in mean predicted probabilities for magical thinking among evangelical Protestants between completely agree and completely disagree as well as among non-evangelical Protestants between completely agree and completely disagree are statistically significant at $p < 0.05$. (Source: 2020 American Values Survey.)

predicted probability of believing COVID-19 is lab made among nonevangelical Protestants increases by *50 percentage points* ($p < 0.05$) moving from somewhat disagreeing (35 percent) to completely agreeing (85 percent) with the statement (Figure 2.2).

Because the goal of this chapter is to also evaluate whether the effect of magical thinking on the belief in COVID-19 conspiracy theories is stronger among religious adherents than nonreligious adherents, we show graphically this relationship among religious unaffiliated Americans, who do not differ significantly between those who completely agree and those who completely disagree with the statement (Figure 2.2). The same is true among Catholics and members of other religious groups (not shown graphically).

In addition, when examining the joint impact between Manichean thinking and religion on COVID-19 beliefs (Figure 2.3), we only find significant results among Catholics: the mean predicted probability of believing COVID-19 is lab made increases by *54 percentage points* among Catholics moving from somewhat disagreeing (25 percent) to completely agreeing (79 percent) with the statement "It is necessary to believe in God in order to be moral and have good values." Even though there is some variation in Manichean thinking among unaffiliated Americans, these differences are not statistically signifi-

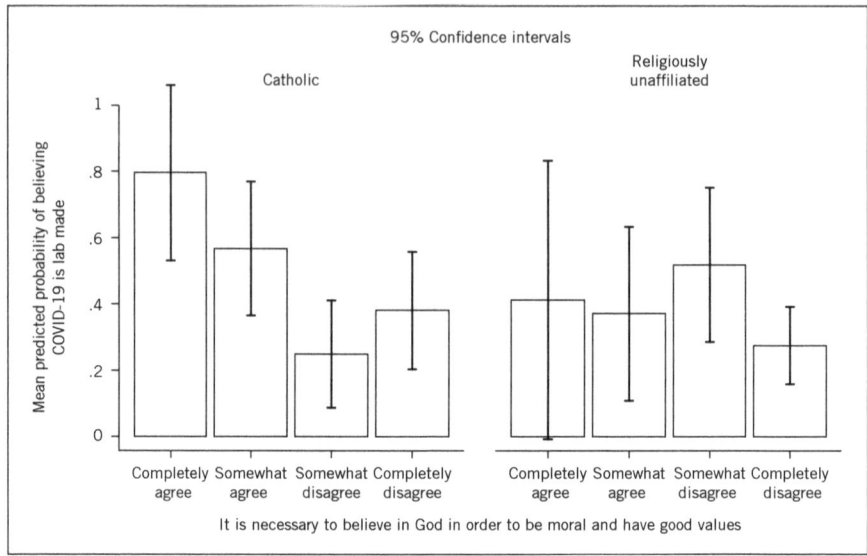

Figure 2.3 Predicted Probability of Believing COVID-19 Is Lab Made by Religious Tradition and Manichean Thinking. Note: Results based on model 5 in the online appendix. Differences in mean predicted probabilities for Manichean thinking among Catholics between completely agree and somewhat disagree are statistically significant at $p < 0.05$. (Source: 2020 American Values Survey.)

cant. These results suggest that Catholics may be particularly attuned to Manichean beliefs compared to other religious groups. Manichean thinking could be one mechanism that helps explain Catholics' COVID-19 conspiracy beliefs.

Other findings from our logit regression models show that those who identify as conservative, mistrust political officials and institutions, and those who approve of President Trump and watch Fox News are more likely to believe that COVID-19 is lab made.

An intriguing and unexpected finding in our models is how attending religious services seems to undermine belief in the COVID-19 conspiracy theory. We find evidence that Americans who attend religious gatherings at least once a week, compared to those who seldom or never attend religious gatherings, are less likely to believe that COVID-19 is lab made, contrary to our expectations. We expected that individuals who engage more with their faith groups would be more inclined to exhibit similar thinking, as likeminded individuals have been found to be exposed to specific rhetoric and more likely to accept these ideas (Swire et al. 2017). However, this could also be an artifact of the regression due to the fact that we are already accounting for religious identification. If the key theoretical linkage between conspiracy theories and religion is the magical and Manichean nature of their beliefs, perhaps more frequent attendance at religious services is simply not an indicator of those particular aspects of religion.

Finally, age, racial identification, and income matter, adding support to previous research suggesting that stigmatized minority groups believe more strongly in conspiracy theories than majority group members (Goertzel 1994; Thorburn and Bogart 2007).

Conclusion

The United States was ripe for conspiracy theories to take hold when the pandemic hit. There was no coherent, unified national message, and the former president—who could have provided that message—instead often repeated misinformation and conspiracy theories regarding the novel coronavirus. But this is not the complete story.

The other unique aspect of the United States is its religiosity. Despite a decrease in religious affiliation among Americans, Americans still remain among the most religious people in the industrialized world. More than half of Americans (55 percent) say they pray daily, compared to 25 percent of Canadians, 18 percent of Australians, and 6 percent of the British (Fahmy 2018). That matters for conspiracy theories because religious beliefs and conspiracy beliefs share two common features: magical thinking, the willingness to believe stories in order to explain or add stability to uncertain situations, and Manichean thinking, the need to sort the world into forces of good and evil. Both are associated with believing that the virus causing COVID-19 was intentionally manufactured in a laboratory.

In addition to the direct linkage between religiously based magical and Manichean thinking and the COVID-19 conspiracy theory, we have shown in these analyses that religious affiliation itself is directly associated with stronger belief in the conspiracy theory. For evangelical and nonevangelical Protestants, there is an interactive effect as well, which shows that stronger magical thinking combined with their religious affiliation makes them more likely to believe in the conspiracy theory.

Layering all of these pieces together—the religiosity of the U.S. population, the connection between religious thinking and conspiracy thinking, and the environment in which U.S. leadership espoused conspiracy theories—created a perfect storm for the U.S. public to believe conspiracy theories. In this light, it becomes less surprising that 50 percent of the country would believe a conspiracy theory that says the virus that causes COVID-19 was intentionally manufactured in a laboratory. And, since believing in COVID-19 conspiracy theories could influence health behaviors and possibly have detrimental health outcomes (Jolley and Douglas 2014), in addition to widespread beliefs that God would protect the faithful, it is likely these mechanisms of thinking have contributed to the United States coping quite badly with the pandemic overall.

3

Religion and Gun Purchasing amid a Pandemic, Civil Unrest, and an Election

ABIGAIL VEGTER AND DONALD HAIDER-MARKEL

As the severity of the COVID-19 pandemic became clear in the spring of 2020, American debate over the freedoms granted by the First and Second Amendments became a nearly daily part of the national conversation. Concerns over empty store shelves and mixed messages from public officials highlighted concerns about personal safety for some. Likewise, restrictions on gatherings during local and state shutdowns, including restrictions for gun shops and religious services, led some to claim that their rights were being unconstitutionally violated. Even with largely ample access to firearm purchasing, many worried that the sales of guns would become limited. The NRA sued the state of New York and others who declared gun stores "nonessential" (Orden 2020). Likewise, some politicians argued that pandemic restrictions were subversive threats to freedoms. President Donald Trump tweeted his support for the "Reopen America" and "Liberate Michigan" campaign in April, linking the shutdowns to gun rights (Shear and Mervosh 2020). Texas attorney general Ken Paxton stated that emergency stay-at-home orders could not be used to close firearm stores in the state (Goldenstein 2020). As churches and gun stores shut down as a result of COVID-19, individuals, activists, politicians, and pastors alike claimed serious threats to First and Second Amendment rights. These claims, however, did not come to fruition as the pandemic has ushered in the highest rates of gun purchasing since such data

---

Material referencing an appendix in this chapter can be found online available here: https://dataverse.harvard.edu/dataverse/epidemic_among_my_people.

began being tracked in 1998. A record breaking 3.9 million firearm background checks were completed in the month of June 2020 alone, and a total of nearly 39.7 million firearm background checks were completed in 2020, beating the previous yearly record by more than 10 million (Federal Bureau of Investigation 2020).[1] Moreover, the Firearm Industry Trade Association estimated that 40 percent of sales were conducted with purchasers who had never previously owned a firearm (NSSF 2020).

To some, the pandemic restrictions also threatened their First Amendment freedom of religious practice. Political and religious leaders around the country opposed various restrictions on group gatherings and religious services. Some religious leaders ignored public officials' orders and held services despite potential legal ramifications (Jacobo 2020) even as gatherings for religious services became noted super-spreader events for the virus (Conger, Healy, and Tompkins 2020).

In addition to the threat of the pandemic, Americans also faced a reckoning with police violence against African Americans. The murder of George Floyd while in police custody in May spurred widespread protests and occasional violence across the country for much of the late spring and summer. For some Americans, the unrest provided another layer of fear and uncertainty in the midst of an election that was argued to be a "Battle for the soul of our nation" (Cummings 2020). Then president Trump explicitly linked religion and civil unrest by having peaceful protesters tear-gassed and forcibly removed from Lafayette Park in order to walk across to St. John's Church for a photo op of himself holding a Bible ("Peaceful Protesters Tear-Gassed to Clear Way for Trump Church Photo-Op" 2020).

As the pandemic raged and civil unrest and the unusual presidential election campaign continued, religion and guns became more intertwined. In addition, recent research suggests that some religious Americans justify their gun ownership using their faith. Vegter and Kelley (2020) find that gun ownership is part of a particular worldview that stems from a posture of fear and a commitment to a higher authority above the law. This particular "ethic," as they describe it, relies on a particular understanding of Christian duty, including the duty to defend. The subjects from whom gun owners feel an obligation to defend themselves and their communities can include Democratic leaders, violent protesters, and, for some, Satan himself. The pandemic presents another set of fears requiring defense, especially concerning individuals' health and safety.

How do these distinct expressions of fear, duty, and divine protection relate to the surge in gun purchasing during the turbulent summer of 2020? To examine this question, we deployed an online survey of a representative sample of American adults in October 2020. Our analysis of the resulting data suggests that evangelicalism significantly predicts the purchasing of a firearm between the months of March and August 2020. Moreover, this relationship varies by religiosity; those who claim that religion is very important in their lives are more likely to have purchased a gun during the spring and summer of 2020. When asked why they purchased a gun, evangelicals were significantly more likely to claim it was due to concerns about civil unrest as a result of police actions toward African Americans and the coming election rather than the threat of COVID-19. In other words, purchasing a gun resulted from a fear of civil unrest and that a Democratic president would "take their guns" rather than the pandemic. Notably, religious importance intensifies this relationship, with the most religious individuals being most likely to purchase a firearm between March and August 2020.

Religion and COVID-19

Religion has been at the center of the COVID-19 pandemic. Religious gatherings have operated as "superspreading events" (Starr 2020), and religious individuals express their opposition toward COVID-19 restrictions in explicitly religious language (Fowler 2020). Polls have shown that evangelicals and those with higher levels of religiosity are more likely to distrust scientific sources about guidance during the pandemic (Burge 2020) and less likely to take recommended health precautions (Perry, Whitehead, and Grubbs 2020a). Meanwhile, Americans who are less religious or not religious at all were more likely to social distance, wear masks, and adhere to the recommendations provided by health experts (Hill, Gonzalez, and Burdette 2020).

Perry, Whitehead, and Grubbs (2020a) provide a robust explanation for the religious response to the global pandemic. The scholars turn to Christian nationalism to explain why some Americans engaged in "incautious behavior" and took fewer precautions than others. The scholars note that Christian nationalism ("an ideology that idealizes and advocates a fusion of American civic life with a particular type of Christian identity and culture") has been "shown to lower Americans' trust in science and scientific expertise; promote a view of (conservative Christian) Americans as God's chosen, divinely protected people; bind them to siding with Trump; and likely reject information put forth by mainstream news media" (2020a, 406). These side effects of Christian nationalism help explain why so many Americans refuse to adhere to COVID-19 safety guidelines.

Additionally, Perry et al. (2020a) find that religious commitment influenced Americans in the opposite direction of Christian nationalism. More devout Americans were more likely to engage in precautionary behaviors. However, it should be noted that this result was found after controlling for Christian nationalism, showing an effect only among the small number of religious Americans who are not Christian nationalists. The evangelical reaction to COVID-19 and the scholarly work illuminating potential causal mechanisms for such findings align well with what the literature suggests about religion's relationship to guns in the United States.

Religion and Guns

Religion has consistently been shown to be a significant predictor of gun ownership in the United States. Young (1989), Little and Vogel (1992), and Cox, Navarro-Rivera, and Jones (2013), among others, have noted that over time Protestants are more likely than members of other religious traditions to own guns and less likely to support gun control; however, few studies move beyond the broad religious category of "Protestant" into other measures of religion, including evangelicalism or religious importance, despite both variables being powerful explanations of political thinking and behavior (Hertzke et al. 2018).

Yamane (2016) concludes that "Protestant" as a measure of broad religious affiliation is irrelevant to gun ownership, controlling for other factors. However, he does find that evangelical Protestants exhibit relatively high levels of personal handgun ownership. Vegter and den Dulk (2020) find that evangelical Protestantism is significantly associated with a gun owner identity as compared to mainline Protestants, which holds important implications for gun control policy attitudes. Moreover, some scholars have suggested that the link between *white* evangelicalism and gun ownership, as well as opposition to gun control, results from an individualist impulse that emphasizes personal responsibility (including, presumably, self-protection) and the role of civil society rather than the state in addressing the root causes of violence (Hempel, Matthews, and Bartkowski 2012; Merino 2018). The interaction of religion and other cultural factors, including the nexus between religion, residence in rural areas, and hunting, are also common in the literature (Young 1989). Taken together, these studies are consistent with broader arguments that attribute patterns of gun ownership and attitudes about guns to tensions between individualist and collectivist cultural traditions in the United States (Celinska 2007).

What are the causal mechanisms that would explain the effects of religious affiliation or religiosity on gun ownership? Some studies have provided a primarily culture-based explanation of these effects. Young and Thompson

(1995) examine support for punitiveness and find that fundamentalism is associated with civic punitiveness among whites, which is in turn associated with gun ownership among whites. Among Blacks, fundamentalism is associated with religious punitiveness and, subsequently, gun ownership. Yamane (2016), however, reports that the influence of religious characteristics on personal handgun ownership is not strongly mediated by punitiveness when civic punitiveness is assessed among all racial groups.

Another approach draws from the literature on social capital and especially social trust. Matthews, Johnson, and Jenks (2011) argue that religiosity is associated with higher levels of generalized social trust and, therefore, less fear of certain types of crime. Hempel, Matthews, and Barthowski (2012) come to a different conclusion, at least about a subset of the faithful. They find that theological conservatism, as a distinctive belief structure, is itself associated with lower levels of generalized trust. One may consider, then, that active religious participation leads to a particular form of trust that reduces the likelihood of gun ownership, unless that participation is within the confines of a belief system that encourages social distrust. While Matthews et al. (2011) or Hempel et al. (2012) suggest these possibilities, neither study addresses gun ownership directly.

Whitehead, Schnabel, and Perry (2018) argue that Christian nationalism is associated with decreased support for gun regulation. They explain that Americans who subscribe to this particular worldview may believe "guns are a God-given right tied to a cultural style tied to deeply held senses of morality, identity, and perceived threat" (9). The particular religious reasoning used to justify gun ownership becomes especially significant when one considers the gun purchasing surge experienced in the spring and summer of 2020.

Gun Purchasing in 2020

Firearm background checks have been a consistent way to measure gun sales in the United States since 1999. With background checks reaching record highs throughout the COVID-19 pandemic, scholars have been interested in assessing this particular "gun-buying" event in relation to others in recent history. Such events include elections, terrorist attacks, and mass shootings (Liu and Wiebe 2019). In the case of the turbulent year of 2020, there was an unprecedented pandemic, a national election, and a wave of nationwide protests for racial justice in the light of police treatment of African Americans. The literature has investigated which types of events trigger gun sales, though, notably, has not investigated what happens when these events happen simultaneously.

Lang and Lang (2020) smartly frame the COVID-19 pandemic as a threat to safety that may trigger firearm sales similar to terrorist attacks and mass shootings. The scholars find the pandemic, as a particular gun-buying event quantified by background checks, had a greater impact on firearm purchases than any other event since 1999. In their multivariate analysis, Lang and Lang (2020) even find that the effects of the COVID lockdown and the George Floyd protests on the increase of firearm purchases was even greater than that of the 9/11 attacks.

Lang and Lang (2020) draw a clear line between COVID and civil unrest as perceived serious threats to personal safety that created the observed historic gun buying of 2020. Indeed, safety concerns have been shown to influence firearm purchasing in the past (Levine and McKnight 2017). Not only do the majority of gun owners cite personal protection as their main justification for owning a gun (Azrael et al. 2017), but scholars have also found that past victimization of crime and fears of future victimization are significant predictors of gun ownership (Hauser and Kleck 2013; Kleck et al. 2011). Lyons et al. (2020) find that the main motivation for gun purchasing between January and May 2020 was protection against people, suggesting threats to safety in myriad forms matter to firearm purchasing.

Political uncertainty has also been shown to influence increases in firearm purchases. Depetris-Cahuvin (2015) finds that gun purchasing increases during election years, as future gun policy is unknown. The 2008 and 2012 election and reelection of Barack Obama were shown to increase firearm purchasing (Laqueur et al. 2019), though this was not true after Trump's 2016 election (Smith 2020). This finding aligns with those of LaPlant, Lee, and LaPlant (2021), who note that gun sale spikes are positively associated with Democratic presidencies, which was predicted throughout the spring and summer of 2020.

The death of George Floyd at the hands of police in May 2020 ignited national protest over police treatment of African Americans in the United States. Lang and Lang (2020) find that the George Floyd protests were associated with an increase in firearm purchasing, distinct from the COVID-19 outbreak. Moreover, the scholars find that there is *not* a partisan dimension to this increase, with Democrat-leaning and Republican-leaning states experiencing similar patterns, a finding they explain by noting both events do not involve gun policy uncertainty. As mentioned, gun sales often spike when gun policy seems uncertain and a Democratic presidency is perceived as a potential threat to gun rights (LaPlant, Lee, and LaPlant 2021), suggesting that there was something distinct about the events of 2020. Violent crime increased that summer

(Federal Bureau of Investigation 2020) and a common narrative attributes the rise in violence to protests against police treatment of African Americans (King 2020). While evidence is inconclusive on how the protests influenced a rise in crime, Lyons et al. (2020) find that a major motivation for gun purchasing between January and May 2020 was fear of crime.

Indeed, considering the potential perceived threat of the COVID-19 pandemic, civilian unrest over police violence, and a contentious election year, we would expect the demand for firearms was high. However, which of these forces, if any, might have had more of an influence on demand? We can gain some insight to this question by examining web searches in 2020.

If we consider that a perceived personal and familial threat from COVID lockdowns and civil unrest might motivate gun purchases, we should expect that interest in guns for personal and family protection would increase. Coinciding with some Protestant Christian traditions, the need for individuals to defend against threats in the twenty-first century might best be resolved by owning a gun. Meanwhile, if the 2020 elections were perceived as potentially creating a change in gun policy, we should expect an interest in guns to be connected to interest in the gun policies of candidates. For conservative Christians, who have aligned themselves with the pro-gun-rights Republican Party, the potential threat of Democratic victory in November might increase the perceived need to purchase a first-time purchase of a gun or add guns to an existing collection (Djupe 2019).

We attempt to break down 2020 interest in guns by examining web searches for guns with Google Trends data. Here we used a search term of "gun for home" as a means of examining gun purchase interest for personal protection. We contrast those searches with searches under "gun policy" as a means to capture interest in the elections and gun positions of candidates. Our effort is similar to that used by Lang and Lang (2020). In Figure 3.1 we display Google Trends results for web searches in the United States using the phrases "gun for home" versus "gun policy" between December 2019 and December 2020. The search volume for each phrase is normalized over the series on a range of 0 to 100 based on the included phrase's proportion to all searches.

The figure reveals a number of peaks in searches for each phrase, with "gun for home" having its highest peaks in March as most of the country went into COVID-induced lockdown and in late May and early June, at the peak of civil unrest over the police killing of George Floyd. Meanwhile, the peaks for "gun policy" searches occur in early 2020 while the Democratic presidential nomination was still contested, again in August as each party held its nominating convention, and in October and November—the peak

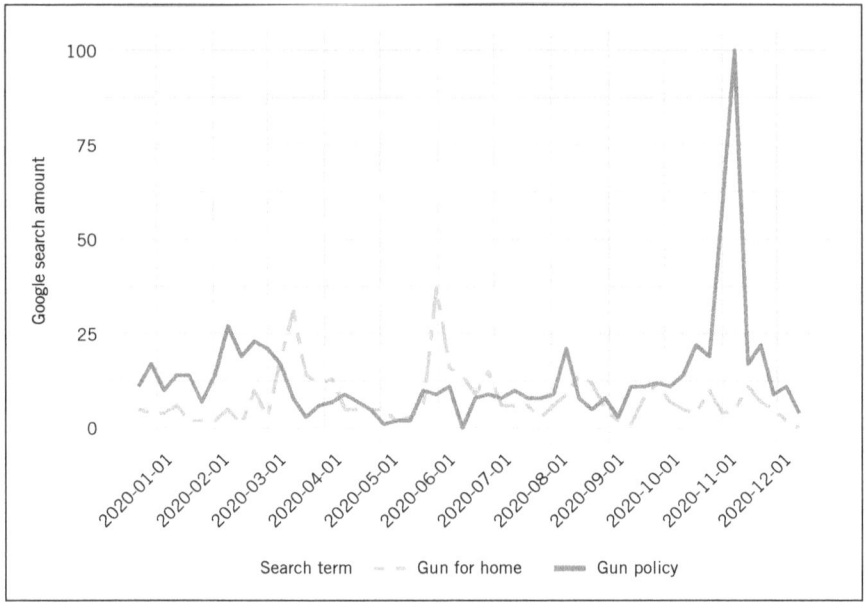

Figure 3.1 Google Trends U.S. Web Searches for Key Terms, December 2019 to December 2020 (Source: Data compiled from Google.)

of attention to the elections. Clearly interest in guns shifted throughout the year. The searches indicate that gun purchasing demand earlier in the year might have been influenced by those looking to buy firearms for personal and family protection, perhaps by first-time gun owners, while gun-related searches later in the year might have been motivated by gun owners and potential gun owners examining the gun policy positions of candidates. We can take a more refined look at these explanations, as well as assess the impact of religion on gun purchasing, using individual-level survey data.

Data and Methods

For our analysis of individuals, our data come from an online survey we commissioned that was administered in October 2020 by Dynata. The survey sample was not a random probability sample of American adults but is representative of the adult population on all major demographic characteristics. Adults were recruited by Dynata, who invited participants via email to complete the survey (see the online appendix). The sample includes 1,784 adults. Of these participants, 513 identified as gun owners, and 150 of these gun owners indicated they purchased a gun between March 2020 and August 2020. Based on this, we estimate that roughly 8 percent of Americans (perhaps over

16 million adults) bought a gun during this time. About half of those who bought a gun during the time frame were first-time gun buyers (42 percent), which suggests that perhaps over 8 million American adults bought a gun for the first time between March and August 2020.

Variable Measurement

Our dependent variables consist of a measure for gun purchases made between March and August 2020 ("Did you buy a gun anytime between March 2020 and August 2020?") and three measures assessing the rationale for that purchase: concern about COVID-19, concern about civil unrest because of police actions toward African Americans, and concern about the outcome of the 2020 election. The gun purchase question is simply dichotomous (0 = no; 1 = yes). The questions on motivation for the purchase allowed respondents to indicate "extremely important" (coded 6) to "not at all important" (coded 1) for COVID-19 concern, unrest concern, and election concern. We model gun purchasing with logistic regression and responses to each concern question with ordered logit.

Our chief independent variables include several measures of religious identification and religiosity. The survey includes the standard question "Would you describe yourself as a 'born-again' or evangelical Christian, or not?" Burge and Lewis (2018) find almost no statistical difference between the full, detailed religious affiliation approach and the simpler scheme that we utilize here. The literature is clear that there is something distinct about *white* evangelicals (Emerson and Smith 2020; Tranby and Harmann 2020), and therefore, we create a dummy variable for white evangelical identification, with all other respondents as the reference category. We investigate both measures of evangelicalism and *white* evangelicalism, recognizing the political relevance of the latter category. We additionally consider religious importance in a respondent's life using the following question: "How important is religion in your life?" Responses were coded as 1 for "not at all important" to 4 for "very important."

We include several variables to control for the demographic considerations shown to be important in research about guns and gun policy (Geier, Kern, and Geier 2017; Goss 2017; Kleck and Kovandzic 2009; Morin 2014; Pederson et al. 2015; Spitzer 2012). We control for race and gender through dichotomous variables in each model (white = 1; female = 1), as well as age (in years), education (on a 7-point scale), and partisan identification of respondents using a 7-point scale, in which strong Democrats are indicated by the highest value.

Results and Discussion

At the bivariate level, evangelicalism is positively associated with buying a gun between the months of March and August 2020 ($r = 0.24$, $p < 0.001$). While this may not initially seem like a particularly strong correlation, it is larger than the correlations for every other variable we consider, including religiosity ($r = 0.23$, $p < 0.001$), race ($r = -0.046$, $p > 0.05$), gender ($r = -0.085$, $p > 0.05$), and partisanship ($r = -0.047$, $p > 0.05$). Shown another way, 43 percent of evangelical Protestants in our sample bought a gun between the months of March and August 2020.

In the multivariate analysis (see full results in the appendix, Table A3.1), religiosity ($\beta = 0.384$, $p < 0.01$) and evangelicalism ($\beta = 0.461$, $p < 0.05$) are the leading predictors for buying a gun between the months of March and August 2020. When we interact evangelicalism and race, comparing white evangelicals to all others in the analysis, white evangelicalism loses predictive power, but religious importance remains significant ($\beta = 0.384$, $p < 0.01$). Women were less likely to purchase a gun during those months in both models ($p < 0.05$). When assessing the predicted probabilities for white evangelicals and others purchasing a firearm between the months of March and August 2020, all individuals who score higher on the religiosity scale experienced an increased likelihood of gun purchase, regardless of religious identity, though white evangelicals are especially impacted by religiosity (see full probabilities in the appendix, Figure A3.1).

Figure 3.2 presents the multivariate models assessing the reasons individuals purchased a firearm between the months of March and August 2020, including models of concerns over COVID-19, concerns over the upcoming 2020 election, and concerns over civil unrest due to police actions toward African Americans (see the full model in the appendix, Table A3.2).

Looking at Americans' citation of concerns over COVID-19 as being an important factor in their decision to buy a gun, the more religious respondents were significantly more likely ($p < 0.001$) to indicate high importance in both the model with evangelicalism broadly and white evangelicalism more specifically. Surprisingly, neither evangelicals nor white evangelicals were significantly more or less likely to assign high importance to COVID-19 ($p > 0.05$). Our other variables do not hold significance in this exploration of COVID-19 as an important rationale for gun purchasing.

Evangelicals were significantly more likely to assign importance to concerns over the upcoming election in purchasing a firearm between the spring or summer of 2020 ($p < 0.10$). White evangelicals, however, do not have a significant relationship with this particular rationale. In addition, more religious

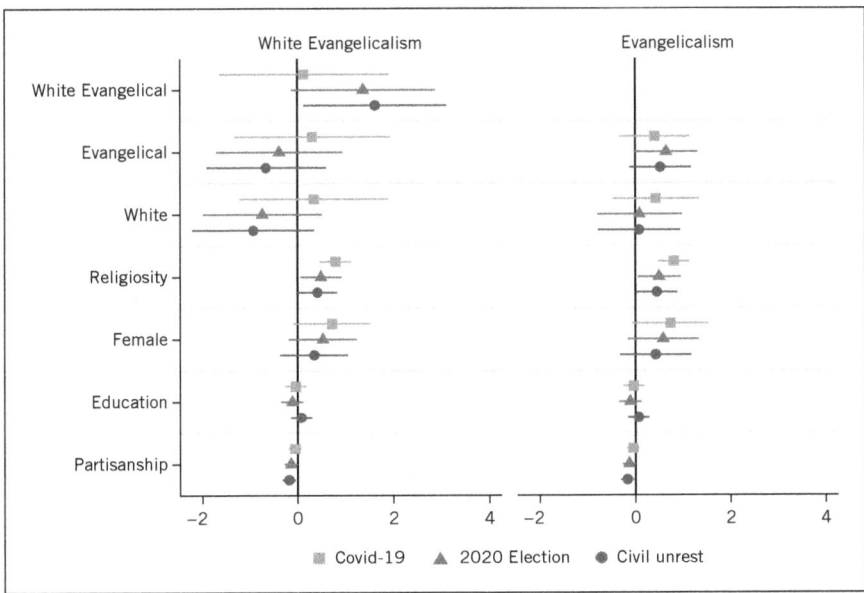

Figure 3.2 Estimated Effects on the Three Rationales for Gun Purchases (Source: KU 2020 survey.)

respondents were more likely to indicate the elections as of high importance in their firearm purchase ($p < 0.05$) in both models. Other variables do not reveal any predictive power.

Model 3 investigates the role of concerns about civil rest over police actions toward African Americans in the purchasing of a firearm. White evangelicals were significantly more likely to cite concerns over civil unrest ($p < 0.05$), though importantly not evangelicals broadly, suggesting a racialized reaction to civil unrest as a motivator for gun purchasing. Religious respondents were also likely to utilize this rationale in both models ($p < 0.05$); meanwhile, Democrats were less likely to assign high importance to concerns over civil unrest in their decision to purchase a firearm in both models ($p < 0.05$).

Conclusion

Gun sales in the United States have sharply risen throughout the COVID-19 pandemic (Lyons et al. 2020). Americans also witnessed widespread civil unrest over police violence and a contentious election in 2020, perhaps motivating some to consider purchasing firearms. Given the exciting literature on religion and guns, we considered the role of religion in gun purchasing during 2020 and what events were more important for those American who did purchase a firearm. Our analysis of data from a representative sample of American adults allows us to draw several tentative conclusions.

First, based on commonly used measurements of gun purchases, gun buying in 2020 was historic (Lang and Lang 2020). Based on the results of our survey sample of 1,784 American adults, we estimate that about 8 percent (perhaps 16 million adults) purchased a gun between March and August 2020. About half of those that bought a gun during the time frame were first-time gun buyers (42 percent), which suggests that over 8 million American adults bought a gun for the first time between March and August 2020.

Second, our analysis suggests that evangelicals were more likely to purchase firearms in 2020. In addition, those with higher religious commitment were more likely to purchase a gun. Given the linkages found between religion and gun ownership, this finding is consistent with existing literature (Yamane 2016) and suggests that the pandemic did not change this previously observed relationship.

Third, we asked those who did purchase firearms whether concern over events in 2020 influenced their decision to buy a gun. Evangelicals were more likely to say their purchase resulted from concerns surrounding the upcoming election, with white evangelicals suggesting the civil unrest relating to police treatment of African Americans motivated their purchase. Neither evangelicals broadly nor white evangelicals specifically cited concerns about the pandemic. This suggests that evangelicals perceived events in 2020 differently than did others who purchased guns.

Evangelicalism's individualist cultural tendencies, as opposed to a collectivist perspective (Emerson and Smith 2001), help explain evangelical gun purchasing in 2020. The emphasis on the individual involves a particular self-protectionist approach to unrest. When considering how evangelicals, perhaps especially those who adopt a Christian nationalist ethic (Perry, Whitehead, and Grubbs 2020a), respond to the COVID-19 pandemic, it is clear that the belief that America is uniquely protected by God precludes the need for self-protectionist action (i.e., purchasing a gun). However, the other forms of unrest experienced during the spring and summer of 2020, including protests over police violence toward African Americans and uncertainty about the outcome of the 2020 presidential election, apparently *do* require action to protect oneself and one's way of life. Exercising a God-given right to purchase a firearm is a seemingly meaningful way to protect the distinct culture that white evangelicals subscribe to—one in which gun ownership is a natural continuation of an emphasis on the individual (Celinska 2007).

Fourth, among religious gun purchasers, concerns about the global pandemic and the 2020 election appear to have played a greater role in motivating their purchase than did civil unrest. In light of this result, it does appear that religious importance has a unique relationship with the justification for purchasing a firearm, one that is distinct from evangelicalism. Unlike evangelicalism broadly or white evangelicalism specifically, religiosity is positively and significantly associated with the expression that concern over COVID-19 was important in the decision to buy a gun. Matthews, Johnson, and Jenks (2011) argue that religiosity is associated with higher levels of generalized social trust and, therefore, less fear of certain concerns, such as crime. When one considers the nature of the pandemic, fear of COVID-19 becomes less about particular and potentially controllable instances of threat. Therefore, the generalized social trust common of the religiously committed may not mitigate the fears of COVID-19, leading to a concern that may inspire a gun purchase. While this is a possible explanation, there are concerns about statistical power given the small sample size. More exploration is certainly needed.

Finally, our study does have limitations. One data limitation already mentioned is the relatively small sample size of gun owners and recent purchasers. Even though our survey sample was representative of American adults, a larger overall sample would have allowed us to better assess the motivations of those respondents that purchased firearms in 2020. In addition, a more systematic analysis could also include direct measures of Christian nationalism and more traditional religion measures. Other researchers should consider including these measures in future research examining the role of religion in gun purchasing.

We do think this project is an important initial step in understanding the gun purchase spike in America during the turbulent year of 2020. Many of the concerns aroused in 2020 will continue, including political polarization, the ongoing threat of COVID, and civil unrest over social justice issues. Social scientists should continue to consider how events are interpreted through religion and how these factors may shape future gun culture.

4

Christian Nationalism and the COVID-19 Pandemic

ANDREW L. WHITEHEAD, SAMUEL L. PERRY,
AND JOSHUA B. GRUBBS

In the waning months of 2020, the United States added over 170,000 new COVID-19 cases and over 1,300 deaths each day. At this point the United States was entering a third upswing in its numbers, unable to maintain any substantial flattening of the curve. By then, over 14 million had been infected and over 270,000 Americans had died. The reality that this pandemic is ongoing and these numbers continue to climb so quickly makes sharing them here somewhat futile. Nevertheless, we do so to anchor just how wildly unsuccessful the United States was at limiting the spread of COVID-19 since it first appeared in the United States in early 2020. Some health experts predict the pandemic—and the need for a coordinated response—will still be with us into 2022. This suggests our exploration into the anemic response of the United States to the COVID-19 pandemic will still be applicable even if the numbers above change.

There are several reasons why the United States responded so poorly. One of the most obvious is the ineffective, and even counterproductive, efforts of then president Trump and his administration. The administration's constant questioning of public health experts, as well as its blatant disregard for common COVID-19 precautions, drastically reduced any likelihood most Americans would unify to suppress infections. Following the lead at the federal level, another reason for the unmitigated spread of the virus was ineffectual responses at the state level, particularly in more conservative states. A third and related reason was how quickly the COVID-19 pandemic was subsumed by the culture wars, where many Americans interpreted various actions aimed at reducing the likelihood of spreading the virus through the lens of their chosen political party or religious group.

Generally, more conservative states with Republican governors were less likely to impose movement and gathering restrictions while more progressive states and Democratic governors did the opposite. Yet some Republican governors, perhaps in response to a less conservative population, did embrace social distancing and masking guidelines. In this sense, political partisanship was not the whole story. While politics were front and center regarding why many Americans took such divergent views of the pandemic, religion played an important role, too. Some faith groups were much more likely to distrust the national media and scientific professionals while others took an opposite view. Several well-known conservative evangelical religious leaders made headlines by continuing to meet in person during the pandemic—in some cases violating state, city, and local ordinances limiting gatherings of large groups—or refusing to encourage mask wearing out in public. John MacArthur, an evangelical megachurch pastor and prolific author, went so far as to claim during an in-person worship service in August 2020, "There is no pandemic." However, many conservative evangelical congregations and leaders sought to abide by the public health guidelines. We cannot merely reduce the underlying influence of religion to religious affiliation or some other aspect of religiosity.

We make the case that a particular political theology and conception of public religion, Christian nationalism, continues to play a powerful role in understanding Americans' responses to the COVID-19 pandemic. We show Christian nationalism is consistently one of the most important predictors of (1) the precautions Americans did (and did not) take to respond to the pandemic, (2) Americans' views toward federal and local governmental response to the pandemic and their priorities, and (3) the explanations Americans embraced regarding the cause of the virus—which were often overtly xenophobic and racist—and why minority communities were being disproportionately affected. To begin, however, we first quickly define what Christian nationalism is and theorize why it is so strongly associated with behaviors and beliefs regarding the COVID-19 pandemic.

Christian Nationalism in the United States

Defining Christian Nationalism

Christian nationalism is a cultural framework—a collection of myths, narratives, symbols, traditions, and value systems—that advocates for a close relationship between American civic life and a particular interpretation of

Christianity (Whitehead and Perry 2020a). We specify "particular interpretation" because studies repeatedly find the "Christianity" of Christian nationalism brings with it assumptions about nativism, patriarchy, white supremacy, militarism, authoritarianism, and heteronormativity. In the minds of those Americans who embrace Christian nationalism, to be truly American, one must generally be white, native-born, and culturally and politically conservative. Groups outside these boundaries are identified as Other and routinely denied equal access to cultural and political power in America.

There are several ways researchers measure Christian nationalism. In most of our work, we rely on a scale consisting of a handful of questions concerning respondents' views toward the relationship between religion and the public sphere. For instance, we ask Americans how much they agree with the following statements:

- "The federal government should declare the United States a Christian nation."
- "The federal government should advocate Christian values."
- "The federal government should enforce strict separation of church and state [reverse coded]."
- "The federal government should allow prayer in public schools."
- "The federal government should allow religious symbols in public spaces."
- "The success of the United States is part of God's plan."

Respondents can strongly agree, agree, disagree, strongly disagree, or state they are undecided. We then assign point values to each response and combine them to create a scale. Americans who score low on the scale mostly reject Christian nationalism, while those on the upper end of the scale wholly embrace it. See Whitehead and Perry (2020a) for a more extensive discussion of this measurement strategy.

A dynamic literature around Christian nationalism finds it is influential in understanding Americans' attitudes toward a broad number of topics. Social scientists find Christian nationalism is consistently important when examining such topics as racial inequality (Davis and Perry 2020; Perry and Whitehead 2019), support for gun control (Whitehead, Schnabel, and Perry 2018), punitive beliefs (Davis 2018), immigration (Dahab and Omori 2019; Sherkat and Lehman 2018), gender attitudes (Whitehead and Perry 2019), same-sex marriage (Whitehead and Perry 2015), and religious minorities (Stewart, Edgell, and Delehanty 2018). There is evidence Christian nationalism has diffused across American culture (Delehanty, Edgell, and Stewart 2019; Whitehead and Perry 2020a) and is not solely located in one religious tradition or sociodemographic group. In fact, some find Christian nationalism is equally or at times even more influential outside of organized religion (Braunstein and Taylor 2017; Stroope et al. 2020).

Christian Nationalism and Epistemic Authority

A fundamental aspect of Christian nationalism is power, the ability to direct the course of the country in a particular direction despite resistance. Power, however, must be legitimized in some way. Therefore, arguments for a more "Christian" nation necessarily include claims around which sources of authority should be central. Recent work demonstrates Christian nationalism is a key mechanism explaining the ongoing perceived "conflict" between science and religion, two sources of epistemic authority some Americans view as oppositional. Christian nationalism seeks to enshrine a specific moral order based on particular interpretations of the Christian Bible. Any alternative source of authority, like science, is an epistemic threat that must be opposed. It is no surprise Baker et al. (2020a) find Christian nationalism is one of the strongest predictors of believing scientists are hostile to faith, creationism should be taught in public schools, and our country relies too much on science over religion. To achieve the desired end—asserting a dominant moral and cultural authority around conservative Christianity—only particular sources of authority are acceptable.

The relationship between Christian nationalism and science is fundamental to understanding the social and cultural divides regarding COVID-19 across the American population. Embracing Christian nationalism leads to a tribalism that denies the authority of scientists and public health experts. This has grave consequences for any coordinated effort around a public health crisis. As with many other significant social problems, Christian nationalism serves as a lens through which the pandemic—including its causes, consequences, and the proper individual and social responses to it—is refracted. Throughout the rest of this chapter, we explore some of these issues, beginning with the personal actions Americans did and did not take to stop the spread of the COVID-19 virus. First, a quick word on the data we use in each of the following sections.

Christian Nationalism and COVID-19 Pandemic Data

The data in each of the three sections below are from the third wave of the Public Discourse and Ethics Survey (PDES) collected in May 2020. This wave of the PDES was a supplemental wave to gather data on the experiences and interpretations of the COVID-19 crisis and followed the first wave collected in August 2019 and the second wave collected in February 2020. It is a nationally representative panel survey of American adults collected by YouGov, an international research data and analytics company. The original data collection included 2,519 respondents with 1,533 respondents in wave 3 due to sample attrition. For more information about the PDES, see Perry and Grubbs (2020).

Christian Nationalism and COVID-19 Behaviors

When COVID-19 first arrived in the United States, there was little concerted effort at the highest levels of government to send a consistent message to citizens concerning how they should respond. Public health officials at the Centers for Disease Control and other federal agencies warned of the seriousness of the COVID-19 virus and suggested Americans wear masks, limit gathering in groups outside their immediate family, and suspend much of their normal day-to-day activities, especially travel. However, then president Trump would routinely question or even downplay these and other precautionary behaviors, saying the virus would soon disappear, perhaps even on its own. While the federal government declined to make an effort to combat the spread of COVID-19, many states, businesses, and localities took drastic steps. Mask requirements, spacing guidelines, and even closing or limiting the number of people in various establishments soon gained traction. While many Americans supported taking—and in some cases even mandating—certain precautionary behaviors or limiting incautious behaviors, this support was not uniform across the population. In fact, we find Christian nationalism was a key factor in explaining the divides across the American public regarding ignoring recommended precautions and acting incautiously (Perry, Whitehead, and Grubbs 2020b).

In the PDES we asked how often in the last two weeks respondents performed the following behaviors—what many health experts labeled as incautious during the pandemic:

- ate inside a restaurant
- attended a gathering of ten or more people
- visited family or friends in person
- went shopping for nonessential items
- went to a medical appointment

- went to a place of worship
- went to a drug store
- went to work outside my home

We then also asked them how often they performed several precautionary behaviors:

- washed my hands more often than typical
- avoided touching my face
- used hand sanitizer more than usual
- wore a mask in public

When we combine each of the first eight measures into an "incautious behaviors" scale, we find even when accounting for various sociodemographic measures, politics, and religiosity, Christian nationalism was the strongest predictor in the entire model. We found Americans who embrace Christian nationalism were much more likely to report eating inside a restaurant, attend gatherings of ten or more people, visit family or friends in person, or shop for nonessential items at least weekly during one of the heights of the COVID-19 pandemic.

While Americans who embrace Christian nationalism are more likely to behave incautiously, it does not also mean they refused to take precautionary behaviors. Perhaps these Americans took precautionary measures like washing their hands more often, wearing a mask, and avoiding touching their face despite not practicing social distancing. We find, however, they did not. Embracing Christian nationalism is also significantly associated with refusing to practice precautionary behaviors. We found embracing Christian nationalism meant someone was *less* likely to wash their hands more often than typical and avoid touching their face. Most importantly, we found that the more Americans subscribe to Christian nationalist ideology, the more likely they were to abstain from mask wearing, even when it was highly encouraged or even mandated.

One final important finding is Christian nationalism and religious practice are not similarly associated with taking various precautions during the COVID-19 pandemic. Once we account for Americans' embrace of Christian nationalism, we find those who practice their religion more regularly—attend religious services, pray, and say religion is important to them—are *more* likely to take precautionary measures. We explore this tendency for religious practice and Christian nationalism to work in opposing directions elsewhere (Whitehead and Perry 2020a).

It is clear that during the first national peak of the pandemic in May 2020, Christian nationalism was one of the most important ideological factors structuring Americans' personal behaviors surrounding COVID-19. There are a number of possible explanations for this strong association. As discussed previously, Christian nationalism is strongly associated with skepticism toward science and scientists, seeing them as an alternative source of authority who should not be easily trusted (Baker et al. 2020a). Other work highlights how Christian nationalism is linked to a distrust of the mainstream news media and is a consistent predictor of support for Trump, who routinely cast doubt on the seriousness of COVID-19 and the necessity of taking precautionary behaviors (Baker, Perry, and Whitehead 2020b; Whitehead et al. 2018).

Americans' behavioral responses to COVID-19 were and continue to be polarized. This polarization was and is powerfully shaped by Christian nationalism. The implications are clear: American lives were lost due to the inability of all citizens to mount a collective response. Despite Biden's win in the November 2020 election and his quick promise to dramatically change the federal government's response to the pandemic, the collective response of all Americans "will potentially remain limited as long as the recommended behaviors are connected to Americans' fear of cultural, epistemic, and political threat" (Perry et al. 2020b). Next, we turn to how Christian nationalism is associated with Americans' views on governmental restrictions around the COVID-19 pandemic.

Christian Nationalism and Governmental Restrictions Due to COVID-19

Americans' views toward if and whether governmental restrictions in response to the COVID-19 pandemic were necessary or legal were as quickly polarized as the individual actions they mandated. Controversy raged over whether federal, state, or local government had the right to dictate if and where citizens had to wear a mask, how large of a group they could congregate with, or if they had to self-quarantine after potential exposure to the virus. Those on the political and religious Right were vociferous in their opposition to any governmental involvement in how Americans responded to the pandemic. Republicans were much more critical of governmental restrictions and worked to limit or lift those restrictions as soon as possible, citing concerns about the economy and the importance of individual liberty (Evans and Hargittai 2020). Former GOP presidential candidate and politically conservative cable news pundit Mike Huckabee claimed governmental restrictions were violating the U.S. Constitution by limiting Americans' civil liberties (Nelson 2020a). The president of a conservative think tank in Wisconsin—who sued Governor Tony Evers over his mask mandate—claimed, "There is no pandemic exception to the rule of law or our Constitution" (Associated Press 2020).

Those on the religious Right echoed these concerns, especially citing fears of limitations on "religious freedom" given many congregations would not be allowed to meet with certain restrictions in place. John MacArthur, well-known pastor of a conservative evangelical megachurch in California, connected the dots regarding the importance of individual freedom and liberty in light of COVID-19 restrictions:

> Just terrify people that they might die and they'll all roll over in complete compliance. They'll give up their freedoms, they'll put on silly masks, they'll put gloves on their hands, and they'll sit in their house for as long as you tell them to sit there. You can conquer an entire nation in fear. . . . Whatever happens in terms of the future of America, we're going to enjoy probably less and less freedoms anyway. There may be speedups to the robbing us of those freedoms coming through something like [COVID-19]. (MacArthur 2020)

He and his congregation chose to meet in person during the pandemic and ended up suing the local government over COVID restrictions. Echoing the theme of individual liberty and freedom of choice, Franklin Graham—head of the Billy Graham Evangelistic Association—shared, "If a pastor and his congregation felt that it was important to meet, I guess that's their business" (Janes 2020). This is notable because at the time Graham was strongly urging Americans to wear masks and practice social distancing, underscoring the seriousness of COVID-19.

The libertarianism and neoliberalism inherent within Christian nationalism help illuminate the clear overlap in these almost identical responses from both political and religious conservatives. Scholars highlight how libertarianism became coterminous with "Christian" at a particular moment in American history. Kruse (2015) and Marti (2020a, 2020b) trace their emergence during in the middle of the twentieth century as the United States began to (re)define itself as a Christian nation. Individual liberty, free-market capitalism, and fear of government overreach became intimately intertwined with a specific understanding of the United States as one favored by the Christian God and destined to shine as a light to the world.

We again turn to the PDES to explore these relationships. Respondents shared their views on various imposed social distancing restrictions embraced by many states and localities. These questions generally coalesced around whether Americans thought it was imperative to protect the economy, individual liberty, or the vulnerable. To measure "protect the economy," we stated, "We must lift social distancing restrictions as soon as possible in order to avoid economic collapse," and "Saving the economy by lifting social distancing restrictions is worth the health risk to older Americans." To measure "protect liberty," we stated, "Governments have the right to restrict our businesses and travel for the sake of minimizing COVID-19 infections," which we reverse coded, and "Citizens have the right to expose themselves to risk if they would prefer to work and travel freely." And finally, to measure "protect the vulnerable," we asked for respondents' agreement with the statements, "Those who are protesting social distancing restrictions are endangering others with their ignorance," and "States should continue social distancing restrictions as long as necessary in order to protect the vulnerable." Respondents could strongly disagree to strongly agree, and we averaged each pair of measures together to create scales.

There is a clear relationship between embracing Christian nationalism and whether Americans are more likely to protect the economy, liberty, or the vulnerable. As you can see in Figure 4.1, as Americans embrace Christian nationalism more strongly, they are much more likely to agree protecting the economy and protecting liberty are most important when considering social distancing restrictions. The opposite is true regarding protecting the vulnerable. Progressing higher on the Christian nationalism scale equates to a greater likelihood of disagreement that protecting the vulnerable is most important. It is important to note that the relationships depicted in the figure take into account respondents' political views, religiosity, and sociodemographic characteristics like age, gender, and education. The underlying statistical models demonstrate Christian nationalism is not merely one factor to consider to understand these attitudes—it is consistently the *most* important factor to consider (Perry, Whitehead, and Grubbs 2021). Christian nationalism is powerfully associated with Americans' propensity to prioritize protecting the economy and individual liberty during the COVID-19 pandemic over and against protecting vulnerable populations like the immune-compromised or elderly.

Yet again, we find in our statistical models that religiosity inclines Americans to be *more* likely to want to protect the vulnerable rather than protect the economy or individual liberty (Perry et al. 2021). While religiosity—frequency of worship service attendance or prayer—is correlated with prioritizing the economy and liberty over protecting the vulnerable, once we account for Americans' embrace of Christian nationalism the relationship completely reverses. This suggests religious practice is not connected to libertarian values

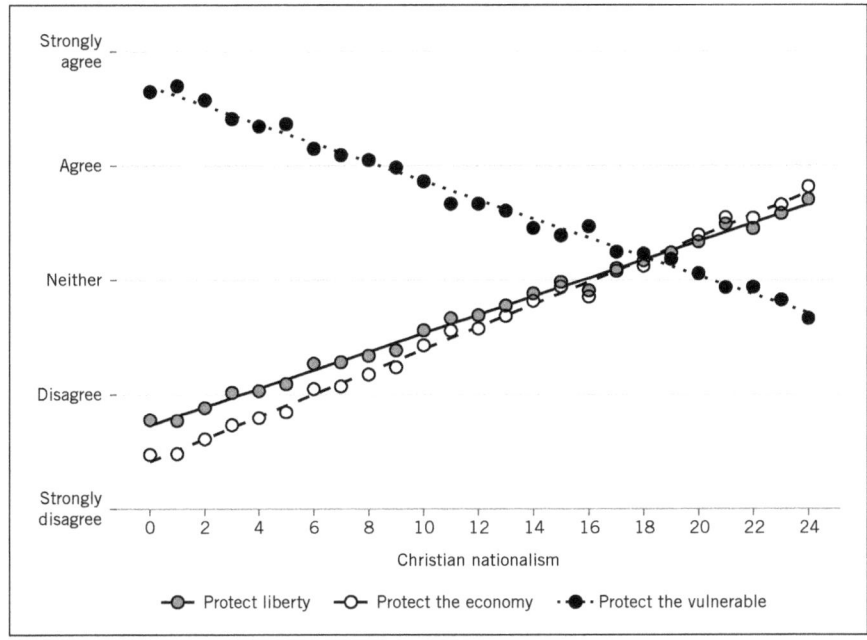

Figure 4.1 Christian Nationalism and Americans' Views toward Governmental Social Distancing Restrictions. Note: Models control for race, age, gender, marital status, children, education, income, region, employment, political party, political ideology, religious affiliation, and religiosity. (Source: 2020 Public Discourse and Ethics Survey.)

in response to COVID-19. Rather, Christian nationalism accounts for the tendency of religious Americans to espouse more libertarian ideology regarding governmental responses to the pandemic.

The role Christian nationalism plays in making sense of Americans' individual behavioral responses to the COVID-19 pandemic and their views toward governmental intervention regarding social distancing restrictions carries with it implications for future research on health care topics generally and health care policy in particular. Recent research demonstrates Christian nationalism is strongly associated with antivaccine attitudes (Whitehead and Perry 2020b) and plays an important role in whether Americans reject a COVID-19 vaccine (Corcoran, Scheitle, and DiGregorio 2021). Americans' views of the Affordable Care Act (ACA) might also be related to the strength of their embrace of Christian nationalism. As portions of the ACA are still debated in various court battles, understanding public perception of the landmark health care law continues to be of consequence.

In the next section, we turn to explanations of the origins of the virus. We find among Christian nationalists such explanations are increasingly racialized.

Christian Nationalism, Racism, and Xenophobia Surrounding COVID-19

From the very beginning of the COVID-19 crisis, then president Trump and his coterie of supporters routinely broadcast both racist and xenophobic explanations alongside questionable solutions for limiting its spread. On multiple occasions—even in a church—Trump referred to COVID-19 as the "China virus," the "Chinese virus," and the "Kung flu" (Lee 2020). Charlie Kirk, Tucker Carlson, and Kevin McCarthy joined him in this messaging (Perry, Whitehead, and Baker 2020). Charlie Kirk, cofounder of Liberty University's now-defunct Falkirk Center for Faith and Liberty, suggested a wall on the southern border of the United States was needed now more than ever. Trump agreed. While never delivering on the promise, then president Trump assured all immigration from China would be suspended: "We would've had thousands of people additionally die if we let people come in from heavily infected China. But we stopped it. We did a travel ban in January. . . . By closing up, we saved millions, potentially millions of lives." In reality, more than 8,000 Chinese and foreign nationals and over 27,000 Americans arrived in the United States from China after the "restrictions" were put in place (Braun, Yen, and Woodward 2020).

The racial disparities in COVID-19 infections and deaths throughout the COVID-19 pandemic continue to be profound (Kendi 2020). By the fall of 2020, Black Americans were dying at 2.2 times the rate of white Americans, followed by American Indian or Alaska Natives, and Hispanic or Latino Americans, with rates of each group exceeding whites by 1.5 (COVID Tracking Project 2020). Infection rates for minority groups also consistently exceed white Americans. The virus continues to ravage prison populations, and the overrepresentation of racial and ethnic minorities in prison only adds to the racial disparities in COVID-19 infection rates and death (Dall 2020). The explanations for these disparities ranged from blaming personal behaviors—like Black Americans do not wash their hands enough—to the biological, that some minorities have a predisposed weakness to the virus. Some went even so far as to say prisoners did not deserve protective measures (Paxton 2020).

We find Christian nationalism is a crucial factor to understanding these various racist and xenophobic attitudes and interpretations of the COVID-19 pandemic. Prior research on Christian nationalism repeatedly demonstrates its strong and enduring association with both racist and xenophobic attitudes and beliefs (Dahab and Omori 2019; Perry and Whitehead 2019; Sherkat and Lehman 2019). Christian nationalism demarcates boundary lines around American identity that highlight ethnocultural markers, including race, nativity, and religious background. Generally, Christian nationalism is interested in a "Christian nation" where white, native-born, and culturally Christian citizens enjoy privileged access to the levers of power.

We asked respondents for their level of agreement with various common racist interpretations of the originating cause of the pandemic and the reason for its continued spread:

- It is racist to refer to COVID-19 as "the Chinese virus."
- The fact that poor, minority communities are more likely to be infected with COVID-19 is a symptom of our unjust society.
- Black Americans are being infected with COVID-19 at higher rates largely because they are not behaving responsibly.
- Some racial minority groups may have a biological susceptibility to COVID-19.
- The fact that COVID-19 is spreading rapidly among prison inmates should be the least of our concerns.
- If prison inmates are being infected with COVID-19 at higher rates, that could be a form of divine justice.

We also asked questions tapping into xenophobic views of the COVID-19 pandemic. We combined these questions into a scale measuring Americans' belief that restricting immigration is a solution to the virus:

- Our lax immigration laws are partly to blame for the COVID-19 crisis.
- All immigration should be halted at least temporarily to protect American jobs during this time.
- One way to prevent further pandemics in the United States would be to build the wall along our southern border.

Even when accounting for a host of other possible explanations for the COVID-19 crisis—age, gender, race, education, income, political ideology, political partisanship, religiosity—in *every single one* of our multivariate statistical models, Christian nationalism is not only an important predictor; it is the *single strongest predictor* (Perry, Whitehead, and Grubbs 2020a). Interestingly, we also find the influence of Christian nationalism on racist and xenophobic interpretations of the COVID-19 pandemic differs across racial and ethnic groups, especially for white and Black Americans. Christian nationalism is particularly powerful among white Americans (see Figure 4.2). White Americans at the upper ends of the Christian nationalism scale are much more likely to disagree it is racist to call COVID-19 "the China virus" or that the higher minority infection rate is the symptom of an unjust society. These same people are much more likely to agree that restricting immigration—lax immigration laws are partly to blame, immigration should be halted to protect American jobs, and building a wall on the southern border would prevent further pandemics—is a solution to the pandemic and higher prisoner infection rates should be the least of our concerns.

Christian nationalism, embraced to some extent by over half of white Americans, clearly defines exclusionary boundaries around race and ethnicity, and this has serious implications for views surrounding the COVID-19

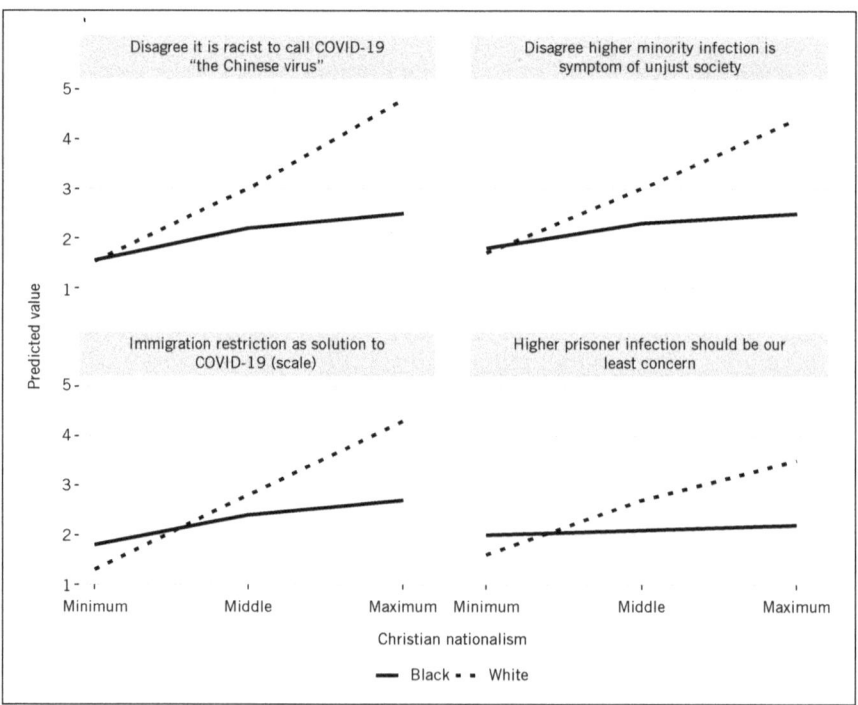

Figure 4.2 Christian Nationalism and Racist or Xenophobic Evaluation/ Interpretation of COVID-19 by Race/Ethnicity. Note: Models control for race, age, gender, marital status, children, education, income, region, political party, political ideology, religious affiliation, and religiosity. (Source: 2020 Public Discourse and Ethics Survey.)

crisis and how to mitigate its effects. Yet again, once we account for Americans' embrace of Christian nationalism, the effect of religiosity on each of these measures is opposite of Christian nationalism. Devout Americans who reject or resist Christian nationalism are much less likely to espouse racist or xenophobic interpretations of the COVID-19 pandemic (Perry et al. 2020a). This suggests that for researchers to understand the influence of religion on racialized explanations of the COVID-19 pandemic, it is essential they account for Christian nationalism.

Conclusion

As we write this chapter in late 2020, there appears to be a ray of hope on the horizon regarding the COVID-19 pandemic. Two pharmaceutical companies report evidence of vaccines that are 90–95 percent effective with an estimated arrival to the public in early 2021. Of course, only time will reveal whether each vaccine lives up to these early reports to company stockholders. It could be that by the time this book reaches its readers, one or more vaccines will have been on the market for over a year. Of course, Christian nationalism significantly alters even this possibility for hope: Americans who embrace Christian nationalism are much more likely to espouse antivaccine attitudes (Whitehead and Perry 2020b). Given that over half of Americans are generally amendable to Christian nationalism, with a fifth strongly embracing it, the likelihood of their delaying or outright refusing to accept a COVID-19 vaccine is high. Recent research shows that the COVID-19 vaccine is yet another example of the polarization of the COVID-19 pandemic with Christian nationalism playing a vital role (Corcoran et al. 2021). This clearly dovetails with our findings from this chapter, which show individual behaviors, attitudes toward governmental responses, or espousing overtly racist and xenophobic explanations for the pandemic are all polarized and Christian nationalism is essential to those relationships.

It is also important to note that in each of the above sections, religious practice operates differently compared to Christian nationalism. To understand the effect of religion on Americans' behaviors and beliefs about COVID-19, researchers must account for public expressions of religion, like Christian nationalism, alongside private expressions of religion. Once we account for Americans' embrace of Christian nationalism, how often they attend religious services or pray tends to be significantly and powerfully associated with taking more precautionary actions and limiting incautious behaviors, wanting to protect the vulnerable rather than the economy or personal liberty, and rejecting racist and xenophobic explanations of COVID-19's spread. This is true even when we account for political party and political ideology.

It is impossible to predict exactly how COVID-19 will continue to shape social life around the globe over the next months and even years. We can be sure, however, Christian nationalism will continue to be near the center of that story in the United States.

5

Syndemics during a Pandemic

Racial Inequity, Poverty, and COVID-19

DILARA K. ÜSKÜP AND RYON J. COBB

Black Americans are nearly three times as likely to be hospitalized and nearly twice as likely to die from COVID-19 as their white, non-Hispanic counterparts (Centers for Disease Control and Prevention 2021). These disparate outcomes are not unique to the COVID-19 pandemic. In fact, across multiple health conditions, Black Americans have an earlier onset of disease and worse outcomes than white Americans (Adams and Simoni 2016). In contrast to their white counterparts, Black Americans experience severe disparities in overall well-being and health, having "higher rates of impairment, illness and death" (D. Williams 2012).

We define health disparities as "differences in health outcomes that are closely linked with social, economic, and environmental disadvantage—[often] driven by the social conditions in which individuals live, learn, work and play" (World Health Organization 2021). We differentiate health disparities from health inequities, which are the results of structural and institutional factors and systems of oppression that disproportionately harm certain groups over others. As such, a health inequity is a state of unfairness.

Health inequities can perpetuate racial health disparities. The racial disparities in COVID-19 health outcomes are inextricably tied to Black Americans' prior experiences in the health care system, preexisting health conditions, and historical racial oppression. This chapter examines the ways preexisting social determinants of health and medical mistrust created a ripe environment among already vulnerable communities for the COVID-19 pandemic to result in disproportionate rates of infection, hospitalization, and death. This environment further suffered from failures at the federal level, where former president Trump's COVID-19 response was to spread false information, de-emphasize scientific public health approaches, and emphasize conspiracy theories in lieu of a concerted federal effort. While minorities may not have approved of Trump and been distrustful of Trump's false COVID-19 assertions, they remained reluctant to become vaccinated and had serious reservations about the vaccine. Medical mistrust specific to COVID-19 has been prevalent during the pandemic, particularly among Black Americans (Bogart et al. 2021). This mistrust has extended to COVID-19 vaccines. In a poll conducted by MassINC Polling Group in Massachusetts in December 2020, only 20 percent of Black women and 20 percent of Latina women opted to take the COVID-19 vaccine as soon as possible. Participants cited concerns that the vaccine had not been thoroughly tested and expressed a disinclination to trust the U.S. government on health care issues.

In this chapter, our discussion will focus on Black Americans' disproportionate COVID-19 burden and health inequities. We will touch on how Latino communities have been adversely affected by racial/ethnic oppression and the COVID-19 pandemic. Finally, we will consider the role of clergy in the COVID-19 pandemic by utilizing the March and October 2020 survey data from Djupe, Lewis, and Burge to examine whether Americans trust clergy and health professionals to have their health interests at heart.

Preexisting Pandemic Conditions

Entrenched institutional and social factors influence health behavior, health care access, and health status, setting the stage for pandemic vulnerability. The COVID-19 pandemic precipitated social, economic, and environmental factors that existed before the pandemic that led to increased risk of contraction of and death from COVID-19 within Black and Latino communities. These factors are the social determinants of health—the conditions in the environments where people are born, live, learn, work, play, worship, and age that affect a wide range of health, functioning, and quality-of-life outcomes and risks (U.S. Department of Health and Human Services 2021). Figure 5.1 groups the six domains of the social determinants of health: (1) economic stability, (2) neighborhood and physical/built environment, (3) education quality and access, (4) food quality and access, (5) community and social context, and finally (6) coverage of and access to high-quality health care.

The social determinants of health directly contributed to COVID-19 racial and ethnic disparities. Working in essential fields that were not easily transferred

Economic stability	Neighborhood and physical environment	Education	Food	Community and social context	Health care system
Employment	Housing	Literacy	Hunger	Social integration	Health coverage
Income	Transportation	Language	Access to healthy options	Support systems	Provider availability
Expenses	Safety	Early childhood education		Community engagement	Provider linguistic and cultural competency
Debt	Parks	Vocational training		Discrimination	Quality of care
Medical bills	Playgrounds	Higher education		Stress	
Support	Walkability				
	Zip code/ geography				

Health outcomes
Mortality, morbidity, life expectancy, health care expenditures, health status, functional limitations

Figure 5.1 Social Determinants of Health (Source: Artiga and Hinton 2018.)

to remote work, a situation significantly more common among Black and Latino Americans than their white counterparts (U.S. Bureau of Labor Statistics 2020), led to increased exposure to the virus. Racial/ethnic disparities in educational attainment drive employment type and limit access to higher-paying jobs with benefits. In frontline roles disproportionately occupied by Black or Latino Americans, such as warehouse, trucking, postal service, and building cleaning services jobs, individuals are more likely to continue working through illness, as many do not have access to worker's compensation or leave policies (Rho et al. 2020).

Neighborhood and physical environment also directly impacted exposure and infection. Residential crowding brought on by racial segregation, redlining, and a lack of affordable housing multiplies the number of individuals in a given area and increases the risk of virus spread. On the macro level, discrimination, structural and institutional racism, income inequality, and violence also contribute to chronic stress, wearing down immunity and making the body susceptible to infectious diseases (Bae et al. 2019). Racism, in particular, has negative effects on mental and physical health (Williams and Mohammed 2013). Finally, lack of access to health insurance (including the affordability of routine visits, medication, and medical devices/equipment to manage chronic disease) and underinsurance coupled with chronic and preexisting conditions, including unmanaged asthma or diabetes, to result in increased risk for more severe or deadly coronavirus infections (Maragakis 2020).

Even when people of color can access health care, they may experience provider bias. Provider bias is a form of implicit bias, attitudes or stereotypes that affect our understanding, actions, and decisions in an unconscious manner. Provider bias can impact health outcomes—examples include undertreating pain (Hirsh et al. 2015) and ignoring birth complications in the case of Black maternal and infant health and mortality (Maina et al. 2018). People of color tend to be less satisfied with their interactions with health care providers, as "dominant communication styles, fewer demonstrated positive emotions, infrequent requests for input about treatment decisions, and less patient-centered care seem to characterize patient provider interactions involving people of color" (Hall et al. 2015).

While we recognize people of color may experience higher burdens of chronic health conditions, including lung disease, heart disease, and asthma, that may be associated with poorer outcomes from COVID-19, the social determinants of health provide a framework to shift our analysis from the individual to the broader system. Social factors influence health outcomes, both directly through the living conditions they create and indirectly by shaping individual behaviors, creating a chronic cycle where health inequities lead to health disparities. In this next section, we specifically discuss how racism and discrimination have led to medical mistrust, which impacted health outcomes in the Black community.

Historical Discrimination Leads to Mistrust

Medical mistrust is animated by a distrust of medical providers, treatments, and health care systems. The absence of trust creates an environment wherein patients become skeptical that providers and organizations genuinely care for patients' interests, are honest, practice confidentiality, or have the proficiency to produce the best achievable outcomes. Medical mistrust is not just a lack of trust in the medical system and personnel but the belief that medical professionals are willingly acting with ill intent toward them. This mistrust often extends to the pharmaceutical industry and government. It is considered "an active response to direct or vicarious (e.g., inter-generational or social network stories, collective memory) marginalization" (Benkert et al. 2019).

Experiencing actual or perceived discrimination is associated with higher mistrust. Mistrust is not necessarily harmful. In fact, skepticism can be healthy when it leads to seeking second opinions, asking questions, seeking additional explanations, or further services. Mistrust can empower individuals for change when channeled effectively. Also, mistrust can serve as a protective or survival mechanism in the face of historical and ongoing oppression.

Yet mistrust can have devastating impacts on health behaviors and outcomes, especially among groups that are already socially and economically marginalized: "Whether the genesis of the mistrust is based on fact or fallacy, the results may be similar. There are myriad negative consequences associated with medical mistrust, including lower utilization of healthcare and poorer management of health conditions" (Jaiswal 2019). Mistrust explains the association between discrimination and certain health behaviors (e.g., longer time between medical exams, lack of seeking treatment, or nonadherence to treatments). Medical mistrust is an important, albeit not exclusive, explanation for staggering racial health disparities and COVID-19–related outcomes.

Among Black Americans, high levels of medical mistrust are a response to historical injustices, ongoing discrimination, and systemic racism. While the medical and public health literature largely cites the U.S. Public Health Service and the Centers for Disease Control and Prevention study at Tuskegee University[1] as the primary provocation for "persistent health-related mistrust among people of color and other groups who experience social and economic vulnerability" (Jaiswal et al. 2019), we briefly outline below additional, historical events and oppression that contributed to ongoing medical mistrust among Black Americans.

The period of African enslavement in America was a medically managed enterprise. Doctors "inspected" people who were enslaved before they were forcibly taken to slave ships. Moreover, doctors were employed to ensure the "cargo" remained alive and healthy during transport. In fact, the Dolben Act (referred to as the Slave Carrying Bill) in 1788 mandated all English slave ships have a doctor on board (Rediker 2008). Capitalism served as the catalyst for medical practice during enslavement, and doctors were rewarded: "The more you [the doctor] preserve of them [people who were enslaved] for the Plantations the more Profit you [the doctor] will have, and also the greater reputation and Wages another voyage" (Sheridan 1985).

Medical practice was integral to the economic success of the plantation, too. The partnership between the slaveowner and doctor played a key role in establishing "soundness at the auction block." When people who were enslaved became ill or died, this was considered a significant financial loss for the slaveowner. To reduce costs incurred by the owner, slaveowners sought to avoid professional medical care for people who were enslaved (Washington 2006). Thus, people who were enslaved were often first attended to by other people who were enslaved using traditional methods passed down over generations. People who were enslaved avoided harsh "treatments" from their owners. If a doctor was called and unable to provide assistance, people who were enslaved were admitted to poorly resourced "slave hospitals." At most plantations, enslaved Black women were designated as midwives to attend births of enslaved women, as well as slaveowners' wives and mistresses, and were assigned to care for their babies and children.

Moreover, medical experimentation was common on enslaved Black people. The "Father of Modern Gynecology," Dr. J. Marion Sims, founded the New York Women's Hospital (Washington 2006). He owned slaves and did experiments on them without anesthesia, including on eleven Black women, to develop and refine the repair of vesicovaginal fistula. He also conducted surgical experimentation on babies to learn about "newborn" tetanus. Black bodies sustained abuse by the medical establishment even after death (Clark 1998). The panicked need for bodies to practice various procedures and anatomy created an appetite at the expense of Blacks and poor whites. This made Black and poor white people wary about going to hospitals—that they would be unnecessarily experimented on or allowed to die so they could be used for practice. The practice of "grave robbing" and worry about the "night doctors" emerged. These bodies were often shipped to medical schools in the North as well—medical schools advertised that they had "dissecting material."

Up until the 1960s, hospitals were rigidly segregated by race (Duke University 2021). In the south, per Jim Crow laws, separate hospitals existed for Black patients, where Black doctors could train. In the North, training opportunities and staff privileges at historically white institutions were offered only to whites, helping ensure separate and unequal care. The emergence of Black hospitals called "the Black Hospital Movement" (1865–1960s), established by the Medical Division of the Freedmen's Bureau, was brought on to improve the health of Black people (Duke University 2021).

With the passage of the Medicare program in the 1960s, desegregation of hospitals was swift. While the Johnson administration's Office of Equal Health Opportunity sought to ensure that hospitals were in compliance with the law, and thus eligible for federal funds, other medical injustices remained. The legacy of medical experimentation without informed consent continued until 1974 (Washington 2006) with the passage of the National Research Act, which established Institutional Review Boards. Specific, unethical experiments include the "Tuskegee Study of Untreated Syphilis in the Negro Male" (Brandt 1978) conducted by the U.S. Public Health Service and the Centers for Disease Control and Prevention (1932–1972), untreated syphilis on Guatemalan prison inmates and psychiatric patients in the 1940s (Selyukh 2011), Henrietta Lacks's cervical cancer cells taken without her consent becoming the first immortalized cell line in 1951 (Skloot 2011), and "the pill" studies in Puerto Rico in 1955 (Roberts 1998).

Eugenics and reproductive coercion were at the center of "reproductive health care" in the twentieth century. "Well-born" (i.e., eugenics) and other government-sanctioned programs (Washington 2006) throughout most of the twentieth century included compulsory surgical sterilizations of communities considered "unfit" to reproduce—disproportionately Black women. The North Carolina Eugenics Commission sterilized 8,000 mentally disabled persons throughout the 1930s; 5,000 were Black. The Southern Poverty Law Center estimates 100,000–150,000 women were sterilized annually for decades using federal funds, half of whom were Black (Day 2001). Many sterilizations, however, happened outside of the law at the discretion of physicians, referred to euphemistically as a "Mississippi appendectomy." Governmental public assistance programs also linked sterilizations to welfare benefits (Roberts 1998).

Margaret Sanger, founder of Planned Parenthood, moved from women's reproductive rights to eugenics. Her American Birth Control League merged with another organization and developed the "Negro Project," which set up birth control clinics in Black neighborhoods around the country. The pill and other contraceptive methods were made available to Black women with low incomes for free or at low cost through government-sponsored Planned Parenthood clinics. This raised community concerns about a de facto genocide in these clinics (Roberts 1998). In 1990, the first new contraceptive in twenty-five years was brought to market. Legislation in some states proposed to "incentivize" Norplant use for people on public assistance, and North Carolina even mandated it for women on Medicaid who had an abortion. Legislators also made Norplant expensive to remove. Medicaid reimbursed providers for removals only if Norplant had been in for five years. Norplant was promoted throughout urban areas, leading to a groundswell of opposition by advocates and community groups. Eventually, Norplant was discontinued in 2002 after multiple class-action lawsuits and concerns about its adverse side effects.

These historical injustices directly contribute to a sustained, engrained memory of racial oppression. Medical "mistrust, which originates in systemic racism, is a rational coping response to centuries of oppression, starting with slavery, and includes historical and ongoing police brutality, high incarceration rates, poverty, and racial residential segregation of Black people" (Bogart et al. 2021).

Impacts of Politics on Public Health Beliefs

The unique political landscape of the COVID-19 response intensified mistrust. The politicization of virus reduction efforts, including social distancing, mask wearing, and stay-at-home orders, directly contributed to the spread of the virus. Then president Donald Trump even contracted COVID-19 after failing to wear a mask or social distance and attending rallies en masse. In a COVID-19 and mistrust survey conducted by Bogart (2020), nearly all participants (97 percent) endorsed at least one general COVID-19–related mistrust belief, and over half endorsed at least one COVID-19 treatment or future vaccine hesitancy belief. Almost two-thirds reported at least one negative, social, economic, or health-related impact from COVID-19 (Bogart et al. 2021). Health care and social service providers were more likely to be trusted than other sources of information, including elected officials, who were more likely to be thought of as dishonest. Government was the least trusted source. This is unsurprising as former president Trump made unsubstantiated claims such as "the virus would just go away" (Rev 2020), called the virus "the China virus" manufactured in a "Chinese lab" (Rev 2020), touted the benefits of hydroxychloroquine to treat and prevent COVID-19 (Cathey 2020), suggested that bleach and UV light can treat COVID-19 (News 2020), and provided inadequate resources because "increased testing" would lead to more "COVID-19 cases" (Trump 2020a).

COVID-19–related mistrust includes conspiracy beliefs/theories around the origin, prevention, and treatment of COVID-19 (e.g., COVID-19 is manmade; a cure is being withheld from Black people; and vaccines change the structure of DNA). Conspiracy beliefs, much like mistrust, do not necessarily have to be false, harmful, unjustified, or irrational; however, when medical mistrust and conspiracy beliefs impact health outcomes, they can become harmful. The manifestations of these phenomena include lower health care / primary care utilization, greater delays in age-appropriate screens and other preventive services, and lower adherence to medical advice, prescription refills, and treatments (Bogart et al. 2021). With respect to COVID-19, medical mistrust may persist among Black Americans due to concerns about inequitable treatment vis-à-vis whites. Moreover, mistrust may influence vaccine hesitancy, with those reporting higher levels of mistrusting the government response and the origins of the pandemic being more reluctant to seek treatment or vaccines (Bogart et al. 2021).

Having explored the history and impact of medical mistrust in the Black community, we now turn to the role of the Black church. The Black church has long been known as a protective organization for the community, addressing individual needs as well as representing the community's interests to the public (Lincoln and Mamiya 1990). Nowhere has this been more apparent than during the Civil Rights movement, and many Black clergy have run for public office, including the late John Lewis, Jesse Jackson, and Raphael Warnock, among many others. Given the threat the coronavirus posed to the Black community, we suspect that clergy addressed the issue with their congregations. We get a sense for whether clergy promoted cooperation with health professionals or skepticism by assessing whether trust in clergy regarding individuals' health interests is positively or negatively associated with trust in medical professionals. If the relationship is negative, that suggests clergy may be fostering medical skepticism or that the church may be seen as a substitute for medical professionals.

We draw on data collected in March and October 2020 by Djupe, Lewis, and Burge that has been discussed extensively in this volume (see Chapter 1). What is particularly useful for this analysis is that they asked for agreement or disagreement with the statements "I trust clergy to have my best health interests at heart" and "I trust the medical professionals and scientists who have sounded the alarm about the dangers of the coronavirus." With sizable samples (and weights in October 2020), we can assess how extensive trusts are and how they are linked across racial groups.

Kindly note that despite the pandemic, Americans found a way to connect with their clergy. Trust is not contingent on in-person interaction, but large numbers of Americans contacted clergy through worship at the height of the pandemic in the fall. In the October survey, 37 percent of attenders (those who attend more often than never) indicated that in-person worship had not been canceled, and 32 percent were attending in person. Also, among attenders, 61 percent of attenders suggested their congregation offered online services in the past six months, and 49 percent of attenders said they attended those online services. Online options were slightly higher among white respondents by 10 percent or less (only 5 percentage points less for Black respondents), though these differences were not significant. This evidence suggests that many kept a connection with their congregation and clergy through this difficult period.

Trust and Admiration in 2020

While our goal is to assess patterns of trust, we start by looking for signs that the pandemic was an object of concern. Toward that end, we determine the proportion of Asian, Black, Latino, and white respondents who reported their clergy addressed the COVID-19 outbreak in their houses of worship in March and October 2020. In March, Asian and Black Americans were more likely than whites to report hearing their clergy discuss the pandemic (the survey language was "the coronavirus"). Given the willingness of clergy serving Black and Asian respondents to address COVID-19, these clergy could serve as key partners in COVID-19 health promotion and disease mitigation. However, their concern evidently waned across the year; we see large drop-offs in Asian and Black respondents' reports of hearing their clergy address COVID-19 by October 2020. In contrast, whites and Latinos remained unchanged in their reports of their clergy discussing the pandemic between March and October 2020. It is also notable that no group had a majority of respondents report that their clergy addressed the pandemic and that this measure of concern dropped to below one-third by October for all respondent groups except Latinos.

With these results in mind, we might expect variation by and within racial groups in whether they trust their clergy with their health interests. That is what Figure 5.2 shows, though overall trust in clergy is much higher than we might anticipate given that no group had a majority of respondents report that their clergy addressed the pandemic. There are very few respondents from any racial group who outright disagree that clergy have their best health interests at heart—no more than 25 percent. Conversely, thin majorities agree that they do trust clergy in this way, and there is little variation across racial groups in March. Most groups retain majority agreement except for Asian Americans, whose trust plummets 20 percentage points over the period from March to October. It is also worth noting that all groups except Black Americans express more disagreement in October compared to March. In both surveys, clergy who were heard addressing the pandemic received more trust, so it is likely that the decline in hearing clergy's concern contributed to the somewhat greater distrust late in 2020. It is also worth noting that a large number of respondents (about one-third) were either ambivalent about clergy or had no opinion—they took the middle option of the response options ("Neither agree nor disagree").

Since a majority of respondents trusts their clergy with their health, clergy can serve as trusted liaisons translating medical information and as voices of reason when misinformation exists within their congregations. This may be especially effective with the most engaged congregational members. Respondents who are engaged in their faith community trust their clergy most to help them with their health.

Arguably the most important results are in Figure 5.3, where we examine whether people trust medical professionals and scientists by race. There is considerably more fluctuation in trust of medical professionals and scientists

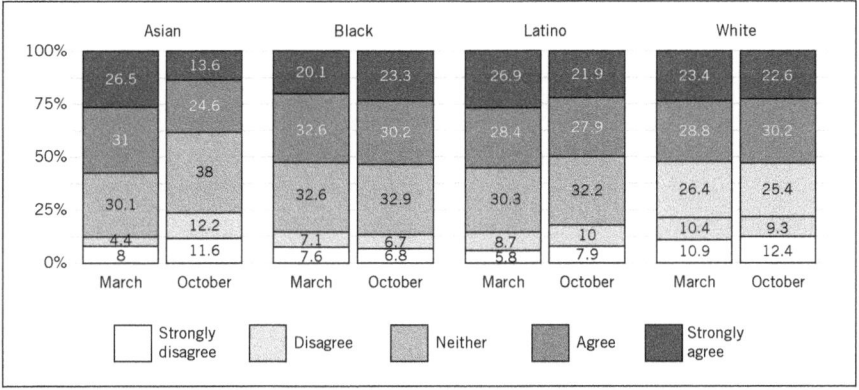

Figure 5.2 Whether People Trust Their Clergy with Their Health, by Race and Survey: "I trust clergy to have my best health interests at heart." (Source: March and October 2020 surveys.)

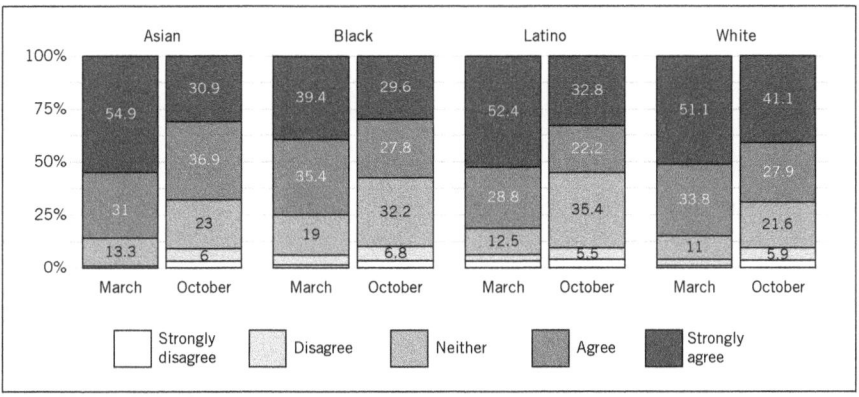

Figure 5.3 Whether People Trust Medical Professionals, by Race and Survey: "I trust the medical professionals and scientists who have sounded the alarm about the dangers of the coronavirus." (Source: March and October 2020 surveys.)

across 2020—it was much higher in March 2020 (over 75 percent reported trust across all racial groups) than in October 2020. By October, trust reported by Black and Latino Americans had declined significantly. Whites and Asians maintained higher trust, though still evidenced a decline. While there were few respondents in either survey who outright distrusted health professionals, ambivalence clearly grew by October across all racial groups, especially among Latinos. Still, trust of medical professionals and scientists is considerably higher than trust of clergy. Accordingly, leveraging trust of medical professionals, scientists, and clergy within the setting of a congregation could be useful for relaying information about COVID-19 and mitigating disease.

Next, we assess whether the two are linked—is trust in clergy a substitute for trust in medical professionals or a complement? In Figure 5.4, we examine whether trust in clergy is linked to trust in medical professionals and scientists by race. There is a positive relationship between the two beliefs in March, where more trust in clergy is linked to greater trust in medical professionals, yet the relationship changes by October in revealing ways. In most cases, there is a noticeable decrease in trust in medical professionals by October, except, among Black Americans (and maybe Latinos), trust in clergy may help buoy trust in medical professionals. While it is surprising that as the election nears, the Democratic candidate, Joe Biden, emphasizes the seriousness of the COVID-19 pandemic and the Republican candidate, Donald Trump, de-emphasizes COVID-19, we assert that reduction in Black Americans' and Latinos' trust of medical professionals and scientists is likely motivated by overall medical mistrust and not partisan attitudes and beliefs. Clergy-distrusting Black and La-

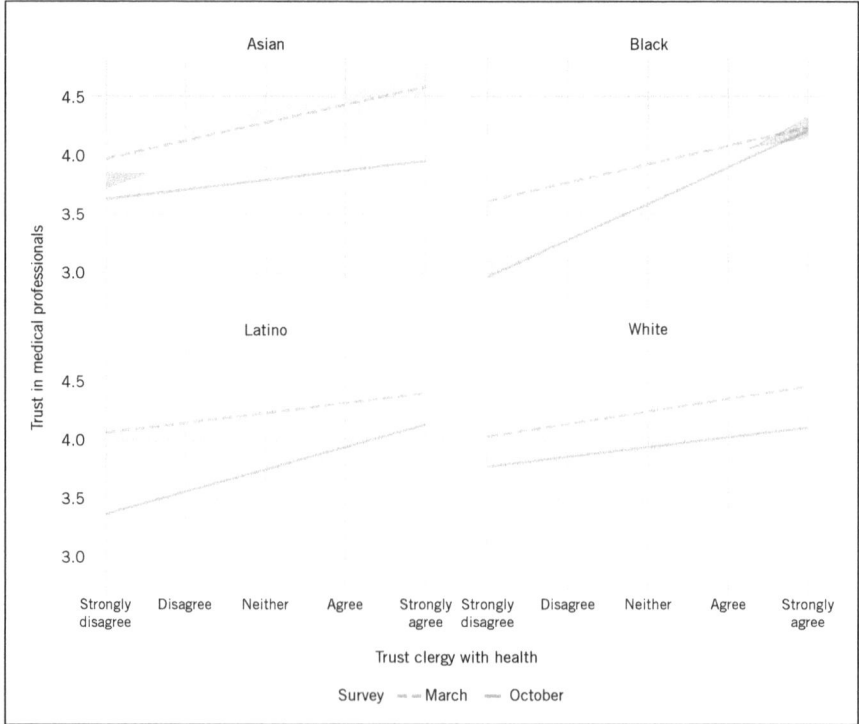

Figure 5.4 Is Trust in Clergy Linked to Trust in Medical Professionals? By Race across Surveys (Source: March and October 2020 surveys.)

tino Americans show the greatest decrease in trust in medical professionals, while the clergy-trusting maintain similar levels to March of trusting medical professionals. Among whites and Asians, however, trust in the two groups starts to delink and appears closer to uncorrelated by October. Thus, trust in medical professionals drops the most for whites and Asians among those who trust their clergy the most. These findings could reflect a growing opposition to health orders over the course of the pandemic (for examples, see the Introduction and Chapters 7, 8, and 9).

Conclusion: On Building Trust and Beyond

Since COVID-19 arrived in the United States in March 2020, the country's Black and Latino communities have been hardest hit. Their disproportionate representation as essential workers and other systemic, institutional, and social factors have left their communities more susceptible to disease and death from the virus. COVID-19 disparities will continue to widen unless public health officials earnestly engage with "culturally congruent, tailored approaches, including effective strategies, sources, and messaging, to deliver evidence-based information and overcome mistrust around COVID-19" (Bogart et al. 2021). Studies on medical mistrust related to COVID-19 using large-scale nationally representative samples of Black Americans and small-scale, in-depth, qualitative focus groups are needed to inform interventions and policy solutions at both structural and individual levels to address mistrust and reduce COVID-19 disparities.

The bioethical principle of justice and a commitment to elimination of health inequity are critical to this effort. Trust building and trustworthiness are processes that build on principles of ethical community engagement and community-based participatory research. Efforts to partner with community agencies, social organizations, and faith-based/placed organizations are key to providing a sound and timely response to COVID-19 in Black and Latino communities.

Our survey results highlight that clergy are reserves of goodwill, though they are not nearly infinite; nor have they been immune to the challenges of the pandemic. There was little decline in trust in clergy and a significant decline in trust in the medical community across 2020. Similarly, trust in clergy may have acted to sustain trust in medical professionals, though not quite evenly across racial groups. To our surprise, it is in the Black and Latino communities where trust in clergy appears to have played the strongest role in maintaining trust in medical professionals—the very groups that have the most troubled history with medical practitioners. Overall, we see little evidence that Americans are choosing either clergy or medical professionals to trust. When they trust one, they trust the other, reflecting the power of social organizational involvement, such as that offered by the Black church.

Finally, we cannot allow those that are hardest hit to be hardly reached. While several efficacious vaccines have been developed and are being disseminated, Black and Latino communities remain at the back of the line. Black and Latino communities must be prioritized to reverse the pandemic's devastating effects.

6

Is the Effect of Religion "Raced" on Pandemic Attitudes and Behaviors?

Angel Saavedra Cisneros, Natasha Altema McNeely, and Paul A. Djupe

Though the novel coronavirus pandemic has spared no group, racial and ethnic minority communities have been disproportionately affected due to existing systemic inequalities like unequal access to health care and personal health status inequalities (Alimi et al. 2020; Substance Abuse and Mental Health Services Administration 2020; see also Chapter 5). Existing work has documented that Hispanics have been disproportionately affected by COVID-19 throughout the United States and especially in Texas (Andres-Henao and Crary 2020; Villarreal 2020). Black communities, especially, have been disproportionately affected by COVID-19 (Boorstein 2020; Moore et al. 2020; Wright and Merritt 2020), bearing a high rate of infection and fatalities. And Asian communities in the United States have faced tremendous prejudice in reaction to former president Trump's labeling of the coronavirus the "Asian flu" and a Chinese conspiracy against him and the world.

In the face of such inequities, community leaders often play an important role exposing the nature of problems, calling for their redress, and guiding their communities. In the Black community, congregations and religious leaders have performed this service, in part due to the oppression that limited the development of Black leadership in other institutions (e.g., Lincoln and Mamiya 1989). These dynamics may not be limited to the Black church, of course,

---

Material referencing an appendix in this chapter can be found online available here: https://dataverse.harvard.edu/dataverse/epidemic_among_my_people.

since all congregations are formed within communities with particular sets of concerns. At the same time, congregations are not just neutral in their outreach and seek to impart worldviews that guide thought and action (Leege and Kellstedt 1993), some of which may be opposed to engaging with the world. That is, we cannot assume that all congregations promote robust individual citizenship, trust in governmental institutions, and social action (e.g., McRoberts 2003). Some develop a reliance on the church and faith as sources of healing and protection (see Chapter 1), some encourage social action, and some pursue other ends. This leads to a puzzle regarding the coronavirus pandemic. If religion is particularly important in minority communities, did social distancing and other public health measures undermine a key source of community influence? Was religion able to rise to the occasion to champion public health measures equally across racial groups, or did it work against public health measures as competitors with religious worldviews?

Religion Is Raced?

As a result of the racial animus that has been at the heart of American politics since the beginning, religious institutions have often developed separately across communities formed largely along racial and ethnic lines. Christianity was imposed by white slaveholders, but congregations became incredibly important resources for the Black community under slavery and after it (e.g., Lincoln and Mamiya 1989). White oppression imposed a political leadership and civil society vacuum that the Black church swelled to fill. Therefore, it is no surprise to find much political leadership in the Black community with various ties to the church. Given the heavy concentration of Latinos in the Catholic Church, we do not find the same tight connection of church and political leadership, though the Catholic Church has been helpful in knitting the community together (Djupe and Neiheisel 2012; Jones-Correa and Leal 2001). Nevertheless, urban religious organizations play an important social and political role for Latinos. It is notable that involvement in Protestant congregations does not have the same effect on Latinos as in Catholic parishes (DeSipio 2007), which may point to the power of a link to the community.

Perhaps because religious institutions have been at the core of social support, it has been widely documented that racial minorities are more religious than white Americans on most measures. The Pew Religious Landscape Study finds that while 49 percent of white Americans report that religion is very important in their lives, 59 percent of Latinos and 75 percent of African Americans report this to be true, though only 36 percent of Asians do (Pew Research

Center 2014). Across a variety of measures, Black Americans report the highest levels of religious behaviors, and yet their political attitudes and behaviors differ in important ways from those of other religious Americans. Even so, we cannot assume anymore that racial/ethnic minorities are attending racially homogeneous congregations. As Pew Research Center's (2021) *Faith among Black Americans* report makes abundantly clear, historically Black churches command a minority of Black membership and may not even be the plurality among younger African Americans. Even greater numbers of Latinos appear to be worshipping in multiracial congregations (Wong 2018, 20).

Since racial minorities have disparate life circumstances from whites in the United States, on balance, their religious communities are likely to take on a different set of priorities that are likely to collect under a social justice umbrella. That is, we would expect congregations with a greater number of minorities to advocate for civil rights, equality, and a more robust social welfare system. That does not mean that they will be more liberal on all issues, and many racial minorities, especially evangelical identifiers, take conservative stances on social issues like abortion and same-sex marriage (see Wong 2018 for a comprehensive look).

Some of these patterns have been affirmed by congregational data. Moreover, not all congregations become social service providers. For example, many of the connections Black congregations make with community organizations involve civil rights organizations and a sizable number do not partner with an organization (Lincoln and Mamiya 1990, 151). In turn, such partnerships are important linkages, with the congregation offering social services as well as willingness to seek government funding for those initiatives (Owens 2007). Rates of community engagement may be higher in the Black community, but congregations are not invariant.

It is no surprise that congregations take the needs of their congregations seriously, and their concern can take many forms, from the material to the symbolic. Religious organizations have historically created successful partnerships with health organizations (Solari-Twadell, Djupe, and McDermott 1990) and public schools (Galiatsatos et al. 2020). For our purposes, researchers have noted the importance of partnerships between public health and government officials with cultural as well as faith-based groups to increase compliance with COVID-19 guidelines (Alimi et al. 2020). One benefit is the mitigation of the spread of misinformation among vulnerable groups, including racial and ethnic minorities (Clark-Ginsberg and Petrun Sayers 2020). Preliminary evidence demonstrates the effectiveness of successful partnerships between public health organizations and faith-based organizations to increase compliance with COVID-19 guidelines within the African American community, while also providing needed resources to its members (Akintobi et al. 2020; Thompkins et al. 2020).

In politics, clergy tend to take greater representational roles for their congregations when they lack it locally. That is, clergy are more likely to take community leadership roles in communities with fewer active leaders (Olson 2000), and clergy step up their representation roles when their congregations are in the minority locally (Djupe and Gilbert 2003). If these dynamics exist across the religious spectrum for white clergy (Djupe, Burge, and Calfano 2016), it is highly likely that we would see it replicated in minority communities as representational roles have been documented historically (e.g., Morris 1984).

This is another way to say that there is real religious variation within minority communities. Partly due to small sample sizes of racial minorities in samples, but also because "differences across Protestant affiliations pale in comparison to structural and cultural similarities resulting from the legacy of racial discrimination and inequality" (Shelton and Cobb 2018, 737), it was common practice to identify a singular category of Black Protestants. From a religious perspective, that assumption is untenable, and there is a wealth of religious variability within the Black community. For instance, Black Methodists (e.g., the African Methodist Episcopal Church [AME]) and Black Baptists developed apart and differed in the degree of denominational organization as well as on whether clergy should be specially educated (Shelton and Cobb 2018). Moreover, Black denominations tend to differ in their public theology, with some affiliates, like Church of God in Christ (COGIC), less likely to support political activity than AME affiliates, thought to be linked to the "other worldliness" of COGIC (McDaniel 2003).

One of the key remaining questions pushes us to consider the endogeneity claim—that the politics of minority religious groups is simply a function of who sits in the pews. We wonder whether minority religion is, in itself, important to consider. Does religion work differently in minority communities? Existing research is suggestive on this point but unable to answer this question definitively because political stances are quite often overdetermined—there are many forces acting on the politics of racial minorities. That is, it is hard to set aside the American political context that is so thoroughly shaped by racial politics. Put another way, Black presidential vote choice has been almost unanimous for Democratic candidates for decades and pays no regard to variation in religious identity, belief, or behavior (McDaniel and Ellison 2008).

Studying religious influence on political attitudes often runs into this problem—many of the issues have been around for decades. So, associations between religious identities and attitudes may be the result of long-running socialization, critical events that have long passed, or other undocumented forces that happen to correlate with religion. These problems, therefore, help provide guidelines to studying religious influence: (1) we can gain greater confidence when issues are novel; (2) we need to be able to document religious input into the system ("exposure"); and (3) we need to assess whether that input was adopted to shape attitudes or behavior.

In this regard, the coronavirus pandemic may be particularly useful, especially at the beginning of its spread. As we will show, the racial disparities exposed as the pandemic progressed had not revealed themselves in late March, which was, depending on the state, about two weeks into lockdowns. The threat perceived from the pandemic was near universal, and the response from congregations was manifestly similar, if certainly not unanimous. Therefore, the early stages of the pandemic provide us with an essential baseline to assess whether religious responses varied upon widespread perceptions of threat.

The Argument

We examine how religious experiences impact COVID-19 attitudes and behaviors among non-Hispanic white, Latino, Black, and Asian Christian believers. Focusing on religious and political predictors without taking into consideration how race and ethnicity shape the American religious experience can obfuscate dynamics that are important to understanding American reactions to COVID-19. We build from the recognition that places of worship can help bridge information gaps for disadvantaged communities. That is, since minority communities have been hit hard by the pandemic, we expect that their religious organizations will pay special attention to the pandemic and provide religious justifications for taking public health seriously. We expect that those who hear their clergy engage the pandemic will assess the virus as a more serious threat and take personal and collective health seriously. This response should be particularly strong within racial minority communities, as clergy have historically been community leaders, and their messages will resonate with the problems people are facing.

Yet religion is not infinitely flexible and may not respond in the same way to community needs. That is, some religious communities are constrained by their beliefs. For instance, a growing number believe that religious belief is sufficient to ensure health, that sickness is a sign of sin, and health is a sign of godliness. This belief, often referred to as the Prosperity Gospel, is particularly common among racial minorities and white evangelicals (see Chapter 1). We suspect that belief in the Prosperity Gospel will procure a more defiant pandemic response equally across racial groups.

Data and Measurement

More and more survey efforts are taking religion seriously, but few include questions sufficient to understand what religion institutions are doing. That is clearly a pressing matter in the pandemic and central to our chapter. Fortunately, the late March 2020 survey from Djupe, Lewis, and Burge included such questions, which enable an assessment of whether religious institutions in which racial/ethnic minorities worship are responding differently than whites' houses of worship (whites = 2,049; Blacks = 353; Latinos = 208; and Asians = 113). Critically, the survey asked respondents whether their clergy had addressed the coronavirus at all.

It is important to acknowledge that using respondent reports is not a silver bullet for capturing exposure to communication within religious institutions—it is likely to come with measurement error. As Djupe and Gilbert (2009) point out, there is rampant misperception of what clergy and congregations are doing from the viewpoint of congregants. They sometimes pay little attention, they downplay communication they disagree with, and sometimes they aren't in the pews when a message is delivered. Still, asking congregants is at least one way in which we can get leverage on this important question.

We consider several responses to the pandemic. The survey asked whether the respondent was being encouraged to attend services in person (just who was doing the encouraging is left unspecified). It also asked whether the respondent was social distancing, which was defined as "staying home as much as possible, avoiding social contact." And it asked about whether their congregation should defy state orders to close, should they be made.

They were in the field again in October (n = 1,790) and repeated some, but not all, of the questions asked in March. While just before the presidential election, it was also a time when COVID-19 cases were reaching stratospheric heights, far greater cases of infection than in the spring. By October, disparities across racial/ethnic groups were well established. Where we can, we compare the March numbers with those found in October.

It is not sufficient to merely examine the difference of means between racial/ethnic groups since engagement with religion differs among these groups, and the level of exposure to institutions will affect what messages get through. Therefore, we examine whether clergy were more likely to engage given respondents' level of attendance at worship services.

Results—Clergy Engagement

Our key hypothesis is that racial/ethnic minorities will report their houses of worship addressing the pandemic at higher rates. Figure 6.1 shows this first

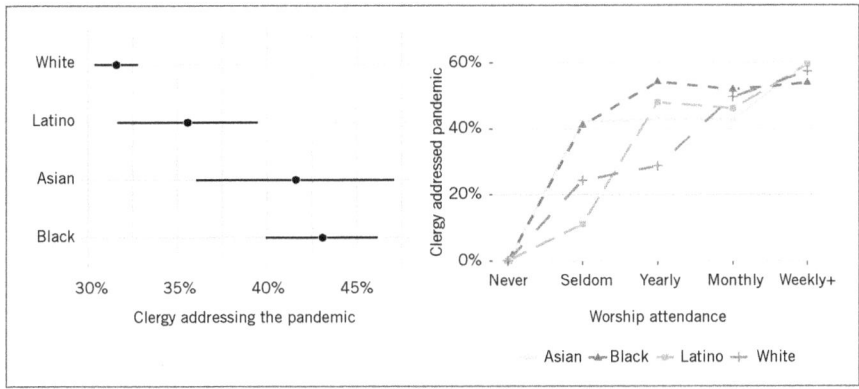

Figure 6.1 Report Their Clergy Addressing the Pandemic by Racial Group and Worship Attendance (Source: March 2020 survey.)

for each racial/ethnic group and then when incorporating worship attendance rates (in the right panel). The results confirm that whites were the least likely to report hearing their clergy address the pandemic (only 33 percent). Latinos report pandemic engagement at a higher rate than whites, but the gap is not significantly larger (because of the small sample size). But both Asians (43 percent) and African Americans (46 percent) reported distinguishably higher rates than whites did. It may be surprising that it is not higher, but, again, some of this may be due to variation in worship attendance—you cannot hear a message when you're not in the pews.

The right panel of Figure 6.1 shows how these reports differ when we consider worship attendance levels. Among those who attend weekly or more often, there is no difference in reports of clergy pandemic engagement among racial/ethnic groups with nearly 60 percent reporting it. The differences between groups only grow at lower rates of attendance to the point where about 20 percent more Black and Asian Americans (compared to Latinos and whites) reported clergy pandemic engagement among those who attend only a few times a year.

This pattern is suggestive of the frequency of engagement with the pandemic. For infrequent attenders to report hearing a message at nearly the same rate as frequent attenders, the message must be on heavy rotation. Without a prominent and lasting place on the clergy's agenda, infrequent attenders would simply miss it, as appears common among Latinos and whites. But this pattern also suggests that not all religious institutions were discussing the pandemic. If they were, then the rate of clergy pandemic engagement would be much higher among persistent attenders.

By October, the rate at which clergy addressed the pandemic "in your house of worship this year" had declined across the board. Only 30 percent of African Americans and whites, 27 percent of Asians, and 35 percent of Latinos reported their clergy addressing the coronavirus. The same link to prepandemic worship attendance remained, but a combination of service cancellations and weaker engagement with online worship surely cut into hearing from clergy.

In-Person Worship

One of the key and most controversial recommendations from public health officials was to limit social gatherings in size and frequency to "flatten the curve." As we have read about in multiple chapters in this book, these recommendations and mandates were not taken particularly well from some sectors. Religious conservatives were arguably the most incensed. The survey asked respondents whether they were being encouraged to attend worship services in person. Again, the source of this encouragement was not specified, so we cannot pin it on clergy, but we can assess whether it was more likely to be reported by frequent attenders.

Racial minorities were more likely to report encouragement to attend in person than whites, though only significantly so for Latinos—37 percent of Latinos reported encouragement, which is about 10 percent more than Black and Asian Americans (see Figure A6.1 in the appendix). A not inconsequential 23 percent of whites reported this encouragement. It is no surprise that receiving encouragement increases by typical (prepandemic) worship service attendance, though the increase is much more muted among African Americans—a 5 percent increase versus approximately 20 percent among the other groups. At best, this is modest evidence that religious effects vary by race but generally highlights that people who are deeply engaged in religious (or other) institutions will receive a greater pull to remain involved in person.

Actual reports of in-person worship in March were higher than one might expect. Upward of 90 percent of Asians, whites, and Latinos reported that in-person worship had been canceled by the time of the survey, though only 80 percent of Black Americans so indicated. From another measure, Black Americans were attending in person in late March at higher levels—25 percent—compared to 17 percent of whites and 19 percent of Asians. By October, despite the rapidly swelling caseloads, in-person worship had drastically increased so that 48 percent of Black Americans reported attending in person, which was not much higher than the 44 percent of whites, 40 percent of Latinos, and 37 percent of Asians. We do not know the extent to which in-person worship was socially distanced and operating at full capacity, but we can tell that these patterns of worship during the pandemic reflect prepandemic worship rates.

Prosperity Gospel

One of the weaknesses of the clergy pandemic engagement item, of course, is that we do not know the content of the message. Did they sound the alarm about the pandemic and encourage compliance with public health orders? Or did they throw sand on the whole project and downplay the severity of the threat posed by the virus? One way we can approximate content is by examining whether reports vary by religious beliefs. Perhaps the most important religious belief in this pandemic is the Prosperity Gospel—the belief that health and wealth on earth are the payout for fervent belief in God (see Chapter 1 for discussion and measurement details; see Chapter 2 for further results). Given the structure of this belief system, we suspect that the links with pandemic responses will not vary by race. Prosperity gospel believers will be fervent advocates of continuing in-person worship and will receive encouragement to remain so.

That is precisely what we find from a statistical model that controls for worship attendance and demographics (see Figure A6.2 in the appendix). Though Latinos report more encouragement to attend in person across the board, the three other racial/ethnic groups show steadily increasing encouragement as their Prosperity Gospel belief grows. About 40 percent of the most committed prosperity gospelers of any race report being encouraged to attend in person. That drops to close to zero for all groups except for Latinos at the lowest level of Prosperity Gospel belief.

Social Distancing

By late March, most religious organizations were complying with public health orders (or recommendations) and closed to in-person worship. By April, estimates are that 90 percent of congregations stopped offering in-person worship (PRRI 2020), though, as we see in Chapter 16, perhaps three-fifths were able to pivot to remote-access worship in some form. That does not mean that everyone was on board with this decision, and it does not necessarily imply that members took this lesson to heart in their lives outside of the congregation.

We can ask about social distancing in a survey, but we should be aware that the responses are likely to be inflated by social desirability bias—people knew it was the right thing to say. Still, there was some variation in the responses, which we chart according to prepandemic worship attendance and whether their clergy engaged with the pandemic. Figure 6.2 highlights that clergy pandemic engagement helped sustain social distancing. With the exception of Latinos, among whom attendance and clergy engagement has no effect, those attending more often where the clergy avoided talking about the pandemic showed a decreased commitment to social distancing compared to those who attend less often. However, when their clergy engaged, then commitment to distancing remained as high as it did for infrequent attenders.

That is, church attendance could be considered a measure of sociability or of the need for social interaction. Some make this case when they link religion with pro-social behavior (e.g., Saroglou et al. 2005; Shariff and Norenzayan 2007). But in the case of the pandemic, we also have the competing interpretation that attenders are being defiant about closing congregations to maintain their treasured social gatherings (see also Chapter 1). Even so, it seems clear that clergy were trying to encourage members to follow public health orders beyond the congregation since reported social distancing behavior is higher when they report their clergy engaging the pandemic. Moreover, there's not much evidence that this effect differed by race, at least not

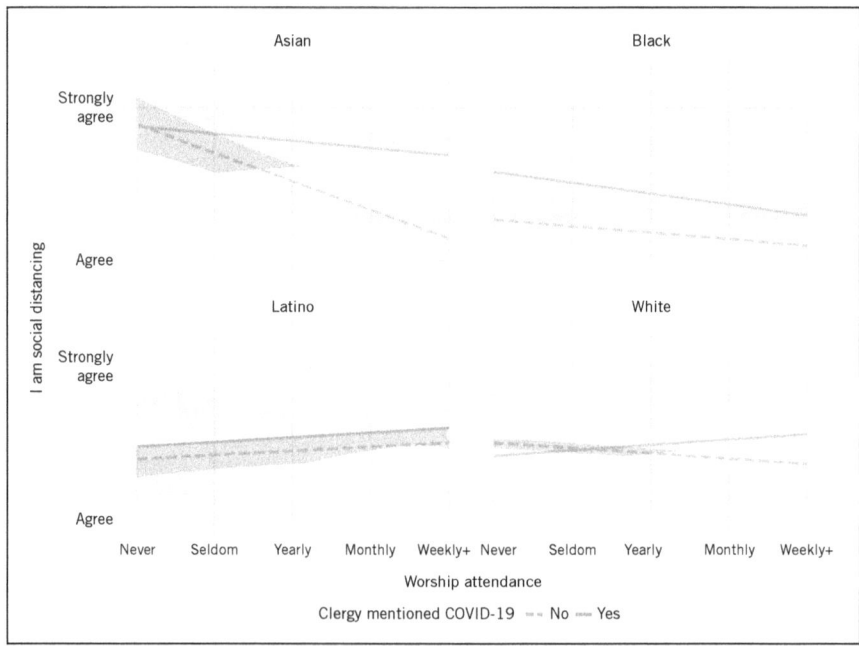

Figure 6.2 Does Religious Engagement and Communication Affect Social Distancing by Race? (Source: March 2020 survey.)

in the sense that it reflects the severity of the pandemic for minority racial communities. For Asians and whites, clergy engagement changed the effect of attendance. Without clergy engagement, more attendance drove *down* social distancing. But when clergy engaged, that decline was arrested, and, for whites, the effect of attendance became slightly positive (more commitment to distancing). For Black and Latino Americans, there was a slight bump in commitment to distancing when their clergy engaged, but it was constant across attendance levels.

Defying Public Health Orders

One of the most notable stances of religious organizations during the pandemic was defiance. Though not practiced by many, there were high-profile instances of holding services despite closure orders that resulted in at least one arrest in Louisiana (e.g., Associated Press 2020b). Even if the incidence of actual defiance of health orders was evidently low (perhaps 10 percent of congregations were open and not all states required closure), the attitude that congregations should be defiant was quite a bit higher in our March sample—22 percent agreed that "If the government tells us to stop gathering in person for worship I would want my congregation to defy the order." That figure varied by race, with racial/ethnic minorities taking stances of greater defiance—about 30 percent of minorities took the defiant stance versus 18 percent of whites. Did clergy pandemic messaging change the link between religious engagement and defiance of health orders?

As Figure 6.3 shows, the effect of more religious observance is to drive *up* the prospect of defiance of government public health orders, though it is important to note that none of these groups are estimated to have a majority opposing health orders. In most cases, weekly attenders show from half to a full scale point (12–25 percent) more support for defiance than those who never attend.

The effect of clergy engagement is interesting. In contrast to select media reports of clergy openly resisting closures, when clergy are reported to have engaged the pandemic, defiance drops. In most every case in Figure 6.3, support for defiance is lower when clergy engage—in the case of Blacks and whites, it is a fairly dramatic difference (about half a scale point at its maximum). Still, in all cases except for Asians, more attendance drives up a defiant stance even when clergy engage. That either means the content of what clergy are urging is different in high-attendance churches or clergy are unable to arrest this sentiment among their most faithful members.

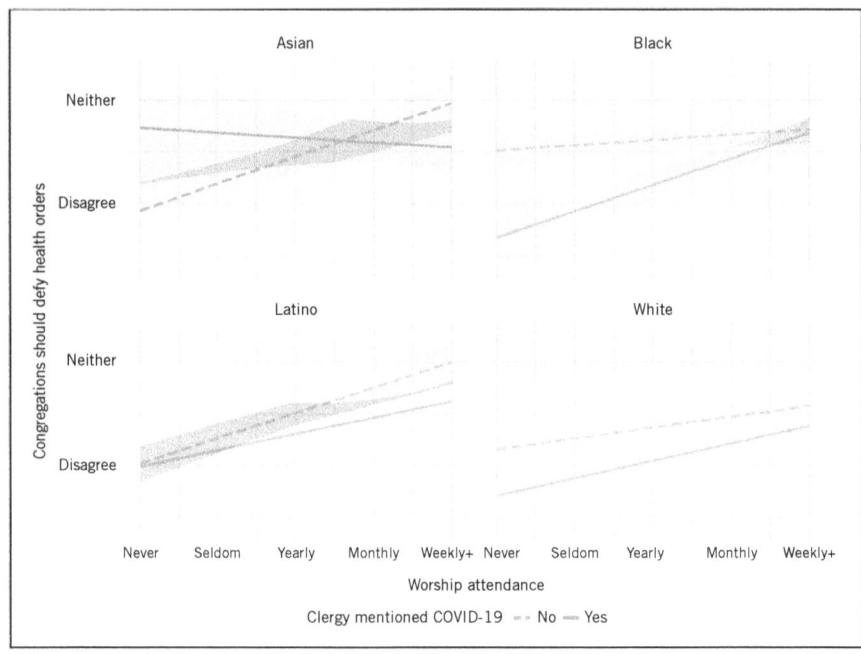

Figure 6.3 Does Religious Engagement and Communication Affect Defiance of Public Health Orders by Race? (Source: March 2020 survey.)

Notably, this pattern changed by October 2020 (results not shown). For Asian Americans, worship attendance is linked to a less defiant stance, as it is among Latinos whose clergy talked about the pandemic. Attendance has no effect among whites but has opposite effects among Black Americans depending on clergy engagement. African Americans whose clergy talked about the pandemic provided a *more* defiant stance against public health orders, while attendance is linked to a less defiant stance without clergy engagement. It seems clear that the community circumstances were not the same in October across racial groups.

Conclusion

One unequivocal lesson from the 2020 pandemic experience is that it hit minority communities harder than white ones, though the virus reached every corner of the United States and the world. As a result, it is natural to suspect that religious organizations would reflect this distribution and engage with the pandemic in different orders of magnitude. Religious organizations have been central to racial/ethnic minority civil society in the United States, demonstrated still by higher levels of religiosity. This creates an analytical problem, however. Does diversity in the pandemic response among racial/ethnic groups reflect the community, in which the religious organization happens to be apart? Or does the local religious organization have a value-added response to the pandemic?

Our tack was to first check whether congregations engaged with the pandemic, which seems to be a necessary condition for asserting their effect (see, e.g., Wald, Owen, and Hill 1988). In March 2020, only a minority indicated that their clergy spoke about the pandemic, though it was higher among Black and Asian Americans, which is what we would expect. That level, though, was purely a function of religiosity levels. Then we tested what kind of pandemic response was linked to that communication. We expected that religiosity would be related to different responses by race that reflected the seriousness of the problem in the community but found little evidence of it.

Weekly attenders of all racial/ethnic groups reported the same level of clergy engagement. There were gaps at lower levels of attendance, however. A sizable minority reported being encouraged to attend in person, which violates the conventional wisdom that social distancing would help limit the spread of the virus. Again, there were few differences among frequent attenders of any race, though Latinos reported the highest rates of encouragement to attend in person. One thing that appears to help unify responses across racial groups is adherence to the Prosperity Gospel. Higher adherence to that worldview is associated with greater encouragement to worship in person and about equally among racial/ethnic groups.

This set of results brings us in line with the findings from Khari Brown and colleagues' investigations of immigration attitude variation by race and exposure to cues in churches (Brown 2010; Brown and Brown 2017; Brown et al. 2017). They find, in broad brush, that the efficacy of clergy communication hinges on different measures of threat, such as financial precarity. In our study, different racial groups reported almost identical levels of threat from the coronavirus, varying less than a tenth of a point from each other on a 1–5 scale. With that knowledge, it is perhaps unsurprising that at this early stage of the pandemic, religious cues had roughly the same effects across groups.

Moreover, clergy communication appears to be largely in sync across groups. We can only infer the content of that communication because it was not asked in the survey. But the patterns are relatively consistent that clergy are consistent promoters of public health messages. That does not mean that everyone was on board with closures and other public health measures, but respondents were more cooperative when clergy engaged—expressing more commitment to social distancing and less defiance to state orders to stop holding in-person worship.

This chapter continues the conversation about whether and how religion in the United States is raced (e.g., Brown et al. 2017; McKenzie and Rouse 2013). It highlights the analytical importance of having some measure of exposure—here, explicit engagement with the pandemic by clergy. Once we have that and can account for the differences in religious engagement across racial/ethnic groups, then we find little evidence that congregational responses across the United States varied by race. Of course, this does not mean that this same pattern will be found in other issue areas. But this is arguably a strong signal given the immediate and strong impact the pandemic has been having on minority communities.

PART II

Elite Actions and Messaging

7

Precedent, Performance, and Polarization

The Christian Legal Movement and Religious Freedom Politics during the Coronavirus Pandemic

ANDREW R. LEWIS AND DANIEL BENNETT

During the earliest days of the 2020 coronavirus pandemic in the United States, state and local governments enacted restrictions on large gatherings to slow the spread of the virus. Restaurants were closed, concerts and sporting events canceled, store capacities limited, and religious services halted. It was a sudden and seismic shift in the American way of life.[1]

Religious Americans generally complied with orders pertaining to worship services, but many also expressed concerns about this regulation of religious life. Across several national surveys, white evangelicals were more likely than others to support churches defying government restrictions (Djupe 2020). Moreover, there were clear partisan gaps coinciding with support or opposition to these restrictions (Pew Research Center's Religion and Public Life Project 2020), and another study connected defiance to trust in Fox News (PRRI 2020). In general, the politics of COVID-19 restrictions on churches reflects the growing polarization of religious freedom, one that is poised to play a major role in future—and, in many ways, current—culture wars (see Castle 2019).

In culture wars, political issues draw on competing conceptions of fundamental values and identity, and the sides are often structured around religion (Hunter 1991; Layman 2001). Of late, religious freedom has been integrated into these broader debates. As such, in conflicts over religious liberty, there are two, often simultaneous conversations going on, one legal and one political.

Following the outbreak of the coronavirus pandemic, while most places of worship transitioned to online or distanced outdoor meetings to meet the requirements of local ordinances and recommendations (Cox, Bowman, and Clemence 2020), others fought back. Some argued that these rules violated their rights under the First Amendment, while others said that these rules were evidence of the persecution of people of faith (for more on this, see Chapter 8). The details constituting these legal fights are different across venues, but the houses of worship at the center of these disputes tend to make a similar argument, that state orders regulating places of worship differently than other entities—or even regulating them at all—run afoul of the First Amendment.

This is an argument the Christian legal movement (CLM) has been more than happy to make in its lawsuits and amicus briefs on behalf of houses of worship. Following other research, we define the CLM as legal advocacy organizations that are distinctively Christian and exist to litigate primarily on behalf of Christians (e.g., Bennett 2017). These include groups like Alliance Defending Freedom, the Thomas More Law Center, First Liberty, and Liberty Counsel, among others.

Its legal arguments notwithstanding, the CLM often stokes culture war fears over religious freedom when appealing to a broader audience. This two-pronged dialogue has in-group advantages, to be sure, but it may also hamper efforts to construct useful (and necessary) coalitions and build stable religious liberty jurisprudence in the years to come. When religious freedom becomes polarized, it is less likely to have broad support in the courts.

In what follows, we examine the interplay between the legal and political conversations among conservative Christians, including the CLM. We evaluate this movement's response to COVID-19–related regulations on places of worship in the United States, incorporating public opinion data about restrictions on religious life. We suggest that the conflict over public health orders during the COVID-19 pandemic was a symptom, not a cause, of the growing partisan polarization of religious freedom in the United States. These public legal arguments have the potential to emphasize culture war rhetoric over religious freedom, continuing to polarize this topic with damaging consequences not only for public health but also for the prospect of robust protections for free exercise in the years to come.

The Prepandemic Politics of Religious Freedom

The polarization of religious freedom has happened among both elite political activists and rank-and-file citizens. Among the legal activists on the Right, there has been a growing emphasis on reframing cultural battles as the protection of fundamental rights, particularly the rights to religious liberty and free speech. This has taken hold particularly among conservative Christian activists (see, e.g., Brown 2002; Lewis 2017), though it is also present within the broader conservative legal movement (see Decker 2016; Hollis-Brusky 2015; Southworth 2008). As religious freedom is increasingly used as constitutional leverage in our legal culture wars, particularly in cases involving conflicts over sexuality, critics have charged that the Right is misapplying religious freedom. The *New York Times* and *The Atlantic* have characterized the Right as "weaponizing" the First Amendment and religious freedom (Gillman and Chemerinsky 2020; Liptak 2018). Democrats in Congress have called for an amendment to the 1993 Religious Freedom Restoration Act that restored broad religious freedom protections through a bipartisan effort—the amendment would limit the application of religious freedom claims as a defense against discrimination (Dallas and Brown 2019).

Within public opinion, there is also a growing divide over religious freedom. Over the past decade, surveys from the Pew Research Center and the Public Religion Research Institute have found growing partisan division over religious freedom protections, particularly over the requirement for religious business owners to provide services for same-sex weddings (Mitchell 2016). This picture fits with other analyses that suggest partisanship and religion are driving not only division but polarized attitudes toward religious freedom (Castle 2019; Lewis 2020).

There is not just a divide over religious freedom but also who should be protected. As religious freedom has become a part of the culture wars, white evangelical Christians express that their rights are under threat, even more than traditional minority groups like Muslims (e.g., Green 2017). Studies also find that higher levels of authoritarianism (Castle 2017) and traditionalism (Goidel, Smentkowski, and Freeman 2016) are related to greater support for religious freedom and the free exercise of religion. This combination of traditionalism, populism, and Christian nationalism (Guth 2019; McDaniel, Nooruddin, and Shortle 2011; Whitehead and Perry 2020) is likely why groups like evangelical Christians are less tolerant of Muslims and their religious rights (Shortle and Gaddie 2015; Uddin 2019). Moreover, experimental studies show that support for religious freedom in public accommodations is not driven by religion as much as other types of discriminatory views (Powell, Schnabel, and Apgar 2017) or disgust for outgroups (Djupe et al. 2021).

In 2020, the COVID-19 pandemic intersected with the two-pronged dynamic of polarized religious freedom. Activists from the CLM were ready to apply their thirty years of litigation experience to challenging pandemic restrictions as unconstitutionally violating sincerely held religious convictions. At the same time, Republicans, and especially white evangelicals, had a growing sense that religious freedom was under threat by secularists and Democrats. During the pandemic, this feeling was exacerbated by President Donald Trump, leading Republican officials, and many CLM organizations.

The Christian Legal Movement and Religious Freedom Politics

The Christian legal movement advocates for issues important to (conservative) Christians in the United States and around the world. The CLM is generally focused on issues aligned with conservative Christians, such as supporting a strong understanding of religious freedom; promoting traditional conceptions of sexuality, gender, and the family; and opposing legal abortion in the name of defending the sanctity of human life. This movement is composed of legal interest groups, law schools, and legal training programs, all with the purpose of building a support structure for the movement (Hollis-Brusky and Wilson 2020).

Even though groups like Alliance Defending Freedom get the lion's share of attention and do the heaviest lifting in court, one must also pay attention to the CLM to understand how the rhetoric from this movement shapes ongoing culture war controversies. For example, it was the relatively minor organization Liberty Counsel that drew national attention for its defense of Kentucky clerk Kim Davis, who refused to issue marriage licenses following *Obergefell v. Hodges* (Lopez 2015). Liberty Counsel and groups like it may not have the pedigree or credibility of larger, more successful organizations, but they can shape the cultural narrative nonetheless. And given the competition for limited resources among like-minded interest groups, it is only natural for smaller, less influential organizations to sometimes make more hyperbolic and outlandish arguments to secure attention and support (e.g., McCarthy and Zald 1977).

The CLM and the Politics of Opposing COVID-19 Restrictions on Religious Gatherings

Perhaps because of the desire to carve out a niche in an otherwise crowded community, several Christian legal groups have been active in litigation on behalf of churches challenging pandemic regulations. Liberty Counsel was involved in one of the country's first lawsuits on these questions, jumping to the defense of a Virginia pastor who faced penalties for continuing to hold in-person church gatherings in violation of state orders (Liberty Counsel 2020a). Alliance Defending Freedom represented two churches who sued Oregon's governor for maintaining restrictions on churches (Alliance Defending Freedom 2020b) and has since defended a church challenging Nevada's person limit on attendance (Alliance Defending Freedom 2020b). First Liberty Institute won a restraining order against a Kentucky policy limiting in-person services (First Liberty 2020a). And the Thomas More Society touted its efforts defending California pastor John MacArthur, whose church fought, unsuccessfully, virtually all of California's restrictions against in-person gatherings (Thomas More Society 2020).

One of the earliest legal challenges to pandemic-related restrictions took place in Virginia, after the pastor of Lighthouse Fellowship was cited for holding an in-person service with sixteen people, exceeding the ten-person limit set by the state (Jouvenal 2020). Liberty Counsel represented the church, focusing its arguments on the religious freedom rights of the church and the pastor. Core to the legal argument was that Virginia exempted "essential retail businesses" from the ten-person limitation but did not do so for religious gatherings. Requiring church meetings to abide by the ten-person limitation resulted in "discriminatory restrictions on religious worship services" (Liberty Counsel 2020b).

At the same time, Liberty Counsel's legal approach stoked anger over perceived government persecution of churches. Appearing before the Fourth Circuit Court of Appeals, Liberty Counsel argued that Virginia's governor "continu[ed] to place his thumb on houses of worship" (Liberty Counsel 2020b). Liberty Counsel also praised the Trump administration for the Department of Justice's involvement, as well as Vice President Pence's statements of support, elevating the administration's support for religious freedom in the face of discrimination. "It is reassuring," declared Mat Staver, the founder of Liberty Counsel, "to have an administration that supports religious freedom" (Liberty Counsel 2020c).

This pattern of coupling legal defense with culture war politics—the escalation of cultural tensions especially between the faithful and the secular—was followed by other Christian legal groups. In the spring, First Liberty Institute defended churches in Kentucky opposing Governor Andy Beshear's restrictions. The lawsuit emphasized the churches' religious freedom and assembly rights under federal and state constitutions. Simultaneously, First Liberty used the events to elevate religious freedom threats and polarize conservatives against liberals (First Liberty 2020b). Debates over public health restrictions on churches were described as an "all-out war on faith" (Gomez 2020a), and the group claimed to have exposed the "real agenda of our opponents: to keep our churches shut down indefinitely and attack religious freedom in America" (Gomez 2020b). The American Center for Law and Justice, meanwhile, also emphasized the polarization of religious freedom to promote its work, arguing that "extremists on the Left are using the coronavirus as an excuse to attack Christians" (Sekulow 2020).

Such polarizing claims did not necessarily originate with the CLM, but they did find favor with elected Republicans. Though the CDC issued measured guidance for churches considering holding in-person services, President Trump emphasized political division, leveraging religious freedom rhetoric for political gain. On May 22, President Trump mirrored the arguments of Christian legal groups about churches being excluded from essential status, declaring that if governors did not allow churches to open immediately, he would "override the governors" (Gearan et al. 2020). In August, Trump told the Catholic cable network EWTN that Democrats were using the coronavirus to "put the churches out of business" (Czachor 2020). And at the Republican National Convention, Donald Trump Jr. echoed this argument, citing recent protests over racial injustice: "People of faith are under attack. You're not allowed to go to church, but mass chaos in the streets gets a pass" (Jenkins 2020).

Partisan Religious Freedom Advocacy and Public Support for Religious Exemptions to Public Health Protocols

There are consequences to the rhetoric by CLM organizations and Republican politicians, particularly in public opinion. Within weeks of the pandemic hitting the United States, surveys found that a strong majority of churches reported meeting virtually or canceling services (Cox, Bowman, and Clemence 2020; Djupe 2020; Lifeway Research 2020a). That consensus, however, gave way to cautious reopening for many congregations and resistance to health protocols by some (Djupe and Burge 2020; Lifeway Research 2020b). The resistance rhetoric mapped onto party politics. Folding religious freedom rights into divisive partisan rhetoric seems to have contributed to public division over religious freedom and public health, and it has the potential to strain broad support for religious liberty.

The Partisan Evolution of Supporting Religious Freedom Exemptions to COVID-19 Restrictions

To analyze the relationship between partisanship and support for the rights of churches to circumvent COVID-19 protocols, we turn to two surveys conducted in the spring and fall of 2020. In March and October 2020, we, along with some colleagues, conducted two national surveys that asked about support for religious practices during the coronavirus pandemic. We asked a battery of items on both surveys to tap support for the religious freedom rights to meet in person (for additional, related analyses, see Djupe and Burge 2020). The survey questions asked the following items, with responses ranging from strongly agree to strongly disagree:

- The freedom to worship is too important to close in-person religious services due to the coronavirus.
- The government should tell churches and houses of worship that they should stop meeting in person to prevent the spread of the coronavirus (reverse coded).
- If the government told us to stop gathering in person for worship, I would want my congregation to defy the order.

We used these items to construct an additive religious freedom index, and statistical measures confirm that the index holds together well.[2] The index ranges from 0 (strongly support closure of in-person services) to 12 (strongly support religious freedom rights to meet in person). In March, sentiment was more favorable to religious services being closed, with the mean response being 4 out of 12. By October, support for congregations opening and resisting public health recommendations had grown to 5.5 out of 12—more than a 30 percent increase.

Republicans were much more likely to move toward supporting religious freedom rights to resist COVID protocols, as is clear from Figure 7.1. In March, there was only about a half-point difference between Democrats (3.83) and Republicans (4.42), with the Democrats more supportive of the government closing houses of worship. In October, sentiment had shifted toward resisting closure. Democratic support for resisting public health measures increased slightly from 3.83 in March to 4.29 in October, while Republican support dramatically increased from 4.42 in March to 6.95 in October. Independents, too, were much more supportive of resisting closure. The political changes were clearly not reserved for legal filings but had filtered into public opinion, where they were structured by partisanship.

Multivariate models with standardized independent variables help solidify the effects of partisanship, while controlling for trust in health professionals, religious affiliation and attendance, and demographic factors. Figure 7.2 layers the results from the March and October surveys for comparison, with the *solid dots* representing the results from the March survey and *hollow squares* representing the results from the October survey. In March, partisanship was a significant predictor of support, where the *solid, horizontal line* is to the right of the *vertical dashed line* (overlap with that dotted line symbol-

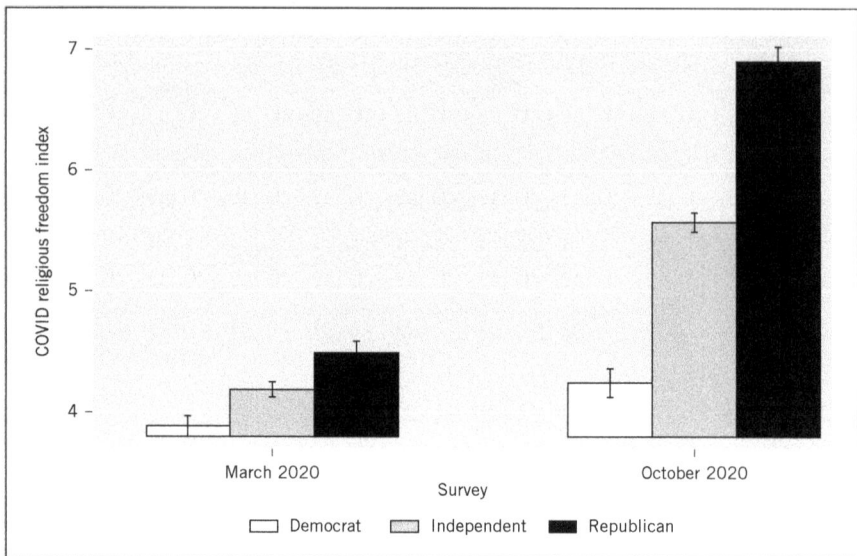

Figure 7.1 Mean of COVID Religious Freedom Index by Party Identification in March 2020 and October 2020 Surveys. Note: Comparing two confidence intervals produces a 90 percent test. (Source: March and October 2020 surveys.)

izes no effect) and does not cross it (meaning it has a positive and statistically significant effect). People who were more Republican were more likely to support religious freedom exemptions. The magnitude of this effect was small, though (similar to being Catholic or evangelical), and substantially trailing the effect of more frequent church attendance.

By October, the effect of partisanship had become more pronounced. In the fall, partisanship outpaced religious identity in its link to support for religious freedom exemptions. It matched the effect of religious attendance—a large change from the spring. In fact, partisanship had the largest movement from the spring to the fall, one of only a few variables to have a significant difference between the two surveys. Only trust in health professionals (less supportive of religious freedom exemptions and defiance) and education (more supportive) showed significant change from March to October.

How Partisanship Alters Public Support for Religious Freedom

In addition to the cross-sectional surveys, evidence from a survey experiment in the October 2020 survey also supports the role of partisanship in structuring public opinion on religious freedom. Participants were asked whether they

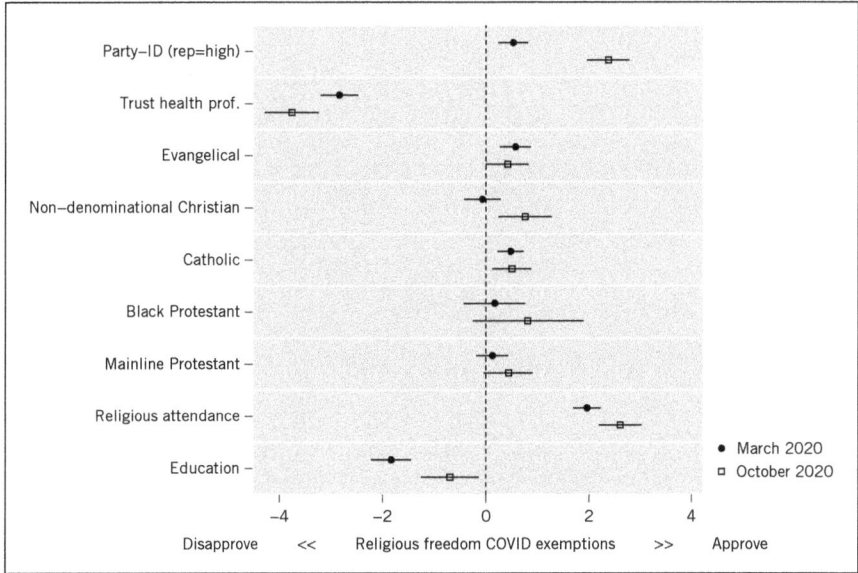

Figure 7.2 Multivariate Models of Support for COVID Religious Freedom Index. Note: 90 percent confidence intervals. Controls for other religion, Jewish, unclassified religion, race, sex, and age are not displayed. (Source: March and October 2020 surveys.)

agreed with a positive, boilerplate statement about religious freedom from a political candidate. The source of this statement was randomly assigned to be either a generic "both candidates" or the Republican or Democratic candidates for president, Donald Trump or Joe Biden, respectively. The experiment was separated from the COVID religious freedom index items (used above) by several minutes, though the topics of the survey and the real-world context were likely to link the general religious freedom candidate statements to the religious freedom disputes over public health disputes for some. However, the correlation between the index and agreement with the candidate statement is a modest 0.26.

Beyond the linking of general support for religious freedom to COVID-19 conflicts, there are clear partisan divisions over general support for religious freedom. Partisans were more supportive when their candidate made a pro-religious freedom statement, but, importantly, opinions were particularly polarized when President Trump supported religious freedom. Figure 7.3 shows the marginal effects, where Republicans were more likely to support Trump's religious freedom statement while Democrats were more likely to oppose it.

More follow-up questions in this religious freedom battery confirm the general finding. Partisan cues polarize religious freedom, especially when they

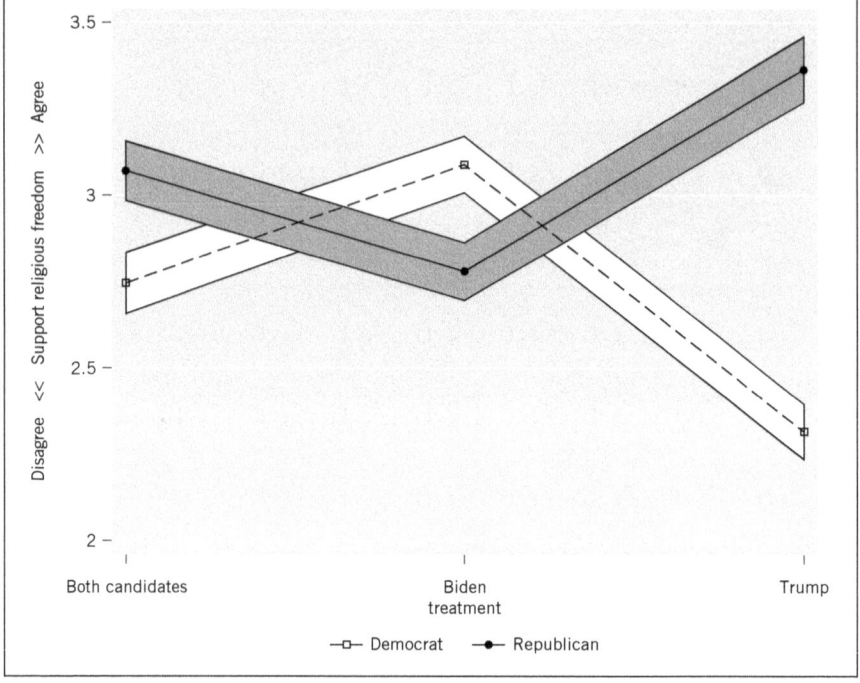

Figure 7.3 Marginal Effects of Candidate Statements Affirming Religious Freedom on Public Support. Note: Comparing two confidence intervals produces a 90 percent test. (Source: October 2020 survey.)

are tied to President Trump (Lewis 2020). In addition, follow-up questions indicate that partisans expressed differences on the groups who are perceived to benefit from religious freedom protections. Republicans consistently thought white Christians would be the beneficiaries, while Democrats were more likely than Republicans to select Muslims as beneficiaries when a Democratic presidential candidate expressed support. In total, evidence from the coronavirus pandemic suggests that more specific religious freedom disputes during the pandemic were structured by partisanship, especially by fall of 2020. If support for a constitutional protection like religious freedom is linked to what group might benefit and is conditional on partisanship, this is concerning indeed.

Discussion

Polarizing religious freedom comes at a cost. For one thing, while the public was predictably divided over these issues, legal actions and rhetoric in some cases have obscured legitimate concerns where religious congregations were overburdened. For example, in the summer of 2020 a Nevada church challenged state restrictions limiting indoor church gatherings to fifty persons, while restricting much larger venues (such as casinos) to 50 percent capacity (Liptak 2020). Though the Supreme Court denied injunctive relief, the Nevada church had a far better legal argument than, say, John MacArthur's California megachurch, which refused to abide by virtually any pandemic regulation, including those related to gathering size, mask wearing, and social distancing (Shimron 2020).

Not surprisingly, this polarization of religious freedom threatened to diminish the stark reality of the pandemic, potentially leading people of faith to downplay just how serious the health crisis was at its apex. MacArthur himself repeatedly cast doubt on the seriousness of the situation, telling congregants in an August 2020 sermon that the numbers of COVID-19 deaths were inflated before concluding, "There is no pandemic" (Wingfield 2020). Additionally, research has highlighted a growing divide over the reasonableness of restrictions on churches during the pandemic. Partisanship plays an important role, as do prosperity gospel beliefs (Djupe and Burge 2020). The marriage of religious freedom polarization and COVID denialism threatened to unnecessarily exacerbate the crisis during the winter months, just ahead of the release of vaccines to the public.

These tensions only amplified as the pandemic raged on. Late in 2020, the Supreme Court weighed in on New York's restrictions on in-person worship, enjoining the ten- and twenty-five-person limits on attendance and finding that these restrictions are likely to be unconstitutional upon closer review (*Roman Catholic Diocese of Brooklyn v. Cuomo* 2020). "Even in a pandemic," reads the court's per curiam opinion, "the Constitution cannot be put away and forgotten. The restrictions at issue here, by effectively barring many from attending religious services, strike at the very heart of the First Amendment's guarantee of religious liberty." And though the dissenting justices argued that the court's decision was both ignoring the government's concern for public health and unnecessary given recent changes to the policy, Justice Gorsuch memorably wrote that the restrictions treat houses of worship different from their nonsectarian counterparts. "Who knew," Gorsuch facetiously asked, "public health would so perfectly align with secular convenience?"

Notably, Washington University's John Inazu agreed with the court's decision yet played down its widespread importance, referring to it as "fairly fact-specific injunctive relief" before adding, "It's hard to generalize much from this decision, and I'm concerned that public messaging about it will fuel a broader culture wars narrative" (Inazu 2020). And that's precisely what happened. Following the decision, the Alliance Defending Freedom declared,

"The Constitution forbids government officials from treating religious Americans like second-class citizens" (Alliance Defending Freedom 2020c), while First Liberty Institute added, "Government officials may not abuse their emergency powers to discriminate against Americans of faith" (First Liberty 2020c).

On the other side, though, the *New York Times* columnist Paul Krugman tweeted, "The first major decision of the Trump packed court—and naturally it will kill people" (Krugman 2020), while New York governor Andrew Cuomo dismissed the court's ruling because of Trump's Supreme Court's appointments and the majority's conservative ideology (McKinley and Stack 2020). Rather than interpreting the decision as a limited defense of the First Amendment during an unprecedented health crisis, both sides of the divide sought to capitalize on the most extreme readings of the decision and to use it as an example of why "the other side" must be defeated at all costs. As we have suggested in this chapter, this is a problem for the future of religious freedom in the United States.[3]

Conclusion

When houses of worship and Christian legal groups challenge reasonable restrictions and link their efforts to partisan politics and cultural polarization, they hamper efforts to vouchsafe religious freedom writ large and build support for the broader cause. Legitimate questions are not only dwarfed by the propensity by some churches and advocacy groups to rebuff any government regulation, but such actions inhibit broader political support for religious freedom. And limited political support will, in time, diminish legal protections. Moreover, even when courts invalidate problematic restrictions, advancing a culture war narrative connected to religious freedom only furthers this problematic divide. Put differently, the increased connection between religious freedom and partisan politics is a troubling development for a robust and widespread free exercise clause.

The polarization of religious freedom did not begin with the arrival of COVID-19, but it certainly did not diminish during the pandemic, either. The CLM may win smaller battles and garner immediate political support by fighting tooth and nail against even the most minute public health regulation, but this strategy does little to win the larger war for expanded religious freedom protections for all.

8

A Tale of Two Burdens

COVID-19 and the Question of Religious Free Exercise

JENNA REINBOLD

The emergence of COVID-19 has exacerbated a number of long-standing social and political fault lines within the United States. Yet, notwithstanding such fault lines, almost all Americans can agree on one thing: gatherings on remote venues such as Zoom are not the same thing as in-person gatherings. This has been the case for everything ranging from school classes to movie-watching parties to Thanksgiving dinners, and it is certainly the case for religious services. In other words, there is no question that the strictures that have unevenly blanketed the United States in the wake of the spring 2020 eruption of COVID-19 have imposed a burden on many religious communities—initially in the form of stay-at-home orders and, gradually, in the form of persisting social-distancing requirements. But, while there is little doubt that particular religious communities have been burdened in the era of COVID-19, it is the decision to take this burden into the courts that has raised a truly difficult question: What does this burden on religion mean in the eyes of the law?

An exploration of this question raises a whole set of other questions: How much of a burden does a particular COVID-19–related restriction place on a particular religious community? Are members of that community obligated to prove that they are being *significantly* burdened rather than merely inconvenienced? If so, how does one "prove" the significance of a burden? Do burdens on the practice of religion warrant a different kind of consideration than those inflicted on secular practices and, if so, why? In the face of a deadly pandemic, do such burdens, religious or otherwise, even matter? All these questions fall under the umbrella of the First Amendment to the U.S. Constitution—specifically its free exercise clause. Because this clause is practically as old as the Constitution itself, the questions raised by COVID-19 are in a sense both old and new; COVID-19 has inflamed preexisting conflicts surrounding the Constitution that reach all the way up to the U.S. Supreme Court and well back into American legal history. Thus, however we may feel about the resistance among particular religious communities to COVID-19 regulations, it is important to recognize that such resistance implicates long-standing and unsettled questions in American law.

The Contours of Free Exercise

The U.S. Constitution contains two clauses designed to outline the protections afforded to religious beliefs and practices and the relation of such beliefs/practices to the government. The wording of each clause is minimal, which has given rise to a variety of interpretations of the specific church-state contours embedded in this founding document. Broadly speaking, however, the establishment clause prohibits the government from "endorsing" one religion over others while the free exercise clause prohibits the government from "burdening" citizens' religious beliefs and practices unless certain conditions are met.

The question of how one determines what constitutes a free exercise burden and which specific conditions must be met to render such a burden acceptable are complex and contentious. Nearly sixty years ago, the U.S. Supreme Court devised a "test" to translate the somewhat vague language of the free exercise clause into a more concrete mechanism of adjudication. The so-called Sherbert test (named after the 1963 case in which the Court formulated this mechanism) attempts to balance the competing interests of a religious claimant and the government in the following way:

- if the claimant can show that their *sincere* exercise of religion is being *substantially burdened* by the government policy in question,
- then the government must demonstrate that it has *a compelling reason* for creating such a burden and
- that there was not *some alternative way* it could have accomplished its goal that would have created less of a burden for the claimant.

The italicized words represent points of particular importance. The person raising a free exercise claim must be sincere, and they must be able to show that their exercise of religion is being substantially burdened, not merely inconvenienced. If they can demonstrate these two things, the government is put to a strenuous test: it must prove not merely that it has a reason for engaging in an action that burdens the exercise of religion but that it has a "compelling" reason to be engaging in this action—a word that triggers legal scrutiny of the highest order. And, even if the government is able to meet this exacting level of scrutiny, it must also prove that its policy could not have been more narrowly tailored to accomplish its goal in some less burdensome way.

In the early 1990s, the Sherbert test went through a fairly dramatic transformation, so today there is a more complicated legal edifice in place for analyzing free exercise claims. However, in circumstances related to COVID-19 restrictions, it is almost certain that the tenets of the Sherbert test still apply.[1] What this means is that state and local governments can be and have been called upon by U.S. courts to give serious consideration to the religious burden caused by their COVID-19–prevention policies. This, in turn, entangles the measures we take to contain COVID-19 within a broader and much more long-standing legal debate over the nature of free exercise burdens, the appropriate mechanisms for assessing them, and the limits of the government's obligation to remedy them.

The Two Burdens of COVID-19

What exactly does a burden on the exercise of religion look like in the era of COVID-19? From among a series of cases that reached the U.S. Supreme Court in 2020, two main complaints emerge. In the first place, claimants describe COVID-19–related regulations as inhibiting practices that are not merely important to them but are in fact central to the religious life of their community. As Agudath Israel Synagogue put it in one recent case, "Synagogues are a necessary and essential component of religious practice for thousands of Orthodox Jews."[2] Many Orthodox Jews pray "every day" in the local synagogues, and "the services that the synagogues conduct on Saturdays and Jewish holidays form a vital part of Orthodox religious worship."[3]

The Roman Catholic Dioceses of Brooklyn describes COVID-19 restrictions as mechanisms that deny to parishioners access to "in-person Mass," a practice that is "'absolutely essential' to the Catholic faith tradition."[4] Even as churches within the diocese had willingly altered the means by which the sacrament of Holy Communion is administered—refraining from distributing wine or placing the Communion wafer directly on parishioners' tongues—the denial of access to in-person Mass has been described as a bridge too far, severely limiting the diocese's ability to sustain the religious life of the community.[5] Since "receiving the Holy Communion for a Catholic is the essence of what it means to be Catholic," the diocese describes virtual substitutes such as livestreaming as "inadequate" and even "impossible" because "the priest has no way of bringing Communion to every household."[6]

Calvary Church, an evangelical church in Nevada whose case was ultimately denied a hearing by the Supreme Court in both 2020 and 2021, describes virtual or drive-in services as practices that fail to "meet the Bible's command that Christians gather together for corporate prayer, worship, and scriptural teaching."[7] As they put it in their legal brief, "Ekklesia," the Greek word in the New Testament translated as "church," means "assembly." And Calvary Chapel views church gatherings as sacred assemblies that embody Christ on earth and are the best expression of "His image and likeness." If a body of believers fails to hold in-person gatherings, Calvary Chapel views it as ceasing to be a church in the biblical sense.[8]

As with Agudath Israel Synagogue and the Roman Catholic Diocese of Brooklyn, Calvary Church's claim about the religious necessity of in-person gatherings reflects an orientation that is widespread within its respective religious tradition. The biblical textualism manifest in the reference to the New Testament's commands and etymology has been a key feature of Protestant Christianity spanning all the way back to its origins, just as the corporeal administration of the Eucharist and the communal observation of the Jewish holidays are venerable features of, respectively, Roman Catholicism and Orthodox Judaism.

Of course, none of this is to say that the emphasis placed on in-person practice in these cases is universal or even indisputable; that is certainly not the case, as numerous retorts from Protestants, Catholics, and Jews have made clear. Indeed, on the very same day on which the Court released its opinion on the *Roman Catholic Diocese* case, none other than Pope Francis expressed opposition to the idea that the values of "autonomy or personal freedom" would outweigh the cultivation of care for the health and dignity of others that God demands of all Christians.[9] Francis's position on the specific free exercise dynamics of COVID-19 regulations was left oblique in his op-ed, though his reference to the misplaced values of autonomy and personal freedom strongly smacks of a criticism of the religious claims in these cases. And, when combined with public assurances made at the very beginning of the pandemic that the *Catechism of the Catholic Church* permits people to appeal "directly to God" if they are unable to undertake in-person confession, the head of the Catholic Church certainly appears not to identify a substantial free exercise burden in even the strictest COVID-19 regulations.[10]

The combination of the palpable public health threat of COVID-19 and the contestability of the claims about how central in-person worship is to particular religious traditions, such as Catholicism, might tempt us to dismiss or even disparage concerns like the ones raised in these cases. This impulse, however, flies in the face of a key tenet of U.S. free exercise jurisprudence—namely, the idea that courts have no right to pass judgment on the veracity of religious claims. As the U.S. Supreme Court put it in a seminal case from 1944, the principle of free exercise categorically prohibits people from being "put to the proof of their religious doctrines or beliefs."[11]

> The Fathers of the Constitution were not unaware of the varied and extreme views of religious sects, of the violence of disagreement among them, and of the lack of any one religious creed on which all men would agree. They fashioned a charter of government which envisaged the widest possible toleration of conflicting views. Man's relation to his God was made no concern of the state. He was granted the right to worship as he pleased and to answer to no man for the verity of his religious views.[12]

What this precedent amounts to on a practical level is that, as long as free exercise claimants are sincere in their beliefs, their understanding of the actual operation of their religion—including which elements of doctrine or practice are indispensable—is beyond the purview of legal assessment. This principle applies to members of a religious tradition with an official leader, such as Catholicism, no less than it applies to members of less hierarchical religions, such as Judaism and Protestantism. Thus, while the fact that members of a particular religious tradition can and do disagree on the severity of the burden posed by COVID-19 restrictions is certainly an interesting feature of the COVID-19 landscape, this contestability is, ironically, not a feature that is likely to enter into the legal assessment of burden.

This brings us to the second burden claim that has surfaced in response to COVID-19 regulations. If the first formulation of religious burden focuses on the beliefs and practices of particular communities (whether or not a given community holds a unanimous opinion about such things), the second formulation focuses on the perception of a burden that is being placed upon "religion" in general. This formulation of burden rests on the idea that the United States has been witnessing a long-standing trajectory of both social and political discrimination against religion and that today's COVID-19 regulations are merely the latest manifestation of this discrimination. This is a narrative whose broader contours have been espoused for decades by members and allies of the so-called religious Right. Ranging from Ronald Reagan's

1980 lament that, "under the pretense of separation of Church and State, religious beliefs cannot be advocated in many of our public institutions but atheism can" to Mitt Romney's 2007 warning about the impending establishment of a "religion of secularism," this narrative attributes Christians' declining demographic and cultural power as the result of a rising anti-religiosity, particularly among America's liberals.[13] This "religious discrimination" complaint has held sway among particular Christian communities—especially Protestant communities—since well before the onset of COVID-19. To raise just one example, a 2017 survey conducted by PRRI found that 57 percent of white evangelical Protestants and 40 percent of nonwhite Protestants believe that Christians face "a lot of discrimination" in the United States.[14] Like all emerging church-state controversies, the issue of COVID-19 regulations has played into these preexisting perceptions in its own unique way.

If it seems outlandish to imagine that houses of worship could claim that they are being burdened both in a substantive sense pertaining to particular religious practices *and* in this more generic way, it is worth noting that a growing segment of justices on the U.S. Supreme Court appear strongly sympathetic to just such an argument. The crux of this argument is that certain COVID-19 regulations simultaneously impede central features of religious life while favoring central features of secular life. As Justice Brett Kavanaugh put it in one recent case, such regulations reflect the sensibility of a society that "assum[es] the worst when people go to worship but assum[es] the best when people go to work or go about the rest of their daily lives in permitted social settings."[15] This assumption is the product of a pervasive favoritism of, in Justice Neil Gorsuch's words, "secular convenience" over religious necessity.[16] Kavanaugh's and Gorsuch's characterizations of secular favoritism strongly resonate with the religious discrimination narrative described above, but it is Justice Samuel Alito who has made this connection in a particularly high-profile way. In November 2020, Alito delivered an uncharacteristically political address to the Federalist Society in which he pointedly situated the management and litigation of COVID-19 within a broader context of religious discrimination. COVID-19 restrictions, he asserted, demonstrate that "religious liberty is fast becoming a disfavored right" in the United States.[17]

One of the initial flashpoints for this confluence of COVID-19 and the religious discrimination narrative was the question of "essentiality"—the question of which types of organizations are providing services so important as to be exempted from both early shelter-in-place mandates and other COVID-19–related regulations. Though the answer to the question of whether houses of worship belong in the same category as grocery stores and hospitals may seem to many to be an obvious no, the very notion of state and local governments assuming the power to exclude in-person worship from the category of "essential" services is a scenario almost perfectly calibrated to trigger complaints of religious discrimination.

In fact, the political category of "essentiality" triggers this narrative in two different ways. In the first place, it appears to dismiss the profundity of the role that religion plays in the lives of many Americans—particularly in times of crisis. In the words of one widely circulated California petition, "the Christian church and other faiths have been relegated to 'nonessential' status by governing agencies throughout the United States" in stark contrast to their own understanding of religion's social function.[18] This complaint has been echoed by Michael J. McConnell, former federal judge and current professor at Stanford Law School: "The real problem here, [which] is quite disturbing from a constitutional point of view[,] . . . is that many governors have taken the view that religious activity may be completely banned because it is essentially voluntary. It is treated the way you might treat going to a movie."[19] Even as McConnell has voiced support for COVID-19 regulations, he has decried the governmental categorization of essentiality as a profoundly subjective maneuver that is almost always bound to diminish the significance of religion.

The category of essentiality also triggers the religious discrimination narrative in a more tangible way. After all, notwithstanding the understandable differences of opinion as to whether religion does indeed play an essential role in human life, it is important to bear in mind that the category of essentiality functions not merely as a descriptor but also as a justification for state intervention and even punishment in the event of noncompliance. In other words, whether or not one is convinced by the charge that there is a kind of "semantic" favoritism at stake in the category of essentiality, there is no question that the exclusion of houses of worship from the category of essentiality opens the door to real-world governmental punishments, such as the leveraging of fines. The specter of a government-wielded categorization that opens the door to punitive measures against religious communities is something that, even under the most bipartisan of circumstances, has the potential to engender anxiety and even outrage.

Ironically, the momentum of the free exercise resistance to COVID-19 regulations has only increased as the United States has moved from initial emergency shelter-in-place measures into more protracted mitigation measures in the weeks and months following the initial outbreak. As states have worked to create regulations capable of protecting the public while also remaining responsive to fluctuating case numbers, they have inevitably confronted the need to categorize businesses, houses of worship, and other venues in some more granular way than a simple essential/nonessential binary. This, of course, has raised a new set of disputes about whether and how the government goes about determining the status of houses of worship in comparison to other venues. In this context, the claim of semantic favoritism recedes; after all, there is no judgment of essentiality at stake when a church is classified as similar to a hardware store in terms of the duration of time typically spent inside of each venue. However, the regulations that have arisen in the aftermath of states' initial shelter-in-place orders have raised their own set of legal questions, each of which is likely to breathe new life into the religious discrimination narrative.

For one thing, whatever regulatory systems states devise to make the long journey from emergency closure to postvaccine herd immunity will be in place for a protracted period of time, effectively placing houses of worship on an indeterminate trajectory of regulation at the discretion of government. Indeed, the more flexibility a state or local government builds into its particular phased reopening plan, the more it invites charges that it is subjecting religious communities not merely to the regulatory powers of the government but also to its caprice. After all, the very purpose of a flexible reopening plan is to give government officials as much latitude as possible in balancing, on the one hand, the workaday well-being of their districts and, on the other, the privations required to prevent the spread of COVID-19. This scenario is almost perfectly tailored to engender anxiety and suspicion about which facets of communal well-being governors will prioritize—and, moreover, how long such governmental discretion will endure. When combined with the fear that political officials will be inclined to prioritize profit-generating venues over other venues, the scene has been set for a potent free exercise dispute.

These dynamics featured prominently in the cases that came before the Court in 2020. In *Calvary Chapel v. Sisolak*, for example, the governor of Nevada categorized houses of worship in such a way that they were placed under heavier restriction than the state's casinos. Though Governor Sisolak argued that casinos are, as a rule, much more heavily regulated than houses of worship and would therefore be easier to monitor and even quickly shut down in the event of rising COVID-19 cases, this regulatory framework all but invited an incensed Justice Gorsuch to raise the specter of "[a] world in which the Constitution permits Nevada to favor Caesar's Palace over Calvary Chapel."[20] In *Roman Catholic Diocese of Brooklyn v. Cuomo*, Gorsuch depicted New York's targeted reopening plan as emblematic of a regulatory landscape in which governors across the United States have, "at the flick of a pen, [a]sserted the right to privilege restaurants, marijuana dispensaries, and casinos over churches, mosques, and temples."[21]

Gorsuch's combative language draws the deprivations that COVID-19 has created for particular Protestants, Catholics, and Jews into alignment with perennial American anxieties about governmental overreach. Importantly, this generalized anxiety is by no means limited to evangelical Christians: Americans from across the religious spectrum evince discomfort over the idea of unrestrained governmental incursion into the realm of religion. The advent of COVID-19 has not necessarily changed this.

For example, when presented with questions that referenced the tension between religious free exercise and COVID-19 restrictions, respondents from across religious traditions voiced substantial—though far from unanimous— support for religious communities' free exercise (Djupe, Burge, and Lewis 2020). Indeed, in a political climate in which evangelicals are so often highlighted as today's biggest free exercise stalwarts, sizable minorities of Black Protestants, Catholics, and those of an "other faith" expressed support for the idea that the freedom to worship is "too important to close in-person services due to the corona virus" (35.5 percent, 35.9 percent, and 41.7 percent compared to 28.9 percent among evangelicals). Though such objections undoubtedly vary in relation to specific state regulations and specific developments in the ongoing pandemic, these responses serve as a reminder of the broader landscape of anxieties and free exercise commitments at stake in the era of COVID-19.

The Future of COVID-19 Regulations?

The legal navigation of religious free exercise in the era of COVID-19 has revealed that the question of burden involves a mixture of, on the one hand, substantive claims grounded in particular religious traditions and, on the other, more generic claims about government discrimination against religion as a whole. Arguably, these are two very different types of burden, but they are easily conflated; indeed, powerful legal voices like Justices Gorsuch, Kavanaugh, and Alito have already laid important groundwork for a conflation of these two conceptions of burden, and there is little reason to believe that this move will prove any less appealing to conservative colleagues, such as Justices Clarence Thomas and Amy Coney Barrett.

This twofold logic of burden is intertwined with the Court's long-standing commitment to viewing the free exercise clause as something that prohibits the government from questioning the veracity of religious claims. This commitment, as we have seen, takes a legal inquiry into the substance of the claims themselves off the table—effectively granting to religious communities that the deprivation of in-person worship is indeed a substantial burden, whether or not this claim is universally held within a given community.[22] What this leaves on the table is a legal inquiry into the question of whether the government has a compelling reason to be burdening a religious community and whether it could not have accomplished this interest in a less restrictive manner. This legal inquiry is precisely what the Court has now demanded of state and local COVID-19 regulations in the wake of its *Roman Catholic Diocese* and *Agudath Israel* decisions.

However, even as they are highly likely to side with claimants on the matter of the centrality of in-person worship, the Court's most conservative members have now tied their legal assessment of COVID-19 regulations to a much more sweeping logic of discrimination against religion. Unlike the refusal to question the veracity of religious claims, this formulation of religious discrimination does not stem from a long-standing jurisprudential commitment; it reflects a much more contemporary development in the Court's understanding of the Constitution's religion clauses. The array of legal, political, and social factors that have contributed to the emergence of this approach is complicated: it includes the decline of the social and political hegemony of white American Christians,[23] the rise of influential Christian advocacy groups that have crafted new legal strategies to navigate this waning sociopolitical hegemony,[24] the emergence of deep rifts among legal professionals about how to navigate the free exercise clause in the era of rising support for LGBTQ rights,[25] and a shift in the Court's reading of the establishment clause that has opened the door to all manner of "accommodations" of religion within the public sphere.[26] Where COVID-19 regulations are concerned, these various developments cohere into a baseline assumption that not only must religious facilities be subject to the same regulations as comparable secular facilities but that houses of worship are likely to be perpetually threatened by state and local governments' tendency to categorize in a way that favors "secular" metrics of well-being over "religious" ones.

In this understanding of things, the free exercise clause requires courts to be especially protective of religion and, by extension, especially skeptical of any policies geared toward the regulation of houses of worship. This highly defensive approach to the free exercise clause is what we might call the "courtroom" version of a broader religious discrimination narrative, and it has already featured prominently in the assessments that the Court's more conservative members have offered of particular COVID-19 regulations. Such assessments range from Kavanaugh's indictment of Nevada for its "implicit judgment that for-profit assemblies are important [while] religious gathering are less so" to Gorsuch's excoriation of New York's "color-coded executive edicts that reopen liquor stores and bike shops but shutter churches, synagogues, and mosques."[27]

In such instances, the burden at issue is just as much about governmental disrespect and overreach as it is about the inhibition of particular religious practices. Ultimately, such characterizations of burden make clear that the advent of COVID-19 has opened yet another front on a much more long-standing culture war over the separation of church and state.

9

High Stakes

Christian Right Politics in 2020

Angelia R. Wilson

American politics changed in unimaginable ways in 2020: the arrival of COVID-19, the Black Lives Matter (BLM) protests, and the rise of right-wing conspiracists questioning democratic elections. Those with "best laid plans" for the U.S. presidential election season found them "often going awry." Keeping the political messaging on course despite the oddities of the pandemic and protests may have seemed like a daunting task. And yet more citizens heeded the call to vote than ever before. That is an impressive outcome for both Democrats and Republicans alike. To better understand how the pandemic shaped the political communication, I consider the messaging of two Christian Right political organizations responsible for mobilizing Republican ground troops.

Evidence examined includes key public statements and over five hundred emails sent to supporters by the Family Research Council (FRC) and the Faith and Freedom Coalition (FFC). The identification and qualitative evaluation of strategic themes from this material draw upon my experience conducting participant observation at Christian Right political events. While various doomsday statements were voiced by evangelical pastors about coronavirus, these two organizations represent the most important, strategically reasoned, and influential Christian Right political voices in contemporary politics. FRC's president, Tony Perkins, was tapped by Trump to chair the U.S. Commission on International Religious Freedom. Ralph Reed, former executive director of the Christian Coalition, established FFC in 2009, growing it into the leading social conservative "get out the vote" organization. Both organizations have multimillion-dollar budgets raised through large contributions and endless pleas for financial donations through direct mail, email, publications, and training events. Both organizations gave President Trump full-throated support throughout his presidency.

The outcome of this assessment of FRC and FFC political messaging demonstrates that support for Trump's presidency continued despite the external shocks of the pandemic and BLM protests. FRC and FFC messaging included familiar political issues—abortion, antitransgender rights, and religious liberty. However, COVID-related restrictions brought a new urgency to concerns over religious freedom. Likewise, BLM protests presented new opportunities to highlight threats to "law and order" as well as the hypocrisy of the "liberal Other" (constructed as concerned about COVID contagion in church congregations but not among BLM protesters). Each of these, the pandemic and BLM protests, became manifestations of forewarned threats of social chaos at the hand of "pro-abortion," "socialist," "radical," and "secular" enemies. Therefore, understanding their reaction to the pandemic and BLM protests offers insights about how familiar political messaging is deployed to frame external shocks to maintain momentum and motivate supporters. Having warned of political and social threats for years, FRC and FFC interpreted these events as manifestations of threats from a foreign and domestic Other. And the articulated threats became prophesy to prime supporters to expect election fraud and to question the legitimacy of the election.

Our Guy

The day after Trump's first impeachment, December 18, 2019, Mark Galli, then editor in chief of *Christianity Today* (CT), wrote: "Whether Mr. Trump should be removed from office by the Senate or by popular vote next election—that is a matter of prudential judgment. That he should be removed, we believe, is not a matter of partisan loyalties but loyalty to the Creator of the Ten Commandments." Claiming that Trump had "dumbed down the idea of morality in his administration," and just as CT had spoken out against Nixon and Clinton, Galli found Trump unfit for office. Immediately, over two hundred evangelical leaders penned a letter of outrage, defending their support of Trump:

> We are Bible-believing Christians and patriotic Americans who are simply grateful that our president has sought our advice as his administration, has advanced policies that protect the unborn, promote religious freedom, reform our criminal justice system, contribute to strong

working families through paid family leave, protect the freedom of conscience, prioritize parental rights, and ensure that our foreign policy aligns with our values while making our world safer, including through our support of the State of Israel. (Becker et al. 2020)

Signatories included Christian Right political stalwarts, such as Tony Perkins, Ralph Reed, Gary Bauer, James Dobson, Franklin Graham, Jerry Falwell Jr., Mike Huckabee, Robert Jeffress, Richard Land, and Eric Metaxas. The historian John Fea (2020) likened evangelical Trump supporters to the "ruthless fawning flatters" of the medieval Europe court clergy who "took so keen an interest in the affairs of state that he neglected chanting the liturgy."

Throughout 2020, Perkins and Reed echoed this pro-Trump message. In August, Perkins explained the integration of "Bible-believing Christians" in the Trump administration: "The administration is filled . . . Mark Meadows, long time friend of mine . . . the vice president . . . Mike Pompeo . . . Dr. Carson . . . Some may not like me to say this but unfortunately the administration has cherry picked a lot of our people" (Perkins 2020c). Perkins agrees with "98% of the administration policies," which could explain why FRC spent "over $20 million in this election cycle" (Perkins 2020c).

Published for the campaign season, Ralph Reed's (2020b) *For God and Country* explained the Christian case for Trump. As a "strong supporter and good friend of his," it was Reed who had hosted Trump's debut on the evangelical political stage at an FFC policy conference in June 2011 (Reed 2020b). Reed likens the discrimination against socially conservative Christians to persecuted Catholics during Kennedy's campaign and to African Americans fighting for civil rights. When discussing Trump, Reed (2020b:14) references Oskar Schindler, whose "shortcomings did not rob his righteous acts of their rich moral content." For Reed (2020c), Trump:

> puts America first, defends our country, keeps us from being ripped off by China, turns the economy around . . . stands for innocent human life, appoints originalists to the court, defends Israel, dismantles ISIS and supports our First Amendment right to freedom of speech and religion.

Reed's (2020b) book closes with "Promises made. Promises kept"—listing Trump administration achievements. Perkins echoes this, claiming Trump is the "best President Christians have ever had" with "promises made, promises kept" (Perkins 2020a). FRC's voter guide details "the Trump administration accomplishments on life, family and religious freedom." One of the many benefits Trump bestowed was an executive order setting aside the Johnson amendment, which prohibits 501(c)(3) nonprofits from endorsing or opposing political candidates. Therefore, by the 2020 campaign, FRC and FFC could legally and openly endorse candidates.

FRC and FFC highlight three key concerns addressed by Trump: abortion, antitransgender equality, and religious freedom. On the first, immediately following inauguration, Trump reinstated the "gag rule"—blocking U.S. aid to international organizations performing or "promoting" abortion. The Trump administration targeted the "Obamacare HHS [Health and Human Services] contraceptive mandate," exempting organizations from purchasing insurance that included coverage for contraceptives and abortions. Trump officials supported the Hyde Amendment, designed to ensure federal tax dollars were not used to support abortions. Further changes to HHS included protections for pro-life health care groups from federal discrimination; termination or changing research contracts that involved the use of fetal tissue from abortion; promises to veto any legislation that weakened federal pro-life policies; and, on a global stage, the administration endorsement of the Protecting Life in Global Health Policy.

Trump became the first sitting president to give a pro-life speech at the March for Life in Washington, DC. On September 29, 2020, FRC emailed supporters a Witherspoon Institute comparative voter guide—"The 2020 Election: a clear distinction on abortion"—emphasizing Trump's pro-life actions and warning that Biden was "actively promoting federal funding for the abortion industry" (Closson 2020). Abortion, always a key focus of Christian Right intervention, continued to be used to rally voters (S. Diamond 2000; Lewis 2017; Wilson and Djupe 2020). In line with the finding of the Wilson and Djupe study examining FRC emails to supporters, my review of the 462 emails FRC sent to supporters in 2020 indicates that 38 percent of those included the word *abortion*. This issue was only overshadowed by the mentions of Trump, which appeared in over 50 percent of FRC emails, increasing in frequency in the last six months of 2020. Trump's action on pro-life issues clearly reflected FRC values.

The second Christian Right concern voiced by the Trump administration was opposition to transgender equality (Castle 2019). Various Trump directives reinterpreted federal antidiscrimination policies. For example, the Departments of Justice (DoJ) and Education rescinded guidance allowing transgender students to use the bathrooms of their choice. The DoJ and the Department of Defense changed policies that allowed transgender military personnel to continue to serve and prohibited those diagnosed with gender dysphoria to join the military unless they serve according to their biological sex. HHS removed nondiscrimination requirements that adoption and foster care providers receiving government funding must not discriminate on the basis of same-sex marriage or transgender identity. During 2020, USAID updated its Gender Equality and Women's Empowerment Policy to note biological differences between males and females and reiterate the importance of the heterosexual family. On May 27, 2020, FRC praised Trump's "pro-religious freedom pivot from his predecessor's disastrous policies" and the HHS for protecting the medical community who "want to be faithful to their religious beliefs and a biological understanding of sex."

Christian Right opposition to transgender equality is now ubiquitous. During participant observation at FRC's 2019 Values Voters conference, I listened as keynote speakers repeated concerns about increasing expansion of transgender rights—including a workshop entitled Speech, Sex and Silenced Parents: The Darkening Landscape of American Education. Post-*Obergefell*, Christian Right organizations dialed back antihomosexual rhetoric and dialed up antitransgender rhetoric. Trump administration policies reflected this agenda.

Thirdly, FRC celebrated the Trump administration's defense of religious liberty. Within the first few months, Trump signed the Religious Liberty Executive Order requiring federal agencies to promote and protect religious liberty and free speech. The DoJ issued guidelines and a Religious Liberty Task Force to implement them. Secretary of State Pompeo and Attorney General Barr both made religious liberty a focus in international forums (e.g., International Religious Freedom Alliance) and Supreme Court advocacy (e.g., *Masterpiece Cake Shop v. Colorado Civil Rights Commission*, *Espinoza v. Montana Department of Revenue*). FRC was delighted with the appointment of Perkins as chair of the U.S. Commission on International Religious Freedom. Samah Norquist, wife of Americans for Tax Reform founder Grover Norquist, was appointed to USAID as chief adviser for religious freedom. According to the USAID (2020) press release, this "elevated the U.S. Government's prioritization of religious freedom as a moral and national security imperative . . . [and] solidifies religious freedom as a foundational principle of American foreign policy." Celebrations of the Trump administration's defense of religious liberty intensified as state and local responses to the pandemic attempted to curtail church gatherings.

The Trump administration's most long-lasting contribution to Christian Right politics was the appointment of approximately 193 federal judges, 51 federal appeals court judges, and 3 Supreme Court justices. Most of these, and significantly all Supreme Court appointments, are constitutional originalists, active in The Federalist Society and expected to support Christian Right positions on abortion, transgender identity, and religious freedom. On June 26, 2020, FRC emailed supporters about the importance of "taking policy over personality" in their praising of Trump's judicial appointments. Trump had matched "Obama's record in judicial appointments in just 3.5 years. . . . Just imagine what President Trump could do if he gets another term." During congressional hearings for Brett Kavanaugh and Amy Coney Barrett, all questioning from Democratic senators was dismissed as "Trump bashing" (FRC email, Sept. 29, 2020). Looking to the Georgia runoff held in January 2021, Ralph Reed warned that Democrats "will also expand the number of seats on the Supreme Court so they can pack the Court with a majority of radical Left Justices" (FFC, Nov. 10, 2020). Republican-appointed justices do not always ensure favorable outcomes, but for the Christian Right, it is better than the alternative.

Election year partisanship is usual, but the intensity of the Christian Right support for an incumbent Republican president is a little unusual. Unlike Reagan, Bush Sr., and Bush Jr., Christian Right leaders agreed that, after four years in office, Trump had delivered on campaign promises. He had made a deal with them and delivered on that deal. Their organizations and their issues were enjoying unprecedented political success. Therefore, despite a prior visible lack of a theology-based morality, Trump was now firmly their guy.

Pandemic Freedom

Going all in for Trump in 2020 limited the possible responses to the pandemic by the Christian Right. Neither Trump nor the Christian Right could ignore it. As a result, FRC and FFC messaging focused on articulating the enemy (i.e., China and congressional liberals) and how these were threatening the free exercise of religion. The BLM protests, discussed below, gave them a respite, first, to shift the political narrative away from Trump's response to COVID-19 and, second, to establish a correlation between COVID-19 and voter fraud.

From the start, FRC rhetoric followed that of the White House. Throughout February and March, for example, FRC emails echoed Trump, referring to COVID-19 only as the "Chinese coronavirus." On March 3, the advice parceled out in FRC emails and the radio program *Washington Watch* similarly echoed Trump: guest Rep. Greg Murphy (R-NC), a medical doctor, likened COVID-19 to "the regular old flu" and dismissed the need for masks: "Those are totally not necessary. The face masks do . . . nothing to prevent somebody from getting the virus" (FRC email, Mar. 3, 2020). By May, FRC claimed that Trump had "solved the supply problem, the equipment problem, the ventilator problem" (FRC email, May 19, 2020). Alternatively, FFC, whose operational priority is voter turnout, was almost silent on the pandemic with emails mentioning coronavirus only twice—both times in relation to early-voting mail-in ballots and the need to begin get-out-the-vote efforts early.

In February, only four FRC emails mentioned the coronavirus, but this jumped to over twenty-five emails per month in March, April, and May as Congress debated COVID-related stimulus packages. The stimulus legislation presented opportunities to target Democrats, who FRC claimed were using stimulus money for "Planned Parenthood loans, taxpayer-funded abortion, cash for illegal immigrants, marijuana banking, state bailouts, rigged elections, freed felons, and a complete redefinition of the family" (FRC email, May 15, 2020). While FRC occasionally appeared to advocate for some economic stimulus, they simultaneously dismissed it as a ruse for Democrats to pursue "immoral actions." With the stimulus discussion quieter after May, the average mention of the pandemic in FRC emails fell to approximately eight per month for the remainder of the year.

FRC and FFC continued to convey a pro-Trump, anti-Democrat theme. For example, in early October, when Trump and the First Lady had contracted COVID-19, FRC issued a prayer request for their recovery, but the rest of the email focused on the Democrats' approach to the stimulus bill: "Anyone who would take a deadly situation and use it to push a grab bag of liberal non-starters cares about campaigning—not compromise. We're grateful for the White House's adamance that any agreement with Pelosi must be pro-life, pro-family, and pro-freedom" (FRC email, Oct. 2, 2020). Messaging focused on Planned Parenthood and Pelosi rather than, for example, the lack of personal protective equipment.

While direct mentions of the coronavirus in FRC emails waned in the second half of the year, worries about the impact of local and state regulations on church gatherings rose to the fore. Social distancing restrictions presented a strategic opportunity to sing another politically familiar tune: religious liberty. Many churches moved to online services to ensure support and community for isolated members (see Knoll's Chapter 15 here). Others found regulations limiting gatherings as an afront to the First Amendment right to exercise religion. On May 21, FRC hosted a meeting between Trump and thousands of conservative pastors after which the president told reporters: "The churches are not being treated with respect by a lot of Democrat governors. . . . I want to get our churches open" (Dupree 2020). FRC expressed outrage that regulations on in-person gatherings stifled the "essential church" worship while allowing "for casinos, tattoo parlors, abortion clinics, and liquor stores to operate with little or no restrictions, while churches around the country are still being held to a different—and even discriminatory—standard" (FRC email, Oct. 10, 2020).

The protestations appear to be based on political objections, but notably much of this outrage focused on (immoral) businesses, which were permitted to remain open, while church services—where collection plates serve as essential financial income—were not. The Alliance Defending Freedom and others supported church ministers to sue public officials in sixteen states—from California to Maine and Minnesota to Mississippi—"claiming that stay-at-home orders and safer-at-home restrictions violate their religious freedom rights" (Posner 2020). The threat to religious freedom became *the* interpretive lens for understanding the threat of the pandemic.

Religious liberty is familiar Christian Right rhetoric, and FRC deployed it regularly in celebrating Trump administration interventions during the pandemic (Wilson and Djupe 2020). For example, Trump's Commission for International Religious Freedom, chaired by Perkins, called on North Korea, Iran, and Russia to release those imprisoned because of their religious faith to protect them from the pandemic. Trump officials appealed to the UN to ensure abortion was not defined as an "essential service" during the pandemic. While those international interventions were celebrated, the primary focus of FRC communication to supporters was the protection of religious liberty at home.

One significant win came when the Small Business Administration confirmed that churches and religious groups would be eligible for coronavirus relief. FRC ensured that Planned Parenthood would not be eligible for similar relief under the CARES Act. FRC sang the praises of the Trump administration as DoJ interventions focused on the right of congregations to worship despite state or local bans on large gatherings. They praised HHS, who pushed hospitals to allow clergy to see patients despite health-based prohibitions on visitors. They applauded as the Department of Homeland Security and DoJ deemed clergy as "essential," allowing them to minister to their congregations and to those in the hospital. Twelve states deemed worship as an "essential service," thus exempting them from social distancing guidelines. FRC wrote to supporters praising Trump warning state officials to "do the right thing. . . . Allow these very important, essential places of faith to open right now for this weekend. If they don't do it . . . I will override the governors" (FRC email, May 27, 2020).

In early October, Perkins hosted evangelical pastors at "Freedom Sunday" held at Calvary Chapel Chino Hills, challenging "unconstitutional steps to restrict . . . and silence" churches and calling for "the resumption of church services in obedience to the scripture," citing Hebrews 10:25, which called believers to be "not neglecting to meet together" (FRC email, Oct. 11, 2020;

Hernandez 2020). As Wilson and Djupe (2020) note, the FRC deployment of religious freedom rhetoric signals a shift in understanding themselves as a persecuted minority. Here, as the election tightened, the religious freedom rhetoric located an actual threat: if you stop supporting Trump, Democrats will restrict your right to worship. Postelection, this justification for supporting Trump because he protected religious freedom is understood as prophecy: they took away our right to worship, so we lost.

While FRC voiced concern about the threat to religious gatherings, they appeared cognizant of organizational responsibilities, or perhaps insurance liabilities, in the face of the pandemic. FRC moved their political gathering, Values Voters 2020, online. They reduced the content to evening sessions with keynote speakers and offered all content for free to those who shared contact data. This public call for religious freedom enabled FRC to capitalize politically on concerns of local pastors/supporters wanting to worship, while avoiding potential liabilities of an outbreak at their own events. The business of religion, for both pastors dependent on the offering plate and for political leaders concerned about organizational liabilities, should continue.

Dogged support for Republican handling of a health crisis is not unusual for Christian Right organizations. During the 1980s, as Reagan refused to listen to scientific explanations for the spread of HIV and the AIDS crisis ravaged thousands of American citizens, Christian Right leaders seized the opportunity to link health and moral behavior. Then, the message was clear: the Lord will protect his own. During the pandemic, support for Trump echoed this suspicion of science and the need for moral behavior—church attendance—without which the immoral Democrats would prevail.

Despite Trump heeding scientific advice early in the pandemic, as the election season progressed and the economic impact of COVID-19 became clear, Trump's messaging shifted: the COVID obsessed should not be allowed to undermine American economic and religious freedom. Social distancing and mask wearing were for the weak. Christian Right churches, local and megachurches, needed congregations. Just as they had followed Reagan's cues, Christian Right leaders again seized the opportunity to assert the rights of the religious against the advice of science. Both Trump, FRC, and FFC seemed to welcome the opportunity presented in the summer to shift the message to more comfortable terrain: "law and order" and liberal hypocrisy.

Riot Resistance

On May 25, George Floyd was arrested for allegedly passing a counterfeit twenty-dollar bill. During that arrest, the police officers held him down, putting a knee on his neck for almost nine minutes, killing him. Floyd's death was one of many high-profile deaths of African Americans, which gave birth to the BLM movement. Over the summer, BLM protests took place across America with the *New York Times* estimating 15–20 million participating in the "largest movement in US history" (Buchanan, Bui, and Patel 2020). The BLM protests became infused with anti-Trump sentiment and met with white-led counterprotests. According to Pew Research, in June, support for BLM was high among all adults (67 percent), both white (60 percent) and Black (86 percent) (Thomas and Horowitz 2020). However, this support among whites was clearly partisan, with Democrats far more supportive (92 percent) than Republicans (37 percent). This mild support among white Republicans dropped over the summer, with only 16 percent in support of BLM by September.

FRC messaging offers insight into reasons fueling this decline. In a May 30 email, Tony Perkins, a former Louisiana police officer, expressed concern about Floyd's "death from excessive force by Minneapolis police officers." In early June, Perkins penned a piece for the *Washington Times* explaining that "mob violence and police brutality result from a morally bankrupt America" (Perkins 2020b). Perkins began with a recognition of the personal and systemic problems in the police department:

> As one who served as a police officer for over a decade on the street, I would say that if the department approved of the tactic of kneeling on the neck of a man who was handcuffed and on the ground, there are bigger problems in Minneapolis than Derek Chauvin. The failure of the other officers to intervene would suggest this type of brutality is pervasive. (Perkins 2020b)

Perkins understood the "breakdown of law and order" as the consequence of removing "God from public life" (FRC email, June 16, 2020). By September, the law-and-order rhetoric was dialed up. Correlating with a shift in Republican concerns, FRC emails claim that Trump's call for law and order is misread by the Left as a "racist message" (Sept. 3, 2020), where calls for "restoring order isn't just controversial but racist too" (Sept. 4, 2020). Defending Trump's law-and-order position comes to overshadow Perkins's previous recognition of police brutality.

Throughout the summer, concerns over law and order intensified the symbiotic political relationship between Christian Right leaders and Trump. On May 31, protesters in Washington, DC, set fire to St. John's Episcopal Church, the "Church of the Presidents." The fire was quickly extinguished, and damage was minimal. Nevertheless, for Christian Right leaders, the assault on this place of worship became symbolic that protests had gone too far.

On the morning of June 1, Charlie Kirk of Turning Point USA and Liberty University's Falkirk Center, tweeted a call for Trump to use the Insurrection Act against protesters. On the same morning, Christian Right–endorsed Sen. Tom Cotton (R-AR) urged Trump to use the Insurrection Act "to deploy active-duty military forces to these cities to support our local law enforcement and ensure that this violence ends tonight, not one more night" (Carney 2020). Later that day, Trump berated governors' responses to violence as "weak" and conveyed the need to "dominate" protesters, offering to send National Guard troops (Idliby 2020).

While none of the above is meant to imply cause, they do give a glimpse of the political atmosphere on the morning of June 1. That afternoon, Trump gave a law-and-order speech in the Rose Garden and then walked to St. John's for a photo opportunity. Layfette Park, sitting between the White House and St. John's, was full of peaceful protesters. Trump directed Park Police and National Guard troops to drive protesters out of the park. Police with riot gear began shooting tear gas. Protesters were beaten. And a path was cleared for Trump. In the iconic photo, Trump holds up a Bible in front of the church. Without speculating as to Trump's intent, the visual can be read as a nod to his religious base. Having once boasted that he could commit murder in Times Square and still have loyal followers, he could now deploy federal force to clear peaceful protesters while holding the "sword of the Spirit" (Ephesians 6:17).

Christian Right leaders responded with praise for Trump. Johnnie Moore, of the President's Evangelical Advisory Board, lauded him as being in "total command" and "defying those who aim to derail our national healing by spreading fear, hate, and anarchy" (Gjelten 2020). Franklin Graham and Pastor Robert Jeffress echoed that Trump was "absolutely correct" in removing protesters (Jenkins 2020). Perkins (2020b) claimed in his *Washington Times* op-ed that very morning that "mob violence and police brutality result from a morally bankrupt America." He did not respond directly to Trump's actions. His email to supporters the following day, entitled "What We Need Is Hope," did not mention Trump's clearing of Layfette Park (FRC email, June 2, 2020). The only reference to the events of the previous day was a brief lamentation over the small fire set by protesters threatening this piece of history with going "up in flames" (FRC email, June 2, 2020). Perkins repeated the "mob" rhetoric, keeping the focus of his constituents on the enemy of "law & order" rather than Trump's controversial clearing of Layfette Park.

Ralph Reed (2020c), who spent much of the summer promoting his book *For God and Country*, responded to Trump's walk to St. John's: "It was symbolic, that is important. . . . The bully pulpit of his office conveys a message. . . . We are not going to allow our country . . . to be run over by rioters and looters and terrorists, and I'm glad he did it." He echoed concerns about religious liberty: "I think it was good for him to go to a house of worship, particularly when liquor stores and massage parlors and abortion clinics have been allowed to be open during the COVID-19 pandemic, but churches have been ordered closed and Christians have been arrested and given citations for trying to worship" (Reed 2020c). When asked about the violence, Reed responded:

> I agree with what the president said yesterday. We need to take our streets back. . . . We need to restore order first and after that we need to look towards an agenda that will ensure police brutality is dealt with. . . . I personally am a strong supporter of school choice and allowing young African American children . . . We need to allow them to go to a home school or private school or Christian school where they can learn and get off on the right foot . . . but first we have to secure the streets.

Reed deftly weaves together the fundamentals of the Christian Right worldview with seemingly unrelated issues of violent protesters, racial tension, moral corruption, homeschooling, economic and religious freedom, and law and order.

In supporter emails, Reed mentioned the protests only twice before the election, and each time he stayed focused on the get-out-the-vote message: "Despite the pandemic, national unrest while rioters destroyed cities over the summer, and more—we have never wavered in our commitment to getting Christian voters to the polls" (FFC email, Oct. 29, 2020). However, after the November elections, with the Georgia Senate runoff election looming, Reed invoked the protests, regularly claiming, "for months we've watched as radical Democrats have been rioting in the streets, tearing our beloved nation apart, and trying to steal the election" (FFC email, Nov. 11, 2020). Reed threatened that the radical Left would "close the doors to our churches," "impose cruel abortion policies," and, in an indirect appeal to white Christians, "destroy the prosperity and the freedom that you and I have enjoyed" (FFC email, Dec. 15, 2020). Arguably, with the possibility of a Democratic Senate, Reed chose to deploy threat-laden messaging to motivate Republican voters.

During some of the protests, activists vandalized federal buildings or toppled statues of white leaders seen to symbolize racism and oppression. On June 25, President Trump signed an executive order titled Protecting American Monuments, Memorials and Statues and Combating Recent Criminal

Violence, which clearly linked the protests throughout the summer with "left wing extremists," "Marxism," and a "mob" with "ignorance of our history." The order implies that these same protesters "indiscriminately" vandalized those who fought against civil rights, communism, and were now targeting statues of Jesus in houses of worship. Jurisdictions that "permit the desecration of monuments" or refuse to prosecute protesters for these acts would not receive federal grants (Trump 2020b).

Following Trump's intervention, and in the context of Independence Day, Christian Right outrage at the BLM protests assumed a patriotic tone. Perkins expressed concerns about the destruction of "statues of great men" and the "renaming of important landmarks," which "erase American history" (FRC emails, June 25 and July 2, 2020). Perkins asked, "When angry mobs tear down our statues and vandalize monuments, it's 'justice?'" (June 26, 2020). FRC celebrated Trump's position: "While Virginia tries to flush its history down the city's tubes, the administration is coming after anyone who defaces, damages, or tries to remove any monument by force" (FRC email, July 15, 2020). Perkins noted that President Trump had made it clear: "If these agitators want to vandalize sacred places, they'll pay for it. . . . As President Trump pointed out, there isn't a shortage of ignorance among these rioters" (July 15, 2020).

The law-and-order rhetoric offers a flexible language for identifying the enemy. Following Trump's Fourth of July speech, FRC sung his praises: "Passionate at times, eloquent at others, it was the speech of a man who realized it wasn't just his presidency at stake—but his country" (FRC email, July 7, 2020). The same email identified the "liberal" enemy: "Meanwhile, no one is quite sure what the mob's solution to this crisis is (if they seek a solution at all). Their idea of justice divides. Their idea of equality silences. . . . And maybe for angry liberals, that's the point" (FRC email, July 7, 2020). FRC reiterated this message of the "liberal," "socialist" threat in approximately 30 percent of emails to supporters in 2020.

Throughout the summer, FRC railed against professional baseball players' symbolic protest in support of BLM and claimed BLM desires to "annihilate America" through violent revolution (July 27, 2020). FRC asserted that BLM activists were Marxists and had financial connections to China (Gonzales 2020). China, first responsible for coronavirus, was now responsible for BLM protests. "America's civil unrest," FRC supporters were told, "has been fomented by foreign agents or Marxist ideologues" (Sept. 25, 2020). Yet FRC made a careful distinction between admonishing racism and denouncing the BLM movement. For years the Christian Right movement has pointed out that Margaret Sanger, founder of Planned Parenthood, advocated eugenics to control the Black population (reiterated in FRC email, Sept. 3, 2020). FRC continued to link the issues of racism and abortion—wondering why it is OK to question the death of one man, George Floyd, but wrong to protest "millions" of deaths through abortions (June 11, 2020). FRC drew a careful distinction between BLM and the importance of *all* God's children: "Americans overwhelmingly agree that the lives of black people have as much value as the lives of white people and people of every skin color. Black lives don't just 'matter' (that's such a utilitarian word); they are precious in God's sight because they reflect his image" (Sept. 25, 2020).

The BLM protests gave Christian Right political leaders an opportunity to shift the discussion away from the pandemic and to reiterate familiar rhetoric about political threats. For example, the juxtaposition of the BLM crowds protesting and the COVID-19 restrictions on church gatherings outraged Perkins:

> after months of force-fed fearmongering, the outbreak found itself in an unusual place: the backburner. Suddenly, concerns about social distancing were non-existent. Liberal leaders, who were doing everything they could to keep Americans locked down, were standing behind podiums, urging people to get out and protest. Now, after a couple of weeks of mob demonstrations, the Left wants to blame someone else for the surge of infections: Donald Trump. (June 23, 2020)

Perkins blamed the rise in cases on the protests, particularly among young people, ironically wondering, "Maybe people believe that the virus wasn't that bad at the riots" (June 23, 2020). Perceived threats to religious freedom, exacerbated by COVID-19 social distancing regulations, were set in contrast to BLM protest and presented an opportunity to call out the unfair treatment of (white) evangelicals and, ultimately, a threat to the Christian Right worldview.

High Stakes

FRC and FFC emails help trace the reaction of the Christian Right to the atmosphere of the public square in 2020. The staple issues (e.g., abortion, antitransgender rights, and religious freedom) provided organizations with a familiar language to animate voters. But the two key external events—the pandemic and the BLM protests—provided unique opportunities to confirm President Trump as an ally in the moral fight. COVID-19, the "China virus," intensified apprehensions of a threatening foreign Other and of science-based policies threatening religious liberty. BLM intensified threats to law and order from largely African American protesters. At first glance, the account above may not be that different from previous campaigns, not that different from the expected behavior of interest groups, not that different from reactions to previous external disruptions to the familiar political rhythm. But in 2020, the stakes of strategic politics turned out to be just a little higher than previous electoral cycles.

Political responses to COVID-19, such as attempts to ensure enfranchisement, presented an opportunity to prime FRC and FFC supporters with a narrative explaining electoral defeat. Throughout the campaign, Trump raised the possibility of voter fraud due to the increase of mail-in ballots. Over the summer, both FRC and FFC parroted the worry that the election could be "stolen" from Trump. On September 14, Reed's emails predicted "rampant voter fraud" in Georgia. Two weeks later, he repeated this worry:

> President Trump said, there *"is going to be fraud like you've never seen. . . . We might not know for months because these ballots are going to be all over."* . . . Voter fraud is going to be rampant this year due to changes in many state's early-voting policies, the expansion of mail-in voting, and the early reports we've already heard of Trump ballots being dumped. (Sept. 30, 2020; emphasis theirs)

According to a video obtained by the *Washington Post* of a Council for National Policy meeting in August, Reed advocated "ballot harvesting," collecting and delivering absentee ballots: "Our organization is going to be harvesting ballots in churches. . . . We're going to be specifically going in not only to white evangelical churches, but into Hispanic and Asian churches and collecting those ballots" (Williams 2020). Note that the call did *not* mention Black churches. This may indicate an expectation that Hispanic and Asian evangelicals were more likely to support Trump (see Burge 2017). In Georgia, the law only allows a third party to return a ballot if the voter is disabled or in the hospital and then only by a family or household member. If anyone else returns the ballot for the voter, it is tampering. If Reed's team planned to ballot harvest in Georgia, it was not difficult for him to predict election tampering.

FRC first mentioned the "enormous potential for voter fraud" in emails on May 6 and then at least once a month until August. In September, FRC emailed approximately twice per week warning of voter fraud. For example, FRC claimed that George Soros had "advocated for widespread 'vote-by-mail' which can be ripe for fraud" and would lead to a "socialist, godless state" (Sept.

17, 2020). Senator Josh Hawley (R-MO), the first to announce he would object to the certification of President Biden, spoke at FRC's Values Voter Summit (VVS) in September. Other voter fraud conspiracy theory advocates, Rep. Jody Hice (R-GA), Rep. Mike Johnson (R-LA), Rep. Chip Roy (R-TX), Rep. Steve Scalise (R-LA), and White House Chief of Staff Mark Meadows, joined President Trump as speakers at VVS 2020. Again, following the election, FRC emailed twice per week about voter fraud. With the Georgia runoff election on the horizon, Perkins emailed supporters that "voters saw how Democrats abused the process in the name of COVID, how they twisted and changed election laws without legislatures' consent" (Dec. 8, 2020). *Washington Watch* and FRC events regularly hosted election fraud proponents, such as Rep. Louie Gohmert (R-TX) and the American Conservative Union lobbyist Matt Schlapp.

On November 9, Ralph Reed emailed: "We put everything into the 2020 elections, and you and I both know that Donald Trump won re-election in reality. We CANNOT allow the Democrats to steal these seats from us too." Reed's emails continued to claim the election was stolen throughout November and December. Each email warned of the dangers of losing the Senate; in December Reed wrote: "Radical extremists Jon Ossoff and Raphael Warnock are doing everything they can to BUY the election and steal away victory from conservatives David Perdue and Kelly Loeffler" (Dec. 28, 2020). Reed's rhetoric warned of the "radical policies" and the threat to Christian values from Democrats.

These warnings fed into the postelection Stop the Steal movement, reaching a crescendo as Congress prepared to certify the Electoral College ballots on January 6. As protesters gathered in Washington, DC, on the evening of January 5, 2020, Perkins broadcast an intercessory prayer event live from the Mall. Perkin's guests were Senator Marshall (R-KS), Representatives Jody Hice (R-GA) and Gohmert (R-TX)—all adamant that there was "massive" election fraud and all who, the next day, voted to reject the Electoral College outcomes in Arizona and Pennsylvania (Perkins 2020d). The event reflected FRC's call to action: "Pray. Vote. Stand." The slogan evokes Ephesians 6:13: "Therefore take the whole armour of God, that you may be able to withstand in the evil day, and having done all, to stand." During the election, Perkins had repeated this phrase incessantly in his radio broadcasts, on Facebook videos, in supporter emails, in almost every in-group publication, and via the FRC "Pray. Vote. Stand." speaker series.

In October, Chino Hills pastor Jack Hibbs had cohosted "Freedom Sunday" with Perkins, encouraging evangelical pastors to "open their doors" and let congregations worship without masks or social distancing. On January 5, Perkins and Hibbs prayed:

> Against all of the reports that is a foregone conclusion . . . that you would shock, Lord, America with your grace and your mercy . . . spare judgement . . . and remove from power those that are against the unborn child's life . . . a miracle that would rock this nation . . . shake us to the point . . . and establish righteousness . . . give senators strength, backbone and frankly guts to do the right thing . . . may people throw off the yoke of playing it safe and be men and women of God and do the right thing. (Perkins 2020d)

Perkins then claimed that the nation is in a "predicament" because churches closed their doors and now believers must have "courage and boldness."

Interest groups are by their nature oppositional and rally supporters with calls to action that articulate potential threats. The evocation of Ephesians 6 as a call to action is not surprising or out of character for FRC to deploy in an election year. There is no evidence in group emails or other communications gathered for this research of either Perkins or Reed advocating violent insurrection. In fact, immediately following the events of January 6, both Perkins and Reed denounced the violence at the Capitol. Reed emailed supporters the next day with a clear message: "The violence at the U.S. Capitol is an assault on everything we stand for. It has no place in the life of our nation, and I condemn and repudiate it. It does not represent our movement or the cause of Christ" (Jan. 7, 2020). Likewise, Perkins wrote: "The violence at the U.S. Capitol building against Congress and Capitol Police is wrong and dangerous for our republic. Lawlessness is not the way, and such actions makes it difficult for law-abiding Americans to fight the good fight" (Jan. 7, 2020).

Having said that, FRC and FFC rhetoric priming supporters for electoral fraud raised the electoral stakes. Standing on the Mall on the evening of January 5 repeatedly claiming a fraudulent election offered a theological endorsement for calling American democracy into question. Casting one's lot in presidential politics is always risky. But at present, both Perkins and Reed continue with their high-stakes endorsement of Trump as "the best President Christians ever had."

Conclusion

This examination of the political messaging of the FRC and the FFC sheds light on the professionalism of these organizations and how they adapt to external shocks by offering supporters a consistent lens for interpreting political events. Both Reed and Perkins were absolutely clear that Trump had been the most Christian Right–friendly president ever. In the words of both Reed (2020b) and Perkins (2020a): "Promises made. Promises kept." Trump was their guy.

While COVID-19 threatened to hijack any campaign agenda, both Trump and Christian Right political leaders were able to shift the narrative to the familiar tropes of anti-intellectualism/antiscience, the lack of values of liberal hypocrites, and threats to religious freedom. The discussion of BLM explains the correlation between this need to shift the message away from the threat of the pandemic and toward the emerging threat of BLM and liberals. Attempts to ensure voter enfranchisement during the pandemic presented an opportunity to prophesy—priming supporters with an explanation for electoral defeat. Close examination of the language in emails and public statements demonstrates how political messaging was deployed to frame external shocks and offer a familiar lens—of the threatening other—with which supporters could understand current events. The Christian Right response to COVID-19 and to BLM protests, therefore, echoed their ongoing moral agenda, where the threat to conservative Christian values had already reached pandemic proportions.

10

Faith, Source Credibility, and Trust in Pandemic Information

JIANING LI, AMANDA FRIESEN, AND MICHAEL W. WAGNER

One of the greatest mass communication challenges during the COVID-19 pandemic was information fragmentation. While most news organizations were reporting about the contagiousness of the virus and strategies to prevent becoming infected with the virus, some outlets, like Fox News, were downplaying the severity of COVID-19. Sean Hannity regularly told his viewers that predictions about the seriousness of the virus were "wrong" and expressed doubts about taking a vaccine. Laura Ingraham tweeted that the pandemic was a good time to fly (though she later deleted the tweet). One of the leaders of the federal government's Coronavirus Taskforce, Dr. Anthony Fauci, called some of Fox's reporting "outlandish" (Stelter 2020). Of course, it wasn't just Fox News spreading misinformation about COVID-19. The president of the United States, Donald Trump, was regularly minimizing the severity of the pandemic and promoting untested and potentially dangerous treatments and alleged preventive behaviors. While there were times that the president indicated the virus was serious and that people should wear masks, he usually quickly pivoted back to downplaying the virus's severity.

Material referencing an appendix in this chapter can be found online available here: https://dataverse.harvard.edu/dataverse/epidemic_among_my_people.

There was considerable variation at the state government level as well. For example, the Republican-led state legislature in Wisconsin took the state's Democratic governor to court, overturning a stay-at-home order. In short, Americans heard mixed messages about COVID-19 from different levels of government, different branches of government, the two major parties, and news sources. Of course, people do not consume news coverage in a vacuum. People's news use is partially driven by predispositions and individual identity characteristics (Shah et al. 2017). As such, how individual identities are related to the trust people have in leaders, news sources, and scientific organizations that provide information about COVID-19 is important to understand. One identity that has the potential to shape how individuals evaluate their major sources of information about the pandemic is their religious identity. In particular, one's religion and their religiosity may be related to the trust and attention people place in various sources related to the pandemic.

Moreover, faith leaders exhibited considerable variation in the messages they gave to their flocks about the coronavirus. One Maine pastor, presiding over what National Public Radio (2020) called a "superspreader wedding event," attacked public health officials for intervening in church business, saying, "You're looking at a liberty lover! I—love—liberty. And I want the people of God to enjoy liberty" (All Things Considered 2020). In Wisconsin, a coalition of faith leaders called on the state's legislature to do more to clear up confusion and help keep their parishioners safe (Gunn 2020).

Who did Americans of different faith traditions trust to tell them the truth about COVID-19? In this chapter, we provide evidence about the answers to these questions using an online national survey that asks about respondents' religious faith, media use, media trust, and trust in various leaders to tell the truth about COVID-19. We show that even though there were not meaningful differences about how much people trusted their most trusted news source to tell them the truth about the coronavirus, evangelical Christians are more likely than others to rely on news sources that provide mixed messages about best practices during the pandemic. We also find that identifying as an evangelical Christian and holding literal views of the Bible were positively associated with trusting Donald Trump to provide good information about the pandemic. Even so, levels of trust were higher for the Centers for Disease Control than the president with respect to COVID-19 information. Levels of trust were also higher for individuals' most trusted media source than for President Trump regardless of religious beliefs and affiliations. We also show how both religious affiliations and trust mattered, as we present evidence highlighting how Catholics, people trusting Donald Trump, and other groups were more likely to underestimate the severity of the pandemic.

Religious Americans and the News Media

Though scholars continually debate media effects on political phenomena, there is evidence that when it comes to policy knowledge, the coverage and salience of news increases individual learning (Barabas and Jerit 2009). Regarding health-related policies, there are differences depending on where individuals get their news. For example, in a study of Zika virus coverage, Jerit et al. (2019) found that local news (*Tampa Bay Times*) printed audience-specific, in-depth prevention coverage, compared to the *New York Times*. But both papers similarly used "sensationalist language and imprecise risk information" (Jerit et al. 2019, 1).

For religious Americans, particularly conservative Christians, selecting a news source for policy information can be influenced by perceptions of media bias toward their beliefs and groups. Indeed, those high in religiosity rate broadcast, print, and internet news as more untrustworthy, as compared to their less religious peers (Golan and Day 2010). Stefanone, Vollmer, and Covert (2019) showed the higher one's religiosity, the more one found fake news credible and the more likely one would share the information.

Moreover, both political and religious elites often signal distrust in mainstream media sources, dissuading their followers from tuning in (Gaskins 2019). High religious service attenders and self-identified evangelicals consider the media hostile to their beliefs and that the media are often factually inaccurate in their stories (see also Ladd 2012). These behaviors are associated with lower political knowledge for highly religious individuals, though it is important to note like many political knowledge scales taken from large publicly available surveys, these items focus on major political figures and institutions, factors that are often less relevant to effective political decision-making (Gaskins 2019; Lupia 2016).

The scholarship on understanding when and how conservative Christians or evangelicals seek or avoid political content has not considered these effects in light of a major health crisis, a time when trust in news sources is directly related to health outcomes (Young and Bleakley 2020). With respect to source trust itself, Krause et al. (2019) found that when asked about the kinds of people they generally trust to "tell the truth," scientists are one of the most trusted groups, even when thinking about scientific issues that can be polarizing. Yet Cacciatore et al. (2018) found that evangelical Christians use media coverage about science differently than non-evangelicals and are less likely to trust scientific sources of information.

The distrust of the news media sown by many religious elites and partisan political leaders is connected to various religious groups' media attitudes. Mormons feel the mainstream media are hostile to their beliefs and politically biased and therefore consider these sources less trustworthy and credible (Golan and Baker 2012). The relationship with religiosity and media trust is more mixed (Golan and Day 2010). Evangelical Christians are more trusting of religious authority figures to tell the truth about scientific information, though they are only slightly less likely than non-evangelicals to trust scientific authorities for the same information (Cacciatore et al. 2018). Evangelicals also tend to use mediated information differently than non-evangelical Christians.

Certain religious beliefs may structure media preferences as well. For example, Christians who hold literal views of the Bible also may be attracted to information sources that display authoritarian themes (for a discussion, see Djupe and Burge 2021). Those with these literal and dogmatic orientations may be more likely to look to the Trump administration or Fox News for their pandemic guidance rather than a scientific, deliberative body like the Centers for Disease Control.

Modality (Talk Radio, TV, Online, Newspaper)

Given the drastic growth of media choices and the rise of niche markets in the contemporary information environment (Stroud 2011), it is imperative to update our understanding of how individuals' media diet can be shaped by their religious beliefs. Research shows that today's audiences structure their media repertoires based on both ideology and modality (talk radio, TV, online, print) (Edgerly 2015). While social media and online news websites increasingly outpace print newspapers in attracting audiences, radio and TV—despite being "older" media than online platforms—still take the lion's share of Americans' media diets (Shearer 2018). In 2018, more than 80 percent of Americans aged twelve or older listened to AM/FM radio in a given week (Pew Research Center 2019). In particular, news/talk formats—where such conservative commentators as Rush Limbaugh and Sean Hannity are prominently featured—are highly influential in the public political discourse (Sobieraj and Berry 2011). Conservative talk radio and Christian radio constitute a substantial proportion of a conservative media diet together with Fox News and conservative blogs (Edgerly 2015).

For our purposes, much of the work on religiosity and news modality preferences has not been updated (see Golan and Day 2010 for a review). For example, there were positive relationships between high religious service attenders and newspaper readership (Finnegan and Viswanath 1988; Sobal and Jackson-Beeck 1981), and religious people eschew the internet in favor of news from print and television/radio (Armfield and Holbert 2003). In 2008 and 2012 national surveys, highly religious Americans were more likely than the less religious to listen to radio for news but no more likely to tune into Fox News once partisanship was taken into account (Gaskins 2019). Part of this chapter's contribution is to update the connections between religious belief and media consumption.

Religion and Trust

Though news and social media are important distributors of policy-related information and knowledge, government agencies also have their own messaging strategies and channels. This is particularly the case with a public health crisis like the COVID-19 pandemic. Individuals are bombarded with messages from the Centers for Disease Control, their state and local public health departments, university medical centers, clinics and hospitals, and local, state, and federal public officials. But reception of those messages hinges on trust—perhaps a generalized trust of others or a specific trust in government entities.

The literature on religious individuals and political and social trust is mixed (see Hsiung and Djupe 2019 for a discussion). While some scholars argue that political trust should be separately understood from social trust (Newton 1999), it is not clear in the case of information about a pandemic whether this trust should be classified as political or not. In fact, the politicization of COVID-19 has been the topic of much discussion—a phenomenon that should be about health and prevention has become polarized by belief and suspicion.

Hsiung and Djupe (2019) argue that variation in social and political trust cannot be neatly organized into the believing, behaving, and belonging categories often describing religion and politics in the United States (Layman 2001). They point to evidence from Traunmüller (2011), which suggests trust increases when religious people feel they are in the majority. In the case of evangelical Christians and the Trump administration, we can expect they will put their trust in Republican-affiliated government officials and only media where they feel part of this majority (e.g., Fox News). Trust in government closely follows partisan control, but also white evangelical Christians were overall less trusting of government (Hsiung and Djupe 2019). More recent evidence from the Pew Research Center (2020) shows that white evangelical Christians hold more positive views of President Trump and are more agreeable with President Trump on important issues, compared to other religious groups and those who are unaffiliated.

With respect to COVID-19, DeFranza et al. (2020) find that religiosity is associated with a decreased likelihood in following shelter-in-place orders as the orders are interpreted as a violation of personal and religious freedom, topics regularly raised in conservative media ecologies (Jamieson and Cappella 2010). Further, trust in these sources tends to be asymmetric, with conservatives trusting talk radio and Fox News at significantly higher levels than moderates and liberals (Pew Research Center 2020d).

Expectations and Open Questions

Given the strong relationship between political and religious identity (Margolis 2018) and the increasing likelihood that religious traditionalists identify as Republicans, we expect evangelical Christians to be more likely to trust the Republican president, Donald Trump, as a source of information about COVID-19. It is less clear what to expect regarding non-evangelical Christians, given the diversity of their partisanship and media use. We also expect that those with more literal views of the Bible will express more trust in President Trump to tell them the truth about COVID-19. Because evangelicals tend to interpret scientific information differently than others (Cacciatore et al. 2018), exhibiting less trust in scientific authority, we expect evangelicals to be less likely than others to trust the CDC to tell them the truth about COVID-19. We do not expect there to be differences in trust of one's most trusted news source based on religious identity or affiliation, although it will be important to compare differences in which sources are trusted the most by religious groups.

Sample and Methods

In April 2020, we conducted a survey of U.S. adult respondents recruited by LHK Partners, with one-third of participants from counties with zero local newspapers, one-third from counties with one local newspaper, and one-third from counties with more than one local newspaper (n = 2,063). These three groups of counties were prematched with a genetic matching algorithm to ensure that they share similar demographic and geographic characteristics despite differing in the number of local newspapers they have. The sampling procedure was developed for another purpose, but the size and makeup of the sample can provide useful insights about how various religious groups approach trusting sources to tell them the truth about important public health issues.

Each respondent was asked to rate how often they access twenty-five different news sources—from talk radio to blogs to television shows—and how much they trust each source. We also asked participants how much they trust the following to "tell you the truth about COVID-19": President Trump, the U.S. Centers for Disease Control and Prevention, and the news source the respondents had indicated that they trusted the most (a source they indicated to us earlier in the survey from a list of twenty-five sources we provided).

Measures

Religious groups. We categorized religious groups using two survey questions. The first question asked respondents whether they would describe themselves as a born-again or evangelical Christian or not, and the second question asked respondents to choose their religious preference from Protestant, Roman Catholic, Jewish, Muslim, Mormon, other Christian religion, other non-Christian religion, no religion, and don't know. Those who answered yes to the first question *and* chose Protestant, other Christian religion, or don't know for the second question were coded as "evangelical Christians" (26.27 percent). Those who answered no or don't know to the first question *and* chose Protestant or other Christian religion for the second question were coded as "non-evangelical Protestants" (22.69 percent). Those who chose Roman Catholic were coded as "Catholics" (19.78 percent). Due to small sample sizes, we collapsed Jewish, Muslim, Mormon, and other non-Christian religion to create the "other religion" category (8.48 percent) and collapsed no religion and don't know (who also did not identify as evangelical) to create the "nones" category (22.78 percent).

Biblical literalism. Respondents answered the question "Which of these statements comes closest to describing your feelings about the Bible?" by choosing from "the Bible is the actual word of God and is to be taken literally, word for word" (24.48 percent, coded as 3), "the Bible is the inspired word of God but not everything in it should be taken literally, word for word" (50.41 percent, coded as 2), and "the Bible is an ancient book of fables, legends, history, and moral precepts recorded by men" (25.11 percent, coded as 1).

Most trusted news sources. Respondents answered the question "Of all of the news sources listed, which one do you trust the most?" by selecting one answer from the list of twenty-five items (see Figure 10.1).

Trust in institutions or person to tell the truth about COVID-19. On a 5-point scale, respondents answered the question "How much do you trust the following people and institutions to tell you the truth about COVID-19?" for President Trump, the CDC, and their answer to the most trusted news source question. Their answers were recoded so that 1 equals completely distrust and 5 equals trust completely ($M_{Trump} = 2.71$; $SD_{Trump} = 1.49$; $M_{CDC} = 3.77$; $SD_{CDC} = 0.99$; $M_{News} = 3.72$; $SD_{News} = 0.92$).

Estimates of confirmed COVID-19 cases in the United States. Based on the COVID-19 Data Repository by the Center for Systems Science and Engineering at Johns Hopkins University, we calculated the average number of confirmed COVID-19 cases in the United States during the period of our survey. We then computed an index for each respondent by dividing their estimate of cases by the documented number of cases. Using one-third quantiles of the distribution of this index, we created three categories to describe the accuracy of a respondent's estimate. If a respondent's index fell under the one-third quantile, they were categorized as giving an "underestimate." If a respondent's index fell between the one-third and two-thirds quantile, they were categorized as giving an "about right estimate." If a respondent's index fell above the two-thirds quantile, they were categorized as giving an "overestimate."

Control variables. We asked respondents to report their partisan identification and recoded the items to a 7-point scale (1 = strong Democrat; 7 = strong Republican; M = 4.23; SD = 2.11). Respondents also reported their political interest (1 = Follow politics hardly at all; 4 = Follow politics most of the time; M = 3.29; SD = 0.90), age (M = 52.02; SD = 16.94), gender (55.12 percent female), education (5-point scale; M = 3.10; SD = 1.43; 80.85 percent with at least some college), race (17.30 percent nonwhite), and household income (7-point scale; M = 3.26; SD = 1.66; 57 percent below $75,000).

Results

We asked our participants to identify, of the twenty-five information sources we provided, the one that they trusted the most. For evangelical Christians, television is king. Figure 10.1 shows that Fox News was the most trusted option by far, followed by local television news and national network television news. CNN, national newspapers, local newspapers, and conservative talk radio were also chosen in moderately high numbers. News content on social media, entertainment and late night programming, daytime talk, and various political blogs were chosen least often as the most trusted news source for evangelicals.

Turning our attention to non-evangelical Protestants, the diversity of media choice is notable, though once again television sources are the most likely to be named as one's most trusted source. Figure 10.1 also shows that mainstream network television news, the third most popular choice for evangelical Christians, came out on top for non-evangelical Protestants. While Fox News was the most trusted choice for evangelical Christians and the third most trusted among non-evangelical Protestants, non-evangelicals also exhibited notable trust in MSNBC, highlighting the ideological diversity of news content preferred by non-evangelical Protestants. Local television news was the second

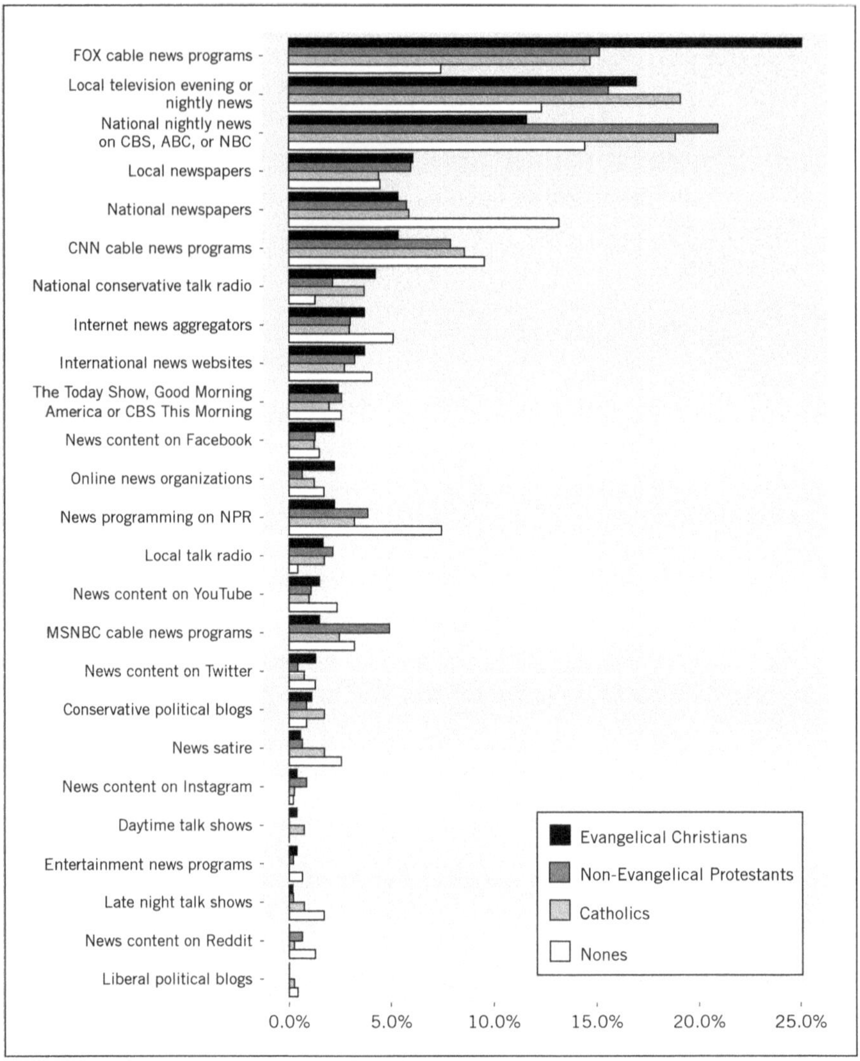

Figure 10.1 The Most Trusted News Sources for Evangelical Christians, Non-evangelical Protestants, Catholics, and Nones (Source: April 2020 survey.)

most popular source. CNN, National Public Radio (NPR), and local and national newspapers were also commonly selected as trusted sources of news.

Similar to non-evangelical Protestants, Catholics also demonstrate a relatively diverse pattern of news trust as compared to evangelicals. Local television news was the most trusted among Catholics, followed by mainstream network television news as a close second. Interestingly, FOX and CNN came in as the third and fourth most popular sources, reflecting the ideological diversity and the strong dominance of television sources in news trust among Catholics. The nones' most trusted news sources reflect even more diversity of information outlets. National mainstream network news was the most trusted source, but national newspapers were close behind, as were local television news, CNN, Fox News, and NPR. Nones also selected international news sites, MSNBC, and internet news aggregators more often than evangelicals, non-evangelical Protestants, and Catholics.

Given the considerable demographic differences regarding typical evangelical Christians as compared, for example, to the average none, we want to more systematically understand whether religious orientations or demographics are more central explanations of correlates of trust in various sources of information about COVID-19. Focusing on whether one identifies as an evangelical Christian or not, Table 10.1 provides estimates for correlates of trust in Donald Trump, the CDC, and one's most trusted news source to tell individuals the truth about the COVID-19 pandemic. The first column estimates factors associated with trust in President Trump to tell the truth about COVID-19. As we expected, evangelical Christians were significantly more likely to trust Trump than others, and, of course, Republicans were more likely than Democrats to trust the Republican president. Those with more education were less likely to trust the president to tell the truth about the pandemic. No other variables were significantly different from zero in the model.

Moving to the middle column and factors associated with trust in the CDC, being an evangelical Christian was negatively signed, as expected, but was not statistically significant. Republicans and respondents who were not white were less likely to trust the CDC. Those with higher incomes and more education were more likely to trust the CDC's COVID-19 statements. In the right-hand column, our analysis reveals that older individuals, men, Democrats, and those interested in politics were more likely to trust their most trusted news source to tell them the truth about COVID-19.

In addition to comparing evangelical Christians to others, we also break down our results by more specific religious traditions. Figure 10.2 suggests a notable difference between the level of trust evangelicals place in Donald Trump as compared to non-evangelical Protestants, who are less trusting in the former president. Evangelical Christians trust Trump to tell the truth about COVID-19 more than any other Christian group. The only group that reported higher levels of trust were Muslim respondents, though this may be an artifact (note the wider error bars) of the small number of such respondents in our data.

TABLE 10.1 TRUST IN TRUMP, CDC, AND TRUSTED NEWS TO TELL THE TRUTH ABOUT COVID-19 BY WHETHER ONE IDENTIFIES AS AN EVANGELICAL CHRISTIAN OR NOT

	Trust in Trump	Trust in CDC	Trust in Their Most Trusted News Source
(Intercept)	0.868 ***	3.862 ***	2.891 ***
	(0.140)	(0.128)	(0.117)
Evangelical Christians	0.221 ***	−0.012	−0.011
	(0.058)	(0.052)	(0.048)
Age	−0.003	0.000	0.004 ***
	(0.002)	(0.001)	(0.001)
Female	0.069	−0.077	−0.109 **
	(0.050)	(0.045)	(0.041)
Nonwhite	−0.074	−0.176 **	−0.040
	(0.068)	(0.062)	(0.056)
Education	−0.075 ***	0.041 *	0.018
	(0.019)	(0.018)	(0.016)
Income	0.021	0.031 *	0.026
	(0.017)	(0.015)	(0.014)
Partisanship	0.482 ***	−0.066 ***	−0.021 *
	(0.012)	(0.011)	(0.010)
Political interest	0.009	0.009	0.194 ***
	(0.030)	(0.027)	(0.025)
R^2	0.496	0.032	0.067

Source: April 2020 survey.
Note: *** $p < 0.001$; ** $p < 0.01$; * $p < 0.05$. Baseline of comparison is anyone who does not identify as an evangelical Christian.

When we examine average level of trust members of different religious groups placed in their most trusted news source, there is not meaningful variation across religious traditions. Notably, evangelical Christians were more likely to trust Donald Trump with pandemic-related information, as compared to everyone else in our sample, and all of the religious groups (including evangelicals) we examined placed more trust in both the CDC and their most trusted news source than Donald Trump.

Because religious beliefs are correlated with authority given to sources of information (Djupe and Burge 2021), we wanted to compare how different beliefs about the Bible were related to trust in what President Trump, the CDC,

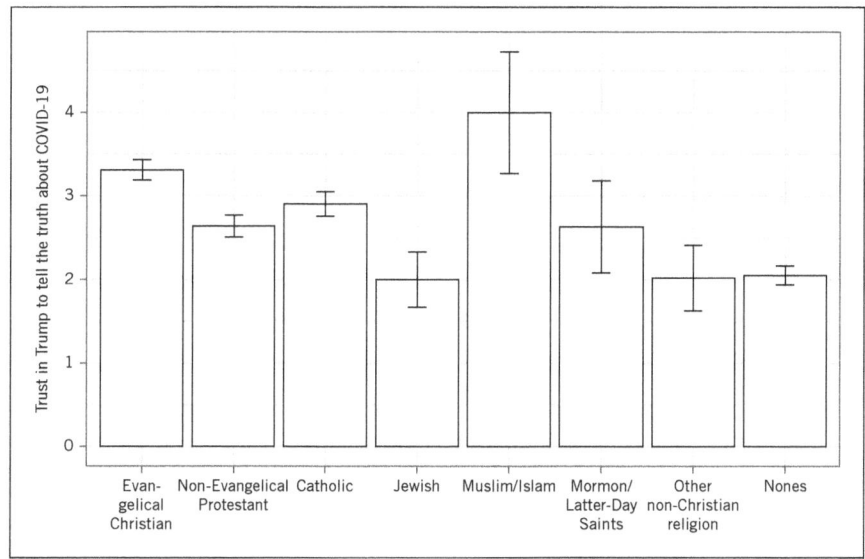

Figure 10.2 Trust in Trump to Tell the Truth About COVID-19 by Religious Groups (Source: April 2020 survey.)

and what one's most trusted media source had to say about the virus. In Table 10.2, the left-hand column examines correlates of trust in Donald Trump to tell the truth about COVID-19. Holding a more literal view of the Bible is positively associated with trusting the then president to tell the truth about COVID-19. When controlling for biblical literalism, only Catholics were significantly more likely to trust Trump as compared to nones, who were the baseline comparison group. The coefficients for evangelical Christians and non-evangelical Protestants were positive but not significant.

The middle column shows that non-evangelical Protestants were more likely to trust the CDC to tell the truth about COVID-19 while evangelicals, Catholics, and those of other religions were not different from zero. Holding other factors constant, biblical literalism has no significant effect on trust in the CDC. Democrats were more likely to trust the CDC while those who are not white were less likely to trust the government organization. Those with more education and higher incomes were also more likely to trust the CDC.

The final column reveals that biblical literalism is positively associated with trust in one's most trusted news source about COVID-19. Similar to findings on trust in Trump, the effect of religious traditions is muted when taking account of biblical literalism. Holding other factors constant, evangelicals, non-evangelicals, and Catholics were no more likely than nones to trust their most trusted news source to tell the truth about COVID-19. Dem-

TABLE 10.2 TRUST IN TRUMP, CDC, AND TRUSTED NEWS TO TELL THE TRUTH ABOUT COVID-19 BY RELIGIOUS GROUPS AND BIBLICAL LITERALISM

	Trust in Trump	Trust in CDC	Trust in Their Most Trusted News Source
(Intercept)	0.457 **	3.865 ***	2.731 ***
	(0.152)	(0.140)	(0.128)
Evangelical Christians	0.164	0.115	−0.063
	(0.089)	(0.082)	(0.075)
Non-evangelical Protestants	0.108	0.193 **	0.008
	(0.078)	(0.072)	(0.066)
Catholics	0.231 **	0.095	−0.010
	(0.082)	(0.076)	(0.070)
Other religions	0.058	0.117	0.126
	(0.099)	(0.091)	(0.083)
Biblical literalism	0.255 ***	−0.035	0.099 **
	(0.044)	(0.041)	(0.037)
Age	−0.003 *	−0.000	0.004 ***
	(0.002)	(0.001)	(0.001)
Female	0.061	−0.080	−0.108 **
	(0.049)	(0.045)	(0.041)
Nonwhite	−0.151 *	−0.177 **	−0.063
	(0.067)	(0.062)	(0.057)
Education	−0.071 ***	0.039 *	0.019
	(0.019)	(0.018)	(0.016)
Income	0.023	0.031 *	0.026
	(0.017)	(0.015)	(0.014)
Partisanship	0.456 ***	−0.067 ***	−0.028 **
	(0.012)	(0.012)	(0.011)
Political interest	0.002	0.008	0.191 ***
	(0.029)	(0.027)	(0.025)
R^2	0.513	0.036	0.073

Source: April 2020 survey.
Note: *** $p < 0.001$; ** $p < 0.01$; * $p < 0.05$. Baseline of comparison for religious groups is nones.

ocrats were more likely to trust in their most trusted news source as were those who were older, had higher levels of interest in politics, and identified as men.

We also examine predictors of the consequences of trusting different sources for information about COVID-19 (tables and figures included in the online appendix). We used the number of COVID-19 cases in the United States at the time of our interview with them as the baseline of comparison. We placed responses into one of three categories: "overestimating" the number of COVID-19 cases (respondent's answer/real number falls above the two-thirds quantile), "underestimating" the number of COVID-19 cases (respondent's answer/real number falls under one-third quantile), and "about right" answers (respondent's answer/real number falls between the one-third and two-thirds quantiles).

More interesting are the factors associated with underestimating the number of COVID-19 cases in the United States. Trust in Donald Trump as a source about the pandemic was positively related to underestimating COVID-19 cases. However, having a high level of trust in one's most trusted news source was correlated with being less likely to underestimate the number of COVID-19 cases; that is, news trust makes people more accurate in their COVID-19 estimates. Catholics were likely to give wrong answers, either overestimating or underestimating the number of COVID-19 cases, rather than giving an about right answer. Finally, evangelical Christians and those identifying with other religions apart from Christianity were more likely to underestimate COVID-19 cases.

Conclusion

Trust in scientific information—on topics ranging from climate change to genetically modified foods to best practices to combat a global pandemic—can serve as a heuristic for people when they consider information they encounter about science (Brossard and Nisbet 2007; Hmielowski et al. 2014). In general, and consistent with past research, the CDC was the most trusted entity when it came to people's evaluations of who would tell the truth about COVID-19 (Krause et al. 2019). Notably, and in conflict with past research, evangelical Christians were not significantly less likely to trust scientific sources like the CDC as compared to other individuals.

People's most trusted news sources were as likely, and in some cases were more likely, to be trusted than the CDC to share accurate pandemic information. If people's most trusted news sources were sharing the verifiable truth with their audiences, this would be little cause for concern. However, evangelical Christians' most trusted news source was Fox News. Increased Fox viewership was associated with a decreased likelihood of staying home in the early days of the pandemic (Simonov et al. 2020). Fox News viewers were also less likely to prepare for the pandemic by purchasing materials that promoted good hygiene and engaging in behaviors that would decrease transmission of the virus (Ash et al. 2020). Thinking about these results in concert with our own—including our demonstration that literal believers in the Bible were more likely to trust their more favored news source on COVID-19—it is possible that evangelical Christians who trusted Fox News and other sources sharing information that played down the seriousness of COVID-19 may have been more likely to avoid pro-social health behaviors or even more likely to become infected with the virus.

Though their faith in their most trusted news source was higher, evangelical Christians, non-evangelical Protestants, and Catholics all were more likely than nones and people of other religious backgrounds to believe that Donald Trump would tell them the truth about COVID-19. The same was true of both Christians who said the Bible should be taken literally and Christians who expressed belief that the Bible was the inspired word of God. This is consistent with the demonstration that religious traditionalists across denominational perspectives are more likely to support Republicans (Layman 2001).

Still, there is considerable heterogeneity in how people of different faith perspectives and varying levels of fervency in their religious beliefs apply their religious lives to their political views (Friesen and Wagner 2012). For those whose religious identities match their political identities, we might expect even higher levels of trust in co-partisan sources of scientific information than those whose religious identity does not perfectly overlap their partisan one. It is important for future research to understand religion's role in how political leaders' rhetoric can cement polarized partisan identities for many while excluding others from a political system that does not represent them (Wagner and Friesen 2021). That is, as scholars continue to demonstrate the political consequences of those who have overlapping identities as compared to those who do not (see Davis and Mason 2016), our evidence suggests that taking account of people's religious belonging and believing are important for creating a more comprehensive accounting of public opinion and political behavior in the United States.

It is also important to note that joining a new faith community or leaving religion behind is often driven by local factors. This is especially true for evangelicals who place a premium on the social and cultural capital they build with fellow members of their congregations (Djupe et al. 2018). Just as polarized attitudes are driven, in part, by local context (Suk et al. 2020), knowing how congregants came to join their current flock (whether they were denomination shopping, invited by a member of their social network, etc.) is critical to placing their religious identity in context. In other words, just as it is the case for trusted news sources, religion can act as an information broker.

To help unpack observational equivalence between the level of trust most of our respondents expressed in the CDC and in their most trusted news source, future research designs might seek to force a choice between different sources of information rather than discretely evaluating trust in each. It would also be helpful to explore a richer set of questions related to religious belief, networks, and context to understand how individuals' various identities—religious, political, and the like—interact with their spiritual, political, and social beliefs. Finally, larger samples of groups like Muslim Americans and Jewish Americans, for instance, are needed to understand how religious faith more fully is associated with believing varying sources of scientific and political information.

PART III

Pandemic Effects on Religious Groups and Individuals

11

Women as Religious Leaders

The Gendered Politics of Shutting Down

CAMMIE JO BOLIN AND KELLY ROLFES-HAASE

As political leaders began to craft policy responses to COVID-19, media outlets quickly identified a global trend in national pandemic responses: many of those countries that had taken early, decisive actions to reduce transmission of the virus, track cases, and build public trust in institutions were led by women (see, e.g., Wittenberg-Cox 2020; Zalis 2020). These actions have included shutdowns of nonessential businesses and other gathering spaces that can facilitate the spread of COVID-19, such as in-person religious services. In the United States, religious leaders in many communities have had the responsibility of deciding how their own congregations would conduct services during the coronavirus pandemic. Given the apparent difference in response between men and women world leaders, this project considers whether women religious leaders have also been more likely than religious leaders who are men to take actions motivated by the public health interests of their constituencies.

In this chapter, we explore the relationship between women's leadership and public health concerns in America's places of worship. Looking to political science literature on women's political leadership, policy priorities, and role model effects, we examine the extent to which these theories of political representation are applicable in a religious context. In particular, we analyze

---

Material referencing an appendix in this chapter can be found online available here: https://dataverse.harvard.edu/dataverse/epidemic_among_my_people.

the relationship between the presence of women's leadership within a congregation and the cancellation of in-person worship due to COVID-19. We expect that places of worship with women serving in leadership roles will be more likely than places of worship that lack leadership by women to cancel in-person services. Relatedly, we are interested in the relationship between women's leadership and congregant trust in their clergyperson to have their best health interests at heart. Using survey data from Paul A. Djupe, Ryan P. Burge, and Andrew R. Lewis, fielded March 23–26, 2020, and linear probability models using multivariate ordinary least squares regression, we find support for both of our hypotheses.

Our analyses suggest that congregants who witnessed women leading in their place of worship were about 5 percentage points more likely to have also experienced cancellation of their in-person services because of the coronavirus. Similarly, we find that congregants who reported seeing women in leadership positions within their congregations were about 5 percentage points more likely to trust clergy to have their best health interests at heart in comparison to congregants who had not seen women leading within their congregations. Though we cannot make causal claims, we find a positive and statistically significant relationship between women's leadership and the prioritization of public health concerns in religious contexts. These findings build on existing research to suggest that gendered trends in women's political leadership may be generalizable to religious settings.

This chapter proceeds as follows: we first discuss literature on women's representation and role model effects as well as initial studies on gender and COVID-19 responses. Next, we outline our hypotheses, describe our data and methodology, and present our results. We end with a discussion of how our findings contribute to our understanding of the relationship between gender and leadership in the case of public health during the coronavirus pandemic.

Political Representation: Women's Issues and Role Model Effects

Are women in positions of political leadership more likely than their peers who are men to make decisions that protect the health of their constituents? The answer is a qualified yes. Women officeholders tend to prioritize issues of health and social welfare, although the stances they take often differ according to partisan pressures. In a political context, women officeholders tend to prioritize issues and policies related to health care, welfare, and women's health and safety (Frederick 2011, 193). Women officeholders' emphasis on these so-called women's issues is seen in their legislative priorities (e.g., Berkman and O'Connor 1993; Kreitzer 2015; Reingold 2000; Reingold et al. 2020; Williamson and Carnes 2013), bill introduction (Thomas and Welch 1991; Vega and Firestone 1995), bill cosponsorship (Swers 2005, 2013), speeches (Osborn and Mendez 2010; Pearson and Dancey 2011), and budgetary allocation (Holman 2014). Although it is important to note that women legislators are not monolithic and their policy priorities are influenced by racial, ethnic, and other identities (Brown 2014; Dittmar, Sanbonmatsu, and Carroll 2018), research consistently suggests that women legislators tend to view themselves as representatives of women—which often means pursuing initiatives that advance the health and well-being of those they represent.

Party and ideology are also important in mitigating and shaping the role that gender plays in legislators' policy priorities and legislative behaviors (Osborn 2012). On the one hand, women officeholders are often seen as more liberal by voters (Sanbonmatsu and Dolan 2009), and there is evidence that women from both parties may hold more liberal policy preferences on so-called women's issues (J. Clark 1998; I. Diamond 1977; Poggione 2004; but see also Osborn 2012). Such work suggests that substantive gendered differences are often more pronounced among Republicans, with Republican women being less conservative, on average, than their colleagues who are men (Poggione 2004). On the other hand, partisanship also influences the kinds of policy approaches championed by women legislators (Osborn and Kreitzer 2014). On abortion legislation, for example, women officeholders tend to lead on both sides of the party divide (Reingold et al. 2020). A recent analysis of congressional voting on abortion-related legislation over a twenty-five-year period between 1993 and 2018 finds gender differences between Republican men and women to attenuate over time (Rolfes-Haase and Swers 2021).

Women's leadership in politics is not only associated with the types of policies officeholders pursue but also with changes in how women in the public perceive and participate in the political arena. Research suggests that the presence of women candidates or officeholders increases women's interest in politics (Campbell and Wolbrecht 2006), political discussion among young women (Wolbrecht and Campbell 2017), levels of political trust (Ulbig 2007), and feelings of political efficacy (Mansbridge 1999; but see also Broockman 2014). These role model effects may be contingent on such factors as the competitiveness of the election (Atkeson 2003), candidates and constituents sharing a partisan identity (Dolan 2006), or the novelty of women candidates (Wolbrecht and Campbell 2017).

Clergywomen: Women's Issues and Role Model Effects

There is reason to suspect that women religious leaders may act similarly to women political leaders on issues related to health and social welfare. Scholars have established a precedent for comparing women leaders in religious and political contexts (e.g., Djupe and Olson 2013). Both religious leaders and political leaders, for example, must maintain a degree of responsiveness to those that they lead to maintain their leadership position (see Djupe and Olson 2013; Djupe and Gilbert 2003; and Olson, Crawford, and Deckman 2005 for more information). Clergywomen tend to be more ideologically liberal on a number of policy issues and are more politically active than clergymen (Deckman et al. 2003; Djupe and Gilbert 2008; Djupe and Olson 2013). These ideological divisions are most striking on abortion, but clergywomen also tend to be more liberal than clergymen on an array of social welfare issues (Deckman et al. 2003; Finlay 1996). These studies echo findings in political contexts of differences in opinion and action between women and men political leaders on so-called women's issues.

When exploring role model effects in a religious context, there is further support for the similarities between women's leadership in political and religious contexts. Knoll and Bolin (2018) find that women's leadership in congregations can have an empowering effect (albeit a modest one) for women congregants in terms of their levels of religiosity, spirituality, and efficacy in their congregations. In both political and religious contexts, diverse leadership can make a difference in the lives of those who are represented. Seeing leadership that reflects one's own identities can affect how someone views an institution and their role within it.

Women's Leadership: COVID-19 Response

Scholars have begun to research the relationship between women's leadership and COVID-19 responses in politics (e.g., Aldrich and Lotito 2020; Bauer, Kim, and Kweon 2020; Coscieme et al. 2020; Johnson and Williams 2020; Piscopo 2020) and in "the workplace" (Brooks and Saad 2020). Although media outlets emphasize the effectiveness of women political leaders' COVID-19 responses (Wittenberg-Cox 2020; Zalis 2020), there is mixed empirical evidence of the relationship between women's executive political leadership and a country's pandemic response.

While Coscieme et al. (2020) find evidence of lower COVID-19 mortality rates among countries led by women, Piscopo (2020) finds that factors such as the state's governing capacity are more likely to drive national pandemic responses. Aldrich and Lotito (2020), similarly, find no relationship between the gender of a nation's leader and the timing of policy responses to COVID-19, but they do find that countries with higher percentages of women in their legislatures closed schools more quickly than did countries with lower levels of women's representation.

Other research analyzes differences in how women and men experience the pandemic, finding that women are less likely than men to believe COVID-19 conspiracy theories (Cassese, Farhart, and Miller 2020), more likely to support government action related to the pandemic (Algara, Fuller, and Hare 2020), and are disproportionately burdened with increased domestic responsibilities during the pandemic (Power 2020). Research by Smothers et al. (2020) explores gender and COVID-19 in a religious context, finding differences in responses to the virus between men and women.

While Smothers et al. (2020) uncover differences between women and men *congregants'* attitudes and religious behaviors in light of COVID-19, our study explores the relationship between women and men's *leadership* within a church and the church's response to COVID-19 as well as congregants' trust in their clergypersons to have their best health interests at heart. In studying the relationship between women's leadership in a religious context and a congregation's COVID-19 precautions, we offer insight into how religious congregations are responding to the pandemic as well as offering further evidence for the comparability of women's leadership in political and religious contexts.

Hypotheses

Following scholarship that finds women political leaders to prioritize women's issues (including health care) during their tenure in office (e.g., Swers 2013, 2005) and scholarship that describes the comparability of political and religious leadership (e.g., Djupe and Gilbert 2003), we expect to find greater concern for public health in congregations with women's religious leadership.

Hypothesis 1: Women's Issues

Respondents who have witnessed women exercising leadership in their religious congregations in the past year will be more likely than respondents who have not to report having had their in-person worship canceled because of the coronavirus.

We look to political science literature on role model effects when developing our second hypothesis. In a political context, the presence of women's leadership is often associated with increases in constituent trust in the political system (e.g., Atkeson and Carrillo 2007). In a religious context, we expect to find a similar relationship between women's leadership and congregant trust.

Hypothesis 2: Role Model Effects

> Respondents who have witnessed women exercising leadership in their religious congregations in the past year will be more likely to report that they "trust clergy to have [their] best health interests at heart."

Data and Methodology

To evaluate the relationships between leadership by women in religious settings and (i) the likelihood that a place of worship canceled in-person services because of the coronavirus and (ii) that congregants trust clergy to have their best health interests at heart, we rely on survey data fielded March 23–26, 2020 (Djupe, Burge, and Lewis 2020). The survey included a battery of questions related to respondents' demographic characteristics, partisan and ideological preferences, religious beliefs, and attendance at religious services. To measure our key independent variable of interest, women's leadership in religious settings, we relied on responses to the following question: "Thinking about any group or organization that you have seen personally in your community in the past year, have you seen women exercising leadership?" and coded the variable 1 for those who responded that they had witnessed women exercising leadership in their religious congregation (i.e., "organizing a small group, activity or serving as clergy").[1] Our two dependent variables are also binary. The first is coded 1 for those who affirmed that "in-person worship has been canceled for now because of the coronavirus." Our second dependent variable is coded 1 for those who either strongly agreed or agreed that they "trust clergy to have [their] best health interests at heart." Descriptively, the survey results align with our hypotheses. Those who reported seeing women exercising leadership in their religious congregation were more likely to have had religious services canceled because of the coronavirus (about 5 percentage points more likely) and to trust clergy to have their best health interests at heart (about 15 percentage points more likely). To control for other factors that may be driving the apparent relationship between women's leadership and our two key dependent variables, we estimate linear probability models using multivariate ordinary least squares regression. This approach allows us to account for a comprehensive set of demographic, political, and religious factors that could be related to both a given respondent's likelihood of having seen women lead in a religious setting and the likelihood that (i) their regular in-person religious services were canceled or (ii) their levels of trust in clergy.[2] In addition to the gender of the respondent, we control for other standard demographic characteristics, including their race, ethnicity, and age. Patterns in both religious affiliation and church attendance by socioeconomic status indicate that family income and educational attainment should be controlled for, as well (Masci 2016; Schwadel et al. 2009).

Research in sociology draws parallels between participation in secular and nonsecular societal institutions, such as workplaces, marriage, and religious organizations, that all integrate individuals into social life (Mueller and Johnson 1975; Schwadel et al. 2009). Therefore, we account for whether a respondent works full-time and their marital status. We also control for region, partisan affiliation, ideological preferences, and the level of attention that respondents pay to politics. Finally, we include their current religious affiliation, attendance, the size of the church they attend, and whether they consider themselves born-again Christians and biblical literalists. We find correlations in our data between respondents' religious behaviors and seeing women engaging in leadership and think it likely that such religious characteristics are related to our outcomes of interest.[3] We use linear probability models because they tend to produce similar estimates as those produced by maximum likelihood estimation with the benefit of being more easily interpretable (Angrist and Pischke 2008).[4] We use robust standard errors.

Analyses and Results

The coefficient estimates shown in Figures 11.1 and 11.2 are for our complete models estimated, including all demographic, political, and religious control variables. Omitted categories for binary variables that occur in a set (e.g., region) are noted below each figure.

The estimates presented in Figure 11.1 evaluate the likelihood that a respondent reported in-person religious services were canceled because of the coronavirus. We find evidence that respondents who reported seeing women exercise leadership in their religious congregations were more likely to have their in-person religious services canceled due to the pandemic even after controlling for our robust battery of potentially confounding factors. More specifically, we find respondents who saw women leading in their congregations to be about 4.8 percentage points more likely than those who did not to report in-person services being canceled. Though the effect appears small, the rates of closure were relatively high at the time of the survey (just under 90 percent of those surveyed in our sample reported in-person services being canceled), so it is revealing to estimate a coefficient of this magnitude given the amount

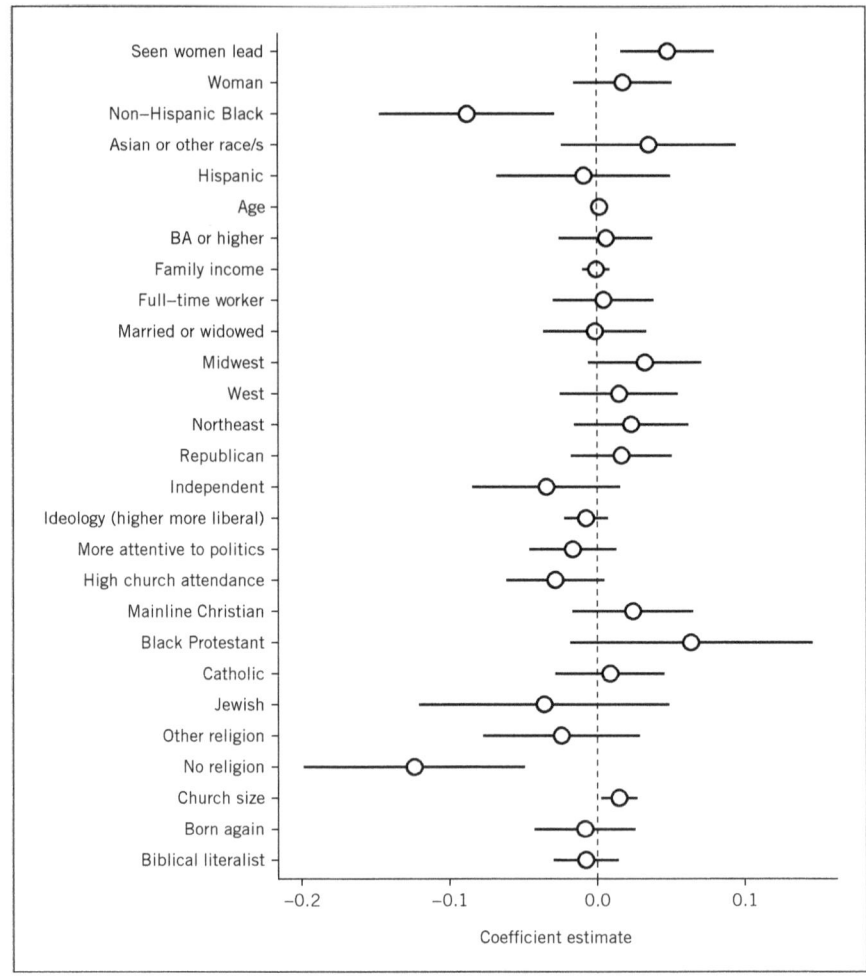

Figure 11.1 Coefficient Estimates for whether In-Person Services Were Canceled. Note: Dependent variable is binary and coded 1 if in-person worship services were canceled due to COVID; confidence intervals for estimates are 95 percent using robust standard errors; omitted race/ethnicity is white; omitted region is South; omitted partisan affiliation is Democrat; and omitted religion is evangelical Christian. N = 1,845. (Source: March 2020 survey.)

of variation left to explain. We also find non-Hispanic Black respondents to be less likely than white respondents to have seen their in-person religious services canceled, those who reported not having a religious affiliation to be less likely than evangelical Christians to have seen in-person services canceled, and church size to be positively related to the cancellation of services.[5]

Women as Religious Leaders | *167*

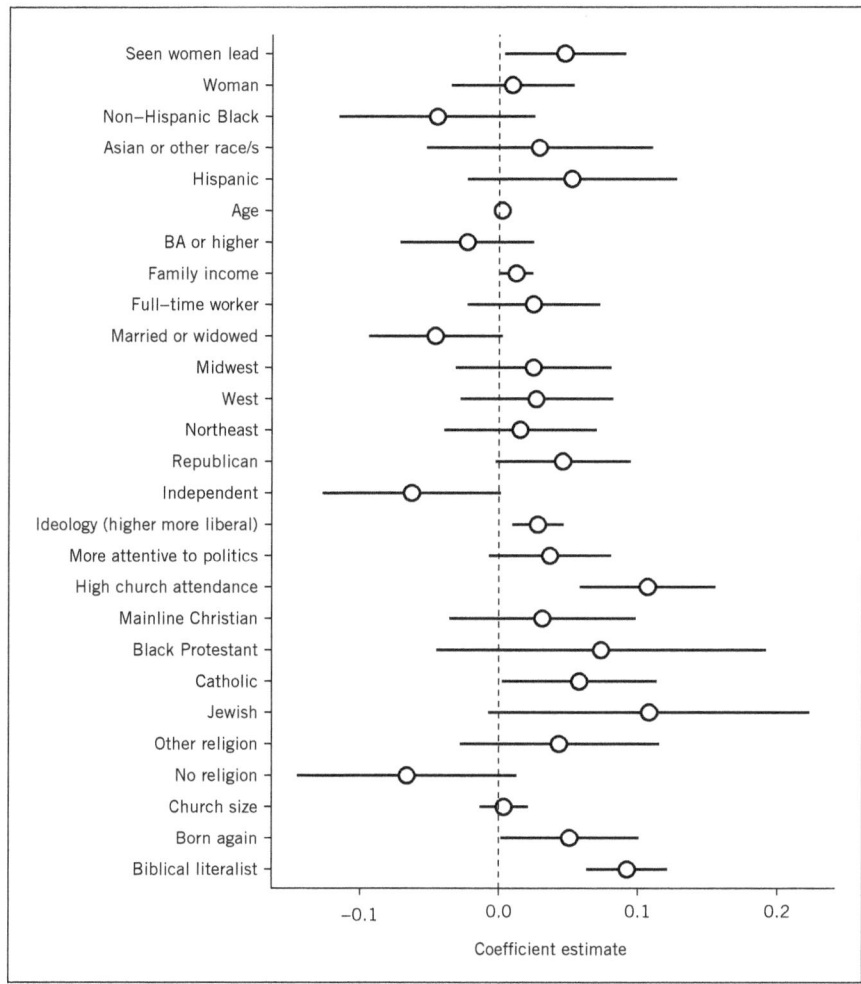

Figure 11.2 Coefficient Estimates for Trust in Clergy to Have Their Best Health Interests at Heart. Note: Dependent variable is binary and coded 1 if respondent trusts that clergy have their best health interests at heart; confidence intervals for estimates are 95 percent using robust standard errors; omitted race/ethnicity is white; omitted region is South; omitted partisan affiliation is Democrat; and omitted religion is evangelical Christian. N = 2,068. (Source: March 2020 survey.)

The estimates presented in Figure 11.2 evaluate the likelihood that a respondent said that they agreed or strongly agreed with the statement "I trust clergy to have my best health interests at heart." Seeing women exercise leadership in their religious congregations is again positively linked to trust in their clergy even after controlling for a variety of demographic, political, and religious factors. In line with our second hypothesis, these estimates suggest that respondents who saw women leading in a religious setting are about 4.7 percentage points more likely to trust their clergy to have their best health interests at heart. This estimate is approximately equivalent to the difference in trust levels reported between Republicans and Democrats, the former being about 4.6 percentage points more likely than the latter to trust clergy to have their best health interests at heart (we find independents to be about 6.3 percentage points less likely than Democrats to trust clergy in this regard).

Our religious control variables also tell an interesting story. Holding constant the other characteristics included in our model, respondents who attend church more regularly, consider themselves to be born-again Christians, and are biblical literalists are more likely to trust clergy to have their best health interests at heart. We find that attending church several times per month or more is associated with an increase in the likelihood that respondents trust clergy to have their best health interests at heart of about 11 percentage points, over twice the magnitude of the relationship we estimate for seeing women lead. The difference between being a born-again Christian and not is also similar to the difference between having seen women lead and not on trusting clergy. Our analyses also suggest that a one-standard-deviation increase on the literalism measure is associated with about an 8-percentage-point increase in the likelihood that a respondent expressed trusting clergy to have their best health interests at heart. Of course, these relationships could be operating in the opposite direction, with individuals who are more likely to trust clergy to protect their health and safety also being more likely to attend church more regularly, consider themselves to be born-again Christians, and take the Bible more literally.

Conclusion

We find evidence of a relationship between women's leadership in a religious congregation and a congregation's COVID-19 response. Respondents who reported seeing women's leadership in their congregation were about 5 percentage points more likely to report that their in-person services had been canceled because of the coronavirus. Although modest in magnitude, it is one of the few covariates to remain statistically significant at conventional levels following the inclusion of multiple demographic, political, and religious controls in our first model. Moreover, this finding supports our women's-issues hypothesis that the presence of women's religious leadership in a congregation is associated with an increased likelihood that a congregation temporarily cancels religious services out of concern for public health.

Our analyses also reveal support for our second hypothesis (i.e., our role-model hypothesis). As expected, we find that respondents who reported seeing women's leadership in their congregation were more likely to "trust in clergy to have [their] best health interests at heart." Congregants who have seen women lead in their congregation in the past year were, on average, about 5 percentage points more likely than those who did not to trust their clergy regarding their health interests. This difference is robust to a comprehensive set of controls and approximately equivalent to the difference in trust levels reported between Republican and Democratic respondents.

These findings also support the overarching hypothesis of this study, that women's leadership in religious contexts can be compared to women's leadership in political contexts and that drawing on political science representation literature can inform research on religious leadership. In both religious and political contexts, seeing women in leadership positions can be associated with how individuals view a given institution and their relationship to it. The positive relationship we find between the presence of women's leadership and cancellation of in-person religious services because of the coronavirus echoes the findings of studies in political contexts that suggest women's political leadership is associated with the increased prioritization of social welfare issues, efforts to protect the health and well-being of seniors, generosity of family and medical leave policies, and public health expenditures (Courtemanche and Green 2017; Giles-Sims, Green, and Lockhart 2012; Holman 2014; Williamson and Carnes 2013). Likewise, our finding that congregants who see women's leadership in a religious congregation are increasingly likely to trust their clergy to have their health interests at heart mirrors findings in a political context where constituents who see women's leadership are increasingly likely to trust their government (Atkeson and Carillo 2007; Ulbig 2007; but see Lawless 2004). Although our results cannot identify causal stories about the impact of women's religious leadership on the cancellation of in-person services and trust in clergy, our analyses support the possibility that women's leadership may matter in relation to the prioritization of public health concerns as well as congregant trust. Future research should continue to explore the relationship between women's religious leadership and congregational responses to other issues related to public health, welfare, education, and women's health to determine whether women religious leaders behave similarly to women political leaders.

Future analysis of religious responses to COVID-19 should explore the relationship between women holding specific leadership positions within a congregation and a congregation's COVID-19 response. While our study analyzed women holding *any* religious leadership role within a congregation (e.g., "organizing a small group, activity or serving as clergy"), it would be interesting to see if women's presence in specific leadership roles is associated with varied COVID-19 responses. For example, within the same denomination or religious tradition, do we find that clergywomen differ from clergymen in their COVID-19 responses? While women remain vastly underrepresented among clergy in America's places of worship (Knoll and Bolin 2018), anecdotal as well as empirical evidence identifies the importance of women serving in all levels of leadership in America's places of worship. Previous research finds that women congregants who see women occupying a majority of lay leadership positions within their congregation report similar levels of trust and commitment to their congregation as women congregants who see a woman serving as their head pastor or priest (Knoll and Bolin 2018). This study, similarly, points to the importance of women's religious leadership—in all forms—within a congregation. Religious responses to COVID-19 provide an additional example of the difference women's leadership can make in the lives of their congregants.

12

Racialized Responses to COVID-19

Shayla F. Olson

Racial inequality has persisted throughout the pandemic. Black, Latino, and Native American communities face significantly higher contraction and death rates from COVID-19 than the white population (Wood 2020). Racist tropes from political elites about the origins of COVID-19 have led to increased discrimination toward Asian Americans (Reny and Barreto 2020). As minoritized communities have been confronted with largely different pandemic circumstances, their responses to the pandemic may also differ from white Americans. In particular, scholars have demonstrated that religion plays a varying role across racial groups (McKenzie and Rouse 2013; Wong 2015; Yukich and Edgell 2020). Holding a consistent religious tradition, such as evangelicalism, does not translate into similar political attitudes among Asian, Black, Latino, and white Americans (Wong 2018a). Additionally, churches have historically been central organizing institutions among minoritized communities. However, the headlining stories about religion have neglected to explore the influence of religious experiences, which are highly racialized, toward a pandemic that has disproportionately affected racial minorities. This leads to a puzzle—have all Christians responded similarly to the pandemic, or do these racial divides within religion also persist amid the coronavirus outbreak?

Material referencing an appendix in this chapter can be found online available here: https://dataverse.harvard.edu/dataverse/epidemic_among_my_people.

In this chapter, I consider how race differentiates Christians' behaviors and attitudes during the pandemic. Using two separate surveys, I evaluate whether there are significant differences between the rates of in-person church service cancellations between Christians of color and white Christians. Related to this, I examine Christians' religious behavior during the pandemic—if they are still attending in-person services—and more generally, what predicts Christians' social distancing behavior. Next, I analyze Christians' attitudes toward the pandemic, how these attitudes vary by race, and what drives these attitudes among Christians of color and white Christians separately. This is an important distinction, because just as the role of religion changes within racial groups, the determinants of pandemic behaviors and attitudes among Christians may vary within racial groups. I conclude my analysis with a look at how the pandemic has influenced the strength of Christians' religious faith. As the church has been a force for political mobilization, group attachment, and well-being, especially among minoritized communities, the coronavirus outbreak provides a relevant case for examining racialized differences among Christians.

Race, Religion, and COVID-19

We should expect race to continue being a differentiating factor in Christians' pandemic responses because religion is a highly racialized experience (Yukich and Edgell 2020). Churches are largely racially segregated (Emerson and Smith 2001; Shelton and Emerson 2012), and the church has been a particularly salient venue for increasing civic engagement and social capital among racial/ethnic minorities (Chan and Phoenix 2020; Djupe and Grant 2001; Gershon, Pantoja, and Taylor 2016; McClerking and McDaniel 2005; Taylor, Gershon, and Pantoja 2014; Valenzuela 2014). For example, attending politically homogeneous churches can increase civic engagement among Asian Americans (Chan and Phoenix 2020). Black congregations are more likely to host voter registration drives than Asian, Hispanic, and white churches (Brown 2009), and higher church attendance among Black Christians is associated with greater political participation (Philpot and McDaniel 2020). In general, churches seek to serve the needs of their communities, and the Black church has historically been an example of how minority churches serve many roles for their communities beyond spiritual care (Fitzgerald and Spohn 2005; Lincoln and Mamiya 1990; Rowland and Isaac-Savage 2014).

Because the coronavirus outbreak has had disparate impacts on communities of color, churches continue to fill different needs for their respective populations. Some of these needs are physical as marginalized racial groups have contracted COVID-19 and died from it at higher rates than white Americans

(Wood 2020), and racial discrimination within the American health care system is well documented (Shavers et al. 2012). But some needs are psychological as well. From the beginning of the pandemic, white conservative elites racialized the coronavirus by referring to it as the "Chinese virus," "Wuhan virus," and "Kung Flu," which increased anti-Asian attitudes and discrimination (Reny and Barreto 2020). Asian Americans, both U.S.- and foreign-born, report increased experiences of discrimination related to coronavirus, and they report increased psychological distress because of it. Further, Black and Hispanic Americans also report higher experiences of stigmatization surrounding coronavirus than non-Hispanic, white Americans (Pan et al. 2020).

The coronavirus could present another case where people turn to their religious communities and beliefs to bring them physical and psychological support. Much of the literature on religion among minoritized groups has focused on historically Black Protestant churches, and the Black church has been a central institution in Black communities (Lincoln and Mamiya 1990). Greater religious social support helps people cope with the anxiety generated by racist experiences (Graham and Roemer 2012; Kim 2017). Clergy of Black churches are aware of the needs of their community and largely see the church as having a role in meeting the health education needs of their congregants (Rowland and Isaac-Savage 2014), and a study of churches in the South found that Black churches are more likely to provide mental health services to their congregants (Blank et al. 2002). The pandemic has amplified needs these churches have historically sought to address, but because public meetings are unsafe during the pandemic, COVID-19 presents a unique challenge for meeting these needs.

Partisanship is also intermixed in the interaction of race and religion within the pandemic. White Christians—even more so, white evangelicals—largely identify with the Republican Party (Layman 2001; Margolis 2018; McDaniel and Ellison 2008). However, despite similar opinions about traditional moral issues and similar religious beliefs, Black Christians largely identify as Democrats (Calhoun-Brown 1998; McDaniel and Ellison 2008). As the coronavirus outbreak has received polarized responses from Democrats and Republicans, it is likely that Christians' partisan loyalties will influence their behaviors and attitudes about the pandemic. Even further, it is possible that Christians' attitudes about the pandemic will merely reflect their partisanship.

For example, the pandemic has brought an onslaught of misinformation to the public sphere, and it has tested the public's trust in science. Conspiratorial thinking among Republicans has increased in relation to the coronavirus outbreak (Miller 2020). Right-wing media often discussed misinformation about the coronavirus, and viewers of right-wing media were, in turn, more likely to believe the misinformation was factual (Motta, Stecula, and Farhart 2020). The same study also found nonwhite respondents to be more likely to believe this misinformation (Motta, Stecula, and Farhart 2020); however, previous research has shown Black and Hispanic Americans to be more likely to defer to science than white and Asian Americans (Blank and Shaw 2015). While experiences of racial discrimination within the health care system could make Black Americans and other minorities more skeptical of the medical community, Black churches have also supported their communities by providing health education (Rowland and Isaac-Savage 2014). Generally, conservatives and those who believe the Bible is the literal word of God hold less trusting attitudes toward science (Blank and Shaw 2015).

Given the current challenge of the pandemic and the previous literature on the role of religion among different racial groups, I hypothesize that race will be a differentiating identity in how Christians respond to the coronavirus. I expect that Christians of color will be more likely to view the coronavirus as a threat and will act accordingly by limiting their attendance at religious services more than white Christians. However, given the historical prevalence of church-based social support among minoritized groups, I expect Christians of color to be less likely to report that their church has closed. Related to this, I expect that Christians of color will rely on their religious experiences more during the coronavirus outbreak, thus leading to reports of stronger faith. I also consider other variables known to be related to coronavirus responses—namely, Republican partisanship should be related to beliefs about the pandemic, while income, age, and education are all related to the severity of the COVID-19 threat in one's daily life.

Data and Methods

Do the racial divides seen among Christians continue amid the pandemic? I provide a descriptive analysis of how Christians' COVID-19 responses vary by race, and I examine the factors driving these decisions. While there are certainly other religious experiences beyond Christianity that have been impacted by the coronavirus outbreak, I focus on Christianity merely for the size of the population and subsequently the samples. The data for these analyses come from two sources, both of which were fielded during the early shutdowns. The first is an original, online survey fielded in late March on 3,136 U.S. adults by Djupe, Lewis, and Burge (2020). Of the respondents, 1,896 identified as either Protestant or Catholic Christians. There are 46 Asian Christians, 194 Black Christians, 112 Hispanic Christians, and 1,288 white Christians. Therefore, the analyses conducted with these data focus on the variation between white Christians and Christians of color. The behavioral outcomes I explore in these data are whether in-person worship has been canceled at a respondent's church, whether they are still attending in-person services, and if they are practicing social distancing. Additionally, I examine Christians' attitudes about the coronavirus outbreak through their agreement or disagreement with three statements: "The coronavirus is a major threat," "Hysteria over the coronavirus is politically motivated," and "I trust the medical professionals and scientists who have sounded the alarm about the dangers of the coronavirus." More conservative stances would be downplaying the threat, great belief that the pandemic is a political ploy, and weakened trust in scientists.

The second data source is Wave 66 of the Pew American Trends Panel (ATP), conducted in late April 2020. The ATP is a nationally representative panel of U.S. adults, and this wave included multiple questions related to COVID-19. I focus on two variables: (1) reports of churches halting in-person services and (2) whether a respondent's religious faith has become stronger or weaker during the coronavirus outbreak. The full sample consists of 10,139 adults, and 6,128 identify as Christians. Among the Christians, 79 identify as Asian, 597 are Black, 1,140 are Hispanic, and 4,078 are white. These sample sizes (with the exception of Asian respondents) allow me to move beyond a dichotomous approach and examine behavior within each racial group.

In the section that follows, I first explore the behavioral outcomes among Christians, and then I turn to their attitudes about COVID-19 and their faith. All models are ordinary least square regressions, and all dependent variables were scaled to between 0 and 1 for ease of interpretation. I present figures of model predictions, but tables for all models can be found in the online appendix. In each figure, I present the fitted values for each model and plot 84 percent confidence intervals, as multiple sources show that comparing two 84 percent confidence intervals is the equivalent of a 95 percent test at the point of overlap (Goldstein and Healy 1995; Knol, Pestman, and Grobbee 2011; MacGregor-Fors and Payton 2013; Payton, Greenstone, and Schenker 2003). In addition to evaluating how Christians' responses vary by race, I interact race with whether a respondent identifies themselves as a born-again Christian—I refer to this group as evangelical Christians (see Burge and Lewis 2018).

Results—Behavioral Outcomes

Figure 12.1 displays the share of Christians who report their church closed because of the pandemic, split by race and born-again identity. The March sample asks individuals to respond to the statement "In-person worship has

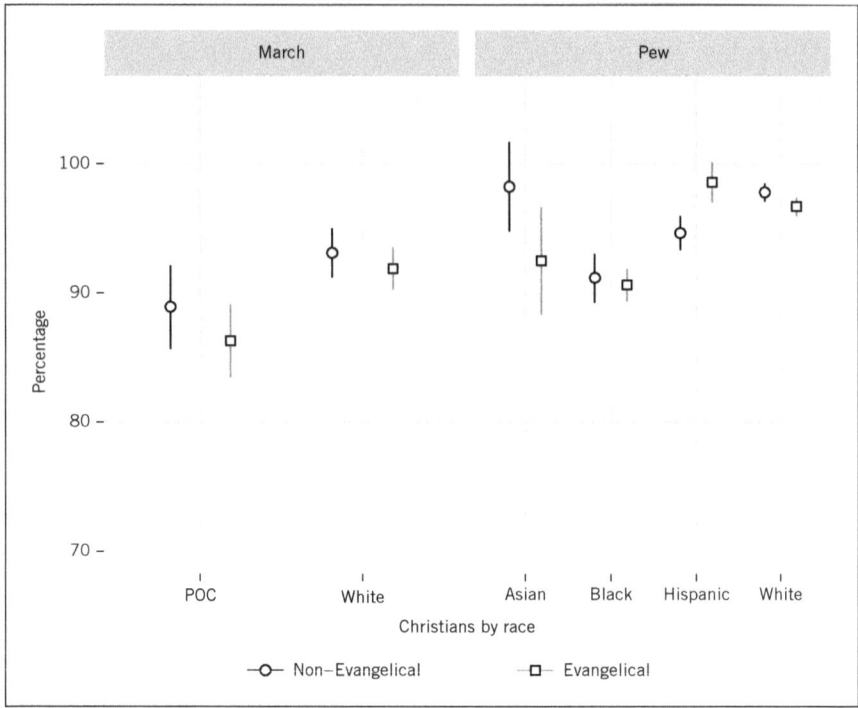

Figure 12.1 Reported Church Cancellations by Race and Evangelical Identification (Source: March 2020, n = 1,367; 2020 Pew ATP, n = 4,735. Model includes control for living in the South.)

been canceled for now because of the coronavirus." The Pew study asks, "Has the congregation or house of worship you most often attend closed its regular religious services to the public in response to the coronavirus outbreak, or are people still gathering there in person?" Both of these variables are coded as binary responses, with 1 indicating the church has closed in-person services. The independent variables include race and born-again indicators, as well as a control for whether the respondent lives in the South. As shown in the figure, a majority of Christians in both samples report that their church canceled in-person services as a result of the pandemic; over 85 percent of all groups report church cancellations. In most cases, born-again Christians are less likely to say their church canceled in-person services, but Hispanic born-again respondents in the Pew sample report higher levels of church closure.

Both samples demonstrate racial differences in Christians' reports of in-person service cancellations. The March data show white Christians are more likely to report cancellation. While this distinction is statistically significant, born-again identity is not a significant variable. The Pew data reveal similar patterns, and these results suggest a significant difference lies between the reports of Black and white Christians. Black Christians report lower levels of church closures than white Christians, regardless of born-again status. Furthermore, Hispanic Christians are the only group of evangelicals who report higher closures than their non-evangelical counterparts.

As reports of church closures more likely reveal the actions of respondents' clergy, I also model whether a respondent is still attending in-person services and whether they are practicing social distancing. A majority of respondents were not attending in-person services in the early weeks of the U.S. coronavirus outbreak. Despite varying reports of church closure, Christians of color and white Christians are responding similarly to the pandemic. Evangelicals of both racial groups attend at higher rates, even after controlling for whether services are canceled and their prepandemic attendance rates. Income is also positively associated with increased attendance, while higher education and older age are associated with decreased attendance.

Beyond religious behavior, I examine self-reported social distancing behavior. Respondents in the March sample are asked on a 5-point scale how much they agree (1) or disagree (0) with the following: "I am practicing social distancing (staying home as much as possible, avoiding social contact)." In addition to analyzing the full sample of Christians, I also split the sample between Christians of color and white Christians to explore the variables driving this behavior among both groups. The models suggest a large majority of Christians are practicing social distancing, though white Christians report slightly higher levels of social distancing than Christians of color ($p = 0.046$).

Of course, we should take a closer examination of possible underlying factors before drawing broader conclusions about the racial differences in social distancing behavior among Christians. The full sample reveals older Christians and those with higher income are social distancing at higher rates. After splitting the sample and analyzing white Christians separately from Christians of color, I find the baseline rate of social distancing among Christians of color and white Christians to be roughly equal. However, income and age remain significantly and positively associated with social distancing among white Christians. This suggests that the racial differences could be driven by the higher levels of income and older age of white Christians compared to Christians of color. White Christians in this sample are much older (fifty vs. thirty-nine) and wealthier on average. Finally, there is a negative association between Republican partisanship and social distancing behavior in the full sample, and this relationship remains significant among white Christians (the estimated effect of partisanship among Christians of color is the same magnitude as it is for whites, but it is not significant).

Results—Attitudes and Beliefs

Next, I turn to Christians' attitudes about the pandemic using three questions about the coronavirus outbreak itself and one question about their religious experiences during the pandemic. Figure 12.2 displays the results for Christians' levels of agreement with the following statements: "The coronavirus is a major threat," "Hysteria over the coronavirus is politically motivated," and "I trust the medical professionals and scientists who have sounded the alarm about the dangers of the coronavirus." All responses are measured on a 5-point scale collapsed to run from 0 (strongly disagree) to 1 (strongly agree).

Just as shown in the behavioral models, there tends to be high levels of agreement among Christians on all attitudinal models. On average, Christians from all groups (by born-again and racial identity) agree that the coro-

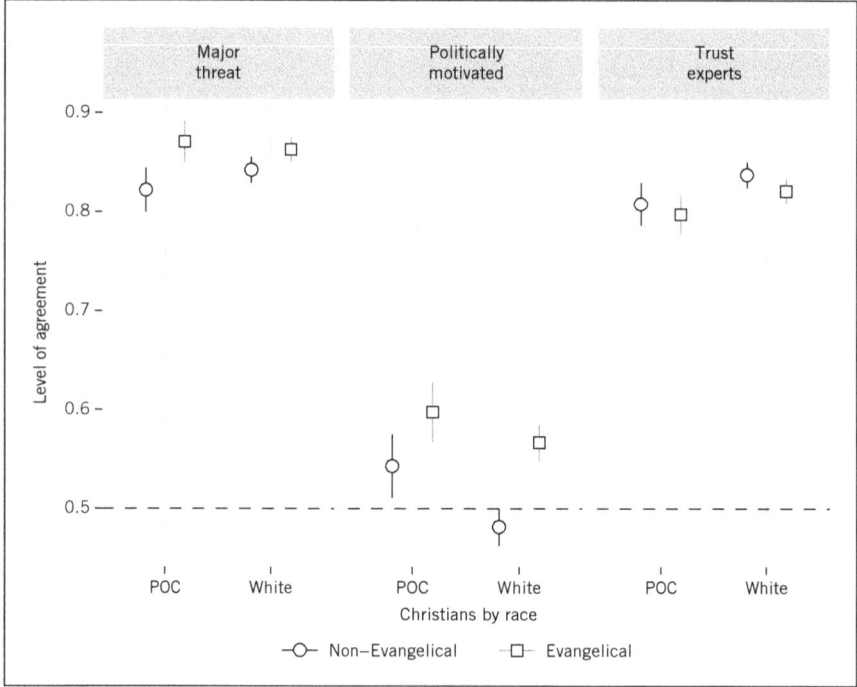

Figure 12.2 Attitudes toward the Coronavirus Outbreak (Level of Agreement) (Source: March 2020, n = 1,711. Models control for church attendance, party ID, age, income, and education.)

navirus is a major threat. While racial identity does not significantly differentiate this belief in the full sample, Christians of color and white Christians are not equally motivated by the same factors. Among all Christians, evangelicals are more likely to agree that the coronavirus is a major threat. Older age and higher income are also associated with higher levels of agreement. Alternatively, stronger Republican partisanship is associated with higher levels of disagreement with the statement among all Christians, Christians of color, and white Christians. Looking within the subsample of Christians of color, born-again identity remains a strong predictor of believing coronavirus to be a major threat, and age is positively associated with this belief. Among white Christians, however, the relationship between born-again identity and this statement is not significant, while age and income hold their statistically strong relationships.

While a majority of all Christians also agree with the statement "Hysteria over the coronavirus is politically motivated," Christians of color are more likely to believe this than white Christians. Additionally, all models—the full sample and those split on race—show higher church attendance to be positively associated with this belief. However, while stronger Republican partisanship predicts stronger beliefs that coronavirus is politically motivated in the full sample, this relationship remains statistically significant only among white Christians. The weak relationship between partisanship and this attitude among Christians of color is likely related to the fact that there are relatively fewer Christians of color who identify as Republican. Among Christians of color, higher education is negatively associated with the belief that the coronavirus is politically motivated.

The right panel on Figure 12.2 displays Christians' responses to the following statement: "I trust the medical professionals and scientists who have sounded the alarm about the dangers of the coronavirus." Christians of color and white Christians hold similar attitudes toward experts. All models show that the stronger Christians identify with the Republican Party, the less they trust experts surrounding the coronavirus. Moreover, among white Christians, age and income again hold a positive relationship; higher income and older white Christians are more likely to trust experts.

In the analyses above, I have examined the reports of church closures, in-person attendance, and social distancing behaviors among Christians, as well as three attitudes about the coronavirus outbreak: the belief that it is a major threat, that it is politically motivated, and that they trust experts who have warned about the dangers of the coronavirus. While Christians of color were more likely to report their church is providing in-person services, they are no more likely to be attending in-person services than white Christians. However, they are less likely to be practicing social distancing, and this may be related to employment and age, as Christians of color report lower income and are younger on average than white Christians in the March sample. While Christians of color and white Christians largely agree in their attitudes about the coronavirus, different variables are more significant predictors among Christians of color and white Christians. While white Christians' beliefs that the coronavirus outbreak is a major threat is significantly predicted by income, it is not as related to the level of agreement among Christians of color. Similarly, age and income influence white Christians' agreement that they can trust experts related to the coronavirus outbreak, while Republican partisanship is the strongest predictor among Christians of color. Finally, Republican partisanship increases the belief that the coronavirus is politically motivated among Christians of color, and education decreases this belief, but among white Christians, born-again identity is positively related to this belief.

Given the disparate pressure the coronavirus outbreak has placed on communities of color, have Christians been turning to the church for support as they have in the past? I conclude my analysis by returning to Christians' religious experiences in the pandemic and examine a broad question about faith amid the coronavirus outbreak. It asks, "As a result of the coronavirus outbreak, has your own religious faith become stronger or weaker (or it hasn't changed much)?" Respondents can select one of these three options, ordered from weaker (value of 0) to stronger (value of 1) in the model. Figure 12.3 displays these results. As this question comes from the Pew data, I first evaluate the full sample of Christians, and then I examine this relationship within each racial group.

Black and Hispanic Christians report their faith being made stronger by COVID-19 significantly more than white Christians. This follows my expectations given previous research showing the role minority churches play in providing social and mental support to their congregants. Among all racial groups, born-again Christians and Christians with higher church attendance are more likely to respond that their faith strengthened because of the pandemic.

While there are only 150 Asian Christians in the model, Asian Republicans' faith reportedly weakened, as did the faith among Black and Hispanic Republicans. However, white Christians who identify more strongly as Republican are more likely to report their faith becoming stronger during the pandemic (see full models in the appendix). This could also be due to the negative effects that political heterogeneity can have within church communities. Attending politically homogeneous churches can increase participation (Chan and Phoenix 2020), and perceived political differences within the

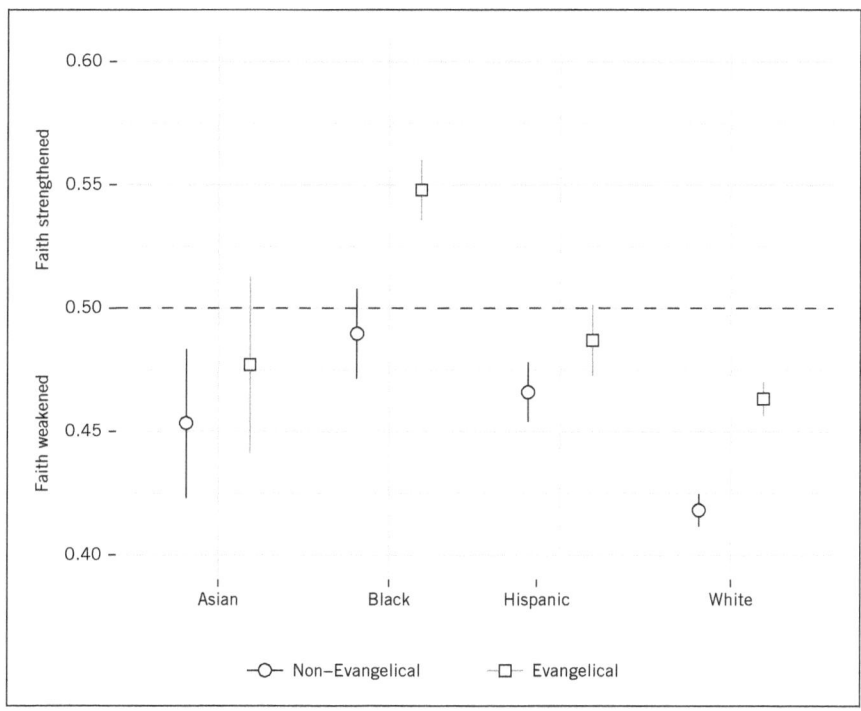

Figure 12.3 Reported Change in Religious Faith during the Coronavirus Outbreak (Source: 2020 Pew ATP, n = 4,408. Models control for church attendance, party ID, age, income, education, and whether church was closed for the COVID-19 pandemic.)

church can lead to disaffiliation (Djupe, Neiheisel, and Sokhey 2018). Churches are often racially homogeneous, and Christians of color are less likely to be Republicans than white Christians. As such, as white Republican Christians are surrounded by people who share similar partisan beliefs about the coronavirus pandemic, they are not feeling cross-pressured by their partisan and religious communities. However, Republican Christians of color are likely feeling conflict between their partisan and religious communities, weakening their religious attachment.

Conclusion

While most Christians responded to the coronavirus outbreak in similar ways, in some cases, Christians' attitudes and behaviors did vary significantly by race. Furthermore, Christians of color and white Christians' decisions were sometimes motivated by different variables. First, I explore Christians' responses to whether their churches had canceled in-person service, whether they are continuing to attend church in person, and the degree to which they are social distancing. Two data sources show white Christians reporting church closures more than Christians of color, and the Pew data suggest this is primarily driven by the differences between Black and white Christians. The largest gap in reported church closures is between Black and white Christians, whereas Asian and Hispanic Christians fall between these groups. However, regardless of racial identity, there is no significant difference in the rates of in-person attendance between Christians of color and white Christians. While white Christians report they are social distancing more than Christians of color, the results suggest this may be driven by the older age and higher income of white Christians compared to Christians of color. Related to this difference in income levels, people of color are more likely to hold employment that is deemed "essential" during the pandemic, which would lead to lower levels of social distancing as they cannot work from home.

Next, I examine three attitudes about the novel coronavirus among Christians. Again, I find that Christians of color and white Christians hold comparable attitudes about the pandemic, but the variables that best predict their attitudes vary. For example, all Christians hold high agreement that coronavirus is a major threat, and born-again identity is positively associated with this sentiment. I also find broad similarities between Christians of color and white Christians' agreement that they trust experts surrounding the pandemic. Additionally, Republicans from all models—Christians of color and white Christians—are less likely to agree that coronavirus is a major threat and are less likely to trust experts. Within-group analyses of Christians of color and white Christians reveal different factors are associated with believing the coronavirus is politically motivated. Among Christians of color, education is negatively associated with a belief that the coronavirus is politically motivated. For white Christians, born-again identity is the strongest variable that is positively associated with this belief. Additionally, higher levels of agreement among Christians of color with the belief that coronavirus is politically motivated may be driven by the increased discrimination they have experienced, which has largely been driven by political elites.

Finally, I present whether Christians' feel their faith has become stronger or weaker amid the pandemic. Here, I find Christians of color to feel their faith has become stronger significantly more than white Christians. Amid a pandemic that has had a disproportionate impact on communities of color, Black and Hispanic Christians report their faith becoming stronger. Additionally, while Republican Christians of color were less likely to report their faith becoming stronger, white Christians' Republican partisanship is positively associated with this response. The relationship between partisan and religious communities may be contributing to this result, where Republican Christians of color are experiencing conflicting viewpoints in their religious communities, but white Republican Christians are finding wider agreement within their church. This assertion is supported by the other attitudinal models, where Republican identity has a consistent effect in Christians' attitudes about the pandemic regardless of racial identity. There are still many consistencies among all racial groups; born-again Christians and those who attend church more often report their faith becoming stronger during the pandemic.

While conventional wisdom points to religious experiences to be highly racialized, throughout these analyses, I find that Christians of all races are responding fairly similarly to the pandemic. A majority of Christians of all races report high levels of church closures, online church attendance, and social distancing behavior. Instead, I point to descriptive differences within these groups that drive their behaviors and attitudes, such as age, income, education, and partisanship. I also support previous literature demonstrating born-again identity has a consistently conservatizing effect, regardless of racial identity. However, while overall trends point to similarity between these groups, we know the coronavirus pandemic has hit communities of color much harder than white communities. While responding similarly to COVID-19 in terms of religious behavior and attitudes, the drastically different contexts of the pandemic among people of color and among whites may influence how Christians in these groups rely on their faith throughout the pandemic.

13

In God "Z" Trusts?

Generation Z's Attitudes about Religion and COVID-19

MELISSA DECKMAN AND STELLA M. ROUSE

Generation Z, which is defined as those Americans born after 1996, makes up more than 20 percent of the U.S. population (Frey 2020). While Gen Z has been spared the worse physical health impacts stemming from COVID-19, as older Americans are far more likely to die or suffer severe complications from getting the coronavirus (Maragakis 2020), Generation Z has incurred several disproportionately negative effects of the pandemic. Gen Z has suffered greater job loss, compared with older Americans as they make up a higher proportion of workers employed in the most hard-hit sectors of the economy, especially young workers of color (Gould and Kassa 2020). Members of Generation Z are also more likely than other generations to report that their mental health has deteriorated over the past year (American Psychological Association 2020).

Given the cross-cutting factors of COVID-19 that have affected Generation Z, it is important to explore how this cohort feels about the strict stay-at-home measures adopted by many state governments around the nation last spring. Although less likely to die from COVID-19, Gen Zers and their slightly older counterparts, Millennials, spread the virus at greater rates than older Americans, largely because they are disproportionately employed in essential service industry jobs (Renner 2020). Support for strict lockdown measures

---

Material referencing an appendix in this chapter can be found online available here https://dataverse.harvard.edu/dataverse/epidemic_among_my_people.

may hinge, then, on Gen Z's willingness to engage in collective social action for the greater good. One driver of selfless and helpful behaviors is religion, as surveys have consistently shown that highly religious people across the world are more likely to engage in helping and caring behaviors, compared to those who are less religious (Pelham and Crabtree 2008).

In this chapter, we consider how religion is shaping attitudes about COVID-19 among this nascent generation. First, using a nationally representative survey of Americans aged eighteen to twenty-four conducted in late May 2020, we paint a religious portrait of Gen Z Americans during the pandemic, sharing descriptive data about their religious identification and frequency of religious attendance. We consider their religious behaviors by race and ethnicity as well, given that Gen Z is also the most racially diverse generation (Wang 2018). Second, we ask whether the coronavirus pandemic has strengthened their religious views and the extent to which Gen Z members have turned to prayer as a way to bring an end to the pandemic. Lastly, we consider how religion shapes their views regarding shelter-in-place laws. We also conduct multivariate analyses to examine how attitudes about and behaviors in response to COVID-19 are influenced by religion, while controlling for other factors.

We find that the largest religious affiliation among Generation Z is *not* being religiously affiliated, especially among white and Asian Gen Z Americans. Furthermore, a plurality across all racial and ethnic Gen Z groups state that they rarely or never attend church services. We find no evidence that religious faith among Generation Z has become stronger or that this cohort is turning more frequently to prayer during this pandemic. While a strong majority of Gen Zers supports shelter-in-place measures to mitigate the spread of COVID-19, there are differences across racial and ethnic groups. White Gen Z Americans are less likely to support these measures, compared to Black, Latino, and Asian Gen Z Americans.

Our multivariate analyses reveal that religious factors, such as religious affiliation, church attendance, and identifying as evangelical affect strength of faith and frequency of prayer among Generation Z. In particular, African Americans and women express praying more often for the end of the pandemic than other racial/ethnic or gender groups. Gen Z conservatives display both an increase in religious faith as a result of COVID-19 and also have a greater tendency toward praying more frequently for the end of the pandemic. Republican and conservative Gen Zers are less likely to support shelter-in-place measures, finding them to be an undue burden on people and the economy. Our results help to illuminate how religion, race/ethnicity, and generation interact to better understand opinions about this once-in-a-lifetime global health crisis.

The Religiosity of Gen Z

One of the largest trends in American religion is the rapid growth of the religiously unaffiliated (Campbell, Layman, and Green 2020), with older Americans being far more likely to identify with a particular religion than Millennials, the youngest full adult cohort (those born between 1980 and 1996). Indeed, Millennials are more than three times as likely than senior citizens aged sixty-five or older to indicate that they are religiously unaffiliated (Cox and Jones 2017). Given the relative youth of Generation Z, much less is known about their religious preferences. In our survey of Gen Z Americans, we asked respondents about both their religious affiliation and how often they attend religious services, while also considering the racial and ethnic dimensions of their religiosity.

We break down our descriptive data by whether respondents are white, African American, Latino, or Asian American for several reasons.[1] First, compared with white Americans and Asian Americans, African Americans and Latinos in the general population are more likely to profess a religious affiliation, attend church, and indicate that religion is very important to their lives (Pew Research Center 2018; Putnam and Campbell 2010). Second, African Americans (Hunt and Hunt 2001; Taylor et al. 1996) and Latinos (Espinosa, Elizonda, and Miranda 2005) often have distinct theological emphases in their faith traditions that have important political implications (Gershon, Pantoja, and Taylor 2016; McDaniel 2009). While white Americans are religiously diverse, holding conservative Christian theological views leads them to be less tolerant and less egalitarian in their views overall. Specifically, McKenzie and Rouse (2013) find that whites who are religiously conservative are significantly less likely to be interested in helping the poor, compared to nonwhites. Religion and race often interact in unique ways with respect to policy attitudes, which leads us to consider how race and ethnicity shape religious behavior overall among Gen Z, the most racially and ethnically diverse cohort in the nation's history.

As Figure A13.1 in the appendix demonstrates, the largest religious affiliation, by far, is religiously unaffiliated: close to 40 percent of Generation Z does not identify with a religion.[2] Roughly 10 percent of Gen Zers are white Catholics, and an additional 12 percent are white Protestant, either evangelical (5 percent) or mainline Protestant (7 percent).[3] About 4 percent of respondents are Black Protestants, and 3 percent identify as Black Catholics. Among Gen Z Latinos, higher percentages are Catholic than Protestant, by almost a two-to-one margin (6.4 percent to 3.3 percent, respectively). Asian Americans who are Catholic make up 3 percent of the sample, followed by 1.3 percent of Asian Protestants. Roughly 5 percent of Gen Z Americans identify as Mormon, while smaller percentages of Gen Z Americans are made up of other Christians (such as the Orthodox), Jews, or adherents to other world religions, such as Muslims, Buddhists, or Hindus. About 2 percent identify as something else, such as being Wiccan. Compared with other national surveys that consider religious identification among Gen Z, our survey has slightly more Mormons and Black Catholics and slightly fewer white evangelicals, but the rest of the categories closely align with other studies.[4]

Figure 13.1 considers the ethnic and racial makeup of religious adherents grouped in one of four categories—Protestants, Catholics, religiously unaffiliated, and other—which reveals some interesting trends. A clear plurality of Gen Z Americans who are white or Asian are religiously unaffiliated. Both African Americans and Latinos among Gen Z are far more likely to identify with a religious group than their white and Asian counterparts. For Gen Z Latinos, Catholicism is still the more frequent religious affiliation—though one in five identify as Protestant. Notably, our study finds that almost one in five African American Gen Zers identify as Catholic, compared with 27 percent who identify as Black Protestant. Despite the historic role that the Black church has played in the political lives of many African Americans, younger Black Americans are also following national trends of being more likely to disaffiliate with a religious tradition than to identify themselves as religious. The same appears true for Latino Gen Z Americans as well.

We also consider how often Gen Z Americans attend church (see Figure A13.2). Given the size of the unaffiliated population, the most frequent category of church attendance among all racial groups is rarely or never, with Asian American Gen Zers recording the highest levels of nonattendance (53 percent), followed by whites (43 percent). Around 31 percent of both African American and Latino Gen Zers report attending church on a weekly basis or more, although African American Gen Zers are more likely to report attending church monthly than all other groups.

A decline in church attendance and growth in religious disaffiliation among Gen Z may be linked to a lack of faith in institutions found more broadly among younger generations. Millennials, for instance, are far less likely to identify with a political party or to engage in traditional forms of politics, such as voting or contacting public officials (Gilman and Stokes 2014), which Rouse and Ross (2018) argue may signal a desire for alternatives to mainstream political institutions. A PRRI (2016) study analyzing the growth of religious disaffiliation in the United States finds that for many Millennials, family dynamics, such as divorce or growing up in a mixed-faith household or with secular parents, lead younger people to disaffiliate with religious institutions. The PRRI

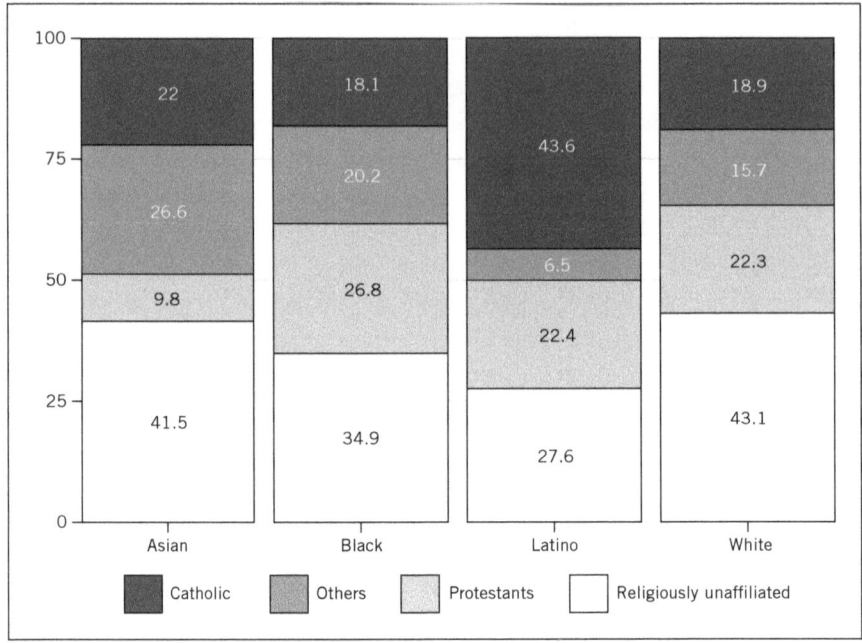

Figure 13.1 Major Religious Traditions among Gen Z, by Race/Ethnicity (Percentages) (Source: 2020 Gen Z survey.)

report also details that the treatment of LGBT Americans by many conservative religious traditions is linked to the decision to religiously disaffiliate for some younger Americans, as is the clergy-sex-abuse scandal among some former Catholics. However, most disaffiliated Americans say that they left their childhood religion simply because they stopped believing in its religious teachings. These disaffiliation trends within Gen Z Americans, then, are an extension of similar patterns among Millennials (Deckman 2020). However, it is important to note that more Gen Z Americans acknowledge some tie with religion than not—and religious affiliation is higher among African American and Latino Gen Zers.

How Has COVID-19 Shaped the Religious Behavior of Gen Z Americans?

We asked Gen Z Americans whether their religious faith has become stronger or weaker during the pandemic; respondents were also given the option of saying that they are not religious. Studies show that during extreme crises, such as pandemics or natural disasters, individuals often turn to their religious faith

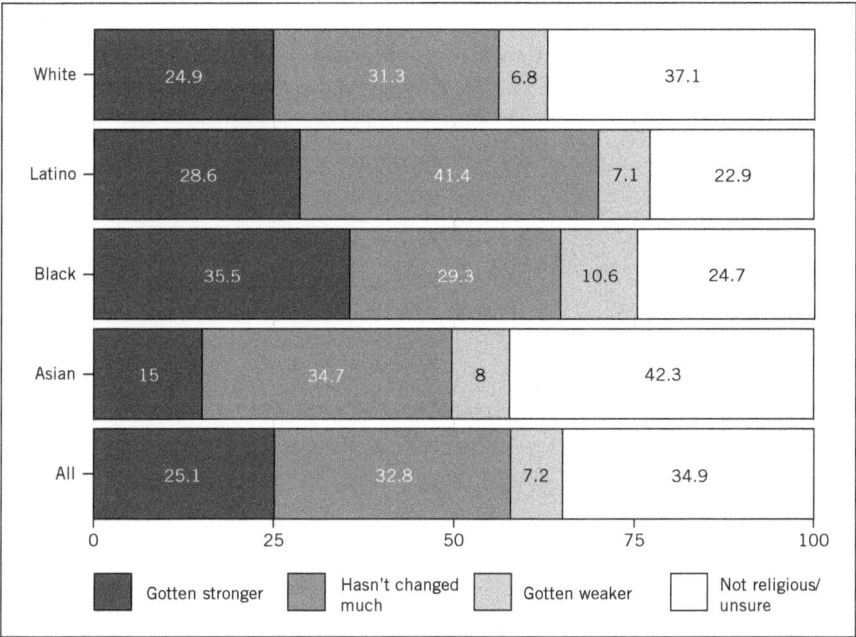

Figure 13.2 Impact of COVID on Religious Faith among Gen Z, by Race/Ethnicity (Percentages) (Source: 2020 Gen Z survey.)

as a coping mechanism in times of uncertainty and anxiety (Ano and Vasconelles 2005; Bentzen 2019). Initial work shows that the pandemic has increased religiosity among Catholics in Colombia (Meza 2020) and among many Americans, particularly Black Protestants (Gecewicz 2020). Figure 13.2 shows the impact of COVID-19 on religious faith based on race/ethnicity and religious affiliation among Generation Z. We have removed those Gen Zers who are not religious (27 percent of the sample) or who indicated they were unsure how their religious faith was impacted by COVID (8 percent of the sample).

Among Gen Zers who profess a religious faith, a slight majority (50.3 percent) indicated that COVID had not changed their religion much. Asian American Gen Zers are the least likely to say that the pandemic has made their religious faith stronger—just 26.1 percent. At the opposite end, 47.1 percent of African American Gen Zers say that their religious faith has gotten stronger as a result of the pandemic. The same is true for 37.1 percent of Gen Z Latinos and 40 percent of Gen Zers who are white. At the same time, relatively few Gen Z Americans who are religious in some way indicate that their faith has diminished or gotten weaker due to the COVID pandemic.

Many individuals may also be turning to prayer specifically as a way to cope with the pandemic. For instance, Bentzen (2020) found internationally that as the seriousness of the pandemic first emerged in March 2020, Google recorded the highest number of searches for prayer in its history. We also asked Gen Z Americans the extent to which they have found themselves praying for an end of the coronavirus to understand whether their own personal religious behaviors have been impacted (see Figure 13.3).

A plurality of both whites and Asian American Gen Zers indicate that they have not turned at all to prayer in response to the pandemic. Solid majorities of African American and Latino Gen Z respondents, however, indicate that they prayed for an end of the COVID pandemic either to some or to a great extent; 36 percent of African American Gen Zers report praying for an end to the pandemic to a great extent. Of course, other work from Pew shows that only a minority of American teenagers pray on a regular basis—indeed, 39 percent report never praying while just 27 percent of teenagers, themselves members of Gen Z, report praying daily (Pew Research Center 2020a). Our data, then, show that at least for younger Americans, there is no evidence of a surge in private religious behavior, such as prayer, even in the midst of a pandemic.

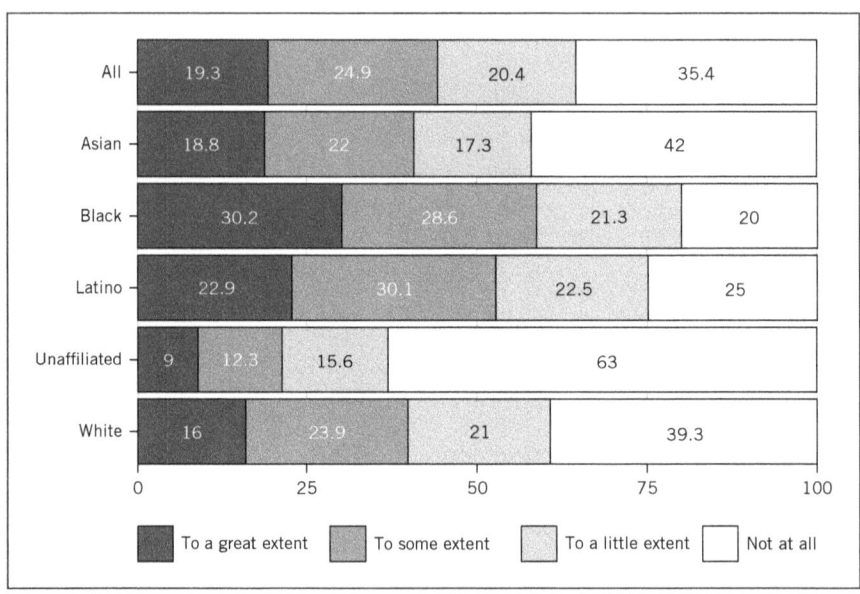

Figure 13.3 Extent to which Gen Z Prays for an End to COVID-19, by Race/Ethnicity (Percentages) (Source: 2020 Gen Z survey.)

Shelter-in-Place Laws and Gen Z

In our final descriptive analysis, we ask Gen Z Americans about their attitudes on shelter-in-place laws—namely, whether they believe that strict shelter-in-place laws are worth it to protect people and limit the spread of the coronavirus or whether those measures are placing unnecessary burdens on people and the economy and are causing more harm than good. At the time of our survey in May 2020, much political debate had ensued about whether such laws in some states were too restrictive, including limitations on gatherings at religious institutions.

While our question asked about Gen Z's attitudes overall on such restrictions—and not specifically about locking down houses of worship—we wanted to see how race/ethnicity and religion shapes those views, if at all. We find that a strong majority of Gen Z Americans—62 percent—believe that the shelter-in-place laws are worth it, compared with just 23 percent who believe such laws are too burdensome on people and the economy. That question came initially from a Kaiser Family Foundation Survey (2020), which found in April 2020 that 80 percent of Americans overall thought the laws are worth it compared with 19 percent who did not. If we remove those respondents who are unsure about which alternative is closer to their views, we find that 72.6 percent of Gen Zers support the laws while 27.4 percent say they are not worth it, so overall it appears that Generation Z is perhaps less supportive of those measures than Americans more generally (data not reported). White Gen Z Americans report being the least likely to think that such laws are worth it (just 58 percent), while Asian American Gen Zers are far less conflicted about those policies (78 percent support the laws).

We also consider how church attendance shapes support for shelter-in-place laws among Gen Z. On the one hand, regular church attenders may be less than thrilled by such strict shelter-in-place measures than those who do not attend regularly because such measures limit access to formal worship in person. On the other hand, regular church attendance may denote a greater ethic of care among respondents, leading them to be more supportive of shelter-in-place laws. For example, Gallup polls conducted in more than 140 countries showed that respondents who were highly religious were more likely to have donated money to charity, volunteered time to an organization, or helped a stranger who needed help (Pelham and Crabtree 2008).

Based on our initial results, weekly Gen Z churchgoers are *not* less supportive of shelter-in-place measures than their counterparts. Notably, weekly attenders share more in common with Gen Z Americans who never attend church or perhaps attend church several times a year in that more than 60 percent support strict shelter-in-place laws. That such a solid majority of weekly attenders back those laws shows potentially that greater religiosity may translate to communal attitudes about responses to the pandemic. These findings are also in line with surveys of other Americans, who have largely been supportive of requiring houses of worship to follow the same guidelines as businesses, schools, or other organizations when it comes to COVID-related restrictions (Pew Research Center 2020b). Our initial findings may also be linked to race and ethnicity, given that African Americans and Latinos attend church at higher levels and are also more supportive of policies to mitigate the effects of COVID-19 (Rouse 2020).

Multivariate Analysis

To further explore the effects of religion on attitudes about COVID-19 among Generation Z, we estimate three regression models that capture the effects of generation on religious faith, prayer, and support for sheltering-in-place measures, respectively, in the presence of other potentially confounding variables. First, we include three religious measures as independent variables: whether respondents are religiously affiliated (coded 1) or not (coded 0), how often they attend religious services (higher values equal more frequent attendance), and whether they consider themselves as born-again or evangelical (coded 1) or not (coded 0). In addition, we control for several common individual factors that may also affect faith, prayer, and opinions about the efficacy of sheltering in place. These include race/ethnicity (Black, Latino, and other, with white as the reference category), gender (coded 1 for cis women; 0, otherwise), party (Republican or independent, with Democrat as the reference category), ideology (7-point scale from extreme liberal to extreme conservative), and family income. Finally, we control for education. However, since a large portion of Generation Z is not old enough to have completed most of their education, we utilize "educational goal," a measure that captures a respondent's plan or hopes for educational achievement (high school to professional degree).

The results of the regression models for all three dependent variables—religious faith, praying, and support for shelter-in-place measures—are presented in the appendix in Table A13.1. We find that members of Generation Z who are religiously unaffiliated are significantly less likely ($p < 0.01$) to say that their religious faith has gotten stronger during the pandemic or that they have found themselves praying to a greater extent ($p < 0.001$) for COVID-19 to come to an end. Conversely, Gen Zers who say they attend religious services more frequently are significantly more likely to say that their religious faith has increased ($p < 0.001$) and that they pray more often ($p < 0.001$) for the pandemic to end. These findings are in line with survey data from Pew Research Center in April 2020 that showed greater religiosity during COVID-19 among respondents who attend church more frequently (Gecewicz 2020). Also, Gen Z respondents who identify as being born-again or evangelical are significantly more likely to say their faith has gotten stronger during the COVID-19 outbreak ($p < 0.001$), as well as state that they have prayed more often for an end to the pandemic ($p < 0.001$).

A few of our dispositional factors influence attitudes about faith, prayer, and support for sheltering-in-place measures. Gen Z African Americans express praying more often to bring an end to the pandemic than Gen Z white Americans ($p < 0.05$), and non–African American/non-Latino minorities (labeled as "other and who identify as Asian Americans, Middle Eastern, Pacific Islander, Native American, or multiracial") are more likely to say shelter-in-place measures are worth it to mitigate the spread of COVID-19 ($p < 0.05$). We also find that women are more likely to say that they are praying more often for an end to the pandemic. Previous research has shown that women are socialized to be more compassionate (Greenlee 2014) and to have greater concern for others (Lizotte 2020); women are also more religious than men (Trzebiatowska and Bruce 2013).

Partisanship is significant in two of our models, while ideology matters in all three models; these two factors sometimes affect our dependent variables in opposite directions. For instance, Gen Z Republicans are less likely to say that their faith has gotten stronger during the pandemic ($p < 0.05$). While at first blush this finding seems counterintuitive, those who are Republican among this cohort may already have high levels of faith that will not be impacted by the pandemic. For instance, 42 percent of Gen Z Republicans report attending church weekly or more compared with just 21 percent of Gen Z independents and 23 percent of Gen Z Democrats. By contrast, members of Generation Z who are more conservative are more likely to state that their faith has gotten stronger during the pandemic ($p < 0.05$). While this finding runs counter to the results for young Republicans, partisanship and ideology are not always synonymous; most people do not think of parties in ideological terms, and parties do not always reflect an individual's belief systems (Iyengar, Sood, and Lelkes 2012).

Ideology is even more complicated by how political beliefs interact with religious beliefs, particularly for different racial and ethnic groups (McKenzie and Rouse 2013). For example, in our survey, only 10.8 percent of African American Gen Z respondents identify as Republican, but 42.9 percent place themselves on the right side of the ideological scale (i.e., more conservative).[5] Similarly, 16.5 percent of Latino Gen Z respondents call themselves Republican, but 35.4 percent identify as conservative. By contrast, white Gen Z respondents have greater congruence between their partisanship (30 percent) and their ideology (36.9 percent identify as conservative). To explore further the effects of ideology on religious faith across groups, we interacted this variable with race and ethnicity in our model. None of the interaction terms yielded significant effects. However, in a logit regression model, we cannot fully establish statistical inferences by simply relying on the interaction terms (Norton et al. 2004). Therefore, as an additional step, we computed predicted probabilities of the different combinations of the interaction term.[6] These results are illustrated in the online appendix Figure A13.4 as pairwise comparisons of marginal effects for the dependent variable outcome of saying religious faith has gotten stronger.[7] In short, these findings confirm that except on a few values of the interaction term, neither ideology nor race/ethnicity consistently drive changes in religious faith among Generation Z. For example, the pairwise comparisons reveal that a conservative non–African American is 19 percent more likely to say their religious faith has gotten stronger during COVID, compared to a liberal African American. Similarly, a conservative non–African American is 18 percent more likely to acknowledge a strengthening of their religious faith during COVID compared to a moderate African American. There was not a statistically significant difference in religious faith between African Americans and non–African Americans with similar ideological beliefs or between African Americans of varying ideological leanings. In the pairwise comparisons for Latinos, we find that a conservative non-Latino is 18 percent more likely to acknowledge a strengthening of their faith during COVID compared to a moderate Latino. Furthermore, a conservative Latino is 16 percent less likely to say their religious faith has gotten stronger during COVID in comparison to a conservative non-Latino. There were no statistically significant differences between non-Latinos and Latinos of similar ideological beliefs.

Turning to the second model, partisanship is not a significant factor in predicting greater frequency of prayer during the pandemic. However, Gen Zers who are more conservative report praying more often ($p < 0.001$) for an end to the pandemic. Since many religious adherents tend to be ideologically conservative, our findings that greater conservatism is linked to stronger religiosity and more prayer are not very surprising.

Both Gen Z Republicans ($p < 0.001$) and Gen Z independents ($p < 0.05$) are less likely to agree that shelter-in-place measures are worth it to allay the spread of the coronavirus. Recent research has found Gen Z Republicans to be less supportive of COVID-19 mitigation efforts (Deckman et al. 2020), which makes sense given that criticism about stringent lockdown measures has most often come from Republican leaders. In contrast to how ideology affects strength of faith and frequency of prayer during the pandemic, conservative respondents are *less* likely to say that shelter-in-place measures are worth it ($p < 0.001$), indicating that these Gen Zers believe that such measures place an unnecessary burden on people and are causing more harm than good. As we noted in the introduction, Gen Zers are disproportionately employed in essential service industry jobs (Renner 2020) while at the same time becoming less sick or less likely to be hospitalized from COVID-19 (Maragakis 2020). These factors may contribute to less support among conservative Gen Zers' attitudes about shelter-in-place measures. Finally, we find that Gen Zers with a higher household income are more likely to support shelter-in-place measures ($p < 0.05$). This finding likely indicates that those with greater economic means believe they are better equipped to absorb restrictive COVID-19 measures that inevitably result in economic hardship for some segments of the population.

Conclusion

There is an old adage that there are no atheists in foxholes. While a pandemic may not be the same thing as a war, the data show that Gen Z is not becoming more religious as a result of this once-in-a century global health crisis. The religious disaffiliation among younger Americans, first witnessed in large numbers among the Millennial generation, continues among Gen Z Americans. Yet religion still matters to Generation Z, as a majority of this cohort affiliates with a religious tradition; a plurality also attends church on a regular basis—particularly African American and Latino Gen Zers. Religious Generation Z respondents view faith to be an important coping mechanism in dealing with the uncertainty that comes with this massive and frightening global health crisis. This tendency is particularly pronounced among born-again Christians. However, for Gen Zers who are not at all religious, there appears to be little movement toward religious activity even in the wake of the uncertainty generated by this pandemic. Finally, with respect to shelter-in-place laws, we find no apparent effect of religion on such attitudes. Instead, partisanship, ideology, and family income matter more in explaining variances in support for such policies among Gen Z.

While young people initially received some mixed messages about their perceived risks of getting sick (Courage 2020), overall, this cohort seems to approve of shelter-in-place measures, perhaps demonstrating that they value the importance of collective social action for the greater good. Religion, then, has some impact on the behaviors of Gen Z during the pandemic but only among those Gen Zers who are religiously inclined to begin with. Religion, overall, has relatively limited explanatory value for understanding how this generation is coping with a crisis that is likely to have significant long-term effects on their economic and social well-being.

14

Who's Allowed in Your Lifeboat?

How Religious Identity Altered Life-Saving Priorities in Response to COVID-19

MATTHEW R. MILES AND JUSTIN A. TUCKER

Not only do Republicans and Democrats disagree about politics; the more ardent partisans express disdain for supporters of the other party. These negative feelings move beyond the political realm into hopes that their children will not marry someone from the opposing political party and beliefs that members of the opposing party are less intelligent and more selfish (Iyengar et al. 2019; Iyengar and Hahn 2009; Iyengar, Sood, and Lelkes 2012; Iyengar and Westwood 2015). One cause of this interparty antipathy is that social identification with a party motivates emotional responses to information. Negative information about the out-group is more easily accepted than positive information (Huddy 2001; Tajfel and Turner 1979). In the United States, some religious groups are closely aligned with political parties (Campbell 2020), which exacerbates in-group and out-group dynamics. Social identity theorists posit that the more salient the group affiliation, the more biased an individual's belief about out-group members will be. As such, it is possible that what appears to be partisan hatred for the other side may simply be another manifestation of religious divisions that spill over into politics. Strong religious identifiers may associate the opposing political party with members of religious groups they dislike. If so, expressing concern that one's child might marry a Democrat could simply be an expression of concern that their child might marry outside of their religion. Is the corona-

---

Material referencing an appendix in this chapter can be found online available here: https://dataverse.harvard.edu/dataverse/epidemic_among_my_people.

virus pandemic any different? Do people prioritize religion over politics in the pandemic?

In this chapter, we exploit an opportunity presented by the COVID-19 pandemic to test the extent to which individuals prioritize saving certain individuals. We embedded a conjoint experiment into a national survey conducted in the middle of June 2020—the point at which U.S. governors were trying to weigh whether their states should reopen while novel coronavirus cases seemed to be on the rise. By experimentally manipulating numerous demographic traits simultaneously and asking participants to indicate which individual they would prioritize saving if the choice were theirs alone, we can estimate the precise amount of interparty hostility that is the result of religious difference. In the case of COVID-19, we find that differences in religious identity explain more of the hostility than do partisan identity differences.

Religious Social Identity and Out-Group Antipathy

The dynamics we are exploring in this chapter fit under the umbrella of political tolerance—putting up with those whom you dislike, perhaps even detest. What causes political intolerance in the United States? Some argue that differing religious beliefs are the primary cause of intolerance (Eisenstein and Clark 2015; Gibson 2010). Other scholars find that belonging and behaving have a strong influence on political intolerance. Religious competition for adherents motivates churchgoing Americans to be less tolerant of nonbelievers (Cox, Jones, and Navarro-Rivera 2015). Others emphasize the importance of values and traits. Individuals who feel disgust are less tolerant (Ben-Nun Bloom and Courtemanche 2015), and because people with exclusive religious values are more likely to feel threatened by religious out-groups (Schaffer, Sokhey, and Djupe 2015), people with religious values that emphasize distinctiveness are less tolerant than those who value religious inclusiveness (Djupe and Mockabee 2015). People with exclusive religious values are more likely to feel threatened by religious out-groups, which in turn motivates greater intolerance toward those groups (Schaffer, Sokhey, and Djupe 2015).

Yet scholars also note that depending on how political tolerance is measured, religious beliefs may not be the primary influence motivating political intolerance (Eisenstein and Clark 2015). Perceptions of threat are consistently the strongest (and least understood) predictors of political intolerance (Gibson 2006). Because threat is a multidimensional concept, Gibson argues that it can be difficult to isolate the conditions under which people perceive a threat. Yet perceived group-level threats—for example, the belief that Democrats will strip Christians of their liberties—tend to be stronger predictors of intolerance than do perceived personalized threats (which are rare in any event). As such, perceived threats to religious group identity could be strong predictors of antipathy toward out-group members. Strong, positive religious in-group identification leads to strong religious out-group negativity. This negativity leads to antipathy toward religious opponents, which heightens perceptions of threat from religious opponents and causes religious intolerance (Gibson and Gouws 2005; Miles 2019).

Muslim religious identity in the United States has also become increasingly racialized (Lajevardi and Oskooii 2018; Selod and Embrick 2013) and conflated with Arab national identity (Calfano and Lajevardi 2019). Thus, non-Muslims may perceive threat as more than competition for adherents but an actual physical or existential threat to Christian American lives and values. Whereas before 9/11 most discrimination faced by Muslims would have largely been based on national origin (e.g., Iranian, Lebanese, etc.), post 9/11 Muslims have been reframed as an Arab and religious out-group that is a threat to American society (Ayers and Hofstetter 2008; Jamal and Naber 2008; Selod 2015).

This reframing influences how the U.S. public views Muslims in the United States. The following figures illustrate the partisan/religious-based hostility toward Muslims in the United States. Pew asked respondents to indicate their feelings toward members of various religious groups in 2014 (N = 35,000) and again in 2017 (N = 4,284). A score of 100 on the thermometer represents very warm, positive feelings toward members of the group, with a score of 0 indicating very cold, negative feelings. A score of 50 means that the person has moderate feelings toward members of the described group (see Figure 14.1).

In 2014, Republican Protestants[1] had slightly warmer than neutral attitudes toward Muslims (53.98), while Democratic Protestants reported feelings 16 points warmer on the 100-point scale (69.96). That is a considerable partisan gap in attitudes toward Muslims. Yet, by 2017 the gap is even larger. In 2017, Republican and independent Protestants report cold feelings toward Muslims (39.75) while Democratic Protestants register cooler feelings toward Muslims (64.38) in 2017 compared to 2014. The large decline in Republican Protestant attitudes toward Muslims yields a large partisan gap of nearly 25 points on the 100-point scale. We are reluctant to attribute all of this change in attitudes to President Trump, in part because Republican presidential candidates have a long history of incorporating anti-Muslim messages in their rhetoric. In 2012, Herman Cain said that he would not appoint a Muslim to his cabinet, Rick Santorum argued that the concept of equality does not exist in Islam, and almost every 2016 candidate for the Republican presidential nomination made anti-Muslim comments (Bush 2015). Clearly, President

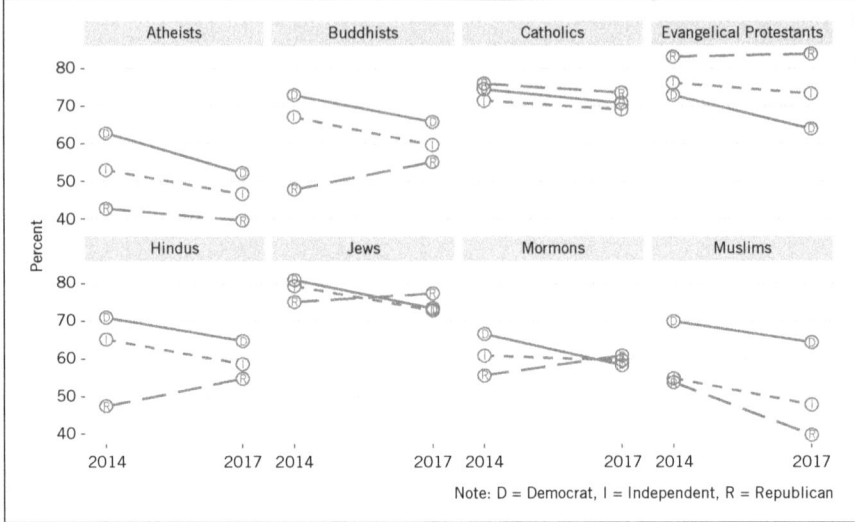

Figure 14.1 The Change in Protestant Attitudes toward Religious Group Members by Partisan Affiliation from 2014 to 2017 (Source: Pew 2014 and 2017 surveys.)

Trump's harsh anti-Muslim rhetoric exacerbated religious divisions, but he was also tapping into sentiment that existed before he entered politics.

In addition, Democratic Protestants report much lower ratings of evangelical Protestants in 2017 than they did in 2014, while Republican Protestants report warmer ones, and Democrat Protestants report colder feelings toward Mormons in 2017 compared to 2014. This suggests that partisanship influences how religious Americans feel about members of religious groups in the United States. Perceptions of religious and other out-groups is contextual and made in comparison to other groups (Calfano, Lajevardi, and Michelson 2019; Kalkan, Layman, and Uslaner 2009). Thus, individual perceptions of others is in part a reference to one's own position as well as a multitude of factors, including, but not limited to, religious affiliation.

To demonstrate the strength of partisan influence on attitudes about Muslims, Figure 14.2 shows the same thermometer rating about Muslims from Catholics, agnostics, and those who do not affiliate with a religion. Not only do Republican Protestants report more negative feelings toward Muslims in 2017 than they did in 2014, Republicans in virtually every religious category did the same. Republican agnostics report a nearly 50-point decline in their attitudes toward Muslims in this three-year period, while Democratic agnostics have much more favorable attitudes toward them. To a lesser degree, those

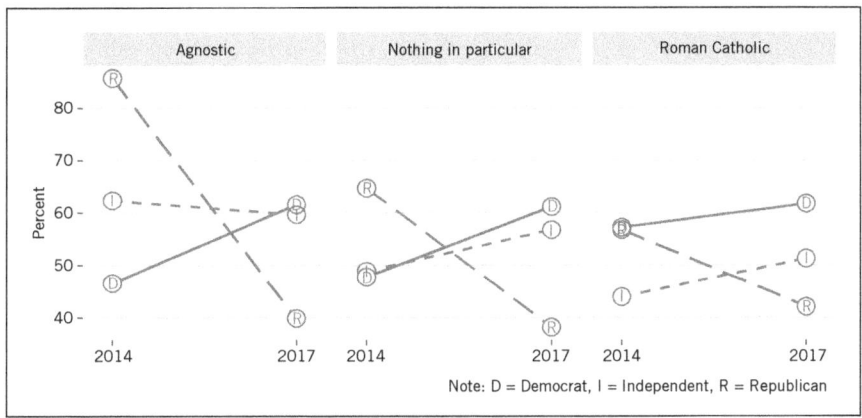

Figure 14.2 Feelings toward Muslims by Religious and Partisan Affiliation
(Source: Pew 2014 and 2017 surveys.)

who are not affiliated with any particular religion show an identical pattern. Democrats become more favorable toward Muslims, while Republicans become much less so. In 2014, there were no real partisan differences in Catholic feelings about Muslims, but by 2017, Republican Catholics report feelings almost 20 points lower than Democratic Catholics.

Strongly identifying with one's religion leads individuals to view members of some groups in the United States more like members of their in-group and other group members more like an out-group. Religious in-groups and out-groups are determined not solely by religious beliefs but also by political alignment. When religious groups compete politically, it magnifies the perceived distance between "us and them" and creates intergroup hostility. Because white evangelical Protestants align with the Republican Party and atheists align with Democrats, there is strong antipathy between the two groups (Campbell 2020). Similarly, as religious groups are perceived to be on one's own side politically, there will be less antipathy between the two religious groups, despite theological divergence.

Social identities are not as stable as beliefs and values, and as the strength of one's identification changes in response to societal conditions, antipathy expressed at one point in time can quickly dissipate as individuals adjust the importance of their various social identities (Miles 2019). That is, prejudice is context specific. Even if religious Americans exhibit prejudice toward members of some disadvantaged groups in society, it is unlikely that it represents a general, stable view.

Affective Polarization

Recent scholarship notes the alarming trend in which members of one political party express surprising negativity toward members of the opposing political party. Partisans report being upset if their progeny were to marry someone from the opposing political party (Iyengar, Sood, and Lelkes 2012), and they are less likely to have friends from the opposing political party (Iyengar et al. 2019). It is tempting to combine this scholarship with findings presented previously and conclude that antipathy toward Muslims is simply the result of partisan affective polarization.

We think that this explanation is too simple and does not adequately explain increased hostility toward Muslims for two reasons. First, the percent of Muslims who identified as Republican in 2007 is roughly the same as in 2017 (Mohamed 2018). If the number of Republican Muslims stayed constant in the three-year period, there is no reason for the affective gap to widen if it is solely driven by partisan affiliations. Second, the gap in partisan affect toward Muslims between Democrats and Republicans is nearly twice as large as it is for other religious groups who are aligned with the Democratic Party. As such, a widening affective polarization gap between Democrats and Republicans between 2014 and 2017 may account for some of the change in attitudes toward Muslims but cannot explain why Republican affect toward Muslims declines more than affect toward other religious groups aligned with Democrats.

As noted previously, out-group antipathy and hostility are context dependent. That which motivates hostility toward an individual who identifies with an out-group in one context would not do so in a different context. Context raises the salience of one identity over another. Something happened within the Republican Party in the three-year period between 2014 and 2017 that caused Republicans to have much more negative feelings about Muslims. As noted previously, many Republican presidential candidates used anti-Muslim rhetoric in their campaigns (Bush 2015), and by the 2018 midterm campaigns, seventy-one Republican candidates for office used anti-Muslim rhetoric in their messaging. Anti-Muslim candidates came from every region of the country, in progressive, conservative, and swing districts, and at every level of government (Muslim Advocates 2018).

Some Protestant clergy employed strong anti-Muslim rhetoric. When Pope Francis declared in 2016 that Islam is not terroristic and that all religions want peace, Franklin Graham, perhaps an extreme example, argued that as individuals "behead, rape, and murder in the name of Islam," they are following the teachings of the Koran (Gibson 2016). The divide has only intensified since the election of President Trump. He tweeted about the threat of radical Islam to the American way of life about once per month.² One of the first things he did in office was to ban Muslims from entering the United States. When political leaders of one's own party employ rhetoric that matches that of their religious leaders, it has a synergistic influence on their attitudes (Campbell 2020; Egan 2020; Nacos, Nacos, and Torres-Reyna 2007; Ocampo, Dana, and Barreto 2018). President Trump's anti-Muslim rhetoric, along with any potential anti-Muslim teachings of evangelical Protestant clergy, causes Republican evangelical Protestants to have much more negative attitudes toward Muslims than they otherwise would. This is not necessarily because of differing values, cultures, or xenophobic tendencies; rather it is because group leaders in both movements use rhetoric to frame Muslims as members of the out-group. And since negative information about the out-group is more easily accepted than positive (Huddy 2001; Tajfel and Turner 1979), this rhetoric might cause some Americans to feel considerable hostility toward Muslims.

How much do some Americans dislike Muslims? How much of the anti-Muslim sentiment is spillover from widening affective partisan gaps? To answer these questions, we employed an experiment during the COVID-19 pandemic to measure intergroup hostility precisely by assessing how Americans would save some Americans rather than others.

Study Design

Participants. A sample of 1,997 subjects was recruited by Lucid to participate in a national political study during June 10–26, 2020. Lucid is an aggregator of survey respondents from many sources, and its respondents are widely used in academic research. It collects basic demographic information from all subjects who flow through their doors, facilitating quota sampling to match U.S. census demographic margins (Coppock and McClellan 2019). Because convenience sample participants might not pay close attention to the survey questions, we included an attention item and filtered out those who were not paying attention. In all, 4,445 began the survey, 2,340 (52.6 percent) correctly answered the attention question, and, of those, 1,997 (85.3 percent) completed the entire survey. A comparison in the appendix shows that our sample is similar to the U.S. population on several key demographic variables.

Procedure. Rather than creating several separate experiments manipulating demographic profiles of people who the individual might prioritize protecting from the virus in turn, we opted for a conjoint experimental design because it allows us to see how each demographic variation works in conjunction with each other (Hainmueller, Hopkins, and Yamamoto 2013). This design allows us to isolate the effects of the different treatments while main-

TABLE 14.1 POSSIBLE TREATMENTS IN THE CONJOINT EXPERIMENT

Gender	Race	Age	Party Affiliation	Religion	Religiosity	Gun Owner	Ideology
Male	African American	18–25	Independent	Evangelical Protestant	Not at all religious	Yes	Moderate
Female	Asian	35–45	Libertarian	Atheist	Somewhat religious	No	Very conservative
	Hispanic/Latino	65–75	Strong Democrat	Catholic	Very religious		Very liberal
	White		Strong Republican	Muslim			

taining a balance of internal and external validity. Randomization means that regression can be used to recover the treatment effects, and the experiment will have higher degrees of realism compared to other experiments that simply vary a single dimension (Bansak et al. 2017, 2018). Table 14.1 describes each treatment to which a participant might be randomly exposed, and Figure A14.1 in the appendix provides an example of what might have been seen by a participant in the survey. The survey was fielded as states were reopening after an initial shutdown but right as numbers of COVID-19 infections were rising once again. At this moment, the public was engaged in genuine debate about whether to prioritize restarting the economy or protecting vulnerable individuals from infection.

After viewing the two scenarios, respondents were presented with a dichotomous choice of which individual to prioritize saving. Although we force a choice in this experiment, results from conjoint experiments that do not force a choice often yield similar results to those that do (Hollibaugh, Miles, and Newswander 2020). The activity was repeated three times in succession, for a total of three choices.

Methods

As we are using a conjoint experiment in our analysis, we estimate average marginal component effects (AMCEs), per the recommendations of Hainmueller, Hopkins, and Yamamoto (2013). The AMCE is an estimate of the average extent to which a particular scenario component (e.g., race, religion, gender, ideology, etc.) affects the dependent variable. Hainmueller, Hopkins, and Yamamoto (2013) show that the AMCEs can be estimated by regressing the dependent variable on sets of indicator variables measuring the levels of each attribute; for example, *Age 35–45*, *Age 65–75* would be included as independent variables in such a regression to capture the effect of the *Age* treatment, with *Age 18–25* as the baseline category.

Each respondent participated in the experiment three times, which gives us a sample size three times as large as the number of respondents in the survey. For all dependent variables, the *forced choice* operationalization is a binary variable indicating which individual they would save. Because each respondent chose from three different pairs, we use the appropriate statistical corrections.

Results

Who does the public prioritize saving from the effects of COVID-19? Figure 14.3 presents the results from the full sample of participants. The *points* in the figure are the estimated probability that someone with that demographic characteristic will be saved, with the *lines* representing the 95 percent confidence interval of the estimate. The *vertical dotted line* at the 0 point of the x-axis represents no effect. If the *solid horizontal lines* overlap with the *dotted vertical line*, the model predicts that there is no difference between someone with that demographic profile and someone with the baseline demographic profile.

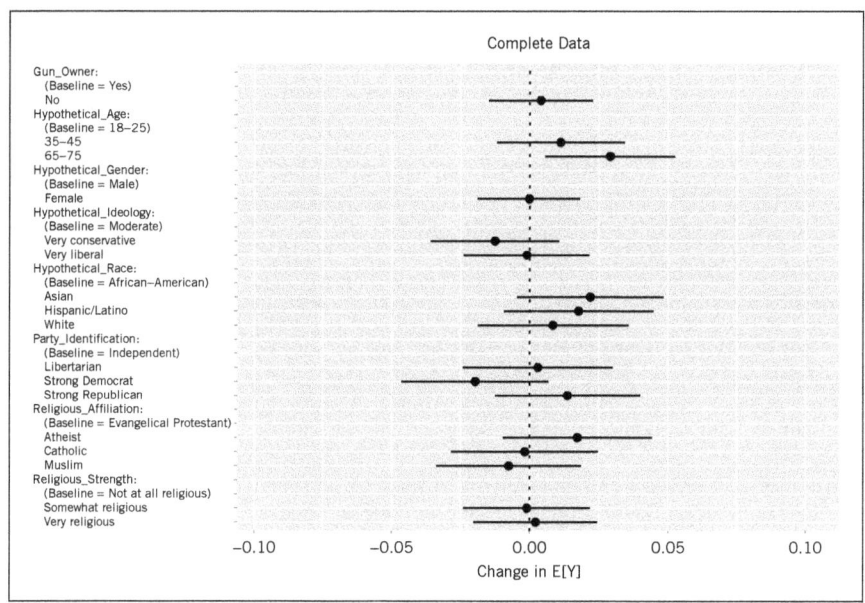

Figure 14.3 The Estimated Effects of Attributes on the Choice to Save an Individual (Source: June 2020 survey.)

On average, Americans are significantly more likely to prioritize saving someone aged sixty-five to seventy-five compared to someone aged eighteen to twenty-five. Yet they are just as likely to prioritize saving someone aged thirty-five to forty-five as they are someone aged eighteen to twenty-five. Specifically, the model predicts that survey participants were 3 percentage points more likely to save an older American. Each of the other demographic characteristics overlaps the 0 point, which means that they do not have an effect different from zero. Broadly, this is encouraging and consistent with expectations. When Americans are forced to make a choice about who to prioritize saving, there is no systematic bias toward any particular partisan or religious identity, but there is toward those most vulnerable to the virus. Since older people were more likely to suffer extreme symptoms from COVID-19, Americans prioritize keeping them safe.

Subgroup Analyses

This experiment provides an opportunity to estimate the degree of out-group hostility some Americans express toward others. It is well documented that Republicans and Democrats are growing less tolerant of each other, and religious intolerance is nothing new. We think it is likely that the same identity-based motivations that cause members of some religious groups to dislike members of other religious groups might motivate them to prioritize saving members of their own religion and not saving members of other religions. We do this by creating subsets of the data and running the same analyses using only members of particular subgroups. Doing so reduces the overall sample size for the analyses and widens the length of the 95 percent confidence interval, which means it also requires a larger substantive effect to achieve statistical significance.

We begin by looking at the responses from people who strongly identify as Democrats. Figure A14.2 in the appendix shows that Democrats make roughly the same judgment call as other Americans. The only group with a model prediction significantly different from zero are people aged sixty-five to seventy-five years old. Democrats are about 4 percentage points more likely to prioritize saving an older person compared to a younger person. We find no evidence of partisan-motivated antipathy toward members of opposing partisan or religious groups. Democrats are just as likely to prioritize saving an evangelical Protestant or a Republican as they are a Muslim or a fellow Democrat. We find the same pattern of findings among Democrats who also have a strong religious identity.

Republicans show no systematic preference toward saving members of any particular group, including seniors. The length of the 95 percent confidence interval is fairly large among this subgroup, but the point estimates in Figure A14.3 in the appendix are pretty close to zero for members of most groups. There really is no evidence that Republicans prioritize saving members of any group over another.

The model predictions displayed in Figure A14.4 in the appendix replicate previous analyses but only on the subset of respondents who indicate that their religion is an important element of their own identity. We subset the data to include only those for whom religion is "somewhat" or "very" important to their sense of who they are. The sample does not include a lot of people from minority religions, and 56 percent of the subset with a strong religious identity are either Catholic or Protestant. The next highest group (17.76 percent) are people who did not select any of the denominational options and call themselves "something else." Less than 3 percent of this group identifies as Muslim, about 8 percent are "nothing in particular," and other religions combine to account for the remaining 15–16 percent of respondents with a strong religious identity. We find that individuals with a strong religious identity are more likely to prioritize saving an evangelical Christian compared to Muslims. We find no evidence that religious identity causes people to prioritize saving Republicans or conservatives from COVID-19. The only substantively large and statistically significant results from any of the subgroup analyses is that individuals with a strong religious identity are nearly 5 percentage points less likely to prioritize saving a Muslim than they are an evangelical Protestant.

Conclusion

Discrimination against Muslim Americans and anti-Muslim sentiment has grown especially acute since 2016 (Lajevardi 2020). Meanwhile, in the 2018 midterm elections, the first two Muslim women to be elected to the U.S. Congress were Democrats. Given the rising antipathy partisans express toward cross-partisans (Iyengar et al. 2019; Iyengar, Sood, and Lelkes 2012), we thought it likely that some of the increasing anti-Muslim sentiment could be explained by the increasing alignment of religious and political identities (Campbell 2020; Egan 2020). Perhaps some Republicans do not dislike Muslims per se, but they equate Islam and Democrats, and this motivates greater antipathy against Muslims because they are political opponents.

The reopening of some states and cities, combined with the rising number of infections of COVID-19 in the early summer of 2020, presented an ideal opportunity to test this hypothesis. Although President Trump and other Republican elites employed partisan rhetoric discussing infection rates, the threat posed by reopening was not clearly partisan or religious in nature. Muslims were not more likely to be infected than Christians; nor were Republicans more likely to be infected than Democrats. Willingness to prioritize saving an individual from one group over another would have to be motivated by underlying biases held by the respondent. There is no other objective, logical rationale for trying to save a Republican other than a preference for Republicans.

Our research design allows us to explore how individuals prioritize protecting some individuals from infection relative to other individuals simultaneously in an experiment. We show that Americans prioritize protecting older Americans from infection. We find no evidence of partisan differences in the willingness to protect the elderly. Furthermore, we demonstrate that partisanship did not influence one's willingness to save a fellow partisan from infection, while allowing a cross-partisan to be infected. Both Democrats and Republicans were equally likely to save cross-partisans from infection.

When asked who they would prioritize saving from a COVID-19 infection, individuals with a strong religious identity were significantly more likely to prioritize saving an evangelical Protestant compared to a Muslim. Juxtaposed with the findings that partisanship does not change which religious groups the individual prioritizes saving, this suggests that religious identity influences life-saving priorities in the early stages of the COVID-19 pandemic. From a broader perspective, this suggests that some anti-Muslim sentiment is motivated more by religious identity than it is by religious beliefs or partisanship. Not only are Muslims closer in belief to religious Americans than are atheists (for whom there was no difference), but we replicated these analyses using belief in God (rather than religious identity) as a predictor and found no effect.

This does not mean that partisan rhetoric has no influence on anti-Muslim sentiment in the United States. Rather, we think that the findings point to the importance of elite rhetoric in guiding anti-Muslim sentiment. When this survey was conducted, Republican elites were engaging in anti-Muslim rhetoric, but it was not clearly connected to the pandemic. Elites were blaming cross-partisans for their handling of the pandemic, but at the time of the survey, it was not as prevalent in the rhetoric as it would become. As other work in this book demonstrates, elite rhetoric would eventually have a stronger influence on attitudes.

This illustrates the importance of context in the study of religion and politics. As others have noted (Abrams and Hogg 1999; Hale 2004), identities develop to fill a psychological need for certainty. Context determines which identities are salient at any given moment. The uncertainty created by the COVID-19 pandemic and the decision to begin reopening caused religious identities to be more salient than political identities were. When asked to decide who should be saved, evangelical Christians with strong religious identities chose to prioritize saving their own. Future work should examine the contexts in which religious identities become more salient than other identities.

15

How the Early Stages of the COVID-19 Pandemic Affected Religious Practices in the United States

Kraig Beyerlein[1] and Jason Klocek

On the morning of Sunday, September 16, 2001, Pastor Tim Keller arrived to a line of congregants out the door of Redeemer Presbyterian Church in Manhattan. The typical crowd of about 2,800 people nearly doubled the first weekend after the September 11 attacks. In fact, so many people showed up that Pastor Keller had to tell those who could not fit inside the church to come back in two hours for another impromptu service. Some 800 people returned (Zylstra 2017).

The spike in turnout at Redeemer Presbyterian Church was neither unique to that congregation nor to New York City. According to a 2001 Gallup poll, religious service attendance rose 6 percent across the United States the Sunday following 9/11 (Walsh 2001). The *Wall Street Journal* reported on a study that found a 25 percent increase across religious congregations and spiritual centers immediately after the attacks (McLaughlin 2001). Regardless of how one measured the initial surge in religious activity, it also proved to be remarkably short-lived. In just two weeks, most U.S. congregations reported that attendance had returned to pre-9/11 levels (Iannaccone and Everton 2004).

The abrupt and fleeting rush to congregations following the September 11 attacks raises important questions about the impact of large-scale catastrophes—such as famines, wars, earthquakes, and pandemics—on religiosity. Yet our ability to test this relationship and draw meaningful conclusions remains limited because we typically lack comparative data from before and after disasters. As such, we still know relatively little about the nature, size, and duration of large-scale tragedies' effects on religious and spiritual practices.

Just as importantly, the empirical study of religious behaviors after wide-reaching crises relies on a relatively limited set of cases. Most existing research focuses on natural disasters that affect a narrow geographic region. The nature of the COVID-19 pandemic, however, introduces unprecedented dynamics. What happens when the majority of congregations in a nation are all suddenly closed or inaccessible? How do people respond when important in-person religious practices they would normally turn to for solace during troubled times pose a significant health risk to themselves and others? Do they replace these practices with safer forms or continue to gather in person and hope they will not be infected?

This chapter draws on representative survey data from U.S. adults collected six weeks into the COVID-19 pandemic to answer these and related questions. We leverage measures asking about religious behaviors in 2019 and six weeks into the coronavirus outbreak among the same respondents to examine whether they increased, decreased, or remained the same. Our over-time analyses focus on four specific religious practices: attending in-person congregational services, viewing virtual religious services, gathering together in person for informal religious activity, and praying privately. Moreover, these analyses are conducted at two distinct levels: (1) *wave* to examine overall change in these practices and (2) *respondent* to identify stability or movement in them among individuals.

The remainder of the chapter proceeds in four parts. In the next section, we summarize extant scholarship on religious responses to crises. Much of that research focuses on how personal trauma, rather than large-scale catastrophes, affects religiosity. The subsequent two sections describe our survey data/methods and findings, respectively. Several wave-level changes in religious practices, including a sharp decline in attending religious services in person and an uptick in viewing virtual religious services during the initial coronavirus outbreak, are in line with theoretical expectations. Others, such as the general stability in private prayer frequency, are more surprising. The final section discusses the implications of our results and identifies areas for future research.

Existing Research on Religion and Crises

Social scientific research on the role of religion in how people experience and respond to crises has developed considerably over the last several decades. Psychologists have carried out the bulk of that work, concentrating on how religious beliefs and practices facilitate coping with illness, the death of a loved one, sexual and physical abuse, or other personal traumas (e.g., see Pargament 1997; Pargament and Raiya 2007). This research has uncovered a range of positive and negative religious methods that people employ to understand and manage unexpected and distressing life events (e.g., see Luhrmann 2013; Pargament 1997; Pargament and Raiya 2007). A considerable amount of attention has also been given to testing empirically the impact of these methods on physical and mental health outcomes (e.g., see Abu-Raiya et al. 2020; Pirutinsky, Cherniak, and Rosmarin 2020). The emerging consensus from this scholarship is that reliance on positive religious coping methods generally has salutary effects in the face of individual trauma.

In the last two decades, natural disasters that strike specific communities have become another area of interest for studying the impact of crises on religious attitudes and behaviors (Belloc, Drago, and Galbiati 2016; Sibley and Bulbulia 2012). Much of the attention has focused on meteorological events, such as floods, droughts, hurricanes, and wildfires. Several studies, for instance, have observed an increase in religious practices (e.g., praying, Bible reading, attending services in congregations) among African Americans living in communities that Hurricane Katrina hit (Alawiyah et al. 2011; Chan and Rhodes 2013). Others have noted a general increase in survivors' self-reported levels of religiosity following the devastation in the U.S. Gulf Coast region in 2005 as well as after the 1993 Mississippi River floods across the Midwest (Kessler et al. 2006; Smith et al. 2000). And one study of Canadians who endured weather-related disasters with significant fatalities found an increase in both religious belief and behavior among respondents (Zapata 2018).

Geological disasters, especially earthquakes, are another focus in the literature regarding how tragedy influences religiosity (e.g., Jang, Ko, and Kim 2018; Stratta et al. 2012). One recent cross-national analysis, for instance, found that individuals in regions with higher earthquake risk tend to be more religious (e.g., believe that God is very important in their lives or attend religious services at higher levels) than those living in lower-risk areas (Bentzen 2019). Another study of the 2011 earthquake in Christchurch, New Zealand, observed that religious affiliation increased in the devastated region, while the rest of the country experienced a net decrease (Sibley and Bulbulia 2012).

Social scientists have paid less attention to religious responses to present-day catastrophes that affect a large segment of the population, a whole nation, or the entire world. This is partly because events of this magnitude remain relatively rare. These events are no less important to understand, and possibly more so, given they have far-reaching and lasting repercussions. As discussed at the beginning of this chapter, 9/11 has been the primary case investigated to understand how contemporary large-scale tragedies influence U.S. religious attitudes and behaviors. This includes a handful of analysts who have documented a brief uptick in religious service attendance (Iannaccone and Everton 2004; Uecker 2008) and others who have shown an increase in self-reported measures of religiosity and spirituality (Bonanno and Jost 2006; Seirmarco et al. 2012; Uecker 2008) after the September 11 attacks.

The COVID-19 pandemic constitutes a new opportunity for scholars to explore how large-scale crises influence religious beliefs and behaviors given its unprecedented dynamics, including the extended period over which the tragedy has unfolded. Additionally, the coronavirus outbreak has involved unique restrictions on in-person access to religious spaces. During the initial weeks of the pandemic in the United States, large numbers of congregations voluntarily suspended services out of an abundance of caution (Mervosh and Dias 2020). The vast majority of them that did not close initially eventually did so in response to states' stay-at-home orders. And even when those constraints were loosened or lifted, many faith communities continued to hold in-person services or placed limits on the number of people who could gather together (Dias 2020). In response, faith leaders significantly expanded online religious services (Estrin 2020). These circumstances raise additional questions. For instance, did those who previously attended in-person religious services seamlessly transition to a virtual platform? Or did they find online services too impersonal? What about the possibility of attracting new people? Will the greater accessibility of streaming services lead those who previously did not attend in-person services to join online more regularly?

Developing research efforts attempt to document and explain changes in religious behaviors in response to the unusual circumstances of the COVID-19 pandemic. Outside of the United States, one study, for instance, found an increase in online searches about livestreamed Catholic masses in Italy during the initial lockdown there (Alfano, Ercolano, and Vecchione 2020). Another observed that Italians who reported a case of coronavirus in their household also reported higher levels of attendance at religious services and frequency of prayer compared to those who reported no household infection (Molteni et al. 2020). Still another recent analysis identified a global rise in Google searches about prayer since March 2020 (Bentzen 2020). Additionally, two recent Pew Research Center studies provide some insight into how the coronavirus outbreak has affected religiosity in the United States. One conducted in March 2020 documents a shift from in-person to online religious services at the very beginning of the outbreak (Pew Research Center 2020b). Another in July 2020 reports that more than half of U.S. adults said they plan to resume going to religious services as often or more often as they did before the pandemic once it is safe to do so (Pew Research Center 2020a).

This nascent research provides a useful starting point for thinking about the impact of the COVID-19 pandemic on religious practices. Most notably, it points to a general expectation of their increase in response to the current crisis. But this research is not without data challenges. One is that collected data are generally for online searches about various religious practices (i.e., prayer and virtual services) rather than people engaging in them. We should not necessarily assume that these are proxies for religious behaviors in real life. In fact, our findings cast doubt that they are. Another limitation is that existing studies draw overwhelmingly on aggregate measures of religious behaviors (at country or regional levels). This limits our ability to infer whether the observed relationships hold at the individual level as well as to determine whether any observed difference is primarily the result of people changing the ways in which they practice their faith or new people engaging in religious practices for the first time. Furthermore, much of the data analyzed thus far come from outside the U.S. context and do not directly compare religious behaviors before and during the COVID-19 pandemic.

Our chapter addresses a number of these concerns. Most importantly, we draw on survey data that asked the same American adults about participation in different forms of religious activity in 2019 and six weeks into the COVID-19 pandemic. We, therefore, examine not only whether such practices as attending in-person or online religious services increased during the initial surge of coronavirus cases in the United States but also whether any such change is due to people participating at the same level at both time points or the movement of different people with varying levels of religious engagement.

Data, Measures, and Methods

We analyze data from the "Religious Practice in the Time of Coronavirus" module that was part of the National Opinion Research Center's (NORC's) AmeriSpeak Omnibus survey fielded between April 30 and May 4, 2020, among 1,002 American adults.[2] AmeriSpeak Omnibus is a representative sample of adults living in U.S. households (for more information, see National Opinion Research Center 2020). Four religious practices for which the same respondents were asked about their participation in 2019 and at the time of the survey are the focus of this chapter: (1) attending in-person religious services, (2) viewing online religious services, (3) gathering in person informally for religious activity, (4) and praying privately. We leverage this research design to analyze the data from *two* distinct perspectives. First, we reshape the original data, stacking respondents' 2019 and time-of-the-survey measures to create a panel-level structure. By doing so, our initial analyses examine wave-level differences in these religious practices. Second, the original data allow us to investigate individual-level differences in these practices between 2019 and six weeks into the COVID-19 pandemic and thus explicate the composition of any observed wave-level differences. For both levels, we also investigate religious tradition differences. All analyses that follow apply survey weights to correct for known demographic discrepancies between our sample and the target population; wave-level analyses also incorporate a panel correction for repeated observations of the same respondents.

Results

We start this section by discussing wave-level and individual-level differences, respectively, including how religious tradition shapes them. Our attention then shifts to the effects of state-level religious regulations and respondent-level congregational closures on in-person religious service attendance during the initial COVID-19 pandemic. Finally, we consider whether the sharp decline of in-person religious service attendance we observe explains the parallel growth in online religious services, as a number of public commentators suggest (e.g., see Gjelten 2020; Yurieff and O'Brien 2020).

Wave-Level Findings

Overall, Figure 15.1 shows a considerable drop in both in-person religious services and informal religious gatherings, an uptick in weekly online religious services, and general stability in prayer. For attending in-person religious services (left-most panel), weekly rates fell from 21 percent in 2019 to 5 percent six weeks into the COVID-19 pandemic. Both monthly and less-than-monthly percentages for this religious activity also declined over time. These declines reflect an over 30 percent increase in those never attending in-person religious services between waves. While less stark, the same basic pattern holds for informal religious gatherings (third panel from the left).

By contrast, we see an 11-percentage-point rise in weekly viewing of streaming religious services six weeks into the coronavirus outbreak. At the same time, less-than-monthly and monthly rates of virtual religious services dropped some between waves. As for private prayer, the right-most panel shows very little change and no overall significant wave-level difference. At 47 percent, the same

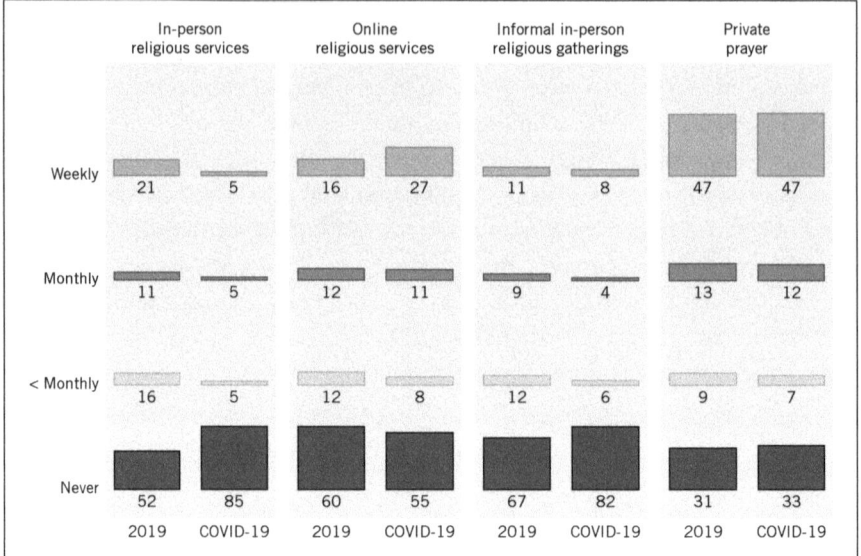

Figure 15.1 Wave-Level Differences in Religious Practices between 2019 and Six Weeks into the COVID-19 Pandemic. Note: Overall differences for all religious practices except private prayer are statistically significant at the $p < 0.001$ level based on a chi-square test; percentages do not always add up to 100 because of rounding. (Source: NORC AmeriSpeak Omnibus Survey, April–May 2020.)

number of American adults engaged in this religious practice weekly *both* before and during the initial phase of the COVID-19 pandemic. Moreover, the remaining participation levels for private prayer do not change by more than 2 percentage points.

The relative stability in private prayer is arguably the most surprising wave-level finding. Numerous studies suggest that people often turn to prayer or pray more often during times of crises (e.g., see Pargament 1997). Furthermore, at least one recent empirical study analyzing aggregate data of daily Google prayer searches for ninety-five countries argues that the COVID-19 pandemic induced more people around the world to pray (Bentzen 2020). This claim is based on the premise that online behavior often reflects what we do off-line, with the study finding a rise in online prayer searches (relative to all other Google searches) for most countries. Our analysis of wave-level data, however, calls into question how well online searches align with changes in prayer frequency, at least in response to the initial surge of coronavirus cases among U.S. adults.

We also analyzed the extent to which religious tradition affected wave-level differences in the four religious practices.[3] While rarely considered in analyses of the relationship between religion and traumatic events (but see Beyerlein, Nirenberg, and Zubrzycki 2021; Uecker 2008), a great deal of prior research in political science and sociology demonstrates the explanatory power of religious tradition (e.g., see Putnam and Campbell 2010; Steensland et al. 2000). Looking at religious traditions represented in our survey data—Black, evangelical, and mainline Protestant, as well as Catholic and the nonreligious—at the wave level reveals three key patterns (results available upon request from the authors). First, we observe religious tradition variation in each of the four practices before the COVID-19 pandemic. Namely, evangelical and Black Protestants tended to be more active than were Catholics and mainline Protestants, consistent with other research (e.g., see Shelton and Emerson 2012). This variation persisted six weeks into the coronavirus outbreak. Second, despite different starting and ending points in levels of religious activity for the different traditions, the same overall pattern of change held for all of them. That is, each religious tradition experienced a steep decline in attending religious services in person and gathering informally together for religious activity, especially weekly participation, a rise in weekly viewing of online services, and stability in private prayer. Third, the magnitude of these changes varied among religious traditions. For instance, evangelical Protestants experienced the largest gain in weekly streaming of online religious services (33 percent before and 52 percent during the pandemic). By comparison, we observe no more than a 15-percentage-point increase among Black Protestants, mainline Protestants, and Catholics for this religious activity.

Individual-Level Findings

The wave-level differences raise questions about movements in people's participation levels. For instance, is the considerable uptick in those never attending in-person religious services between waves due to already infrequent attenders simply choosing not to attend at all during the initial coronavirus outbreak, or are more frequent participants suddenly opting out of in-person religious services? And to what extent do the more stable wave-level findings reflect people engaging in the same level of religious activity before and six weeks into the pandemic? To answer such questions, we turn to individual-level data on religious practices before and during COVID-19.

Four broad patterns emerge in Figure 15.2. First, the pandemic did not generally influence the behavior of those who reported nonparticipation in 2019. For example, 90 percent or more of the nonengaged in 2019 remained so six weeks into the coronavirus outbreak, with the exception of virtual religious services. Second, a substantial number of respondents who attended

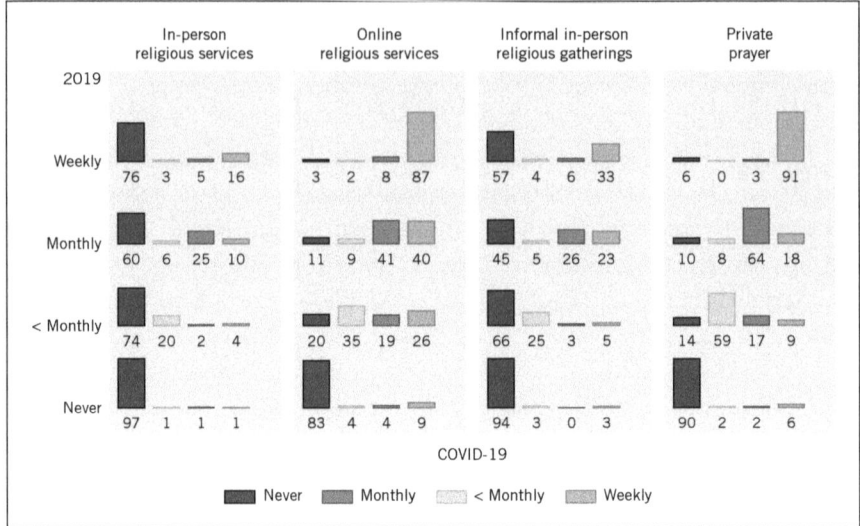

Figure 15.2 Individual-Level Differences in Religious Practices between 2019 and Six Weeks into the COVID-19 Pandemic. Note: Overall differences for all religious practices are statistically significant at the $p < 0.001$ level based on a chi-square test; percentages do not always add up to 100 because of rounding. (Source: NORC AmeriSpeak Omnibus Survey, April–May 2020.)

in-person religious services and gathered together informally for religious activity prior to the initial stage of the COVID-19 pandemic did *not* continue to do so after it. Over three-quarters of Americans attending in-person religious services weekly in 2019, for instance, no longer did so six weeks into the crisis.

Third, looking at the diagonals for the greater-than-never participation categories, we see much higher percentages for online religious services and private prayer. For them, more Americans stayed engaged at prepandemic levels, especially weekly. Over 90 percent of people who prayed weekly in 2019, for instance, continued to do so six weeks into the coronavirus outbreak. Last, we observe some gains in participation frequency across the four different religious practices. The biggest ones are for less-than-monthly and monthly online religious services. We see at least a 40-percentage-point climb in these frequency categories during the initial surge of U.S. coronavirus cases.

Taken together, the results in Figure 15.2 indicate that a good number of Americans maintained prepandemic levels of religious practices six weeks into the COVD-19 pandemic; this was especially the case for those never participating before and weekly participants in virtual religious services and private prayer. At the same time, we see some movement of people in both directions. In-person religious services and informal religious gatherings experienced considerable downward mobility in participation, while some upward shifts occurred for online religious services and private prayer.

Do the above patterns vary by religious tradition? In results not shown but available upon request from the authors, we find that the individual-level findings for religious traditions generally adhere to the same basic patterns found in the full sample. That said, the extent of some of the changes differs across the various religious traditions, particularly for the two in-person measures. For instance, over one-fifth of evangelical and Black Protestants who attended in-person religious services weekly in 2019 continued to do so a month and a half into the initial surge of coronavirus cases. The comparable numbers for mainline Protestants and Catholics are 6 percent and 10 percent, respectively. On the other hand, mainline Protestants, at 42 percent, had the highest weekly continuity rate for informal religious gatherings. Black Protestants ranked second, with more than one-third of members of this religious group gathering together informally for religious activity weekly both before and during the initial stage of the pandemic.

These findings both confirm and add nuance to media accounts focusing on evangelical Protestants for defying state mandates and attending in-person religious services during the early days of the coronavirus outbreak, often in the name of religious freedom (e.g., see Collier, Trevizo, and Davilla 2020). At least among prepandemic weekly attenders, Black Protestants had the same rate of attendance six weeks into the COVID-19 pandemic as did their evangelical counterparts.

State-Level Religious Regulations and Congregational Closures

Based on the advice from public health officials to stem the spread of the coronavirus, many congregations across the country closed their doors either voluntarily or in response to state-mandated lockdown orders. To investigate the impact of this reduced access to congregations on in-person religious service attendance six weeks into the COVID-19 pandemic, we collected, read, and coded executive orders for all fifty states and then merged this coding with the survey data.[4] Our coding scheme differentiated among *four* broad types of regulation operating at the time of the survey.[5] These ranged from allowing religious gatherings or services with no explicit limits, on the one hand, to their total prohibition, on the other hand. The middle categories included executive orders that allowed gathering for religious services but either encouraged or

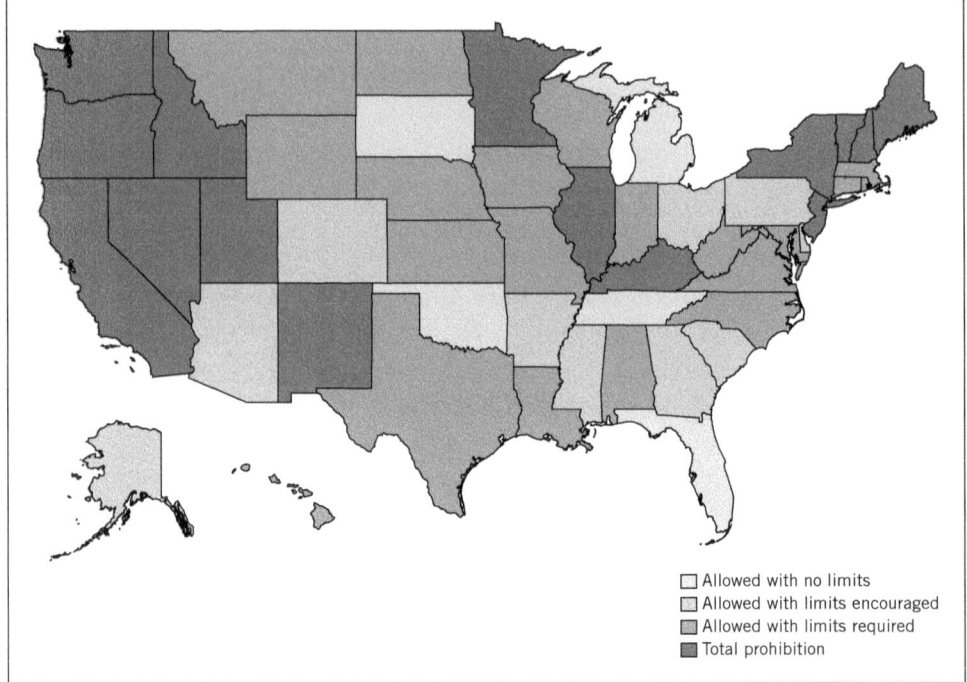

Figure 15.3 State Religious Regulations Six Weeks into the COVID-19 Pandemic (Source: NORC AmeriSpeak Omnibus Survey, April–May 2020.)

required restrictions, such as limiting the number of people who could assemble together in person.

Figure 15.3 shows the distribution of these four categories across the United States. Total prohibitions are most prominent on the coasts. Only five states allowed religious gatherings with no limits six weeks into the COVID-19 pandemic: Florida, Tennessee, Michigan, Oklahoma, and South Dakota. The other two religious regulations—allowed with limits, encouraged or required—are generally distributed evenly among the remaining states.

What effect, if any, did these state-level religious regulations have on Americans' in-person religious service attendance rates a month and a half into the initial coronavirus outbreak? We link the data presented in Figure 15.3 with our survey respondents' state locations to analyze the relationship among those who attended in-person religious services at some level in 2019.[6] Interestingly, in results not shown but available upon request from the authors, we find that the four different types of state-level religious regulations were *not* a significant factor accounting for variation in prepandemic attenders' rates of attending in-person religious services six weeks into the COVID-19 pandemic.

What about closure of respondents' congregations? Did that make a difference in whether U.S. adults who previously attended in-person religious services continued to do so during the initial stage of the COVID-19 crisis? Figure 15.4 demonstrates that it clearly did. Among prior attenders who lost access to their congregations, over 80 percent never attended an in-person religious service six weeks into the coronavirus crisis, while only 6 percent did so weekly (roughly the same number attended less than monthly and monthly). We observe a different story for prepandemic attenders whose congregations stayed open. More than three-quarters of them gathered for in-person religious services at some level during the initial surge of coronavirus cases. Over 40 percent of 2019 attenders whose congregations remained opened attended in-person services weekly a month and a half into the first wave of the COVID-19 pandemic. Another one-quarter attended monthly, and nearly one out of every ten prior attenders gathered in person for religious services at least once during the initial outbreak of the coronavirus. With that said, more than one-fifth of Americans who attended in-person services in 2019 attended *no* in-person religious services at this time despite having the opportunity to do so.

Congregational closures help shed light on the previously discussed religious tradition differences in attending religious services in person. Recall that among prepandemic weekly in-person attenders, evangelical and Black Protestants (at 21 percent each) were more likely to continue attending in-person weekly services during the initial COVID-19 crisis compared to Catholics (10 percent) and especially mainline Protestants (6 percent). Across all religious traditions, we find that the majority of 2019 weekly attenders' congregations, at 85 percent, closed in response to the first wave of coronavirus cases. That said, prepandemic weekly in-person attenders connected to evangelical and Black Protestant communities had greater access relative to others. About one-fifth and one-third of evangelical and Black Protestants who attended in-person religious services weekly in 2019, respectively, reported that their church doors remained open six weeks into the COVID-19 pandemic (results available upon request from the authors). By comparison, the opportunity to attend in-person religious services was considerably lower for Catholic and mainline Protestant prepandemic weekly in-person attenders, at 7 percent and 4 percent, respectively.

Shifts from In-Person to Online Religious Services

Finally, we turn to the question of whether the rise of virtual religious services in the time of the coronavirus crisis reflects a substantive change to the

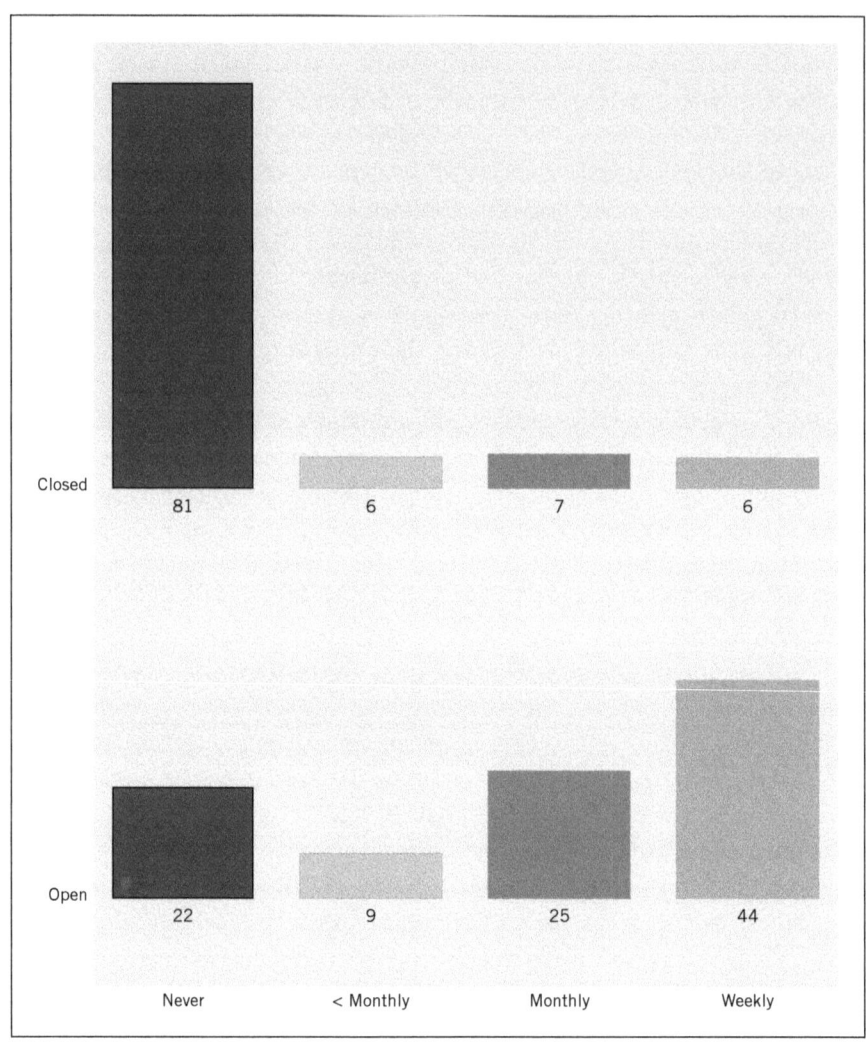

Figure 15.4 Relationship between Closure of Individuals' Congregation and In-Person Religious Service Attendance Six Weeks into the COVID-19 Pandemic. Note: Overall differences are statistically significant at the $p < 0.001$ level based on a chi-square test; results for 2019 attenders only; percentages do not always add up to 100 because of rounding. (Source: NORC AmeriSpeak Omnibus Survey, April–May 2020.)

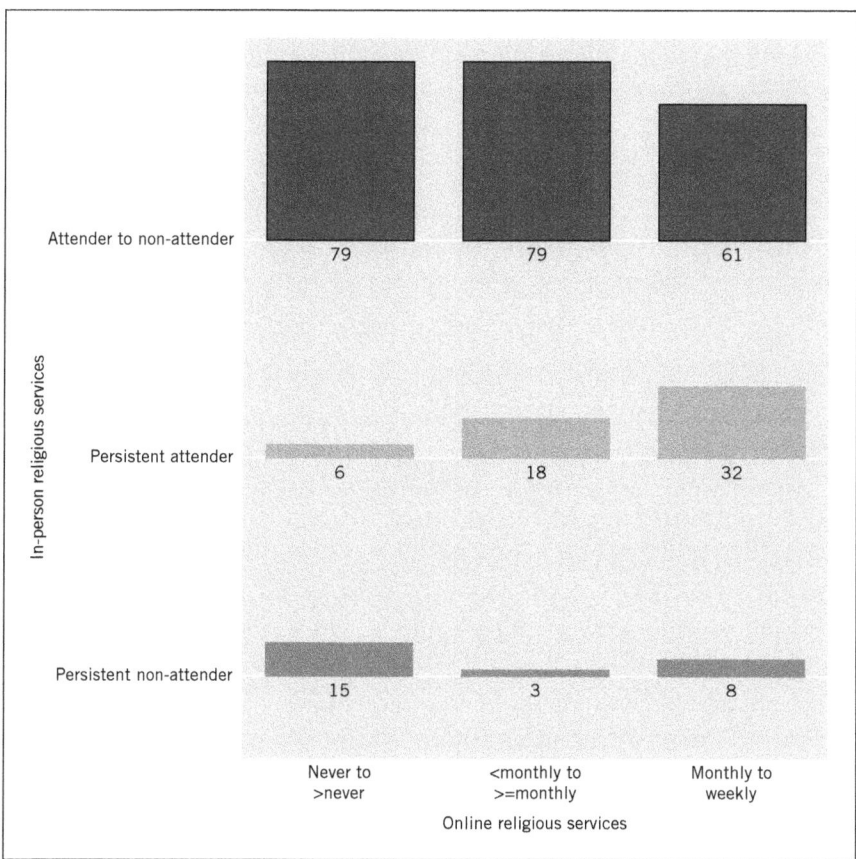

Figure 15.5 Relationship between Types of In-Person Religious Service Attenders and Increased Virtual Viewing of Religious Services Six Weeks into the COVID-19 Pandemic. Note: Overall differences are statistically significant at the $p < 0.01$ level based on a chi-square test; results for those reporting an increase in online religious services between 2019 and six weeks into the COVID-19 pandemic; percentages do not always add up to 100 because of rounding. (Source: NORC AmeriSpeak Omnibus Survey, April–May 2020.)

U.S. religious landscape. Journalists and other public commentators speculated early on that streaming religious services were attracting new viewers, but were these largely those who shifted from in-person to online attendance, or did virtual services also draw in the previously nonengaged (M. Clark 2020; Sherwood 2020)?

As Figure 15.5 shows, nearly 80 percent of the never-to-greater-than-never and less-than-monthly-to-monthly-or-more upward shifts in online services are concentrated among those who attended in-person religious services before *but not* during the initial stage of the COVID-19 pandemic. At 61 percent, the attender-to-nonattender in-person group accounts for over half of the monthly-to-weekly positive change in virtual viewing. It is also noteworthy that American adults who did not attend in-person services both before and during the first outbreak of coronavirus cases compose 15 percent of the never-to-greater-than-never upward shift in online services.

Conclusion

This chapter presented some of the first survey data comparing rates of various religious behaviors before and after the initial surge of coronavirus cases in the United States (see also Chapter 16). Our analyses confirm and challenge conventional thinking about how the COVID-19 pandemic affected Americans' religious practices in the short term. As anticipated, we observed a substantial decline in attending religious services in person and a general rise in the viewing of online religious services during the early stages of the pandemic. Somewhat surprisingly, however, the frequency of private prayer remained stable over time.

Our findings also underscore that individuals were actively navigating the shifting nature of the religious terrain and making choices about how, if at all, to practice their faith during and in response to the crisis. Broad state restrictions were not a significant variable explaining actions related to in-person religious activity.[7] The closure (or not) of congregations to which Americans were *personally* connected had a strong effect, however. People were much less likely to continue to attend in-person religious services—especially at high levels—six weeks into the initial coronavirus outbreak when their faith communities closed for public safety. Furthermore, highly active evangelical and Black Protestants in 2019 remained so during the early stages of the pandemic much more than did those from other religious groups, in part, because their congregations were more likely to remain open.

It is also clear that this factor alone does not fully explain the variation we observe. Nearly one in five Americans actively sought out another place to attend in-person religious services when their regular congregation closed. And a similar number of those whose faith communities remained opened chose *not* to attend in-person religious services. These findings motivate future study of the determinants of religious behaviors during and following large-scale disasters that fundamentally limit in-person access to faith leaders and organizations.

What other factors are at work, influencing whether—and if so how—people practice their faith during a public health crisis? For instance, do people's anxiety about the pandemic or direct experience with the virus influence how willing they are to look for other religious spaces holding in-person religious services when their congregation closes? Are face-to-face religious interactions so important during a pandemic that they even cross denominational lines to secure them?

We also need more data to evaluate the durability of changes. Our survey data focused on religious responses during the initial month and a half of the COVID-19 pandemic. Future studies should explore whether the patterns we observe persist. As the positive case count and death toll rose in the United States before vaccination, did rates of online religious service attendance climb further? Perhaps frequency of private prayer surged months into the pandemic as uncertainty and loneliness became the norm. Did more Americans attend in-person religious services as state regulations loosened and ended at different times and in different ways across the country? And will we witness a lasting transformation of the U.S. religious landscape because of the COVID-19 pandemic?

In particular, journalists and pundits speculate that previous in-person attenders who switched to online services will continue to attend virtually long after the pandemic subsides. Nevertheless, the above-mentioned Pew Research Center poll from July 2020 suggests such speculation may be premature; more than half of U.S. adults reported they plan to resume going to religious services in person as often or more often as they did before the outbreak once it is safe to do so again (Pew Research Center 2020a). As more and more congregations are opening their doors again but encouraging masking and other policies to protect and save lives, will people maintain this commitment to return to in-person services?

To conclude, our chapter captures important short-term consequences of the COVID-19 pandemic for religious practices in the United States. As such, it provides a useful starting point on which future studies analyzing changes in religious behaviors can build, especially those with data spanning longer periods. What short-term shifts that we observed endure over time? Much work remains to be done about how the particular—and unprecedented in the modern era—dynamics of the COVID-19 pandemic are shaping how people practice their faith and what this means for the future of religion, not just in the United States but across the globe.

16

Patterns of In-Person Worship Service Attendance during the COVID-19 Pandemic

The Importance of Political and Religious Context

BENJAMIN R. KNOLL

"Easter's a very special day for me. Wouldn't it be great to have all of the churches full? You'll have packed churches all over our country. I think it would be a beautiful time." This optimistic prediction came from President Donald Trump on March 24, 2020, in an interview with Fox News. Earlier that month, spiking levels of the novel coronavirus pandemic had prompted a critical mass of states and localities to issue shutdown orders and for public schools to transition to online learning. At the time, many Americans (including President Trump) were hopeful that the lockdown measures would be short-lived and that Americans would be able to get back to their regular lives within a few weeks, perhaps even by Easter on April 12.

Of course, these early hopes were dashed as the spread of COVID-19 infections only intensified in the coming weeks and months. Public health experts consistently warned against large, in-person gatherings, religious gatherings included. States took varying approaches to regulating religious gatherings. An analysis by Jenkins (2020b) showed that in April, seven states exempted religious services from the state's shutdown protocols while another ten had limited exemptions. Another eleven states, in contrast, deliberately did *not* exempt religious gatherings from shutdown orders. Given these varying approaches, what did individual worshippers do? Did they continue to worship in person, or did they stay home and take advantage of online religious services? Who were the ones who decided to attend in person against the guidelines offered by public health officials, and how did they differ from those who decided to stay home? These are the central questions of this chapter.

These questions are important because they speak to longer-term trends in American religious behavior. Even before the COVID-19 pandemic, religious service attendance patterns had been in decline for decades. Research has shown that regular participation in religious congregations is strongly habitual and that significant life changes (marriage, relocation, etc.) are the most likely time when these habits can be interrupted, leading adults to make changes in their religious patterns (Putnam and Campbell 2012, ch. 6). The COVID-19 pandemic was a disruptive event in many ways, leading the vast majority of regular worshippers to suspend in-person participation for at least a few weeks in April 2020. While in-person worship experiences decreased as a result of the pandemic, other religious behaviors, such as frequency of prayer, increased substantially (Bentzen 2020; Dallas 2020; Dein et al. 2020). Religious behavioral patterns during the COVID-19 pandemic, especially attendance at religious services, might offer clues about longer-term trends in American religious patterns. In what follows, I draw on available data to track religious behavior during critical periods of 2020.

Late March

Before the COVID-19 pandemic hit, 31 percent of Americans reported that they attended religious services once a week (or more), according to extensive polling by Pew Research, which combined results of multiple surveys from 2018 to 2019. Another 13 percent said that they attended a few times a month, and 20 percent, a few times a year. Those who rarely attended made up 17 percent of Americans, and those who never attended comprised another 17 percent (Pew Research Center 2019). Our baseline, then, is that before the 2020 COVID-19 pandemic hit, about one-third of Americans said they attended religious services on a weekly basis while about half said that they attended only occasionally or not at all.

The March 2020 survey fielded by Djupe, Burge, and Lewis (see Chapter 1) polled 3,065 Americans about their religious activities in the first few weeks of the pandemic shutdown, specifically between Monday, March 23, and Friday, March 27. At this point it had been a full week since the Trump administration's guidelines to limit gatherings to ten people or fewer and included the first weekend that worshippers would have had the opportunity to attend religious services after these guidelines were released. When this question was asked, respondents were likely reflecting on their activities from the previous weekend (a week after the ten-person gathering-size guidelines) and their plans for the upcoming weekend (two weeks afterward). Further, these questions were given only to survey respondents who indicated that they attend religious services at least "seldom" (excluding the 24.8 percent who said they "never" attend religious services aside from weddings and funerals).

The March survey revealed that of the three-quarters of American adults who attend religious services, whether routinely or occasionally, only 12 percent said that their congregation was still open for in-person worship services. Among those whose congregations were still open, roughly one-third (37.5 percent) said that they were still attending in-person services. Interestingly, 18.3 percent of those whose congregations had closed reported that they were still worshipping in-person. While some of this is likely overreporting (common with surveys of church attendance; see Presser and Stinson 1998), it could also mean that some worshippers chose to attend another congregation that was still open during the last two weeks of March. Overall, then, 20 percent of American worshippers reported that they were continuing to attend in person during the last two weeks of March. Who were they?

In terms of religious identity, those with the lowest rates of in-person attendance were mainline Protestants (16.4 percent) and those who do not claim any religious affiliation (16.6 percent). Those with the highest rates of attendance in late March were, interestingly, the "other" category—non-Protestant/Catholic/Jews—at 27.8 percent.[1] While much of the public focused on the public refusal of some evangelical congregations to comply with the shutdown orders, the March survey showed that they were only slightly more likely (17.6 percent) than mainliners and "nones" to report still worshipping in person and lower than either Catholics (22.9 percent) or Black Protestants (19.6 percent). Given the approximately 2 percent margin of survey error, though, evangelicals were statistically indistinguishable from some other major religious groups.

Politically speaking, survey respondents were asked to rate, on a scale of 0 to 100, how supportive they thought that their congregation's "head clergyperson" was of Donald Trump. Those in congregations where the pastor, priest, or other leader was perceived by the respondent to be strongly supportive of Trump (a score of 67 or higher), one-quarter (26.5 percent) were still worshipping in person compared to only one in ten (11.1 percent) among those who perceived their clergyperson to be least supportive of Trump (a score of 33 or lower).

March survey results also revealed a somewhat counterintuitive finding regarding the issue of religious freedom. Much of the litigation surrounding the shutdown orders throughout 2020 centered on religious freedom arguments, arguing either that a prohibition on in-person religious worship violated the First Amendment or that houses of worship were unfairly restricted compared to other businesses or venues. Survey responses, though, revealed no statistically significant difference in worship patterns between those who said that their clergyperson had addressed the topic of religious freedom that year (21.8 percent) and those who had not (19.3 percent).

In contrast, the strongest contextual variable seems to be direct messaging from congregational leaders. One-quarter of respondents (25.7 percent) said that their congregations had *encouraged* them to continue to attend in-person worship because of the virus. Among them, a full half (50.8 percent) continued to do so compared to only 10 percent of those whose congregations had *not* encouraged them to continue to worship in person. Similar to the findings of other research on the effect of religious messaging from congregational leaders (see Knoll and Bolin 2019 for a review), I find here that worshippers were very responsive to the recommendations of their congregations about whether to continue to meet in person, at least initially.

While there was a great deal of uncertainty at the beginning of the pandemic about how the virus affected different communities, one of the more reliable patterns was that older people were more susceptible to contracting COVID-19 and experiencing worse symptoms, including morbidity, than younger people. There seemed to be widespread awareness of this pattern in our survey responses, as only about 7 percent of those over the age of fifty-five said that they were attending worship services in person after the nationwide restrictions on gatherings were put in place the weekend of March 15–16. In contrast, nearly one-third (29.3 percent) of those in their late twenties and thirties continued to attend, and one-quarter (26.2 percent) of those in their late teens and early twenties (remember that these questions are asked of those who said they attend more often than never).

Further analysis showed other patterns that defy conventional wisdom about worship patterns during the early weeks of COVID-19 in the United States. As with so much in contemporary American politics, attitudes toward COVID-19 were politically polarized from the outset. In the second half of March, though, there was a not a strong partisan difference between Democrats/leaners and Republicans/leaners in terms of their worship patterns (although the small difference was statistically significant). While 22.4 percent of Democrats reported continuing to worship in person, 19.1 percent of Republicans did so as well. In comparison, 14.9 percent of self-identified pure independents (excluding those who lean toward one party or another) continued to worship in person.

There were similarly surprising findings when it comes to the respondent's most trusted source of news about current events and politics. Contrary to what many might expect, those who put their trust in Fox News were initially much *more* likely to stop worshipping in person, with only 16.7 percent reporting that they were continuing to do so. This is less than for those who put their trust in outlets with more liberal reputations, such as MSNBC, where 30.7 percent continued to worship in person, or Comedy Central's *The Daily Show* or John Oliver's *Last Week Tonight*, where a full 37.5 percent continued to worship in person. This may be more of an age effect, though, as the Fox News audience skews older, and Comedy Central's audience skews younger (Pew Research Center 2012). For their part, those who trust NPR the most reduced their in-person worship to 6.9 percent.

Worship patterns were also not strongly related to supposed "anti-science" skepticism in March. Survey results showed no statistically significant difference between those who said that they agreed that the virus was a "major threat" (19.8 percent) and those who did not (18.1 percent). There also was only a relatively small and statistically nonsignificant 7-percentage-point difference in worship patterns between those who say that they "trust the medical professionals and scientists" (19.6 percent) and those who do not (26.8 percent).

What *did* make a clear difference, though, were levels of political paranoia around the coronavirus issue. Those who thought that the "hysteria" around the coronavirus was "politically motivated" were 23 percentage points more likely to report continuing to worship in person than those who disagreed with that statement (31 percent to 7.8 percent, respectively) (see Jamieson and Albarracín 2020; and Chapter 2 in this collection by Orcés, Huff, and Jackson for more about the link between conspiracy theory acceptance and COVID-19 attitudes). Further, one of the strongest effects was the respondent's level of belief that the Democratic Party and its leaders were actively persecuting Christians for their religious and political beliefs. Respondents were asked if they believed that a Democratic president would likely "ban the Bible," "force you to pay for abortions," or "take away your guns." They were also asked if they believed that they would "lose their religious freedom if Democrats control the federal government." These responses were combined into a collective index variable of "perceived persecution from Democrats." Among those with the strongest levels of perceived persecution from Democrats (the top third of the scale), a full 40.1 percent continued to worship in person in the few weeks after President Trump's shutdown order, compared to 16 percent of those with moderate levels of perceived persecution and 9.1 percent of those with the lowest levels of perceived persecution. (These figures remain virtually unchanged if we exclude non-Christians from the sample.)

In reporting these various trends in church attendance in late March, it is also important to keep in mind that many of these factors overlap. We saw, for example, that Fox News viewers were actually *less* likely to continue worshipping in person. We also know, though, that Fox News tends to draw an audience that is disproportionately older, and older people were more likely to begin stricter social distancing given that it was clear at the time that they were at a greater risk for contracting COVID-19. Given that reality, Table 16.1 shows the independent effect of each of the various factors considered above.

In this more sophisticated (logistic regression) analysis, we see that there were three key factors that each *independently* predicted whether someone continued to attend in-person religious worship services in the early weeks of the nationwide shutdown: congregational encouragement to attend, age, and perceived religious persecution from the Democratic Party. Specifically, those whose congregations encouraged them to continue to worship in person were 23 percentage points more likely to do so than those whose congregations encouraged them to stay home, even controlling for a variety of other potential factors (described above). The youngest people in the survey (age eighteen) were about 21 percentage points more likely to say that they were continuing to worship in person compared to the oldest (age ninety). Finally, those who strongly perceive that the Democratic Party in the United States is actively seeking to ban the Bible and eliminate religious freedom for Christians were about 20 percentage points more likely to continue to worship in person compared to those who strongly *disagreed* that Christianity is being actively persecuted by Democrats in the United States.

Table 16.1 also shows that a few other factors mattered, although not to the same extent as the three described above. For example, biblical literalists were about 12 percentage points more likely to continue to worship in person than those who believe the Bible is not divinely inspired; those who attended religious services at least weekly *before* the pandemic were about 7 percentage points more likely to say that they were continuing to worship in person compared to those who rarely attended. There are also small effects with men, Republicans, those who think that COVID "hysteria" is politically motivated, and, interestingly, those who say that CNN/MSNBC are their most trusted news sources, each being about 4–5 percent more likely to report continuing to worship in person.

One of the most important revelations from this analysis is the strong influence of context on a person's decision to continue to worship in person during a global pandemic. The context of a person's congregation (whether the congregation chose to specifically encourage people to continue to attend) and the context of the person's information environment (whether they be-

TABLE 16.1 INDEPENDENT EFFECT OF RELIGIOUS, CONTEXTUAL, DEMOGRAPHIC, AND SOCIAL/POLITICAL FACTORS ON IN-PERSON WORSHIP ATTENDANCE

	March 2020	October 2020
Congregation encouragement to attend in person	22.8	NS
Age (oldest to youngest)	21.3	NA
Perceived persecution from Democrats	20.3	21.2
Biblical literalism	12.1	4.4
Typical religious service attendance	7.2	26.2
Gender	5.1	NS
COVID "hysteria" is politically motivated	4.8	13.8
Trusted news source: MSNBC	4.2	NS
Political partisanship	4.1	NS
Gen X cohort	NA	8.9
Clergy has recently preached about religious freedom	NS	8.3
"I trust the medical professionals and scientists who have sounded the alarm about the dangers of the coronavirus."	NS	4.7

Source: March and October 2020 surveys.
Note: Effect sizes displayed here are derived from a logistic regression procedure using in-person worship attendance as the dependent variable (0 = no; 1 = yes) and including each of the variables discussed in this section as independent variables. Displayed factors are those that achieved statistical significance at $p < 0.05$; they depict the predicted probability of the dependent variable as the independent variable moves from its minimum to maximum value. "NA" = "not included in this model." "NS" = "not significant." Unless otherwise indicated, the full models included variables measuring religious identity (tradition/denomination), frequency of worship service attendance prepandemic, biblical literalism, whether the respondent heard pastor talk about religious freedom from the pulpit, respondent perception of clergy support of Trump, whether congregation was encouraging/discouraging in-person worship, size of congregation, gender, race/ethnicity, age, education, income, political partisanship, trusted news source, perception as to whether "hysteria" over coronavirus is politically motivated, perceiving the coronavirus as a major threat, trust in medical professionals, and perceived anti-Christian persecution from Democratic Party.

lieved that Christians were actively under attack by the Democratic Party and its leaders) were two of the three strongest and most consistent predictors of continuing to worship in person.

While there are, of course, legitimate conversations to be had about the important trade-offs between individual liberty and public safety, these results illustrate the strong effect that opinion leaders (whether in religious congregations or political contexts) can have on the public's decisions on matters of public health and safety in the midst of a pandemic. Those whose congregations did not encourage them to continue to attend and who did not perceive an active political attack on Christianity were significantly more likely to stay home and therefore helped prevent further spread of the coronavirus in the early days of the pandemic. In contrast, those whose information ecosystems were actively cultivating a perceived persecution of Christianity and encouraging them to continue to worship in person were much more likely to do so, likely accelerating the early spread of the virus in the United States.

April and Easter Sunday

Easter Sunday took place on April 12, 2020, four weeks after the Trump administration's initial recommendation to limit gatherings to ten people or fewer. The week before Easter, the Public Religion Research Institute fielded a national poll ($N = 1,007$), which included a question asking respondents who say they usually attended worship services at least "a few times a year" whether "the place at which you primarily attend religious services is currently holding in-person gatherings for Easter or other religious occasions in the coming days or weeks?" (PRRI 2020). This survey revealed that fewer than one in ten Americans (9 percent) reported that their congregations were still planning in-person worship services for Easter or other occasions (down a little from the 12 percent who said their congregations were open in the March survey two weeks prior). When asked about their personal plans, only 3 percent of Americans who ordinarily attend religious services at least a few times a year said that they were planning to celebrate Easter or other religious occasions by worshipping in person. Most of the remainder (63 percent) said they planned to celebrate with some sort of online service, and 33 percent said they did not plan to celebrate one way or the other.

The PRRI results further showed that the vast majority of American worshippers planned to either celebrate Easter or other occasions online (or not at all), and the survey results once again show the importance of context: among the 9 percent of regular worshippers who said that their congregations were still planning in-person worship services, nearly one-quarter (23 percent) reported that they were planning on taking advantage of the opportunity and worshipping in person. Only 1 percent of those whose congregations were closed to in-person worship said they planned to worship in person (presumably with a congregation other than their usual one). In other words, when a congregation chose to stay open for in-person worship, one in four planned to attend; when a congregation chose to close for in-person worship, nearly all of its congregants stayed home for Easter or other religious services. This shows once again the strong influence of congregational leaders in a time of a public health emergency—their choice to stay open for in-person worship or to move exclusively online has a strong influence on the choices of worshippers in their congregations and thus also the spread of the coronavirus in their communities (and beyond).

Late October

By late fall of 2020, the United States was well into the third wave of COVID-19 infections, resulting at the time in approximately 80,000 new cases per day (double the rate from only one month previous). In the middle of this spike, the October survey by Djupe, Burge, and Lewis (see Chapter 1) polled 1,800 Americans between October 20 and November 3. Findings from this survey showed consistency in religious behavior from the summer through the fall—roughly one-third (34.2 percent) of American worshippers (i.e., those who say they attend religious services at least "seldom," about 70 percent of all adult Americans in the survey) said that they were back to attending in-person worship services.

In terms of individual religious identification, mainline Protestants were least likely to say that they were worshipping in person in late October, with only one in five (20.2 percent) doing so, again perhaps because mainline Protestants are, on average, older and at a higher-than-average risk for COVID-19. Views of the Bible made a difference, with biblical literalists roughly 30 percent more likely to be worshipping in person than those who say that the Bible is "not the word of God" (49.2 percent to 18.1 percent, respectively). Typical worship service attendance was also strongly related to whether someone is attending in person or not in late October. Of those who attended worship services weekly or more prior to the pandemic, nearly 40 percent more were likely to say that they are worshipping in person than those who attended a few times a year or seldom prior to the pandemic (50.7 percent to 12.3 percent, respectively).

Similar to patterns shown in late March, religious context was an important predictor of in-person worship in October. Those who had heard their pastor mention the topic of religious freedom in his or her sermons were about 20 percentage points more likely to be attending in person than those who had not (48.1 percent to 29.4 percent, respectively). A similar pattern is evident among those who say that they believe that their congregation's clergy are highly supportive of President Trump compared to those whose clergy are not supportive (43.1 percent to 26.4 percent, respectively). Those who attend larger congregations (101 or more on a typical worship service) were about 15 percentage points more likely to be worshipping in person (43.7 percent) than those in smaller congregations (100 or fewer) (27.3 percent)—notable especially because COVID-19 had consistently been shown to spread especially in large gatherings, including religious services.

Of course, one of the most direct contextual factors is whether a congregation chose to remain open for in-person worship services or whether they chose to provide these services online or to suspend services temporarily. By late October, only 27.6 percent of American worshippers said that their congregations were still closed to in-person worship, meaning the other three-quarters were hosting in-person services. Of those whose congregations were open, nearly half (48.5 percent) said that they were attending in person. Interestingly, though, nearly one-third (31.2 percent) of those who said that their in-person worship services had been suspended said that they were attending worship services in person. As we saw in the March data, some of this inconsistency is likely due to respondents overreporting their actual in-person worship behavior due to social desirability concerns, but it is also possible that some of those whose primary congregations had suspended in-person services decided to attend *other* congregations that were open. Indeed, in the late October survey, 12.1 percent of those who said that their primary congregations had suspended in-person worship had switched to a new congregation sometime in 2020.

Given the strong correlation between age and COVID-19 morbidity rates, it is also notable that baby boomers and silent generation worshippers, while ordinarily some of the nation's most consistent worshippers, continued to curtail their in-person worship activities throughout the fall. Less than one-quarter (23.5 percent) of those born before 1965 reported attending in-person worship activities compared to nearly half (46 percent) of Gen Xers and a third (24.1 percent) of Millennials. For their part, only 28.3 percent of Gen Z worshippers were attending in person (see Chapter 12 for more on this group).

Consistent with our March survey results, certain social/political attitudes were strong predictors of in-person worship in the October 2020 survey. For example, those who believe that "hysteria over the coronavirus is politically motivated" were about 35 percentage points more likely to be worshipping in person than those who disagreed with this (50.5 percent vs. 15.7 percent, respectively). Similar to March, a perceived sense of religious, and specifically Christian, persecution from the Democratic Party is especially correlated with decisions to worship in person or online. Nearly three in five (56.4 percent) of those with strong perceptions of Democratic religious persecution were choosing to worship in person compared to nearly one in five (17.4 percent) of those who disagreed with these perceptions.

Politically speaking, there was some partisan difference when it came to in-person worship behavior in October. Republicans (including independents who lean Republican) were about 12 percentage points more likely to be worshipping in person than Democrats, who themselves were about 7 percentage points more likely than pure independents (42.1 percent, 30.5 percent, and 23.9 percent, respectively). As might be expected, Fox News viewers were more likely than others to be worshipping in person (40 percent), but as might *not* be expected, they were attending at the same rate as those who list CNN as their most trusted news source (39.7 percent). We also see, again, that those who look to the *Daily Show* or *Last Week Tonight* were even *more* likely to be worshipping in person (44.8 percent), again perhaps related to the younger audiences that these programs tend to attract. In contrast, the media group least likely to be worshipping in person, though, were NPR listeners, with 17.2 percent.

As with the data in March, it is important to keep in mind that many of these factors are correlated with each other, which could distort our interpretation of the effect of each individual factor on the decision to worship in person or not. For example, those who believe that Democrats are actively persecuting Christians in the United States are *also* less likely to identify as Democrats; which of the two factors is the stronger factor when statistically controlling for the effect of the other?

Shown again in Table 16.1, the logistic regression analysis reveals that the strongest predictor of in-person worship is, as we might expect, typical worship patterns. Those who say that they attended worship services weekly or more prior to the COVID-19 pandemic are 26 percent more likely to be attending in-person worship services than those who typically attended a few times a year. In contrast, typical attendance patterns were a much weaker factor in predicting in-person worship in late March, where frequent attenders were only 7 percentage points more likely to be worshipping in person compared to infrequent attenders.

There is also now an interesting contrast in terms of age. In late March, there was a linear relationship between age and in-person worship patterns—the older you were, the less likely you were to be attending in person. This was also one of the strongest predictors of in-person worship decisions. By late October, though, this pattern had shifted. Table 16.1 shows a curvilinear relationship—those most likely to be worshipping in person were middle-aged Gen Xers, with younger and older individuals both less likely to be attending in person. Indeed, in October the Gen X cohort was 9 percent more likely to be attending in-person services than all other age cohorts when controlling for the various other factors.

Table 16.1 also shows that one consistent factor of in-person worship patterns in the early weeks of the pandemic compared to seven months later was perceived religious persecution from the Democratic Party. In late March, it was one of the three strongest predictors of in-person worship (along with age and encouragement from congregation leaders to attend in person), and it remained so in late October. Those with high levels of agreement that the Democratic Party is actively persecuting Christianity in America were 21 percentage points more likely to be worshipping in person than those with low levels of agreement. It is interesting to note that the third strongest factor was also political in nature—those who strongly agree that "hysteria over the pandemic is politically motivated" were 14 percentage points more likely to be worshipping in person than those who strongly disagree. A third factor was *also* political in nature—those whose clergy had preached recently about religious freedom were 8 percentage points more likely to be worshipping in person than those whose clergy had not.

This again suggests that contextual factors, and political factors specifically, exerted the strongest influence over a person's decision to attend in-person worship services by the beginning of November 2020 (perhaps not surprising in the closing days of a contentious presidential election). Adding the various factors together, someone whose clergy were preaching about the importance of religious freedom, who believed that pandemic hysteria was politically motivated, and who perceived active religious persecution from Democrats were 43 percentage points more likely to be worshipping in person than those who did not report those things. These factors exerted a stronger effect than a person's preexisting religious behaviors and views (normal worship patterns and biblical literalism), which accounted for a 31 percent change in the likelihood of attending in-person worship services.

These findings are also important within the wider context of the relationship between worship patterns and the spread of COVID-19 in 2020. Figure 16.1 shows rates of in-person worship attendance between the different surveys discussed in this chapter, adding additional surveys fielded by Pew Research Center (2020a), Barna (Kinnaman 2020), and the University of Chicago School of Divinity in partnership with AP-NORC (AP-NORC 2020), comparing responses of Americans who attend religious services at least monthly. The general pattern is that in-person attendance for regular worshippers dropped to nearly one-quarter by the end of March and then to low single digits by mid-April. This had climbed to high single digits by the beginning of May, about one-third by the summer, and about half by the fall. For comparison, Figure 16.1 also shows that in-person religious attendance patterns increased steadily just as COVID rates were also exponentially rising throughout the fall of 2020.

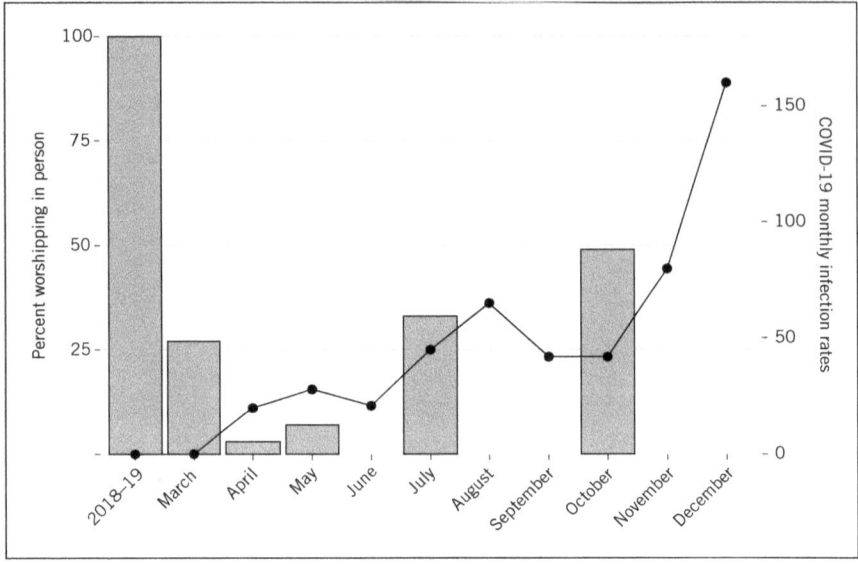

Figure 16.1 In-person Worship Patterns among Regular Attenders Compared to Average Daily COVID-19 Rates throughout 2020. (Source: Data from March and October 2020 surveys [Chapter 1], PRRI, Pew Research Center, Barna, and the University of Chicago School of Divinity in partnership with AP-NORC.)

Conclusion

Collectively, this analysis provides strong evidence of the central role that religious and political leaders play in influencing the religious behavior of Americans, even in the middle of a global pandemic. When religious leaders preach about the importance of religious freedom in a national environment where such arguments were frequently invoked to oppose pandemic-related restrictions on in-person religious services, worshippers in the pews take note and respond accordingly. This also shows that when political or religious leaders politicize religion for partisan purposes by promoting baseless conspiracy theories (such as that a Democratic president would ban the Bible or that coronavirus "hysteria" is politically motivated), many people took note and made special efforts to continue to attend religious services in person in the middle of a pandemic.[2] Had more political and religious leaders instead chosen to support public health officials and emphasized the nonpolitical nature of public health emergencies, in-person worship in the United States would likely have been significantly reduced, thus also significantly reducing the spread of the virus and resulting fatalities.

Conclusion

AMANDA FRIESEN AND PAUL A. DJUPE

Two years after the first novel coronavirus cases were discovered in December 2019, there have been 260 million recorded cases and over 5 million deaths worldwide, with almost 50 million cases and 800,000 deaths in the United States.[1] Though there are global disparities in vaccine availability and access, all Americans over the age of five are eligible, and most can easily access their first round of shots as well as the booster. Around 60 percent of all Americans are fully vaccinated, with 69 percent having at least one dose.[2] Globally, about 50 percent of the population are vaccinated, with wide disparities due to supply and access and, more often than not, vaccine hesitancy and suspicion. Protests have erupted in several European cities as governments circle back to shutdowns in the wake of waves, new variants, and hospitals over capacity. Cases, hospitalizations, and deaths are overwhelmingly concentrated in the unvaccinated. Public health campaigns continue to wage war against misinformation and conspiracy theories. Those vaccinated and even boosted with a third dose also grow tired of the ongoing travel and social restrictions, delays in non–COVID-19 medical care, and the overall persistence of a pandemic that could be better curtailed with cooperation from their fellow citizens. Choosing whether to wear a mask has become a kind of political statement—a shorthand for who to trust, who is a fellow partisan.

It is in this morass that religious communities make decisions about whether to continue to operate, their role in the health of their congregants, and whether to advocate for or against pandemic protocols or remain silent. It is important to remember that in the early days, almost all houses of worship closed, following public health orders (or suggestions in a number of states). That is, the default setting for most congregations was compliance. Many opened again in the fall along with the rest of society. What we haven't known in a systematic way until now is whether clergy stoke these fires, attempt to counter, or remain completely silent. Most appear to have remained silent as only a minority of people report hearing their clergy address the pandemic (see Chapter 6).

Their caution is reflected in the engagement of clergy, which was not nearly unanimous, at least according to those who attend worship services. But this is also what we know about clergy—they face theological limitations that undermine political engagement (Guth et al. 1997; Jelen 1993) and talk about political issues less or at least in a more qualified manner when facing a divided congregation (e.g., Djupe and Neiheisel 2008). The strong, often partisan reactions to the pandemic likely put a lid on how clergy could engage, effectively limiting the public health role of religious institutions. And this comes on top of the contingent that has openly opposed public health measures and are now handing out letters of support for those seeking religious exemptions to vaccine mandates (Bailey 2021).

We can look at this from another angle, which is to start with the degree of threat to a community and gauge the degree of religious engagement with the pandemic. This, then, is one enduring puzzle of the pandemic. The media was full of stories about how racial minority communities were hit hard by the virus, now backed by scientific research (see Chapters 5, 6, and 12), but clergy engagement did not mirror that pattern—frequent attenders across racial and ethnic groups heard their clergy address the pandemic at similar rates. That's curious and not just because the pandemic hit racial minority communities harder. Primarily Black churches also do not suffer the same problems facing political disagreement that other clergy face. That is, since the Black community is almost unanimously Democratic and Black clergy have a long tradition of engagement with pressing problems, why were their rates of addressing the pandemic so (relatively) low? One reason may be the degree of prosperity gospel belief that pervades the Black community (see Chapter 1), but more systematic study is required to make that determination.

We can see the weakness of religious institutions in U.S. pandemic society from the perspective of political theorists from Tocqueville to Neuhaus, who have argued that democracy is only possible within the confines of shared religious values—referred to as the "sacred canopy." Political decisions need "moral legitimation" (Neuhaus 1984), which most often still means a grounding in religion. In response, Ted Jelen (1991) wondered if such a consensus ever existed, and we would add that the pandemic tore gaping holes in that narrative on several fronts. The elevation of radical individual freedom has never had a basis in a world religion but was espoused as religious freedom by those opposed to vaccines. Moreover, it became clear that values, shared or not, were not the operative force as they yielded to institutional interests. The elevation of threat served to keep members beholden to religious and political elites, some pandemic entrepreneurs found an incentive to keep their doors open in opposition to health orders, and still others downplayed the seriousness of the pandemic, at least until they caught the virus themselves, when many changed their tune.

This argument about the weakness of the sacred canopy approach can likely be pushed one step further using the pandemic. At one time, religious involvement was a marker of community integration, which is why religious involvement historically has had such a strong relationship with political participation, civic involvement, civility, and pro-sociality (e.g., Saroglou et al. 2005; Verba, Schlozman, and Brady 1995). But the pandemic appears to show that for a good number of religious adherents, the implicit connection to the community has frayed, perhaps on purpose as Chapter 1 shows. Some worldviews urge an exclusive orientation, keeping society at arm's length. Some worldviews have routed adherents to networks and news sources that are far removed from fact and perniciously promoted the pandemic through conspiracy theories and undermining public health officials (Chapters 2, 9, and 10). And, of course, a sizable contingent of Christian nationalists are fighting against the changing nature of society, which may include the scientific community, looking to enshrine the power of Christian conservatives (Chapter 4). We believe it's fair to say that there is no sacred canopy in the United States, if there ever was one.

Each phase of the pandemic, naturally, has generated new responses from the state and religious groups. The vaccination stage, arriving for most in early 2021, was no different, featuring large numbers of conservatives and especially religious conservatives raising opposition, even a year into vaccinations (PRRI 2021). As a religious historian describes, Bible passages have been "lifted out of context and repurposed to buttress the anti-vaccine movement" (Fea 2021). He also notes that this is nothing new among evangelicals in the United States, whose individualistic faith allows or even promotes "free-wheeling" theological innovation to support preferred outcomes. No small number of religious entrepreneurs have fueled this process and have often attracted large followings. We continue to see evidence of this process unfolding to disastrous public health consequences during the pandemic.

From an academic perspective, one way to read this evidence is a strike against capturing general measures of religiosity. Indeed, from the chapters in this volume, it seems problematic to make blanket assumptions about what the religiously involved experienced or thought. Specific messages and religious beliefs seem to offer much more explanatory power but also enable observers to assess the degree of theological innovation. For instance, there is a wide gap among the unvaccinated, with opposition to vaccination much more likely from their personal religious beliefs versus the "teachings of their religion" (PRRI 2021). Yet widely applicable religiosity measures are still valuable to capture, in part because they offer a way to index the effect of the pandemic on the populace. It interrupted attendance, at least early on, but appears to have had only a marginal effect on belief and affiliation. Of course, these results are not independent of what congregations did—whether they remained open, offered online services, and found creative ways to maintain community.

Our communities were not only beset by pandemic waves. As Vegter and Haider-Markel demonstrate, COVID-19 spread in a year with unprecedented national and international Black Lives Matter protests and a contentious, competitive presidential election (see also Chapter 9). Messaging around racial justice swirled with pleas to "flatten the curve" as centrist Democratic candidate Joe Biden campaigned on unity. While one side responded to 2020 with an ethic of care, the other followed their leader President Trump in downplaying the pandemic, continuing to support police and their actions, and questioning the legitimacy of the election. The latter issues clashed as insurrectionists attacked the U.S. Capitol and its police force on January 6, 2021, claiming election fraud. Christian nationalism reverberates through all these debates, as religious language, imagery, and justification bolster claims that to be American is to be Christian, white, and Republican (Chapter 4). Antipathy toward the Left also surged as frustrations grew around antivaxxers and the "big steal" election conspiracies. Though it is interesting that most people would still offer to save out-partisans, though not Muslims, with their "lifeboats," as Miles and Tucker report in experimental work in Chapter 14.

As evidenced by our chapters on religious freedom and debates about in-person services, 2020 set the stage for more legal arguments about face-to-face worship that are playing out in state legislatures and the courts. With a conservative majority on the U.S. Supreme Court, we are likely to see continued deference to religious freedom claims playing out at the highest levels. Interestingly, those claims have limits as the Supreme Court recently refused to block New York state's vaccine mandate for health care workers that allowed no religious exemptions (Totenberg 2021). Perhaps this decision, though without a formal opinion, starts to clarify the importance of religious burden, which Reinbold discusses in Chapter 8. Successful challenges to state closure orders were brought by religious institutions with an emphasis on liturgy, not those with more individualistic faiths (see Chapter 7 for more). Perhaps the individualistic claims of burden suffered by vaccine mandates are not sufficiently credible to the court. The pandemic is certainly providing them a rich set of cases with which to clarify their views.

We noted in the introduction that the pandemic offered conditions rarely available to researchers: "Everyone is thinking about and reacting to the same thing [and] that thing—the coronavirus—is quite literally 'novel.'" If there was one overarching theme to this volume, it would be the importance of context. As Miles and Tucker argue, "Context determines which identities are salient at any given moment." The role of context is not limited to identity salience, clearly, providing the information, interests, and actors that make up choice scenarios. It has probably never been as important to document individual contexts as well as their understandings of those contexts—perceptions vary widely. What are individuals hearing and facing, and what do individuals think they are facing?

Beyond how religious communities can help or hinder efforts to stem the COVID-19 tide, the pandemic also may have long-lasting impacts on religious life. If we were in the stereotypical coma for a few years, we might not know there was a pandemic from one perspective—surveys in 2021 are reporting a steady rise in religious nones with numbers we could have projected in 2019 (e.g., Smith 2021). It's not that there weren't disruptions during the pandemic; it's that U.S. religion was generally resilient and responded favorably to political and religious encouragement. Then President Trump encouraged people to attend, and so did a small minority of clergy—those parishioners attended in person at much higher rates early in the pandemic (see Knoll's Chapter 16).

The pandemic offered a quite different crisis than previous research had studied, such as 9/11 or natural disasters. Beyerlein and Klocek (Chapter 15) do not see the surge in individual faith that attends such catastrophes and, instead, find individuals picking their way through the pandemic with many online, a small minority of intense believers stubbornly attending in person, and stable rates of private prayer. Perhaps the difference is that the pandemic was largely invisible to most, it decimated communities in slow motion, and some of the most personal impacts came from public health officials (e.g., orders to close). It's entirely possible that the pandemic break early on put some play in the joints and allowed more people to rethink their congregation ties, to try out new congregations, or to cut their congregation loose. Those decisions were likely already in motion, however.

There are so many reasons why a resurgence in interest in religion in minority communities is happening now. Of course, some of the reasons have to do with the Black Lives Matter protests that energized the world to reconsider racial justice. But others argue, rightly, that we don't understand American religion unless we understand race, racism, and racial dynamics in its many forms that permeate American society and politics (see, e.g., Yukich and Edgell 2020). From our perspective, quite a bit of conventional wisdom about the Black community is stuck in a civil rights frame of mind—clergy are expected to be some form of MLK Jr. representing the Black community in full prophetic mode.

While there is some evidence that minority clergy are more likely to represent their congregations in public affairs—that is, as representatives—than whites, that leaves a lot to be explained. Minority Christians are also concerned with teaching the gospel, though it's important to remember how much variation there is among Christians, not to mention the non-Christian religions in the United States. The prosperity gospel, a belief system that is not conducive to following public health orders, has a huge following among African Americans (see Chapter 1). But they are all also concerned with maintaining members against loss to other congregations, which means proving their value on a weekly basis. It's hard to prove your worth if the congregation is closed, so at least some frustration with public health orders was natural. Olson finds minority congregations more likely to be meeting face-to-face early in the pandemic (Chapter 12; see also Chapter 15), which could be the result of the prosperity approach, the religious economy pressures, or some other force. Minority religion is not the same as their white brethren, even within the same religious tradition, but religion in communities of color is also not uniform and solely cut from the civil rights movement cloth. We have much to explore, and the pandemic investigations of minority religion in the United States provides further impetus to do so.

Colloquially, the terminology "in the before times" has developed to describe normal activities before the pandemic. In the "after times," then, do we expect any of these pandemic-induced alterations to remain? For example, with religious communities investing in online infrastructure and improving their virtual service delivery, will this continue once there is no longer COVID-19 spreading concerns? For the elderly or those with disabilities, facing inclement weather, and busy with children, perhaps virtual services will become a way to stay connected to their religious community when they may have otherwise fallen away. Conversely, is there a set of leavers who were just hanging on to church membership that used the pandemic as a way to cut the final thread? Fortunately, researchers are closely attuned to these sorts of questions amid most likely unprecedented data gathering across the social sciences. We'll soon find out.

In the end, we hope this volume has shed light on the continuing role of religion in American public life and how these communities, their leaders, and beliefs shape and are affected by large-scale societal disruptions like the pandemic. We believe they also show the efficacy of continued social-scientific research in such times as especially illuminating about the efficacy and role of religion in public life.

Notes

FOREWORD

1. See Department of Veterans Affairs, Office of Public Affairs, "America's Wars," accessed January 7, 2022, https://www.va.gov/opa/publications/factsheets/fs_americas_wars.pdf.
2. The notable exception to this pattern is the small but growing group of Hispanic Protestants who consistently lean Republican.

INTRODUCTION

1. In an unexpected twist, the Biden administration mandated an investigation of whether COVID-19 was made in the Wuhan lab (Harris and Abutaleb 2021). Regardless of the results of that review, it is important to remember that, "throughout much of the pandemic, the 'lab leak' hypothesis has been ridiculed by scientists as a baseless conspiracy theory, fueled by President Donald Trump in an effort to deflect attention from his administration's botched pandemic response" (Harris and Abutaleb 2021). That is, there was no public evidence at the time of the surveying in 2020, and it was widely acknowledged as a conspiracy theory.

CHAPTER 1

1. Portions of this article have been reprinted with permission by Cambridge University Press. It was originally published as Paul A. Djupe and Ryan P. Burge, "The Prosperity Gospel of Coronavirus Response," *Politics and Religion* 14, no. 3 (2020): 552–573, https://doi.org/10.1017/S175504832000053X. Reproduced with permission. We offer the epigraph as an explanation for the chapter title, which was chosen because it highlights so perfectly the idea that COVID-19 is linked to supernatural forces and the power of religious belief is a sufficient prophylactic.

2. Please see the online appendix for this chapter for an overview of religious belief work that had to be omitted due to space constraints.

3. For about one-third of the sample, there was also a quota for a Hispanic identity. The final returns were very close to the U.S. Census quotas, only missing by a percentage point or two.

4. In an earlier formulation, the question text was not specific enough about when and where blessings would flow from belief. For instance, we had asked, "Our efforts and our sacrifices to God will be richly rewarded." In this survey we asked, "Our efforts and our sacrifices to God will be richly rewarded *in this life*" (emphasis added). We formerly asked, "God will give you what you seek if you give to Him and have faith," but now ask, "God will give you *the material things* you seek if you give to Him and have faith" (emphasis added).

5. The estimate varies with question wording capturing the general concept of the end times. For instance, a 2012 PRRI question asked whether "[T]he end of the world, as predicted in the Book of Revelation, will happen in your lifetime," to which 13 percent agreed. It was only a bit lower from the figure reported by David Barker and David Bearce (2012), who report that 56 percent of Americans believe "in the Second Coming of Jesus Christ—that is, that Jesus will return to Earth someday." It is clearly close to Pew's finding in 2010 that 41 percent believe that by 2050 it is probable or definite that "Jesus Christ will return." It is not clear what exactly generates the variation in response, but the variation does seem to suggest that events heighten agreement in imminent events.

6. The models (coefficients and fit statistics are available in appendix Table A1) also include religious tradition dummies, worship attendance, race, age, gender, and education (the appendix also contains full variable coding). We also decided to square the Prosperity Gospel measure, which allows for nonlinear relationships to emerge. It is important to note that this does not change the estimated effect size; it merely allows for different shapes of the slope to emerge (and it could return a linear slope).

7. In the appendix for this chapter, we have a discussion and present results of an analysis of how the Prosperity Gospel index performs in the context of many other religious measures.

8. The racial composition of the parties looks quite different across the distribution of Prosperity Gospel beliefs—Republicans are uniformly white, but independents and especially Democratic believers are far more likely to be racial minorities (50 percent in the case of Democrats).

CHAPTER 2

1. It is worth noting that more scientific knowledge does not necessarily result in higher acceptance of scientific results and instead may cause the opposite (Landrum and Olshansky 2019). People tend to deny results and use science to confirm their prior beliefs (Lewandowsky, Oberauer, and Gignac 2013).

2. Scholars of conspiracy theories summarize conspiracy thinking as "a political worldview consisting of general feelings of distrust or paranoia toward government services and institutions, feelings of political powerlessness and cynicism, and a general defiance of authority" (Landrum and Oshanky 2019, 194). By contrast, scholars cannot agree on a common definition of religion. Hogg, Adelman, and Blagg (2010, 73) define religion as "a group phenomenon involving group norms that specify beliefs, attitudes, values, and behaviors relating to both sacred and secular aspects of life. . . . Religious groups differ

from other groups in one fundamental way—they invoke the sacred and the divine to render existence meaningful."

3. All interviews were conducted among participants in AmeriSpeak, a probability-based panel designed to be representative of the national U.S. adult population run by NORC at the University of Chicago.

4. This is the only measure related to COVID-19 conspiracy theories in the survey. We recognize the controversy surrounding the idea that the coronavirus was developed in a lab, but as the origins of the virus have not been confirmed, this measure remains in the realm of conspiracy theories.

5. To conduct our statistical analyses, we recoded our dependent variable into 1 and 0. The 0 category, which denotes "the coronavirus developed naturally," includes those who "don't know" or skipped the question due to the very low numbers of cases (18). The inclusion or exclusion of these individuals does not change the results.

6. For example, magical thinking can be present among evangelical Christians who believe in the prosperity gospel. In this chapter, we argue that magical thinking is a cognitive style that is part of the religious thinking of any religion (e.g., belief in a perceived higher power) and it is not only particular to evangelicals.

7. Model 1 in the appendix. Differences in mean predicted probabilities are statistically significant at $p < 0.05$. Evangelical and nonevangelical Protestants are more likely than religiously unaffiliated Americans to believe that COVID-19 is lab made, while there are not statistically significantly differences between those who identify as Catholic, as other Christian (Mormon and Orthodox), or with other religions (Jewish, Muslim, Buddhist, Hindu) from religiously unaffiliated Americans.

CHAPTER 3

1. These statistics represent the number of firearm background checks initiated through the National Instant Criminal Background Check system. These numbers "do not perfectly represent the number of firearms sold" (Federal Bureau of Investigation 2020). Miller, Hepburn, and Azrael (2017) estimated that approximately 20 percent of gun owners reported obtaining their most recent firearm within the previous two years without a background check. It is likely, therefore, that these numbers are underestimates.

CHAPTER 5

1. The usage of "U.S. Public Health Service Syphilis Study" instead of "Tuskegee Experiment" or "Tuskegee Study" is intentional. The often cited "Tuskegee Experiment" places the emphasis on Tuskegee University (a historically Black college/university) and the city of Tuskegee (a historically Black city) regarding the immoral and unethical syphilis experiment. This framing and language deemphasize the role of the U.S. federal government. We honor, recognize, and respond to the way language shapes our ideas about truth in history, ethics, and institutional memory.

CHAPTER 7

1. This chapter has been adapted and expanded from a presentation at the International Conference on Covid-19 Pandemic and Religious Freedom: Reports from North America and Europe, sponsored by Andrews University, the BYU Law School Center for Law and Religion Studies, and the University of Portsmouth, December 2–3, 2020. Portions

of Chapter 7 previously appeared as "The Coronavirus Pandemic and Restrictions on Churches: Evaluating the Christian Legal Movement's Role in Polarizing Religious Freedom," in *Fides et Libertas*, special edition "COVID-19 and Religious Liberty," 2021. Used with permission.

2. In March 2020, the alpha was 0.61, and the eigenvalue was 1.17. In October 2020, the alpha was 0.60, and the eigenvalue was 1.31.

3. For a similar argument about the effects of polarization of reactions to the Supreme Court case dealing with New York's restrictions, see Asma T. Uddin and Andrew Lewis's (2020) *USA Today* op-ed.

CHAPTER 8

1. Indeed, the Court's majority has pointedly located COVID-19 restrictions within the ambit of the Sherbert test. See Reinbold 2021.
2. Agudath Israel of America et al. v. Andrew Cuomo 2020.
3. Agudath Israel of America et al. v. Andrew Cuomo 2020.
4. Roman Catholic Diocese of Brooklyn v. Andrew Cuomo 2020.
5. Roman Catholic Diocese of Brooklyn v. Andrew Cuomo 2020.
6. Roman Catholic Diocese of Brooklyn v. Andrew Cuomo 2020.
7. Cavalry Chapel Dayton Valley v. Steve Sisolak 2020.
8. Cavalry Chapel Dayton Valley v. Steve Sisolak 2020.
9. Pope Francis 2020.
10. Our Sunday Visitor 2020.
11. United States v. Ballard 322 U.S. 78 (1944).
12. United States v. Ballard 322 U.S. 78 (1944).
13. Reagan 1980; Romney 2007.
14. Cox and Jones 2017b.
15. South Bay United Pentecostal Church v. Gavin Newsom 2020.
16. Calvary Chapel v. Sisolak 2020.
17. Alito 2020.
18. Tyler & Bursch, LLP 2020.
19. K. Jones 2020.
20. Calvary Chapel v. Sisolak 2020.
21. Roman Catholic Diocese v. Cuomo 2020.
22. There is every reason to believe that this tendency to defer to religious claimants on the question of whether they are being substantially burdened will increase in coming cases. See Reinbold 2020.
23. See, for example, R. Jones 2016.
24. See, for example, Bennett 2017; FitzGerald 2017.
25. See, for example, Lewis 2017; Reinbold 2018.
26. See, for example, Feldman 2005; Jay Wexler 2019.
27. Cavalry Chapel Dayton Valley v. Steve Sisolak 2020; Roman Catholic Diocese v. Cuomo 2020.

CHAPTER 11

Acknowledgments: The authors would like to thank Paul A. Djupe and Jamil S. Scott for their advice and comments and Paul A. Djupe, Ryan P. Burge, and Andrew R. Lewis for sharing data.

1. While a direct measure of clergywomen within a congregation would be the closest equivalent to women in executive leadership positions in the political realm (e.g., mayors, governors, presidents), a broader measure of "women's leadership" was the closest available measure in the Djupe, Burge, and Lewis (2020) survey. Additionally, in a religious context, there are leadership roles aside from clergy (e.g., deacon) that have similar visibility and functional roles as women legislators. Moreover, using a broader measure of women's leadership allows us to examine the role of women's leadership and COVID-19 responses in more congregations than if we only examined congregations that allow women to serve in the head leadership role. Denominations differ in whether they allow women to serve as clergy (Chaves 1999), but even in denominations that formally allow women to serve as the head pastor or priest, clergymen vastly outnumber clergywomen in America's places of worship. Of Americans who attend worship services, only 9 percent report attending a congregation led by a clergywoman (Knoll and Bolin 2018). In the Djupe, Burge, and Lewis (2020) survey, respondents across religious traditions report similar levels of seeing women lead within their congregations (see the online appendix for more information).

2. See the online appendix for tables containing variable descriptions and measures.

3. The correlation coefficients between whether a respondent had seen women leading and their church attendance, church size, whether they considered themselves to be born-again Christians, and the degree to which they identified as biblical literalists ranges from 0.19 to 0.29.

4. We also estimated logit models. The key coefficients in these models are in the same direction as the key coefficients estimated using linear probability models and have very similar levels of statistical significance.

5. Because there is likely to be a negative relationship between not reporting a religious affiliation and church attendance, responses to the question about in-person services being canceled from individuals who identified as having no religion may be suspect (e.g., perhaps respondents guessed). We therefore estimated this model excluding individuals who reported not having a religion, but the coefficient on having seen women leading in a religious setting remained statistically significant and nearly identical in magnitude.

CHAPTER 13

1. We conducted a nationally representative survey of 1,049 adults, eighteen to twenty-four years old via a Qualtrics online panel during May 19–28, 2020, after shelter-in-place measures were imposed by most U.S. states. While participants in the survey were volunteers (i.e., not a random sample), we constructed the sample to be representative of Gen Z on several metrics (gender, race, socioeconomic status). The data are weighted accordingly. Given our sample size and the corresponding population metrics, we did not have enough respondents to draw reasonable inferences about smaller racial/ethnic groups.

2. In this case, we combine respondents who said they are atheists (7.8 percent), agnostic (7.04 percent), or nothing in particular (24.3 percent) into the religiously unaffiliated category.

3. We first asked survey respondents whether they identified as Protestant, Catholic, Jewish, Mormon, Orthodox Christian, Muslim, Buddhist, Hindu, atheist, agnostic, nothing in particular, or "something else," with the option in the last category to write in their own answers. Given that white respondents make up a larger percentage of the sample, those who answered that they were Protestant or said they were Christian in the something else category were asked whether they identified themselves as an evangelical or

born-again Christian. We classified those respondents who said yes on the latter question as white evangelical Protestants; we classified those who said no as white mainline Protestants.

4. PRRI's 2019 American Values Survey found that 7 percent of Gen Z Americans are white evangelical Protestant, compared with the 5 percent we found in our 2020 survey. Mormons made up 2 percent of PRRI's survey compared with 5 percent in our analysis. Finally, PRRI found that 1 percent of their respondents are Black Catholics, compared with 3 percent in our sample; we have similar measures of Black Protestants in both surveys. Thanks to Natalie Jackson, PRRI's research director, for compiling those numbers for us.

5. The ideological 7-point scale runs from 1 (extremely liberal) to 7 (extremely conservative), with 4 indicating moderate.

6. To interpret more easily the predicted probabilities, we collapsed the ideology measure into three values: liberal, moderate, and conservative.

7. For brevity, we only present and discuss the results for the highest outcome of religious faith—whether a respondent's faith has gotten stronger during COVID. However, the results are similar for the other outcomes of the measure (weakened faith or faith has stayed the same) and are available from the authors upon request.

CHAPTER 14

1. During the analyses, we looked to see if evangelical or born-again Protestants expressed different attitudes; the results are largely the same.

2. See the Trump Twitter Archive for specific tweets: http://www.trumptwitterarchive.com/archive.

CHAPTER 15

1. Order of authorship is alphabetical to denote equal contribution. Direct correspondence to Kraig Beyerlein, University of Notre Dame, Department of Sociology, 4044 Jenkins and Nanovic Halls, Notre Dame, IN 46556.

2. The University of Chicago Divinity School and the Associated Press-NORC Center for Public Affairs Research funded this module.

3. Because information about denominations was not collected as part of the survey, we used race of respondent and self-identification as a "born-again or evangelical Christian" to distinguish among Black, evangelical, and mainline Protestants (Smith et al. 2018).

4. For excellent research assistance for this part of the project, we thank Ella Wisniewski.

5. Twenty states revised their executive orders about religious regulations between the date of their initial enactment in late March and the fielding of our survey. In those cases, we coded the version closest to the date of our survey.

6. Also excluded are respondents who said they typically do not attend a congregation when asked about whether their congregation had closed in response to the COVID-19 pandemic.

7. A survey fielded about a month prior to the one we analyze found that evangelical Protestants were more likely than non-evangelicals to continue in-person religious activity, as well as explicitly support defiance of government restrictions, in states that prohibited religious gatherings or had no restrictions at that time (Djupe 2020).

CHAPTER 16

1. This includes 21.7 percent of Latter-Day Saints, 41.5 percent of Orthodox Christians, 20 percent of Muslims, 26.7 percent of Buddhists, and 10.3 percent of Hindus.

2. This finding is similar to Perry et al. (2020) who found that Christian nationalism—an attitudinal blend of (1) a conception of Americans as God's chosen and protected people, (2) distrust of the news media, and (3) allegiance to President Donald Trump—was the strongest predictor of disregarding recommendations from public health officials when it came to social distancing, washing hands, wearing a mask, and so on. The key difference in our current analysis is that communication from religious and political elites played a key factor in religious behavior during the pandemic while Perry et al. focus on the effect of preexisting political and societal attitudes.

CONCLUSION

1. Johns Hopkins University and Medicine, Coronavirus Resource Center, "COVID-19 Dashboard," last updated June 10, 2022, https://coronavirus.jhu.edu/map.html.

2. Centers for Disease Control and Prevention, "COVID-19 Vaccinations in the United States," COVID Data Tracker, last updated June 10, 2022, https://covid.cdc.gov/covid-data-tracker/#vaccinations_vacc-total-admin-rate-total.

References

Abalakina-Paap, Marina, Walter G. Stephan, Traci Craig, and W. Larry Gregory. 1999. "Beliefs in Conspiracies." *Political Psychology* 20(3): 637–47.

Abrams, Dominic, and Michael A. Hogg. 1999. *Social Identity and Social Cognition*. Oxford: Blackwell.

Abu-Raiya, Hisham, Tali Sasson, Kenneth I. Pargament, and David H. Rosmarin. 2020. "Religious Coping and Health and Well-Being among Jews and Muslims in Israel." *International Journal for the Psychology of Religion* 30(3): 202–15.

Adams, Leah M., and Jane M. Simoni. 2016. "The Need for Multi-Level Mitigation of Medical Mistrust among Social Network Members Contributing to Antiretroviral Treatment Nonadherence in African Americans Living with HIV: Comment on Bogart et al. (2016)." *Social Science and Medicine* 159:58–60.

Agudath Israel of America et al. v. Andrew Cuomo, Governor of New York. S. Ct. 20–3572 (2020). Emergency Application for Writ of Injunction. 2020. Accessed December 16, 2021. https://www.supremecourt.gov/DocketPDF/20/20A90/160811/20201116134517389_Agudath%20Israel%20v.%20Cuomo%20-%20Emergency%20Application%20for%20Writ%20of%20Injunction.pdf.

Akintobi, Tabia Henry, Theresa Jacobs, Darrell Sabbs, Kisha Holden, Ronald Braithwaite, L. Neicey Johnson, Daniel Dawes, and LaShawn Hoffman. 2020. "Community Engagement of African Americans in the Era of COVID-19: Considerations, Challenges, Implications, and Recommendations for Public Health." *Preventing Chronic Disease* 17:10.

Alawiyah, Tuti, Holly Bell, Loretta Pyles, and Ratonia C. Runnels. 2011. "Spirituality and Faith-Based Interventions: Pathways to Disaster Resilience for African American Hurricane Katrina Survivors." *Journal of Religion and Spirituality in Social Work: Social Thought* 30(3): 294–319.

Aldrich, Andrea S., and Nicholas J. Lotito. 2020. "Pandemic Performance: Women Leaders in the Covid-19 Crisis." *Politics and Gender* 16(4): 960–67.

Alfano, Vincenzo, Salvatore Ercolano, and Gaetano Vecchione. 2020. *Religious Attendance and COVID-19: Evidences from Italian Regions*. CESifo Working Paper 8596.

Algara, Carlos, Sam Fuller, and Christopher Hare. 2020. "The Conditional Effects of Scientific Knowledge and Gender on Support for COVID-19 Government Containment Policies in a Partisan America." *Politics and Gender* 16(4): 1075–83.

Alimi, Toni, Elizabeth L. Antus, Alda Balthrop-Lewis, James F. Childress, Shannon Dunn, Ronald M. Green, Eric Gregory, Jennifer A. Herdt, Willis Jenkins, M. Cathleen Kaveny, Vincent W. Lloyd, Ping-Cheung Lo, Jonathan Malesic, David Newheiser, Irene Oh, and Aaron Stalnaker. 2020. "COVID-19 and Religious Ethics." *Journal of Religious Ethics* 48(3): 349–87.

Alito, Samuel. 2020. "Address by Justice Samuel Alito." Federalist Society, November 12, 2020. https://www.youtube.com/watch?v=tYLZL4GZVbA.

Alliance Defending Freedom. 2020a. "ADF to 9th Circuit: Strike Down NV Governor's Rule Treating Churches Worse than Casinos." ADFmedia.org, December 7, 2020. http://www.adfmedia.org/News/PRDetail/11145.

———. 2020b. "Oregon Governor Sued over COVID-19 Order that Allows Numerous Gatherings, Restricts Churches." ADFmedia.org, May 26, 2020. http://www.adfmedia.org/News/PRDetail/11001.

———. 2020c. "US Supreme Court Halts NY Governor's Rules that Treat Churches, Synagogues Worse than Businesses." ADFmedia.org, November 26, 2020. http://www.adfmedia.org/News/PRDetail/11140.

All Things Considered. 2020. "How 1 Maine Wedding Caused Hundreds of Coronavirus Cases and 7 Deaths." NPR, September 16, 2020. https://www.npr.org/2020/09/16/913693778/how-1-maine-wedding-caused-hundreds-of-coronavirus-cases-and-7-deaths.

American Psychological Association. 2020. "Stress in America 2020 Survey Signals a Growing National Mental Health Crisis." APA.org, October 20, 2020. https://www.apa.org/news/press/releases/2020/10/stress-mental-health-crisis.

Andrade, Gabriel. 2020. "Medical Conspiracy Theories: Cognitive Science and Implications for Ethics." *Medicine, Health Care, and Philosophy* 23(3): 505–18.

Andres-Henao, Luis, and David Crary. 2020. "2 Hispanic Churches and Too Many Tears: 100 COVID-19 Deaths." Religion News, May 13, 2020. https://religionnews.com/2020/05/13/2-hispanic-churches-and-too-many-tears-100-covid-19-deaths/.

Angrist, Joshua D., and Jörn-Steffen Pischke. 2008. *Mostly Harmless Econometrics: An Empiricist's Companion*. Princeton, NJ: Princeton University Press.

Ano, Gene G., and Erin B. Vasconcelles. 2005. "Religious Coping and Psychological Adjustment to Stress: A Meta-Analysis." *Journal of Clinical Psychology* 61(4): 461–80.

AP-NORC. 2020. "Religious Practice in the Time of Coronavirus." AP-NORC. Accessed December 12, 2021. https://apnorc.org/projects/religious-practice-in-the-time-of-coronavirus/.

Apuzzo, Matt, and David D. Kirkpatrick. 2020. "Covid-19 Changed How the World Does Science, Together." *New York Times*, April 1, 2020. https://www.nytimes.com/2020/04/01/world/europe/coronavirus-science-research-cooperation.html.

Armfield, Greg G., and R. Lance Holbert. 2003. "The Relationship between Religiosity and Internet Use." *Journal of Media and Religion* 2(3): 129–44.

Artiga, Samantha, and Elizabeth Hinton. 2018. "Beyond Health Care: The Role of Social Determinants in Promoting Health and Health Equity." Kaiser Family Foundation, May 10, 2018. https://www.kff.org/racial-equity-and-health-policy/issue-brief/beyond-health-care-the-role-of-social-determinants-in-promoting-health-and-health-equity/.

Ash, Elliott, Sergio Galletta, Dominik Hangartner, Yotam Margalit, and Matteo Pinna. 2020. "The Effect of Fox News on Health Behavior during COVID-19." Center for Law and Economics Working Paper Series 10, June 26, 2020.

Associated Press. 2020a. "After Trump Diagnosis, Republicans Continue to Fight Virus Restrictions." *Tampa Bay Times*, October 3, 2020. https://www.tampabay.com/news/health/2020/10/03/after-trump-diagnosis-republicans-continue-to-fight-virus-restrictions/.

———. 2020b. "Pastor Defies House Arrest, Again Holds Service during Virus." AP News, April 26, 2020. https://apnews.com/article/8151dfc516d9aad07404f30fd62dceff.

Atkeson, Lonna Rae. 2003. "Not All Cues Are Created Equal: The Conditional Impact of Female Candidates on Political Engagement." *Journal of Politics* 65(4): 1040–61.

Atkeson, Lonna Rae, and Nancy Carrillo. 2007. "More Is Better: The Influence of Collective Female Descriptive Representation on External Efficacy." *Politics and Gender* 3(1): 79–101.

Ayers, John W., and C. Richard Hofstetter. 2008. "American Muslim Political Participation Following 9/11: Religious Belief, Political Resources, Social Structures, and Political Awareness." *Politics and Religion* 1(1): 3–26.

Azrael, Deborah, Lisa Hepburn, David Hemenway, and Matthew Miller. 2017. "The Stock and Flow of U.S. Firearms: Results from the 2015 National Firearms Survey." *RSF: The Russell Sage Foundation Journal of the Social Sciences* 3(5): 38–57.

Bae, Yong-Soo, Eui-Cheol Shin, Yoe-Sik Bae, and Willem Van Eden. 2019. "Editorial: Stress and Immunity." *Frontiers in Immunology* 10:245.

Bailey, Sarah Pulliam. 2020. "What NIH Chief Francis Collins Wants Religious Leaders to Know about the Coronavirus Vaccines." Washington Post, December 12, 2020. https://www.washingtonpost.com/religion/2020/12/12/coronavirus-vaccine-nih-francis-collins-faith-leaders/.

———. 2021. "Religious Exemptions from Coronavirus Vaccines Are Expected to Become a Legal Battleground." *Washington Post*, September 1, 2021. https://www.washingtonpost.com/religion/2021/09/01/religious-exemptions-covid-19-mandates/.

Baker, Joseph O., Samuel L. Perry, and Andrew L. Whitehead. 2020a. "Crusading for Moral Authority: Christian Nationalism and Opposition to Science." *Sociological Forum* 35(3): 587–607.

———. 2020b. "Keep America Christian (and White): Christian Nationalism, Fear of Ethnoracial Outsiders, and Intention to Vote for Donald Trump in the 2020 Presidential Election." *Sociology of Religion* 81(3): 272–93.

Bansak, Kirk, Jens Hainmueller, Daniel J. Hopkins, and Teppei Yamamoto. 2018. "The Number of Choice Tasks and Survey Satisficing in Conjoint Experiments." *Political Analysis* 26(1): 112–19.

———. 2019. "Beyond the Breaking Point? Survey Satisficing in Conjoint Experiments." *Politcal Science Research and Methods* 9(1): 53–71.

Barabas, Jason, and Jennifer Jerit. 2009. "Estimating the Causal Effects of Media Coverage on Policy-Specific Knowledge." *American Journal of Political Science* 53(1): 73–89.

Barker, David C., and David H. Bearce. 2012. "End-Times Theology, the Shadow of the Future, and Public Resistance to Addressing Global Climate Change." *Political Research Quarterly* 66(2): 267–79.

Bauer, Nichole M., Jeong Hyun Kim, and Yesola Kweon. 2020. "Women Leaders and Policy Compliance during a Public Health Crisis." *Politics and Gender* 16(4): 975–82.

BBC News. 2020. "Coronavirus: Outcry after Trump Suggests Injecting Disinfectant as Treatment." BBC News, June 9, 2020. https://www.bbc.com/news/world-us-canada-52407177.

Beck, Sedefka V., and Sara J. Gundersen. 2016. "A Gospel of Prosperity? An Analysis of the Relationship between Religion and Earned Income in Ghana, the Most Religious Country in the World." *Journal for the Scientific Study of Religion* 55(1): 105–29.

Becker, Amy Julia, Dale Hanson Bourke, Mae Elise Cannon, Rob Dalrymple, Richard Foster, Marlena Graves, Chris Hall, Daniel Hill, Evan B. Howard, Sam Logan, George Marsden, Rich Mouw, Natasha Sistrunk Robinson, Ron Sider, and Nikki Toyama-Szeto. 2019. "An Open Letter from Friends of Christianity Today Affirming Mark Galli's Editorial." Religious News Service, December 24, 2019. https://religionnews.com/2019/12/24/an-open-letter-from-friends-of-christianity-today-affirming-mark-gallis-editorial/.

Beckman, Howard B., and Richard Frankel. 1984. "The Effect of Physician Behavior on the Collection of Data." *Annals of Internal Medicine* 101(5): 692–96.

Belloc, Marianna, Francesco Drago, and Roberto Galbiati. 2016. "Earthquakes, Religion, and Transition to Self-Government in Italian Cities." *Quarterly Journal of Economics* 131(4): 1875–926.

Benkert, Ramona, Adolfo Cuevas, Hayley S. Thompson, Emily Dove-Meadows, and Donulae Knuckles. 2019. "Ubiquitous yet Unclear: A Systematic Review of Medical Mistrust." *Behavioral Medicine* 45(2): 86–101.

Bennett, Daniel. 2017. *Defending Faith: The Politics of the Christian Conservative Legal Movement*. Lawrence: University Press of Kansas.

Bennett, Daniel, and Andrew R. Lewis. 2021. "The Coronavirus Pandemic and Restrictions on Churches: Evaluating the Christian Legal Movement's Role in Polarizing Religious Freedom." *Fides et Libertas*. Forthcoming.

Ben-Nun Bloom, Pazit, and Gizem Arikan. 2013. "Priming Religious Belief and Religious Social Behavior Affects Support for Democracy." *International Journal of Public Opinion Research* 25(3): 368–82.

Ben-Nun Bloom, Pazit, and Marie Courtemanche. 2015. "Religion, Morality, and Tolerance." In *Religion and Political Tolerance in America: Advances in the State of the Art*, edited by Paul A. Djupe, 100–16. Philadelphia: Temple University Press.

Bentzen, Jeanet Sinding. 2019. "Acts of God? Religiosity and Natural Disasters across Subnational World Districts." *Economic Journal* 129(622): 2295–321.

———. 2020. *In Crisis We Pray: Religiosity and the COVID-19*. London: Centre for Economic Policy Research.

———. 2020a. "In Crisis, We Pray: Religiosity and the COVID-19 Pandemic." *Journal of Economic Behavior and Organization* 192:541–83.

———. 2020b. "Rising Religiosity as a Global Response to COVID-19 Fear." Vox EU, June 9, 2020. https://voxeu.org/article/rising-religiosity-global-response-COVID-19-fear.

Berkman, Michael B., and Robert E. O'Connor. 1993. "Do Women Legislators Matter? Female Legislators and State Abortion Policy." *American Politics Quarterly* 21(1): 102–24.

Beyerlein, Kraig, David Nirenberg, and Geneviève Zubrzycki. 2021. "Theodicy and Crisis: Explaining Variation in U.S. Believers' Faith Response to the COVID-19 Pandemic." *Sociology of Religion* 82(4): 494–517.

Blank, Joshua M., and Daron Shaw. 2015. "Does Partisanship Shape Attitudes toward Science and Public Policy? The Case for Ideology and Religion." *Annals of the American Academy of Political and Social Science* 658:18–35.

Blank, Michael B., Marcus Mahmood, Jeanne C. Fox, and Thomas Guterbock. 2002. "Alternative Mental Health Services: The Role of the Black Church in the South." *American Journal of Public Health* 92(10): 1668–72.

Bogart, Laura M., Bisola O. Ojikutu, Keshav Tyagi, David J. Klein, Matt G. Mutchler, Lu Dong, Sean J. Lawrence, Damone R. Thomas, and Sarah Kellman. 2021. "COVID-19 Related Medical Mistrust, Health Impacts, and Potential Vaccine Hesitancy among Black Americans Living with HIV." *Journal of Acquired Immune Deficiency Syndromes* 86(2): 200–207.

Bogart, Laura M., and Sheryl Thorburn. 2006. "Relationship of African Americans' Sociodemographic Characteristics to Belief in Conspiracies About HIV/AIDS and Birth Control." *Journal of the National Medical Association* 98(7): 1144–50.

Bonanno, George A., and John T. Jost. 2006. "Conservative Shift among High-Exposure Survivors of the September 11th Terrorist Attacks." *Basic and Applied Social Psychology* 28(4): 311–23.

Boorstein, Michelle. 2020. "Covid-19 Has Killed Multiple Bishops and Pastors within the Nation's Largest Black Pentecostal Denomination." *Washington Post*, April 19, 2020. https://www.washingtonpost.com/religion/2020/04/19/church-of-god-in-christ-pentecostal-coronavirus-kills-bishops/.

Bowler, Kate. 2018. *Blessed: A History of the American Prosperity Gospel*. New York: Oxford University Press.

Brandt, Allan M. 1978. "Racism and Research: The Case of the Tuskegee Syphilis Study." *Hastings Center Report* 8(6): 21–29.

Braun, Stephen, Hope Yen, and Calvin Woodward. 2020. "AP Fact Check: Trump and the Virus-Era China Ban that Isn't." AP News, July 18, 2020. https://apnews.com/article/d227b34b168e576bf5068b92a03c003d.

Braunstein, Ruth, and Malaena Taylor. 2017. "Is the Tea Party a 'Religious' Movement? Religiosity in the Tea Party versus the Religious Right." *Sociology of Religion* 78(1): 33–59.

Broockman, David E. 2014. "Do Female Politicians Empower Women to Vote or Run for Office? A Regression Discontinuity Approach." *Electoral Studies* 34:190–204.

Brooks, Deborah J., and Lydia Saad. 2020. "Double Whammy: Why the Underrepresentation of Women among Workplace and Political Decision-Makers Matters in Pandemic Times." *Politics and Gender* 16(4): 1110–22.

Brossard, Dominique, and Matthew C. Nisbet. 2007. "Deference to Scientific Authority among a Low Information Public: Understanding US Opinion on Agricultural Biotechnology." *International Journal of Public Opinion Research* 19(1): 24–52.

Brouwer, Steve, Paul Gifford, and Susan D. Rose. 1996. *Exporting the American Gospel: Global Christian Fundamentalism.* New York: Routledge.

Brown, Nadia E. 2014. *Sisters in the Statehouse: Black Women and Legislative Decision Making.* Oxford University Press.

Brown, R. Khari. 2009. "Racial/Ethnic Differences in the Political Behavior of American Religious Congregations." *Sociological Spectrum* 29(2): 227–48.

———. 2010. "Religion, Economic Concerns, and African American Immigration Attitudes." *Review of Religious Research* 52(2): 146–58.

Brown, R. Khari., and Ronald E. Brown. 2017. "Race, Religion, and Immigration Policy Attitudes." *Race and Social Problems* 9(1): 4–18.

Brown, R. Khari, Angela Kaiser, Lara Rush, and Ronald E. Brown. 2017. "Immigrant-Conscious Congregations: Race, Ethnicity, and the Rejection of Anti-Immigrant Frames." *Politics and Religion* 10(4): 887–905.

Brown, Steven P. 2002. *Trumping Religion: The New Christian Right, the Free Speech Clause, and the Courts.* Tuscaloosa: University of Alabama Press.

Buchanan, Larry, Quoctrung Bui, and Jugal K. Patel. 2020. "Black Lives Matter May Be the Largest Movement in U.S. History." *New York Times*, July 3, 2020. https://www.nytimes.com/interactive/2020/07/03/us/george-floyd-protests-crowd-size.html.

Burge, Ryan P. 2017a. "Do Americans Believe in the Prosperity Gospel? Here's What the Data Says." *Religion in Public* (blog), November 21, 2017. https://religioninpublic.blog/2017/11/21/do-americans-believe-in-the-prosperity-gospel-heres-what-the-data-says/.

———. 2017b. "How Does Being White Shape Evangelicals' Voting Habits?" *Religion in Public* (blog), November 6, 2017. https://religioninpublic.blog/2017/11/06/how-does-being-white-shape-evangelicals-voting-habits/.

———. 2020. "Where Do White Evangelicals Get Their Coronavirus News? The White House." News & Reporting. May 14. https://www.christianitytoday.com/news/2020/may/evangelicals-trump-media-public-health-response-coronavirus.html.

Burge, Ryan P., and Paul A. Djupe. 2019. "What Is a Black Protestant? Why Are They Their Own Category?" *Religion in Public* (blog), June 24, 2019. https://religioninpublic.blog/2019/06/24/what-is-a-black-protestant-why-are-they-their-own-category/.

———. 2022. "Religious Authority in a Democratic Society: Clergy and Citizen Evidence from a New Measure." *Politics and Religion* 15(1): 169–96. https://doi.org/10.1017/S1755048321000031.

Burge, Ryan P., and Andrew R. Lewis. 2018. "Measuring Evangelicals: Practical Considerations for Social Scientists." *Politics and Religion* 11(4): 745–59.

Burke, Daniel. 2020. "Police Arrest Florida Pastor for Holding Church Services Despite Stay-at-Home Order." CNN, March 30, 2020. https://www.cnn.com/2020/03/30/us/florida-pastor-arrested-river-church/index.html.

Burns, Alexander. 2020. "Trump's Closing Argument on Virus Clashes with Science, and Voters' Lives." *New York Times*, October 28, 2020. https://www.nytimes.com/2020/10/28/us/politics/trump-coronavirus.html.

Bush, Daniel. 2015. "Could Trump's Anti-Muslim Rhetoric Influence Politics Well Beyond 2016?" PBS News Hour, December 11, 2015. https://www.pbs.org/newshour/politics/could-trumps-anti-muslim-rhetoric-influence-politics-well-beyond-2016.

Cacciatore, Michael W., Nick Browning, Dietram A. Scheufele, Dominique Brossard, Michael A. Xenos, and Elizabeth A. Corley. 2018. "Opposing Ends of the Spectrum: Exploring Trust in Scientific and Religious Authorities." *Public Understanding of Science* 27(1): 11–28.

Calfano, Brian R., Nazita Lajevardi, and Melissa R. Michelson. 2019. "Trumped Up Challenges: Limitations, Opportunities, and the Future of Political Research on Muslim Americans." *Politics, Groups, and Identities* 7(2): 477–87.

Calhoun-Brown, Allison. 1998. "The Politics of Black Evangelicals: What Hinders Diversity in the Christian Right?" *American Politics Quarterly* 26(1): 81–109.

Calvary Chapel v. Steve Sisolak. 591 S. Ct. 19A1070. 2020. https://www.supremecourt.gov/opinions/19pdf/19a1070_08l1.pdf.

Campbell, David E. 2020. "The Perils of Politicized Religion." *Daedalus* 149(3): 87–104.

Campbell, David E., Geoffrey C. Layman, and John C. Green. 2020. *Secular Surge: A New Fault Line in American Politics*. New York: Cambridge University Press.

Campbell, David E., and Christina Wolbrecht. 2006. "See Jane Run: Women Politicians as Role Models for Adolescents." *Journal of Politics* 68(2): 233–47.

Carney, Jordain. 2020. "Cotton: Trump Should Use Insurrection Act to Deploy Active-Duty Military to Cities." The Hill, June 1, 2020. https://thehill.com/homenews/senate/500449-cotton-trump-should-use-insurrection-act-to-deploy-active-duty-military-to.

Cassese, Erin C., Christina E. Farhart, and Joanne M. Miller. 2020. "Gender Differences in COVID-19 Conspiracy Theory Beliefs." *Politics and Gender* 16(4): 1009–18.

Castle, Jeremiah J. 2019. "New Fronts in the Culture Wars?" *American Politics Research* 47(3): 650–79.

Cathey, Libby. 2020. "Timeline: Tracking Trump alongside Scientific Developments on Hydroxychloroquine." ABC News, August 8, 2020. https://abcnews.go.com/Health/timeline-tracking-trump-alongside-scientific-developments-hydroxychloroquine/story?id=72170553.

Cavalry Chapel Dayton Valley v. Steve Sisolak, Emergency Application for an Injunction. 2020. https://adflegal.org/sites/default/files/2020-07/Calvary-Chapel-Dayton-Valley-v-Sisolak-Emergency-Application.pdf.

Celinska, Katarzyna. 2007. "Individualism and Collectivism in America: The Case of Gun Ownership and Attitudes toward Gun Control." *Sociological Perspectives* 50(2): 229–47.

Centers for Disease Control and Prevention. 2022. "Health Equity Considerations and Racial and Ethnic Minority Groups." CDC.gov, updated January 25, 2022. https://www.cdc.gov/coronavirus/2019-ncov/community/health-equity/race-ethnicity.html.

---. 2022. "Risk for COVID-19 Infection, Hospitalization, and Death by Race/Ethnicity." CDC.gov, updated June 2, 2022. https://www.cdc.gov/coronavirus/2019-ncov/covid-data/investigations-discovery/hospitalization-death-by-race-ethnicity.html.

Chan, Christian S., and Jean E. Rhodes. 2013. "Religious Coping, Posttraumatic Stress, Psychological Distress, and Posttraumatic Growth among Female Survivors Four Years after Hurricane Katrina." *Journal of Traumatic Stress* 26(2): 257–65.

Chan, Nathan K., and Davin L. Phoenix. 2020. "The Ties that Bind: Assessing the Effects of Political and Racial Church Homogeneity on Asian American Political Participation." *Politics and Religion* 13(3): 639–70.

Chaves, Mark. 1999. *Ordaining Women: Culture and Conflict in Religious Organizations.* Cambridge, MA: Harvard University Press.

Clark, Janet. 1998. "Women at the National Level: An Update on Roll Call Voting Behavior." In *Women and Elective Office: Past, Present, and Future*, edited by Sue Thomas and Clyde Wilcox, 118–29. New York: Oxford University Press.

Clark, Megan. 2020. "Closing Doors Is Boosting Church Attendance, but Can Online Activity Stem Christianity's Decline?" *Newsweek*, February 12, 2020. https://www.newsweek.com/closing-doors-boosting-church-attendance-can-online-activity-stem-christianitys-decline-1497286.

Clark, Peter A. 1998. "A Legacy of Mistrust: African-Americans, the Medical Profession, and AIDS." *Linacre Quarterly* 65(1): 66–88.

Clark-Ginsberg, Aaron, and Elizabeth L. Petrun Sayers. 2020. "Communication Missteps during COVID-19 Hurt Those Already Most at Risk." *Journal of Contingencies and Crisis Management* 28(4): 482–84.

Closson, David. 2020 "The 2020 Election: A Clear Distinction on Abortion." Public Discourse, September 20, 2020. https://www.thepublicdiscourse.com/2020/09/71555/.

CNN. 2020. "Despite Warnings, Churchgoers Explain Why They're Still Going to Services." CNN, April 4, 2020. https://www.cnn.com/videos/us/2020/04/04/ohio-church-service-covid-19-pandemic-tuchman-pkg-ac360-vpx.cnn.

Collier, Kiah, Perla Trevizo, and Vianna Davilla. 2020. "Despite Coronavirus Risks, Some Texas Religious Groups Are Worshipping in Person—with the Governor's Blessing." *Texas Tribune*, February 15, 2020. https://www.texastribune.org/2020/04/02/texas-churches-coronavirus-stay-open/.

Conger, Kate, Jack Healy, and Lucy Tompkins. 2020. "Churches Were Eager to Reopen. Now They Are Confronting Coronavirus Cases." *The New York Times*, July 8, 2020, sec. U.S. https://www.nytimes.com/2020/07/08/us/coronavirus-churches-outbreaks.html.

Coppock, Alexander, and Oliver A. McClellan. 2019. "Validating the Demographic, Political, Psychological, and Experimental Results Obtained from a New Source of Online Survey Respondents." *Research and Politics* 6(1): 1–14.

Corcoran, Katie E., Christopher P. Scheitle, and Bernard D. DiGregorio. 2021. "Christian Nationalism and COVID-19 Vaccine Hesitancy and Uptake." *Vaccine* 39(45): 6614–21.

Coscieme, Luca, Lorenzo Fioramonti, Lars F. Mortensen, Kate E. Pickett, Ida Kubiszewski, Hunter Lovins, Jacqueline McGlade, et al. 2020. "Women in Power: Female Leadership and Public Health Outcomes during the COVID-19 Pandemic." MedRxiv, July 16, 2020.

Courage, Katherine Harmon. 2020. "Why More Young People Are Getting Sick in the Latest Covid-19 Outbreaks." Vox, July 18, 2020. https://www.vox.com/2020/7/18/21328358/covid-19-cases-by-age-florida-arizona-texas-miami.

Courtemanche, Marie, and Joanne Connor Green. 2017. "The Influence of Women Legislators on State Health Care Spending for the Poor." *Social Sciences* 6(2): 40.

COVID Tracking Project. 2020. "The COVID Racial Data Tracker." *The Atlantic*. Accessed November 17, 2020. https://covidtracking.com/race.

Cox, Daniel A., Karlyn Bowman, and Jacqueline Clemence. 2020. "Fear, Frustration, and Faith: Americans Respond to the Coronavirus Outbreak." AEI, April 2, 2020. https://www.aei.org/research-products/report/fear-frustration-and-faith-americans-respond-to-the-coronavirus-outbreak/.

Cox, Daniel, and Robert P. Jones. 2017a. "American's Changing Religious Identity." PRRI.org, September 6, 2017. https://www.prri.org/research/american-religious-landscape-christian-religiously-unaffiliated/.

———. 2017b. "Majority of Americans Oppose Transgender Bathroom Restrictions." PRRI.org, March 10, 2017. https://www.prri.org/research/lgbt-transgender-bathroom-discrimination-religious-liberty.

Cox, Daniel, Robert P. Jones, and Juhem Navarro-Rivera. 2015. "Nonreligious Tolerance." In *Religion and Political Tolerance in America: Advances in the State of the Art*, edited by Paul A. Djupe, 131–50. Philadelphia: Temple University Press.

Cox, Daniel, Juhem Navarro-Rivera, and Daniel Jones. 2013. "Americans Say Better Mental Health Screenings Best Way to Prevent Future Mass Shootings." *PRRI* (blog). 2013. https://www.prri.org/research/january-2013-tracking-poll/.

Coyne, Marley. 2020. "In Idaho, Lawmakers Flout Stay-at-Home Requirements—and Encourage Others to Follow Suit." *Forbes*, April 7, 2020. https://www.forbes.com/sites/marleycoyne/2020/04/07/in-idaho-lawmakers-flout-stay-at-home-requirements--and-encourage-others-to-follow-suit/#6daa4be120cc.

Crary, David. 2020. "Religious Leaders Worldwide, across Faiths Who Died in 2020." AP News, December 31, 2020. https://apnews.com/article/new-york-coronavirus-pandemic-sierra-leone-africa-brooklyn-6b3429c6638f9255da962b808ac890b8.

Cummings, William. 2020. "'Battle for the Soul of the Nation': Before They Were Running Mates, Joe Biden and Kamala Harris Both Used Slogan." *USA Today*, August 13, 2020. https://www.usatoday.com/story/news/politics/elections/2020/08/13/biden-and-harris-both-see-election-fight-soul-nation/3355971001/.

Czachor, Emily. 2020. "Trump Warns Catholic Voters Democrats Want Them 'Out of Business,' Says He 'Saved the Second Amendment.'" *Newsweek*, August 5, 2020. https://www.newsweek.com/trump-warns-catholic-voters-democrats-want-them-out-business-says-he-saved-second-amendment-1523089.

Dahab, Ramsey, and Marisa Omori. 2019. "Homegrown Foreigners: How Christian Nationalism and Nativist Attitudes Impact Muslim Civil Liberties." *Ethnic and Racial Studies* 42(10): 1727–46.

Dall, Chris. 2020. "Studies Spotlight High COVID-19 Infection Rate in US Prisons." Center for Infectious Disease Research and Policy, August 21, 2020. https://www

.cidrap.umn.edu/news-perspective/2020/08/studies-spotlight-high-covid-19-infection-rate-us-prisons.

Dallas, Kelsey. 2020. "More Prayer, Fewer Donations: How the Coronavirus Is Changing People's Religious Habits." *Deseret News*, April 4, 2020. https://www.deseret.com/indepth/2020/4/4/21203565/coronavirus-utah-covid-19-prayer-religion-faith-church-mosque-synagogue-god-research-pew.

Dallas, Kelsey, and Matthew Brown. 2019. "Would the Equality Act Harm Religious Freedom? Here's What You Need to Know." *Deseret News*, March 13, 2020. https://www.deseret.com/2019/3/13/20668346/would-the-equality-act-harm-religious-freedom-here-s-what-you-need-to-know#rep-david-cicilline-d-r-i-center-speaks-during-a-news-conference-to-introduce-the-equality-act-a-comprehensive-non discrimination-bill-for-lgbt-rights-at-the-capitol-on-wednesday-march-13-2019-in-washington.

Davis, Joshua T. 2018. "Enforcing Christian Nationalism: Examining the Link between Group Identity and Punitive Attitudes in the United States." *Journal for the Scientific Study of Religion* 57(2): 300–17.

Davis, Joshua T., and Samuel L. Perry. 2020. "White Christian Nationalism and Relative Political Tolerance for Racists." *Social Problems* 68(3): 513–34.

Day, Katie. 2001. "The Southern Poverty Law Center." *Journal of Religious and Theological Information* 4(2): 49–50.

Decker, Jefferson. 2016. *The Other Rights Revolution: Conservative Lawyers and the Remaking of American Government.* New York: Oxford University Press.

Deckman, Melissa M. 2020. "Generation Z and Religion: What New Data Show." *Religion in Public* (blog), February 10, 2020. https://religioninpublic.blog/2020/02/10/generation-z-and-religion-what-new-data-show/.

Deckman, Melissa M., Sue E. S. Crawford, Laura R. Olson, and John C. Green. 2003. "Clergy and the Politics of Gender." *Journal for the Scientific Study of Religion* 42(4): 621–31.

Deckman, Melissa, Jared McDonald, Stella Rouse, and Mileah Kromer. 2020. "Gen Z, Gender, and COVID-19." *Politics and Gender* 16(4): 1019–27.

Dein, Simon, Kate Loewenthal, Christopher Alan Lewis, and Kenneth I. Pargament. 2020. "COVID-19, Mental Health and Religion: An Agenda for Future Research." *Mental Health, Religion and Culture* 23(1): 1–9.

Delehanty, Jack, Penny Edgell, and Evan Stewart. 2019. "Christian America? Secularized Evangelical Discourse and the Boundaries of National Belonging." *Social Forces* 97(3): 1283–306.

Del Rio, White. 2012. "Separating Spirituality from Religiosity: A Hylomorphic Attitudinal Perspective." *Psychology of Religion and Spirituality* 4(2): 123–42.

Depetris-Chauvin, Emilio. 2015. "Fear of Obama: An Empirical Study of the Demand for Guns and the U.S. 2008 Presidential Election." *Journal of Public Economics* 130(October): 66–79.

DeSipio, Louis. 2007. "Power in the Pews? Religious Diversity and Latino Political Attitudes and Behaviors." In *From Pews to Polling Places: Faith and Politics in the American Religious Mosaic*, edited by J. Matthew Wilson, 161–84. Washington, DC: Georgetown University Press.

Diamond, Irene. 1977. *Sex Roles in the State House.* New Haven, CT: Yale University Press.

Diamond, Sara. 2000. *Not by Politics Alone*. New York: Guilford.
Dias, Elizabeth. 2020. "After Weeks on Zoom, Churches Consider Plans to Reopen." *New York Times*, February 10, 2020. https://www.nytimes.com/2020/05/07/us/church-reopening-coronavirus.html.
Dittmar, Kelly, Kira Sanbonmatsu, and Susan J. Carroll. 2018. *A Seat at the Table: Congresswomen's Perspectives on Why Their Presence Matters*. New York: Oxford University Press.
Djupe, Paul A. 2019. "White Evangelicals Fear Atheists and Democrats Would Strip Away Their Rights. Why?" *The Washington Post*, December 23, 2019. https://www.washingtonpost.com/politics/2019/12/23/white-evangelicals-fear-atheists-democrats-would-strip-away-their-rights-why/.
———. 2020. "Survey Numbers Chart Evangelical Defiance against the States." Religion News Service, November 22, 2020. https://religionnews.com/2020/04/17/survey-numbers-chart-evangelical-defiance-against-the-states.
Djupe, Paul A., and Ryan P. Burge. 2020a. "Church Defiance to Covid-19 Restrictions Is Growing." *Religion in Public* (blog), November 17, 2020. https://religioninpublic.blog/2020/11/17/church-defiance-to-covid-19-restrictions-is-growing/.
———. 2020b. "A Conspiracy at the Heart of It: Religion and Q." *Religion in Public* (blog), November 6, 2020. https://religioninpublic.blog/2020/11/06/a-conspiracy-at-the-heart-of-it-religion-and-q/.
Djupe, Paul A., Ryan P. Burge, and Brian R. Calfano. 2016. "The Delegational Pulpit? Clergy Identifying as Congregational Political Representatives." *Representation* 52(1): 43–69.
Djupe, Paul A., and Amanda J. Friesen. 2018. "Moralizing to the Choir: The Moral Foundations of American Clergy." *Social Science Quarterly* 99(2): 665–82.
Djupe, Paul A., and Christopher P. Gilbert. 2003. *The Prophetic Pulpit: Clergy, Churches, and Communities in American Politics*. Lanham, MD: Rowman & Littlefield.
———. 2008. "Politics and Church: Byproduct or Central Mission?" *Journal for the Scientific Study of Religion* 47(1): 45–62.
———. 2009. *The Political Influence of Churches*. New York: Cambridge University Press.
Djupe, Paul A., and J. Tobin Grant. 2001. "Religious Institutions and Political Participation in America." *Journal for the Scientific Study of Religion* 40(2): 303–14.
Djupe, Paul A., Andrew R. Lewis, Anand E. Sokhey, and Ryan P. Burge. 2021. "Does Disgust Drive Religious Freedom Attitudes? Experimental Results about the Context of Service Refusal Opinion." *Social Science Quarterly* 102(2): 755–70.
Djupe, Paul A., and Stephen T. Mockabee. 2015. "Religious Worldviews and Political Tolerance." In *Religion and Political Tolerance in America: Advances in the State of the Art*, edited by Paul A. Djupe, 117–32. Philadelphia: Temple University Press.
Djupe, Paul A., and Jacob R. Neiheisel. 2008. "Clergy Deliberation on Gay Rights and Homosexuality." *Polity* 40(4): 411–35.
———. 2012. "How Religious Communities Affect Political Participation among Latinos." *Social Science Quarterly* 93(2): 333–55.
Djupe, Paul A., Jacob R. Neiheisel, and Anand E. Sokhey. 2018. "Reconsidering the Role of Politics in Leaving Religion: The Importance of Affiliation." *American Journal of Political Science* 62(1): 161–75.

Djupe, Paul A., and Laura R. Olson. 2013. "Stained-Glass Politics and Descriptive Representation: Does Associational Leadership by Women Engender Political Engagement among Women?" *Politics, Groups, and Identities* 1(3): 329–48.

Dougherty, Kevin D., Mitchell J. Neubert, and Jerry Z. Park. 2019. "Prosperity Beliefs and Value Orientations: Fueling or Suppressing Entrepreneurial Activity." *Journal for the Scientific Study of Religion* 58:475–93.

Douglas, Karen M., and Robbie M. Sutton. 2011. "Does It Take One to Know One? Endorsement of Conspiracy Theories Is Influenced by Personal Willingness to Conspire." *British Journal Of Social Psychology* 50(3): 544–52.

Duke University. 2021. "Black History Month: A Medical Perspective: Hospitals." Duke University, last modified January 14, 2021. https://guides.mclibrary.duke.edu/blackhistorymonth/hospitals.

Dupree, Jamie. 2020. "Trump Presses for Relaxed Virus Restrictions on Churches." Boston 25 News, May 21, 2020. https://www.boston25news.com/news/politics/jamie-dupree/trump-presses/NRNZ47MCPG3JIC7PXSOES3JPAE/.

Dyrendal, Asbjørn, David G. Robertson, and Egil Asprem, eds. 2019. *Handbook of Conspiracy Theory and Contemporary Religion*. Leiden: Brill.

Ecklund, Elaine Howard. 2010. *Religion vs. Science: What Religious People Really Think*. New York: Oxford University Press.

Edgerly, Stephanie. 2015. "Red Media, Blue Media, and Purple Media: News Repertoires in the Colorful Media Landscape." *Journal of Broadcasting and Electronic Media* 59(1): 1–21.

Egan, Patrick J. 2020. "Identity as Dependent Variable: How Americans Shift Their Identities to Align with Their Politics." *American Journal of Political Science* 64(3): 699–716.

Eisenstein, Marie A., and April K. Clark. 2015. "Heterogeneous Religion Measures and Political Tolerance Outcomes." In *Religion and Political Tolerance in America: Advances in the State of the Art*, edited by Paul A. Djupe, 83–99. Philadelphia: Temple University Press.

Emerson, Michael O., and Christian Smith. 2001. *Divided by Faith: Evangelical Religion and the Problem of Race in America*. Oxford: Oxford University Press.

Engel v. Vitale. 1962. 370 U.S. 421. https://supreme.justia.com/cases/federal/us/370/421/.

Enns, Peter K., Paul M. Kellstedt, and Gregory E. McAvoy. 2012. "The Consequences of Partisanship in Economic Perceptions." *Public Opinion Quarterly* 76(2): 287–310.

Espinosa, Gaston, Virgilio P. Elizonda, and Jesse Miranda. 2003. *Hispanic Churches in American Public Life: Summary of Findings*. South Bend, IN: University of Notre Dame.

Estrin, James. 2020. "Staying Apart, but Praying Together." *New York Times*, February 10, 2020. https://www.nytimes.com/2020/11/15/nyregion/nyc-coronavirus-religious-worship.html.

Evans, John H., and Eszter Hargittai. 2020. "Who Doesn't Trust Fauci? The Public's Belief in the Expertise and Shared Values of Scientists in the COVID-19 Pandemic." *Socius* (January 2020).

Fahmy, Dalia. 2018. "Americans Are Far More Religious Than Adults in Other Wealthy Nations." *Pew Research Center*, July 31, 2018. https://www.pewresearch.org/fact-tank/2018/07/31/americans-are-far-more-religious-than-adults-in-other-wealthy-nations/.

Fea, John. 2020. "Courtiers and Kings, Evangelicals, Prophets and Trump." Religious News Service, January 8, 2020. https://religionnews.com/2020/01/08/courtiers-and-kings-evangelicals-prophets-and-trump/.
———. 2021. "Cherry-Picking the Bible and Using Verses Out of Context Isn't a Practice Confined to Those Opposed to Vaccines—It Has Been Done for Centuries." The Conversation, October 4, 2021. https://theconversation.com/cherry-picking-the-bible-and-using-verses-out-of-context-isnt-a-practice-confined-to-those-opposed-to-vaccines-it-has-been-done-for-centuries-168995.
Federal Bureau of Investigation. 2020. "NICS Firearm Checks: Month/Year—FBI." 2020. https://www.fbi.gov/file-repository/nics_firearm_checks_-_month_year.pdf/view.
Feldman, Noah. 2005. *Divided by God: America's Church-State Problem—and What We Should Do About It*. New York: Farrar, Strauss, and Giroux.
Finlay, Barbara. 1996. "Gender Differences in Attitudes toward Abortion among Protestant Seminarians." *Review of Religious Research* 37(4): 354–60.
Finnegan, John R., Jr., and Kasisomayajula Viswanath Jr. 1988. "Community Ties and Use of Cable TV and Newspapers in a Midwest Suburb." *Journalism Quarterly* 65(2): 456–63.
First Liberty. 2020a. "Breaking: Judge Grants Restraining Order against Kentucky Governor in Dispute over In-Person Religious Gatherings." First Liberty, May 8, 2020. https://firstliberty.org/media/breaking-judge-grants-restraining-order-against-kentucky-governor-in-dispute-over-in-person-religious-gatherings/.
———. 2020b. "FLI Sues Kentucky Governor on Behalf of Church." First Liberty, May 6, 2020. https://firstliberty.org/covid-19-fli-sues-kentucky-governor-fb/.
———. 2020c. "U.S. Supreme Court Protects Places of Worship from NY Governor Cuomo's Order." First Liberty, November 26, 2020. https://firstliberty.org/media/u-s-supreme-court-protects-places-of-worship-from-ny-governor-cuomos-order/.
FitzGerald, Francis. 2017. *The Evangelicals: The Struggle to Shape America*. New York: Simon and Schuster.
Fitzgerald, Scott T., and Ryan E. Spohn. 2005. "Pulpits and Platforms: The Role of the Church in Determining Protest among Black Americans." *Social Forces* 84(2): 1015–48.
Fowler, Hayley. 2020. "Here's How Religious Americans View the Coronavirus Pandemic | Charlotte Observer." May 16, 2020. https://www.charlotteobserver.com/news/coronavirus/article242784396.html.
Frederick, Brian. 2011. "Gender Turnover and Roll Call Voting in the US Senate." *Journal of Women, Politics and Policy* 32(3): 193–210.
Frey, William. 2020. "Now, More than Half of Americans Are Millennials or Younger." *The Avenue* (blog), Brookings Institution, July 30, 2020. https://www.brookings.edu/blog/the-avenue/2020/07/30/now-more-than-half-of-americans-are-millennials-or-younger/.
Friedman, Jared Parker, and Anthony Ian Jack. 2018. "What Makes You So Sure? Dogmatism, Fundamentalism, Analytic Thinking, Perspective Taking and Moral Concern in the Religious and Nonreligious." *Journal of Religion and Health* 57:157–90.
Friesen, Amanda J., and Michael W. Wagner. 2012. "Beyond the Three 'Bs': How American Christians Approach Faith and Politics." *Politics and Religion* 5(2): 224–52.
Froese, Paul, and Christopher Bader. 2010. *America's Four Gods: What We Say About God and What That Says About Us*. New York: Oxford University Press.

Furnham, Adrian. 2003. "Belief In A Just World: Research Progress Over The Past Decade." *Personality and Individual Differences* 34(5): 795–817.

Galiatsatos, Panagis, Kimberly Monson, MopeninuJesu Oluyinka, DanaRose Negro, Natasha Hughes, Daniella Maydan, Sherita H. Golden, Paula Teague, and W. Daniel Hale. 2020. "Community Calls: Lessons and Insights Gained from a Medical–Religious Community Engagement during the COVID-19 Pandemic." *Journal of Religion and Health* 59(5): 2256–62.

Gearan, Anne, Lena H. Sun, Josh Dawsey, and Michelle Boorstein. 2020. "Trump Tells States to Let Houses of Worship Open, Sparking Cultural and Political Fight over Pandemic Restrictions." *Washington Post*, May 22, 2020. https://www.washingtonpost.com/politics/trump-tells-states-to-let-houses-of-worship-open-sparking-cultural-and-political-fight-over-pandemic-restrictions/2020/05/22/1ab1c160-9c57-11ea-ad09-8da7ec214672_story.html.

Gecewicz, Claire. 2020. "Few Americans Say Their House of Worship Is Open, but a Quarter Say Their Faith Has Grown amid Pandemic." Pew Research Center, April 30, 2020. https://www.pewresearch.org/fact-tank/2020/04/30/few-americans-say-their-house-of-worship-is-open-but-a-quarter-say-their-religious-faith-has-grown-amid-pandemic/.

Geier, David A., Janet K. Kern, and Mark R. Geier. 2017. "A Longitudinal Ecological Study of Household Firearm Ownership and Firearm-Related Deaths in the United States from 1999 through 2014: A Specific Focus on Gender, Race, and Geographic Variables." *Preventive Medicine Reports* 6(June): 329–35.

George, Carol V. R. 2019. *God's Salesman: Norman Vincent Peale and the Power of Positive Thinking*. Oxford, UK: Oxford University Press.

Georgiou, Neophytos, Paul Delfabbro, and Ryan Balzan. 2020. "COVID-19-Related Conspiracy Beliefs and Their Relationship with Perceived Stress and Pre-Existing Conspiracy Beliefs." *Personality and Individual Differences* 166:110201. https://www.ncbi.nlm.nih.gov/pmc/articles/PMC7296298/.

Gershon, Sarah Allen, Adrian D. Pantoja, and J. Benjamin Taylor. 2016. "God in the Barrio? The Determinants of Religiosity and Civic Engagement among Latinos in the United States." *Politics and Religion* 9(1): 84–110.

Gibson, David. 2016. "Franklin Graham Rebuts Pope on Islam: 'This Is a War of Religion.'" Sojourners, August 1, 2016. https://sojo.net/articles/franklin-graham-rebuts-pope-islam-war-religion.

Gibson, James L. 2006. "Enigmas of Intolerance: Fifty Years after Stouffer's Communism, Conformity, and Civil Liberties." *Perspectives on Politics* 4(1): 21–34.

———. 2010. "The Political Consequences of Religiosity: Does Religion Always Cause Political Intolerance?" In *Religion and Democracy in the United States: Danger or Opportunity*, edited by Ira Katznelson and Alan Wolfe, 147–75. New York: Russell Sage.

Giles-Sims, Jean, Joanne Connor Green, and Charles Lockhart. 2012. "Do Women Legislators Have a Positive Effect on the Supportiveness of States toward Older Citizens?" *Journal of Women, Politics and Policy* 33(1): 38–64.

Gillman, Howard, and Erwin Chemerinsky. 2020. "The Weaponization of the Free-Exercise Clause." *The Atlantic*, September 18, 2020. https://www.theatlantic.com/ideas/archive/2020/09/weaponization-free-exercise-clause/616373/.

Gilman, Hollie R., and Elizabeth Stokes. 2020. "The Civic and Political Participation of Millennials." New America Foundation, accessed December 7, 2020. https://d1y8sb8igg2f8e.cloudfront.net/documents/The_Civic_and_Political_Participation_of_Millennials.pdf.

Gittleson, Ben, Jordyn Phelps, and Libby Cathey. 2020. "Trump Doubles Down on Defense of Hydroxychloroquine to Treat COVID-19 Despite Efficacy Concerns." *ABCNews*, July 28, 2020. https://abcnews.go.com/Politics/trump-doubles-defense-hydroxychloroquine-treat-covid-19-efficacy/story?id=72039824.

Gjelten, Tom. 2020. "'Things Will Never Be the Same': How The Pandemic Has Changed Worship." NPR, February 13, 2020. https://www.npr.org/2020/05/20/858918339/things-will-never-be-the-same-how-the-pandemic-has-changed-worship.

Goertzel, Ted. 1994. "Belief in Conspiracy Theories." *Political Psychology* 15(4): 733–44.

Goidel, Kirby, Brian Smentkowski, and Craig Freeman. 2016. "Perceptions of Threat to Religious Liberty." *PS: Political Science and Politics* 49(3): 426–32.

Golan, Guy J., and Anita G. Day. 2010. "In God We Trust: Religiosity as a Predictor of Perceptions of Media Trust, Factuality, and Privacy Invasion." *American Behavioral Scientist* 54(2): 120–36.

Goldenstein, Taylor. 2020. "Texas AG Ken Paxton Says Gun Sales Can't Be Restricted by Stay-Home Orders." *HoustonChronicle.Com*. March 27, 2020. https://www.houstonchronicle.com/news/article/ken-paxton-gun-sales-stay-at-home-orders-texas-15161765.php.

Goldstein, Harvey, and Michael J. R. Healy. 1995. "The Graphical Presentation of a Collection of Means." *Journal of the Royal Statistical Society* 158:175–77.

Gomez, Jorge. 2020a. "All Out War on Faith: Opponents Use COVID-19 Crisis to Launch Attacks on Religious Freedom." First Liberty, April 3, 2020. https://firstliberty.org/news/covid-19-religious-liberty-attacks/.

———. 2020b. "Opponents of Freedom Use COVID to Attack and Destroy the Religious Freedom Restoration Act." First Liberty, September 11, 2020. https://firstliberty.org/news/opponents-use-covid-to-attack/.

Gonzales, Mike. 2020. "This BLM Co-founder and Pro-Communist China Group Are Partnering Up: Here's Why." Heritage Foundation, September 15, 2020. https://www.heritage.org/progressivism/commentary/blm-co-founder-and-pro-communist-china-group-are-partnering-heres-why.

Goss, Kristin A. 2017. "The Socialization of Conflict and Its Limits: Gender and Gun Politics in America: The Socialization of Conflict and Its Limits." *Social Science Quarterly* 98(2): 455–70.

Gould, Elise, and Melat Kassa. 2020. "Young Workers Hit Hard by COVID-19 Economy." Economic Policy Institute, October 14, 2020. https://www.epi.org/publication/young-workers-covid-recession/.

Graham, Jesse, and Jonathan Haidt. 2010. "Beyond Beliefs: Religions Bind Individuals into Moral Communities." *Personality and Social Psychology Review* 14(1): 140–50.

Graham, Jessica R., and Lizabeth Roemer. 2012. "A Preliminary Study of the Moderating Role of Church-Based Social Support in the Relationship between Racist Experiences and General Anxiety Symptoms." *Cultural Diversity and Ethnic Minority Psychology* 18(3): 268–76.

Gramlich, John. 2020. "Q&A: How Pew Research Center Evaluated Americans' Trust in 30 Sources." Pew Research Center, January 24, 2020. https://www.pewresearch.org/fact-tank/2020/01/24/qa-how-pew-research-center-evaluated-americans-trust-in-30-news-sources/.

Green, Emma. 2017. "White Evangelicals Believe They Face More Discrimination than Muslims." *The Atlantic*, March 10, 2017. https://www.theatlantic.com/politics/archive/2017/03/perceptions-discrimination-muslims-christians/519135/.

Green, Ricky, and Karen M. Douglas. 2018. "Anxious Attachment and Belief in Conspiracies." *Personality and Individual Differences* 125(15): 30–37.

Greenlee, Jill S. 2014. *The Political Consequences of Motherhood*. Ann Arbor: University of Michigan Press.

Gunn, Erik. 2020. "Faith Leaders Join to Lobby Lawmakers for COVID-19 Legislation." *Wisconsin Examiner*, December 17, 2020. https://wisconsinexaminer.com/2020/12/17/faith-leaders-join-to-lobby-lawmakers-for-covid-19-legislation/.

Guth, James L. 2019. "Are White Evangelicals Populists? The View from the 2016 American National Election Study." *Review of Faith and International Affairs* 17(3): 20–35.

Guth, James L., John C. Green, Lyman A. Kellstedt, and Corwin E. Smidt. 1995. "Faith and the Environment: Religious Beliefs and Attitudes on Environmental Policy." *American Journal of Political Science* 39(2): 364–82.

Guth, James L., John C. Green, Corwin E. Smidt, Lyman A. Kellstedt, and Margaret Poloma. 1997. *The Bully Pulpit: The Politics of Protestant Clergy*. Lawrence: University of Kansas Press.

Hainmueller, Jens, Daniel J. Hopkins, and Teppei Yamamoto. 2013. "Causal Inference in Conjoint Analysis: Understanding Multidimensional Choices via Stated Preference Experiments." *Political Analysis* 22(1): 1–30.

Hale, Henry E. 2004. "Explaining Ethnicity." *Comparative Political Studies* 37(4): 458–85.

Hall, William J., Mimi V. Chapman, Kent M. Lee, Yesenia M Merino, Tainayah W. Thomas, B. Keith Payne, Eugenia Eng, Steven H. Day, and Tamera Coyne-Beasley. 2015. "Implicit Racial/Ethnic Bias among Health Care Professionals and Its Influence on Health Care Outcomes: A Systematic Review." *American Journal of Public Health* 105(12): 60–76.

Harris, Frederick. 2010. "Entering the Promised Land? The Rise of Prosperity Gospel and Post-Civil Rights Black Politics." In *Religion and Democracy in the United States: Danger or Opportunity*, edited by Alan Wolfe and Ira Katznelson, 255–78. New York: Russell Sage.

Harris, Shane, and Yasmeen Abutaleb. 2021. "Coronavirus 'Lab Leak' Theory Jumps from Mocked to Maybe as Biden Orders Intelligence Review." *Washington Post*, May 28, 2021. https://www.washingtonpost.com/national-security/wuhan-lab-leak-theory-intelligence-biden/2021/05/28/786d57ac-bfe6-11eb-83e3-0ca705a96ba4_story.html.

Harris-Lacewell, Melissa V. 2007. "From Liberation to Mutual Fund: Political Consequences of Differing Conceptions of Christ in the African-American Church." In *From Pews to Polling Places: Faith and Politics in the American Religious Mosaic*, edited by J. Matthew Wilson, 131–60. Washington, DC: Georgetown University Press.

Harvey, Josephine. 2020. "Rush Limbaugh Claims Health Experts Are Hillary Clinton Allies Trying to Hurt Trump." *Huffington Post*, April 7, 2020. https://www.huffpost

.com/entry/rush-limbaugh-fauci-trump-coronavirus-conspiracy_n_5e8cfc45c5b6e1a2e0fb746e.

Hauser, Will, and Gary Kleck. 2013. "Guns and Fear: A One-Way Street?" *Crime & Delinquency* 59(2): 271–91.

Hellinger, Daniel. 2019. *Conspiracy and Conspiracy Theories in the Age of Trump*. New York: Palgrave.

Hempel, Lynn M., Todd Matthews, and John Bartkowski. 2012. "Trust in a 'Fallen World': The Case of Protestant Theological Conservatism." *Journal for the Scientific Study of Religion* 51(3): 522–41.

Hernandez, M. 2020. "Calvary Pastor Jack Hibbs Challenges U.S. Pastors: 'Open Your Doors' Oct. 25th; 'The People of God Want to Go to Their Churches.'" *Citizens Journal*, October 12, 2020. https://www.citizensjournal.us/calvary-pastor-jack-hibbs-challenges-u-s-pastors-open-your-doors-oct-25th-the-people-of-god-want-to-go-to-their-churches/.

Hertzke, Allen D., Laura R. Olson, Kevin R. den Dulk, and Robert Booth Fowler. 2018. *Religion and Politics in America: Faith, Culture, and Strategic Choices*. New York: Routledge.

Higgins-Dunn, Noah. 2021. "Texas Gov. Abbott Blames Covid Spread on Immigrants, Criticizes Biden's 'Neanderthal' Comment." CNBC, March 4, 2021. https://www.cnbc.com/2021/03/04/texas-gov-abbott-blames-covid-spread-on-immigrants-criticizes-bidens-neanderthal-comment-.html.

Hill, Terrence D., Kelsey Gonzalez, and Amy M. Burdette. 2020. "The Blood of Christ Compels Them: State Religiosity and State Population Mobility During the Coronavirus (COVID-19) Pandemic." *Journal of Religion and Health* 59(5): 2229–42.

Hirsh, Adam T., Nicole A. Hollingshead, Leslie Ashburn-Nardo, and Kurt Kroenke. 2015. "The Interaction of Patient Race, Provider Bias, and Clinical Ambiguity on Pain Management Decisions." *Journal of Pain* 16(6): 558–68.

Hmielowski, Jay D., Lauren Feldman, Teresa A. Myers, Anthony Leiserowitz, and Edward Maibach. 2014. "An Attack on Science? Media Use, Trust in Scientists, and Perceptions of Global Warming." *Public Understanding of Science* 23:866–83.

Hogg, Michael A., Janice R. Adelman, and Robert D. Blagg. 2010. "Religion in the Face of Uncertainty: An Uncertainty-Identity Theory Account of Religiousness." *Personality and Social Psychology Review* 14(1): 72–83.

Hollibaugh, Gary E., Jr., Matthew R. Miles, and Chad B. Newswander. 2020. "Why Public Employees Rebel: Guerrilla Government in the Public Sector." *Public Administration Review* 80(1): 64–74.

Hollis-Brusky, Amanda. 2015. *Ideas with Consequences: The Federalist Society and the Conservative Counterrevolution*. New York: Oxford University Press.

Hollis-Brusky, Amanda, and Joshua C. Wilson. 2020. *Separate but Faithful: The Christian Right's Radical Struggle to Transform Law and Legal Culture*. New York: Oxford University Press.

Holman, Mirya R. 2014. "Sex and the City: Female Leaders and Spending on Social Welfare Programs in U.S. Municipalities." *Journal of Urban Affairs* 36(4): 701–15.

Hout, Michael, and Claude S. Fischer. 2002. "Why More Americans Have No Religious Preference: Politics and Generations." *American Sociological Review* 67(2): 165–90.

Huddy, Leonie. 2001. "From Social to Political Identity: A Critical Examination of Social Identity Theory." *Political Psychology* 22(1): 127–56.

Hunt, Larry L., and Matthew O. Hunt. 2001. "Race, Region, and Religious Involvement: A Comparative Study of Whites and African Americans." *Social Forces* 80(2): 605–31.

Hunter, James Davison. 1991. *Culture War: The Struggle to Define America*. New York: Basic Books.

Iannaccone, Laurence R., and Sean F. Everton. 2004. "Never on Sunny Days: Lessons from Weekly Attendance Counts." *Journal for the Scientific Study of Religion* 43(2): 191–207.

Idliby, Leia. 2020. "Listen: Trump Berates Governors as 'Fools' and 'Jerks.'" Mediaite, June 1, 2020. https://www.mediaite.com/trump/trump-reportedly-berates-governors-as-fools-jerks-in-conference-call-demands-they-dominate-protesters-with-force/.

Inazu, John. 2020. "SCOTUS Gets It Right on Religious Liberty: Church IS Essential." *Christianity Today* (blog), November 26, 2020. https://www.christianitytoday.com/edstetzer/2020/november/scotus-gets-it-right-religious-liberty-church-is-essential.html.

Institute of Medicine (US) Committee on Understanding and Eliminating Ethnic Disparities in Health Care. 2003. *Unequal Treatment: Confronting Racial and Ethnic Disparities in Health Care*. Edited by Brian D. Smedley, Adrienne Y. Stith, and Alan R. Nelson. Washington, DC: National Academies Press.

Islam, Md Saifu, Tonmoy Sarkar, Sazzad Hossain Khan, Abu-Hena Mostofa Kamal, S. M. Murshid Hasan, Alamgir Kabir, Dalia Yeasmin, et al. 2020. "COVID-19–Related Infodemic and Its Impact on Public Health: A Global Social Media Analysis." *The American Journal of Tropical Medicine and Hygiene* 103(4): 1621–29. https://doi.org/10.4269/ajtmh.20-0812.

Iyengar, Shanto, and Kyu S. Hahn. 2009. "Red Media, Blue Media: Evidence of Ideological Selectivity in Media Use." *Journal of Communication* 59(1): 19–39.

Iyengar, Shanto, Yphtach Lelkes, Matthew Levendusky, Neil Malhotra, and Sean J. Westwood. 2019. "The Origins and Consequences of Affective Polarization in the United States." *Annual Review of Political Science* 22(1): 129–46.

Iyengar, Shanto, Gaurav Sood, and Yphtach Lelkes. 2012. "Affect, Not Ideology: A Social Identity Perspective on Polarization." *Public Opinion Quarterly* 76(3): 405–31.

Iyengar, Shanto, and Sean J. Westwood. 2015. "Fear and Loathing across Party Lines: New Evidence on Group Polarization." *American Journal of Political Science* 59(3): 690–707.

Jacobo, Julia. 2020. "California Pastor Found in Contempt for Ignoring COVID-19 Mandates." *ABC News*. December 9, 2020. https://abcnews.go.com/US/california-pastor-found-contempt-ignoring-covid-19-mandates/story?id=74623637.

Jaiswal, Jessica. 2019. "Whose Responsibility Is It to Dismantle Medical Mistrust? Future Directions for Researchers and Health Care Providers." *Behavioral Medicine* 45(2): 188–96.

Jamal, Amaney, and Nadine Naber. 2008. *Race and Arab Americans before and after 9/11: From Invisible Citizens to Visible Subjects*. Syracuse University Press.

Jamieson, Kathleen Hall, and Dolores Albarracín. 2020. "The Relation between Media Consumption and Misinformation at the Outset of the SARS-CoV-2 Pandemic in the US." *Harvard Kennedy School Misinformation Review* 1(3): 1–22. https://misinforeview.hks.harvard.edu/article/the-relation-between-media-consumption-and-misinformation-at-the-outset-of-the-sars-cov-2-pandemic-in-the-us/.

Janes, Theoden. 2020. "Franklin Graham on Easter amid Pandemic: 'God Never Intended for Man to Have Disease.'" *Charlotte Observer*, April 10, 2020. https://www.charlotteobserver.com/living/religion/article241911986.html.

Jang, Mikyung, Ju-Ae Ko, and Eun-jung Kim. 2018. "Religion and Mental Health among Nepal Earthquake Survivors in Temporary Tent Villages." *Mental Health, Religion and Culture* 21(4): 329–35.

Jelen, Ted G. 1991. "Review: Religion and Democratic Citizenship." *Polity* 23(3): 471–81.

———. 1993. *The Political World of the Clergy*. Westport, CT: Praeger.

Jelen, Ted G., and Clyde Wilcox. 1991. "Religious Dogmatism among White Christians: Causes and Effects." *Review of Religious Research* 33(1): 32–46.

Jenkins, Jack. 2020a. "At Republican Convention, a Vision of Faith Under Fire." Religion News Service, August 29, 2020. https://religionnews.com/2020/08/29/at-republican-convention-a-partisan-vision-of-faith-god-gop/.

———. 2020b. "See Which States Have Religious Exemptions in Their Stay-at-Home Orders." Religion News Service, April 9, 2020. https://religionnews.com/2020/04/09/see-which-states-have-religious-exemptions-in-their-stay-at-home-orders/.

———. 2020c. "Trump Faith Advisors Say the President Did the Right Thing." Christian Headlines, June 10, 2020. https://www.christianheadlines.com/blog/trump-faith-advisers-say-the-president-did-the-right-thing-by-visiting-church.html.

Jenkins, Jack, and Claire Giangravé. 2020. "As Coronavirus Death Toll Mounts, Faith Leaders the World over Grapple with Funerals." Religion News Service, March 26, 2020. https://religionnews.com/2020/03/26/as-cornoavirus-death-toll-mounts-faith-leaders-the-world-over-grapple-with-funerals/.

Jerit, Jennifer, Yangzi Zhao, Megan Tan, and Munifa Wheeler. 2019. "Differences between National and Local Media in News Coverage of the Zika Virus." *Health Communication* 34(14): 1816–23.

Johnson, Akilah. 2020. "Coronavirus, on the Minds of Black Lives Matter Protesters." Propublica, June 5, 2020. https://www.propublica.org/article/on-the-minds-of-black-lives-matters-protestors-a-racist-health-system.

Johnson, Carol, and Blair Williams. 2020. "Gender and Political Leadership in a Time of COVID." *Politics and Gender* 16(4): 943–50.

Johnson, Christine. 2014. "FaithWords Celebrates 10 Years of 'Your Best Life Now.'" Christian Retailing, August 11, 2014. https://www.christianretailing.com/index.php/newsletter/latest/27354-faithwords-celebrates-10-years-of-your-best-life-now.

Johnson, Kathryn A., Yexin Jessica Li, and Adam B. Cohen. 2015. "Fundamental Social Motives and the Varieties of Religious Experience." *Religion, Brain, and Behavior* 5(3): 197–231.

Jolley, Daniel, and Karen M. Douglas. 2014. "The Effects of Anti-Vaccine Conspiracy Theories on Vaccination Intentions." *PLoS ONE* 9(2): e89177.

Jones, Kevin J. 2020. "Former Judge: Coronavirus Restrictions Have a Place, but Religion Is 'Essential.'" Catholic New Agency, May 15, 2020. https://www.catholicnewsagency.com/news/former-judge-coronavirus-restrictions-have-a-place-but-religion-is-essential-36424.

Jones, Robert P. 2016. *The End of White Christian America*. New York: Simon and Schuster.

———. 2020. *White Too Long: the Legacy of White Supremacy in American Christianity*. New York: Simon & Schuster.

Jones, Robert P., Daniel Cox, Rachel Lienesch, and Betsy Cooper. 2016. "Exodus: Why Americans Are Leaving Religion—and Why They're Unlikely to Come Back." PRRI.org, September 22, 2016. http://www.prri.org/research/prri-rns-poll-nones-atheist-leaving-religion/.

Jones-Correa, Michael A., and David L. Leal. 2001. "Political Participation: Does Religion Matter?" *Political Research Quarterly* 54(4): 751–70.

Jouvenal, Justin. 2020. "DOJ Claims Virginia Governor Is Violating Religious Freedom with Pandemic Order." *Washington Post*, May 4, 2020. https://www.washingtonpost.com/local/legal-issues/doj-claims-virginia-governor-is-violating-religious-freedom-with-pandemic-order/2020/05/04/2c083b18-8e35-11ea-9e23-6914ee410a5f_story.html.

Kaiser Family Foundation. 2020. "Poll: 8 in 10 Americans Favor Strict Shelter-in-Place Orders to Limit Coronavirus Spread." Kaiser Family Foundation, April 23, 2020. https://www.kff.org/global-health-policy/press-release/poll-8-in-10-americans-favor-strict-shelter-in-place-orders-to-limit-coronavirus-spread-and-most-say-they-could-continue-to-obey-such-orders-for-another-month-or-longer/.

Kaleem, Jaweed. 2020. "Megachurch Pastors Defy Coronavirus Pandemic, Insisting on Right to Worship." *Los Angeles Times*, March 31, 2020. https://www.latimes.com/world-nation/story/2020-03-31/coronavirus-megachurches-meeting-pastors.

Kalkan, Kerem Ozan, Geoffrey C. Layman, and Eric M. Uslaner. 2009. "'Bands of Others'? Attitudes toward Muslims in Contemporary American Society." *Journal of Politics* 71(3): 847–62.

Kallingal, Mallika, Steve Almasy, Faith Karimi, and Marcelo Grande. 2020. "The US Coronavirus Death Toll is Projected to Reach 410,000 in the Next 4 Months if Mask Use Wanes." *CNN*, September 4, 2020. https://www.cnn.com/2020/09/04/health/us-coronavirus-friday/index.html.

Kellstedt, Lyman A., and Corwin E. Smidt. 1993. "Doctrinal Beliefs and Political Behavior: Views of the Bible." In *Rediscovering the Religious Factor in American Politics*, edited by David C. Leege and Lyman A. Kellstedt, 177–98. Armonk, NY: M. E. Sharpe.

Kendi, Ibram. 2020. "Stop Blaming Black People for Dying of the Coronavirus." *The Atlantic*, April 14, 2020. https://www.theatlantic.com/ideas/archive/2020/04/race-and-blame/609946/.

Kenrick, Douglas T., Vladas Griskevicius, Steven L. Neuberg, and Mark Schaller. 2010. "Renovating the Pyramid of Needs: Contemporary Extensions Built upon Ancient Foundations." *Perspectives on Psychological Science* 5:292–314.

Kessler, Ronald C., Sandro Galea, Russell T. Jones, and Holly A. Parker. 2006. "Mental Illness and Suicidality after Hurricane Katrina." *Bulletin of the World Health Organization* 84(12): 930–39.

Kim, Paul Youngbin. 2017. "Religious Support Mediates the Racial Microaggressions—Mental Health Relation among Christian Ethnic Minority Students." *Psychology of Religion and Spirituality* 9(2): 148–57.

King, Danae. 2020. "Coronavirus in Ohio: Some Houses of Worship to Reopen Sunday, Others More Cautious." *Columbus Dispatch*, May 27, 2020. https://www.dispatch.com/story/lifestyle/faith/2020/05/27/coronavirus-in-ohio-some-houses/1125634007/.

King, Maya. 2020. "'It's My Constitutional Freaking Right': Black Americans Arm Themselves in Response to Pandemic, Protests." POLITICO. July 26, 2020. https://www.politico.com/news/2020/07/26/black-americans-gun-owners-380162.

Kinnaman, David. 2020. "What Research Has Revealed About the New Sunday Morning." Barna Group, June 3, 2020. https://www.barna.com/research/new-sunday-morning/.

Kleck, Gary, and Tomislav Kovandzic. 2009. "City-Level Characteristics and Individual Handgun Ownership: Effects of Collective Security and Homicide." *Journal of Contemporary Criminal Justice* 25(1): 45–66.

Kleck, Gary, Tomislav Kovandzic, Mark Saber, and Will Hauser. 2011. "The Effect of Perceived Risk and Victimization on Plans to Purchase a Gun for Self-Protection." *Journal of Criminal Justice* 39(4): 312–19.

Knol, Mirjam J., Wiebe R. Pestman, and Diederick E. Grobbee. 2011. "The (Mis)use of Overlap of Confidence Intervals to Assess Effect Modification." *European Journal of Epidemiology* 26:253–54.

Knoll, Benjamin R., and Cammie Jo Bolin. 2018. *She Preached the Word: Women's Ordination in Modern America*. New York: Oxford University Press.

———. 2019. "Religious Communication and Persuasion." *Oxford Research Encyclopedia of Politics*. New York: Oxford University Press.

Koch, Bradley A. 2009. "The Prosperity Gospel and Economic Prosperity: Race, Class, Giving, and Voting." Ph.D. diss., Indiana University.

Kreitzer, Rebecca J. 2015. "Politics and Morality in State Abortion Policy." *State Politics and Policy Quarterly* 15(1): 41–66.

Krugman, Paul (@paulkrugman). 2020. "The first major decision from the Trump-packed court—and, naturally, it will kill people 1/." Twitter, November 26, 2020, 9:55 A.M. https://twitter.com/paulkrugman/status/1331974982704967681.

Kruse, Kevin M. 2016. *One Nation under God: How Corporate American Invented Christian America*. New York: Basic Books.

Lajevardi, Nazita. 2020. *Outsiders at Home: The Politics of American Islamophobia*. Cambridge: Cambridge University Press.

Lajevardi, Nazita, and Kassra A. R. Oskooii. 2018. "Old-Fashioned Racism, Contemporary Islamophobia, and the Isolation of Muslim Americans in the Age of Trump." *Journal of Race, Ethnicity and Politics* 3(1): 112–52.

Landrum, Asheley R., and Alex Olshansky. 2019. "The Role of Conspiracy Mentality in Denial of Science and Susceptibility to Viral Deception About Science." *Politics and The Life Sciences* 38(2): 193–209.

Lang, Bree J., and Matthew Lang. 2020. "Pandemics, Protests and Firearms." SSRN Scholarly Paper ID 3593956. Rochester, NY: Social Science Research Network. https://doi.org/10.2139/ssrn.3593956.

LaPlant, Kristina M., Keith E. Lee, and James T. LaPlant. 2021. "Christmas Trees, Presidents, and Mass Shootings: Explaining Gun Purchases in the South and Non-South." *Social Science Quarterly* 102(1): 387–406.

Laqueur, Hannah S., Rose M. C. Kagawa, Christopher D. McCort, Rocco Pallin, and Garen Wintemute. 2019. "The Impact of Spikes in Handgun Acquisitions on Firearm-Related Harms." *Injury Epidemiology* 6(1): 35–41.

Lawless, Jennifer L. 2004. "Politics of Presence? Congresswomen and Symbolic Representation." *Political Research Quarterly* 57(1): 81–99.

Layman, Geoffrey C. 2001. *The Great Divide: Religious and Cultural Conflict in American Party Politics*. New York: Columbia University Press.

Lee, Bruce Y. 2020. "Trump Once Again Calls Covid-19 Coronavirus the 'Kung Flu.'" *Forbes*, June 24, 2020. https://www.forbes.com/sites/brucelee/2020/06/24/trump-once-again-calls-covid-19-coronavirus-the-kung-flu/?sh=784040291f59.

Leege, David C., and Lyman A. Kellstedt, eds. 1993. *Rediscovering the Religious Factor in American Politics*. Armonk, NY: M. E. Sharpe.

Levine, Phillip B., and Robin McKnight. 2017. "Firearms and Accidental Deaths: Evidence from the Aftermath of the Sandy Hook School Shooting." *Science* 358(6368): 1324–28.

Lewandowsky, Stephan, Klaus Oberauer, and Gilles E. Gignac. 2013. "NASA Faked the Moon Landing—Therefore, (Climate) Science Is a Hoax: An Anatomy of the Motivated Rejection of Science." *Psychological Science* 24(5): 622–33.

Lewis, Andrew R. 2017. *The Rights Turn in Conservative Christian Politics: How Abortion Transformed the Culture Wars*. New York: Cambridge University Press.

———. 2020. "Donald Trump Hurts Public Support for Religious Freedom." *Religion in Public* (blog), November 2, 2020. https://religioninpublic.blog/2020/11/02/donald-trump-hurts-public-support-for-religious-freedom/.

Liberty Counsel. 2020a. "Criminal Charges against VA Pastor Dropped." LC.org, July 14, 2020. https://lc.org/newsroom/details/071420-criminal-charges-against-va-pastor-dropped.

———. 2020b. "VA Church Goes to Appeals Court." LC.org, June 29, 2020. https://lc.org/newsroom/details/062920-va-church-goes-to-appeals-court-1.

———. 2020c. "VP Pence Supports VA Church Case." LC.org, May 7, 2020. https://lc.org/newsroom/details/050720-vp-pence-supports-va-church-case.

Lifeway Research. 2020a. "Few Protestant Churches Met in Person for Worship Services in April." Lifeway Research, May 1, 2020. https://lifewayresearch.com/2020/05/01/few-protestant-churches-met-in-person-for-worship-services-in-april/.

———. 2020b. "Most Churches Cautiously Holding Services Again." Lifeway Research (blog), July 24, 2020. https://blog.lifeway.com/newsroom/2020/07/24/most-churches-cautiously-holding-service-again/.

Lincoln, C. Eric., and Lawrence H. Mamiya. 1990. The Bla*ck Church in the African American Experience*. Durham, NC: Duke University Press.

Liptak, Adam. 2018. "How Conservatives Weaponized the First Amendment." *New York Times*, June 30, 2018. https://www.nytimes.com/2018/06/30/us/politics/first-amendment-conservatives-supreme-court.html.

———. 2020. "Supreme Court Rejects Nevada Church's Challenge to Coronavirus Shutdown Restrictions." *New York Times*, July 24, 2020. https://www.nytimes.com/2020/07/24/us/supreme-court-nevada-church-coronavirus.html.

Little, Robert E., and Ronald E. Vogel. 1992. "Handgun Ownership and the Religion Factor." *Journal of Applied Social Psychology* 22(23): 1871–77.

Lizotte, Mary-Kate. 2020. *Gender Differences in Public Opinion*. Philadelphia: Temple University Press.

Lopez, German. 2015. "Meet the Little-Known Christian Law Firm behind the New Wave of Anti-LGBTQ Bills." Vox, November 23, 2015. https://www.vox.com/2015/11/23/9770610/liberty-counsel-mat-staver-kim-davis.

Luhrmann, Tanya Marie. 2013. "Making God Real and Making God Good: Some Mechanisms through which Prayer May Contribute to Healing." *Transcultural Psychiatry* 50(5): 707–25.

Lyons, Vivian H., Miriam J. Haviland, Deborah Azrael, Avanti Adhia, M. Alex Bellenger, Alice Ellyson, Ali Rowhani-Rahbar, and Frederick P. Rivara. 2020. "Firearm Purchasing and Storage during the COVID-19 Pandemic." *Injury Prevention* 27(September): 87–92.

MacArthur, John. 2020. "Thinking Biblically About the COVID-19 Pandemic: An Interview with John MacArthur." Grace to You, April 24, 2020. https://www.gty.org/library/sermons-library/GTY176/thinking-biblically-about-the-covid19-pandemic-an-interview-with-john-macarthur.

MacGregor-Fors, Ian, and Mark E. Payton. 2013. "Contrasting Diversity Values: Statistical Inferences Based on Overlapping Confidence Intervals." *PLoS ONE* 8(2): 1–4.

Maina, Ivy W., Tanisha D. Belton, Sara Ginzberg, Ajit Singh, and Tiffani J. Johnson. 2018. "A Decade of Studying Implicit Racial/Ethnic Bias in Healthcare Providers Using the Implicit Association Test." *Social Science and Medicine* 199:219–29.

Malinowski, Bronislaw. 1992. *Magic, Science and Religion*. New York: Waveland.

Mangan, Dan, and Berkeley Lovelace Jr. 2020. "Trump Suspects Coronavirus Outbreak Came from China Lab, Doesn't Cite Evidence." *CNBC*, April 30, 2020. https://www.cnbc.com/2020/04/30/coronavirus-trump-suspects-covid-19-came-from-china-lab.html.

Mansbridge, Jane. 1999. "Should Blacks Represent Blacks and Women Represent Women? A Contingent 'Yes.'" *Journal of Politics* 61(3): 628–57.

Maragakis, Lisa L. 2020a. "Coronavirus and COVID-19: Who Is at Higher Risk?" Johns Hopkins Medicine, December 8, 2020. https://www.hopkinsmedicine.org/health/conditions-and-diseases/coronavirus/coronavirus-and-covid19-who-is-at-higher-risk.

———. 2020b. "Coronavirus and Covid-19: Younger Adults Are at Risk, Too." Johns Hopkins Medicine, December 2, 2020. https://www.hopkinsmedicine.org/health/conditions-and-diseases/coronavirus/coronavirus-and-covid-19-younger-adults-are-at-risk-too.

Margolis, Michele F. 2018a. *From Politics to the Pews: How Partisanship and the Political Environment Shape Religious Identity*. Chicago: University of Chicago Press.

———. 2018b. "How Far Does Social Group Influence Reach? Identities, Elites, and Immigration Attitudes." *Journal of Politics* 80(3): 772–85.

Marsh, Christopher., and Artyom Tonoyan. 2009. "The Civic, Economic, and Political Consequences of Pentecostalism in Russia and Ukraine." *Society* 46(6): 510–16.

Marshall, Katherine. 2020. "Beating Coronavirus Requires Faith Leaders to Bridge Gap between Religion and Science." The Conversation, April 16, 2020. https://theconversation.com/beating-coronavirus-requires-faith-leaders-to-bridge-gap-between-religion-and-science-135388.

Marti, Gerardo. 2020a. *American Blindspot: Race, Class, Religion and the Trump Presidency*. Lanham, MD: Rowman & Littlefield.

———. 2020b. "White Christian Libertarianism and the Trump Presidency." In *Religion Is Raced: Understanding American Religion in the Twenty-First Century*, edited by Grace Yukich and Penny Edgell, 19–39. New York: NYU Press.

Masci, David. 2016. "How Income Varies among U.S. Religious Groups." Pew Research Center, October 11, 2016. https://www.pewresearch.org/fact-tank/2016/10/11/how-income-varies-among-u-s-religious-groups/.

Matthews, Todd, Lee Michael Johnson, and Catherine Jenks. 2011. "Does Religious Involvement Generate or Inhibit Fear of Crime?" *Religions* 2(4): 485–503.

Mayrl, Damon, and Aliya Saperstein. 2013. "When White People Report Racial Discrimination: The Role of Region, Religion, and Politics." *Social Science Research* 42(3): 742–54.

Mazzei, Patricia. 2020. "Florida Pastor Arrested after Defying Virus Orders." *New York Times*, March 30, 2020. https://www.nytimes.com/2020/03/30/us/coronavirus-pastor-arrested-tampa-florida.html.

McCarthy, John D., and Mayer N. Zald. 1977. "Resource Mobilization and Social Movements: A Partial Theory." *American Journal of Sociology* 82(6): 1212–41.

McClendon, Gwyneth H., and Rachel Beatty Riedl. 2019. *From Pews to Politics: Religious Sermons and Political Participation in Africa*. New York: Cambridge University Press.

McClerking, Harwood K., and Eric L. McDaniel. 2005. "Belonging and Doing: Political Churches and Black Political Participation." *Political Psychology* 26(5): 721–34.

McDaniel, Eric L. 2003. "Black Clergy in the 2000 Election." *Journal for the Scientific Study of Religion* 42(2): 533–46.

———. 2009. *Politics in the Pews: The Political Mobilization of Black Churches*. Ann Arbor: University of Michigan Press.

———. 2016. "What Kind of Christian Are You? Religious Ideologies and Political Attitudes." *Journal for the Scientific Study of Religion* 55(2): 288–307.

McDaniel, Eric L., and Christopher G. Ellison. 2008. "God's Party? Race, Religion, and Partisanship over Time." *Political Research Quarterly* 61(2): 180–91.

McDaniel, Eric L., Irfan Nooruddin, and Allyson Faith Shortle. 2011. "Divine Boundaries: How Religion Shapes Citizens' Attitudes toward Immigrants." *American Politics Research* 39(1): 205–33.

McKenzie, Brian D., and Stella M. Rouse. 2013. "Shades of Faith: Religious Foundations of Political Attitudes among African Americans, Latinos, and Whites." *American Journal of Political Science* 57(1): 218–35.

McKinley, Jesse, and Liam Stack. 2020. "Cuomo Attacks Supreme Court, but Virus Ruling Is Warning to Governors." *New York Times*, November 26, 2020. https://www.nytimes.com/2020/11/26/nyregion/supreme-court-churches-religious-gatherings.html.

McLaughlin, Katy. 2002. "The Religion Bubble: Churches Try to Recapture 9/11 Crowds." *Wall Street Journal*, September 11, 2020. https://www.wsj.com/articles/SB1031681981556422835.

McRoberts, Omar M. 2003. *Streets of Glory: Church and Community in a Black Urban Neighborhood*. Chicago: University of Chicago Press.

Merino, Stephen. 2018. "God and Guns: Examining Religious Influences on Gun Control Attitudes in the United States." *Religions* 9(6): 189–202.

Mervosh, Sarah, and Elizabeth Dias. 2020. "From Seattle to Kentucky, Churches Cancel Religious Services." *New York Times*, February 10, 2020. https://www.nytimes.com/2020/03/11/us/coronavirus-kentucky-churches-cancel.html.

Meza, Diego. 2020. "In a Pandemic Are We More Religious? Traditional Practices of Catholics and the COVID-19 in Southwestern Colombia." *International Journal of Latin American Religions* 4(2): 18–234.

Miles, Matthew R. 2019. *Religious Identity in US Politics*. Boulder, CO: Lynne Rienner.

Miller, Joanne. 2020a. "Do COVID-19 Conspiracy Theory Beliefs Form a Monological Belief System?" *Canadian Journal of Political Science* 53(2): 319–26.

———. 2020b. "Psychological, Political, and Situational Factors Combine to Boost COVID-19 Conspiracy Theory Beliefs." *Canadian Journal of Political Science / Revue canadienne de science politique* 53(2): 327–34.

Miller, Matthew, Lisa Hepburn, and Deborah Azrael. 2017. "Firearm Acquisition without Background Checks: Results of a National Survey." *Annals of Internal Medicine* 166(4): 233–39.

Mitchell, Travis. 2016. "Where the Public Stands on Religious Liberty vs. Nondiscrimination." Pew Research Center, September 28, 2016. https://www.pewforum.org/2016/09/28/2-americans-divided-over-whether-wedding-related-businesses-should-be-required-to-serve-same-sex-couples/.

Mohamed, Besheer. 2018. "A Small but Steady Share of U.S. Muslims Are Republicans." Pew Research Center, November 6, 2018. https://www.pewresearch.org/fact-tank/2018/11/06/republicans-account-for-a-small-but-steady-share-of-u-s-muslims/.

Molteni, Francesco, Riccardo Ladini, Ferruccio Biolcati, Antonio M. Chiesi, Giulia Maria Dotti Sani, Simona Guglielmi, Marco Maraffi, Andrea Pedrazzani, Paolo Segatti, and Christiano Vezzoni. 2020. "Searching for Comfort in Religion: Insecurity and Religious Behaviour during the COVID-19 Pandemic in Italy." *European Societies* 23(1): 704–20.

Moore, Sharon E., Sharon D. Jones-Eversley, Willie F. Tolliver, Betty L. Wilson, and Christopher A. M. Jones. 2020. "Six Feet apart or Six Feet Under: The Impact of COVID-19 on the Black Community." *Death Studies* 1:1–11.

Morin, Rich. 2014. "The Demographics and Politics of Gun-Owning Households." Pew Research Center, July 15, 2014. https://www.pewresearch.org/fact-tank/2014/07/15/the-demographics-and-politics-of-gun-owning-households/.

Morris, Aldon D. 1984. *The Origins of the Civil Rights Movement: Black Communities Organizing for Change*. New York: Free Press.

Motta, Matt, Dominik Stecula, and Christina Farhart. 2020. "How Right-Leaning Media Coverage of COVID-19 Facilitated the Spread of Misinformation in the Early Stages of the Pandemic in the U.S." *Canadian Journal of Political Science* 53(2): 335–42.

Mueller, Charles W., and Weldon T. Johnson. 1975. "Socioeconomic Status and Religious Participation." *American Sociological Review* 40(6): 785–800.

Muslim Advocates. 2018. "Running on Hate: 2018 Pre-Election Report." Muslim Advocates, October 22, 2018. https://muslimadvocates.org/2018/10/new-report-documents-nationwide-spread-and-failure-of-anti-muslim-2018-2017-campaigns/.

Nacos, Brigitte L., and Oscar Torres-Reyna. 2007. *Fueling Our Fears: Stereotyping, Media Coverage, and Public Opinion of Muslim Americans*. Lanham, MD: Rowman & Littlefield.

National Opinion Research Center. 2020. "AmeriSpeak Omnibus Survey 2020." AmeriSpeak. Accessed February 16, 2021. https://amerispeak.norc.org/about-amerispeak/Pages/default.aspx.

Nelson, Joshua. 2020. "Huckabee: We Are 'Shredding the Constitution' While Enforcing Quarantine Measures." Fox News, April 13, 2020. https://www.foxnews.com/media/huckabee-enforcement-of-quarantines-should-scare-the-daylights-out-of-us.

Neuhaus, Richard John. 1984. *The Naked Public Square: Religion and Democracy in America*. Grand Rapids, MI: Eerdmans.

Newton, Kenneth. 1999. "Social and Political Trust in Established Democracies." In *Critical Citizens: Global Support for Democratic Governance*, edited by Pippa Norris, 169–87. Oxford, UK: Oxford University Press.

———. 2001. "Trust, Social Capital, Civil Society, and Democracy." *International Political Science Review* 22(2): 201–14.

Norton, Edward C., Hua Wang, and Chunrong Ai. 2004. "Computing Interaction Effects and Standard Errors in Logit and Probit Models." *Stata Journal* 4(2): 154–67.

NSSF: Trade Association for the Firearm Industry. 2020. "Firearm Retailer Survey: First-Time Gun Buyers." NSSF. August 24, 2020. https://d3aya7xwz8momx.cloudfront.net/wp-content/uploads/2020/06/FirstTimeResearch.pdf.

Ocampo, Angela X., Karam Dana, and Matt A. Barreto. 2018. "The American Muslim Voter: Community Belonging and Political Participation." *Social Science Research* 72:84–99.

Ogden, Thomas H. 2010. "On Three Forms of Thinking: Magical Thinking, Dream Thinking, and Transformative Thinking." *The Psychoanalytic Quarterly* 79(2): 317–47.

Oliver, J. Eric, and Thomas J Wood. 2014. "Conspiracy Theories and the Paranoid Style(s) of Mass Opinion." *American Journal of Political Science* 58(4): 952–66.

———. 2018. *Enchanted America: How Intuition and Reason Divide Our Politics*. Chicago: University of Chicago Press.

Olson, Laura R. 2000. *Filled with Spirit and Power: Protestant Clergy in Politics*. Albany: State University of New York Press.

Orden, Erica. 2020. "NRA Suing New York for Deeming Gun Stores Non-Essential Businesses during Coronavirus Pandemic." CNN. April 4, 2020. https://www.cnn.com/2020/04/03/politics/nra-new-york-gun-store-non-essential/index.html.

Osborn, Tracy L. 2012. *How Women Represent Women: Political Parties, Gender and Representation in the State Legislatures*. Oxford, UK: Oxford University Press.

Osborn, Tracy L., and Rebecca Kreitzer. 2014. "Women State Legislators: Women's Issues in Partisan Environments." In *Women and Elective Office: Past, Present, and Future*, edited by Sue Thomas and Clyde Wilcox. New York: Oxford University Press.

Osborn, Tracy L., and Jeanette Morehouse Mendez. 2010. "Speaking as Women: Women and Floor Speeches in the Senate." *Journal of Women, Politics and Policy* 31(1): 1–21.

Osteen, Joel. 2018. *Next Level Thinking: 10 Powerful Thoughts for a Successful and Abundant Life*. New York: FaithWords.

Our Sunday Visitor. 2020. "If You Can't Go to Confession, Take Your Sorrow Directly to God, Pope Says." OSVNews.com, March 20, 2020. https://www.osvnews.com/2020/03/20/if-you-cant-go-to-confession-take-your-sorrow-directly-to-god-pope-says/?fbclid=IwAR3NHwDP4P-XsOByhw6GrlyzDTyb212LpSSAFtKcvkwoQicEtxKbpHr-Ts8.

Owens, Michael L. 2007. *God and Government in the Ghetto: The Politics of Church-State Collaboration in Black America*. Chicago: University of Chicago Press.

Palmer, Ewan. 2020. "Virginia Pastor Dies from Coronavirus after Previously Saying 'Media Is Pumping Out Fear' about Pandemic." *Newsweek*, March 27, 2020. https://www.newsweek.com/virginia-pastor-dies-coronavirus-after-previously-saying-media-pumping-out-fear-about-pandemic-1494702.

Pan, Stephen W., Gordon C. Shen, Chuncheng Liu, and Jenny H. Hsi. 2020. "Coronavirus Stigmatization and Psychological Distress among Asians in the United States." *Ethnicity and Health* 26(1): 110–25.

Pargament, Kenneth I. 1997. *The Psychology of Religion and Coping: Theory, Research, Practice*. New York: Guilford.

Pargament, Kenneth I., and Hisham Abu-Raiya. 2007. "A Decade of Research on the Psychology of Religion and Coping: Things We Assumed and Lessons We Learned." *Psyke and Logos* 28(2): 742–66.

Parker, Kim, and Ruth Igielnik. 2020. "On the Cusp of Adulthood and Facing an Uncertain Future: What We Know About Gen Z So Far." Pew Research Center, May 14, 2020. https://www.pewsocialtrends.org/essay/on-the-cusp-of-adulthood-and-facing-an-uncertain-future-what-we-know-about-gen-z-so-far/.

Paxton, Ken. 2020. "AG Paxton Applauds Fifth Circuit for Prioritizing the Health and Safety of Medical Professionals Combating COVID-19 Crisis over Demands of Prisoners." Press release, April 22, 2020. https://www.texasattorneygeneral.gov/news/releases/ag-paxton-applauds-fifth-circuit-prioritizing-health-and-safety-medical-professionals-combating.

Payton, Mark E., Matthew H. Greenstone, and Nathaniel Schenker. 2003. "Overlapping Confidence Intervals or Standard Error Intervals: What Do They Mean in Terms of Statistical Significance?" *Journal of Insect Science* 3(1): 34–39.

"Peaceful Protesters Tear-Gassed To Clear Way For Trump Church Photo-Op." 2020. NPR.Org. June 1, 2020. https://www.npr.org/2020/06/01/867532070/trumps-unannounced-church-visit-angers-church-officials.

Pearson, Kathryn, and Logan Dancey. 2011. "Elevating Women's Voices in Congress: Speech Participation in the House of Representatives." *Political Research Quarterly* 64(4): 910–23.

Pederson, JoEllen, Thomas L. Hall, Bradley Foster, and Jessie E. Coates. 2015. "Gun Ownership and Attitudes toward Gun Control in Older Adults: Re-Examining Self Interest Theory." *American Journal of Social Science Research* 1(5): 273–81.

Pelham, Brett, and Steve Crabtree. 2008. "Worldwide, Highly Religious More Likely to Help Others." Gallup News Brief, October 8, 2008. https://news.gallup.com/poll/111013/worldwide-highly-religious-more-likely-help-others.aspx.

Perkins, Tony. 2020a. "Evangelical Leaders Praise Trump as Christians' Best Friend in the 21st Century." Life Site, January 7, 2020. https://www.lifesitenews.com/opinion/evangelical-leaders-praise-trump-as-christians-best-friend-in-the-21st-century.

———. 2020b. "Mob Violence and Police Brutality Result from a Morally Bankrupt America." *Washington Times*, June 1, 2020. https://www.washingtontimes.com/news/2020/jun/1/mob-violence-and-police-brutality-result-from-a-mo/.

———. 2020c. "Pray. Vote. Stand. Series: Pray for our Nation." Family Research Council, January 5, 2020. https://www.frc.org/university/pray-vote-stand-january-5.

———. 2020d. "Tony Perkins on Campaign 2020." *Washington Journal*, August 25. https://www.c-span.org/video/?475094-5/washington-journal-tony-perkins-discusses-campaign-2020.

Perry, Samuel L., and Joshua B. Grubbs. 2020. "Formal or Functional? Traditional or Inclusive? Bible Translations as Markers of Religious Subcultures." *Sociology of Religion* 81(3): 319–42.

Perry, Samuel L., and Andrew L. Whitehead. 2019. "Christian America in Black and White: Racial Identity, Religious-National Group Boundaries, and Explanations for Racial Inequality." *Sociology of Religion* 80(3): 277–98.

Perry, Samuel L., Andrew L. Whitehead, and Joseph O. Baker. 2020. "Coronavirus Exposes the Religious Right's Racism." Religion Dispatches, March 14, 2020. https://religiondispatches.org/coronavirus-exposes-the-religious-rights-racism/.

Perry, Samuel L., Andrew L. Whitehead, and Joshua B. Grubbs. 2020a. "Culture Wars and COVID-19 Conduct: Christian Nationalism, Religiosity, and Americans' Behavior during the Coronavirus Pandemic." *Journal for the Scientific Study of Religion* 59(3): 405–16.

———. 2020b. "Prejudice and Pandemic in the Promised Land: How White Christian Nationalism Shapes Americans' Racist and Xenophobic Views of COVID-19." *Ethnic and Racial Studies* 44(5): 759–72.

———. 2021. "Save the Economy, Liberty, and Yourself: Christian Nationalism and Americans' Views on Government COVID-19 Restrictions." *Sociology of Religion* 82(4): 426–46.

Peters, Cameron. 2020. "A Detailed Timeline of All the Ways Trump Failed to Respond to the Coronavirus." *Vox*, June 8, 2020. https://www.vox.com/2020/6/8/21242003/trump-failed-coronavirus-response.

Pew Research Center. 2012. "In Changing News Landscape, Even Television Is Vulnerable: Section 4; Demographics and Political Views of News Audiences." Pew Research Center, September 27, 2012. https://www.pewresearch.org/politics/2012/09/27/section-4-demographics-and-political-views-of-news-audiences/.

———. 2014. "Racial and Ethnic Composition." Pew Research Center. Accessed February 21, 2021. https://www.pewforum.org/religious-landscape-study/racial-and-ethnic-composition/.

———. 2018. "Religious Landscape Study." Pew Research Center. Accessed December 7, 2020. https://www.pewforum.org/religious-landscape-study/.

———. 2019a. "Audio and Podcasting Fact Sheet." Pew Research Center, June 29, 2019. https://www.journalism.org/fact-sheet/audio-and-podcasting/.

———. 2019b. "In U.S., Decline of Christianity Continues at Rapid Pace." Pew Research Center, October 17, 2019. https://www.pewforum.org/2019/10/17/in-u-s-decline-of-christianity-continues-at-rapid-pace/.

———. 2020a. "Americans Oppose Religious Exemptions from Coronavirus-Related Restrictions." Pew Research Center, August 7, 2020. https://www.pewforum.org

/2020/08/07/americans-oppose-religious-exemptions-from-coronavirus-related-restrictions/.

———. 2020b. "Most Americans Say Coronavirus Outbreak Has Impacted Their Lives." Pew Research Center, March 30, 2020. https://www.pewresearch.org/social-trends/wp-content/uploads/sites/3/2020/03/PSDT_03.30.20_W64-COVID-19.Personal-impact-FULL-REPORT.pdf.

———. 2020c. "U.S. Teens Take After Their Parents Religiously, Attend Services Together and Enjoy Family Rituals." Pew Research Center, September 10, 2020. https://www.pewforum.org/2020/09/10/u-s-teens-take-after-their-parents-religiously-attend-services-together-and-enjoy-family-rituals/.

———. 2020d. "White Evangelicals See Trump as Fighting for Their Beliefs, though Many Have Mixed Feelings About His Personal Conduct." Pew Research Center, March 12, 2020. https://www.pewforum.org/2020/03/12/white-evangelicals-see-trump-as-fighting-for-their-beliefs-though-many-have-mixed-feelings-about-his-personal-conduct/.

———. 2021. "Faith Among Black Americans." *Pew Research Center*, February 16, 2021. https://www.pewresearch.org/religion/2021/02/16/faith-among-black-americans/.

Philpot, Tasha S., and Eric L. McDaniel. 2020. "Black Religious Belief Systems and Political Participation." *National Review of Black Politics* 1(3): 374–95.

Pirutinsky, Steven, Aaron D. Cherniak, and David H. Rosmarin. 2020. "COVID-19, Mental Health, and Religious Coping among American Orthodox Jews." *Journal of Religion and Health* 59(5): 2288–301.

Piscopo, Jennifer M. 2020. "Women Leaders and Pandemic Performance: A Spurious Correlation." *Politics and Gender* 16(4): 951–59.

Pope Francis. 2020. "A Crisis Reveals What Is in Our Hearts." *New York Times*, November 26, 2020. https://www.nytimes.com/2020/11/26/opinion/pope-francis-covid.html.

Posner, Sara. 2020. "St. John's Episcopal Church to Pandemic Response." NBC News, June 2, 2020. https://www.nbcnews.com/think/opinion/st-john-s-episcopal-church-pandemic-response-trump-co-opting-ncna1222086.

Powell, Brian, Landon Schnabel, and Lauren Apgar. 2017. "Denial of Service to Same-Sex and Interracial Couples: Evidence from a National Survey Experiment." *Science Advances* 3(12): 1–7.

Power, Kate. 2020. "The COVID-19 Pandemic Has Increased the Care Burden of Women and Families." *Sustainability: Science, Practice and Policy* 16(1): 67–73.

Presser, Stanley, and Linda Stinson. 1998. "Data Collection Mode and Social Desirability Bias in Self-Reported Religious Attendance." *American Sociological Review* 63(1): 137–45.

Public Religion Research Institute (PRRI). 2019. "Fractured Nation: Widening Partisan Polarization and Key Issues in 2020 Presidential Elections." PRRI.org, October 21, 2019. prri.org/research/fractured-nation-widening-partisan-polarization-and-key-issues-in-2020-presidential-elections.

———. 2020. "Vast Majority of Americans Stayed Home for Easter, Oppose Religious Exemptions to Stay-at-Home Orders." PRRI.org, April 15, 2020. https://www.prri.org/research/vast-majority-of-americans-stayed-home-for-easter-oppose-religious-exemptions-to-stay-at-home-orders/.

———. 2021. "Religious Identities and the Race against the Virus: American Attitudes on Vaccination Mandates and Religious Exemptions (Wave 3)." PRRI.org, December 9, 2021. https://www.prri.org/research/religious-identities-and-the-race-against-the-virus-american-attitudes-on-vaccination-mandates-and-religious-exemptions/.

Putnam, Robert D., and David E. Campbell. 2010. *American Grace: How Religion Divides and Unites Us*. New York: Simon and Schuster.

Read, Richard. 2020. "A Choir Decided to Go Ahead with Rehearsal: Now Dozens of Members Have COVID-19 and Two Are Dead." *LA Times*, March 29, 2020. https://www.latimes.com/world-nation/story/2020-03-29/coronavirus-choir-outbreak.

Reagan, Ronald. 1980. "National Affairs Campaign Address on Religious Liberty." American Rhetoric Online Speech Bank, August 1980. https://www.americanrhetoric.com/speeches/ronaldreaganreligiousliberty.htm.

Rediker, Marcus. 2008. *The Slave Ship: A Human History*. New York: Viking.

Reed, Ralph. 2020a. *For God and Country*. Washington, DC: Regnery.

———. 2020b. "Ralph Reed on Evangelical Voters' Support for President Trump." *Washington Journal*, June 2, 2020. https://www.c-span.org/video/?472640-4/washington-journal-ralph-reed-discusses-evangelical-voters-support-president-trump-campaign-2020.

———. 2020c. "Ralph Reed Says President Trump Has 'Advanced Moral Goods and the Common Good.'" Posted by Washington Post Live on September 14, 2020. YouTube video, 2:50. https://www.youtube.com/watch?v=V0955U5IqF0.

———. 2020d. "Why Did Christians Vote for Trump in 2016 and Will They Vote for Him Again in 2020?" Interview by Pat Robertson on CBN News, May 26, 2020. https://www1.cbn.com/cbnnews/us/2020/may/why-did-christians-vote-for-trump-in-2016-and-will-they-vote-for-him-again-in-2020.

Reinbold, Jenna. 2018. "'Honorable Religious Premises' and Other Affronts: Disputing Free Exercise in the Era of Trump." *Studies in Law, Politics, and Society* 79: 31–54.

———. 2020. "For Neil Gorsuch, Religious Freedom Hasn't Gone Far Enough." Religion and Politics, August 25, 2020. https://religionandpolitics.org/2020/08/25/for-neil-gorsuch-religious-freedom-hasnt-gone-far-enough/.

———. 2021. "Religious Conservatives Won the Battle Over COVID-19, But Not the War." *Religion and Politics*, July 13. https://religionandpolitics.org/2021/07/13/religious-conservatives-won-the-legal-battle-over-covid-19-but-not-the-war/.

Reingold, Beth. 2000. *Representing Women: Sex, Gender, and Legislative Behavior in Arizona and California*. Chapel Hill: University of North Carolina Press.

Reingold, Beth, and Jessica Harrell. 2010. "The Impact of Descriptive Representation on Women's Political Engagement: Does Party Matter?" *Political Research Quarterly* 63(2): 280–94.

Reingold, Beth, Rebecca J. Kreitzer, Tracy Osborn, and Michele L. Swers. 2020. "Anti-Abortion Policymaking and Women's Representation." *Political Research Quarterly* 74(2): 403–20.

Renner, Rebecca. 2020. "Millennials and Gen Z Are Spreading Coronavirus—but Not Because of Parties and Bars." *National Geographic*, September 17, 2020. https://www.nationalgeographic.com/science/2020/09/millennials-generation-z-coronavirus-scapegoating-beach-parties-bars-inequality-cvd/.

Reno, R. R. 2020. "Keep the Churches Open." First Things, March 17, 2020. https://www.firstthings.com/web-exclusives/2020/03/keep-the-churches-open.

Reny, Tyler T., and Matt A. Barreto. 2020. "Xenophobia in the Time of Pandemic: Othering, Anti-Asian Attitudes, and COVID-19." *Politics, Groups, and Identities,* May 28, 2020, 1–24. https://doi.org/10.1080/21565503.2020.1769693.

Reuters. 2020. "The Americans Defying Palm Sunday Quarantines: 'Satan's Trying to Keep Us Apart.'" Reuters, April 4, 2020. https://www.reuters.com/article/us-health-coronavirus-usa-palmsunday-idUSKBN21M0OP.

Rev. 2020. "Donald Trump Coronavirus Press Conference Transcript July 28: Talks Kodak, Vaccine, DACA." Rev.com, July 28, 2020. https://www.rev.com/blog/transcripts/donald-trump-coronavirus-press-conference-transcript-july-28.

Rho, Hye Jin, Brown, Hayley, and Shawn Fremstad. 2020. "A Basic Demographic Profile of Workers in Frontline Industries." *Center for Economic and Policy Research* 7:1–10. https://axelkra.us/wp-content/uploads/2020/12/2020-04-Frontline-Workers.pdf.

Roberts, Dorothy. 1998. *Killing the Black Body: Race, Reproduction, and the Meaning of Liberty.* New York: Second Vintage Books.

Rocha, Abby. 2020. "Central Church Hosts More than 1,800 People amid Covid-19 Outbreak." Brproud.com, March 22, 2020. https://www.brproud.com/health/coronavirus/central-church-hosts-1800-people-amid-covid-19-outbreak/.

Rolfes-Haase, Kelly, and Michele L. Swers. 2021. "Understanding the Gender and Partisan Dynamics of Abortion Voting in the House of Representatives." *Politics and Gender* 18(2): 448–82.

Roman Catholic Diocese of Brooklyn v. Andrew Cuomo, Emergency Application for Writ of Injunction. 2020. https://www.supremecourt.gov/DocketPDF/20/20A87/160205/20201109225714204_Diocese%20Application%20TO%20FILE.pdf.

Romney, Mitt. 2007. "Transcript: Mitt Romney's Faith Speech." NPR, December 6, 2007. https://www.npr.org/templates/story/story.php?storyId=16969460.

Rouse, Stella M. 2020. "New Data Finds Black and Hispanic Americans More Likely to Take Precautions against Coronavirus." *Washington Post,* August 10, 2020. https://www.washingtonpost.com/politics/2020/08/10/new-data-finds-black-hispanic-americans-more-likely-take-precautions-against-coronavirus/.

Rouse, Stella M., and Ashley Ross. 2018. *The Politics of Millennials: Political Beliefs and Policy Preferences of America's Most Diverse Generation.* Ann Arbor: University of Michigan Press.

Rowland, Michael L., and E. Paulette Isaac-Savage. 2014. "As I See It: A Study of African American Pastors' Views on Health and Health Education in the Black Church." *Journal of Religion and Health* 53(4): 1091–101.

Safi, Michael, and Milivoje Pantovic. 2021. "Vaccine Diplomacy: West Falling Behind in Race for Influence." *The Guardian,* February 19, 2021. https://www.theguardian.com/world/2021/feb/19/coronavirus-vaccine-diplomacy-west-falling-behind-russia-china-race-influence.

Sales, Ben. 2020. "Brooklyn's Orthodox Neighborhoods Have Especially High Rates of the Coronavirus." Jewish Telegraphic Agency, April 2, 2020. https://www.jta.org/2020/04/02/united-states/brooklyns-orthodox-neighborhoods-have-especially-high-rates-of-coronavirus.

Sanbonmatsu, Kira, and Kathleen Dolan. 2009. "Do Gender Stereotypes Transcend Party?" *Political Research Quarterly* 62(3): 485–94.

Saroglou, Vassilis, Isabelle Pichon, Laurence Trompette, Marijke Verschueren, and Rebecca Dernelle. 2005. "Prosocial Behavior and Religion: New Evidence Based on Projective Measures and Peer Ratings." *Journal for the Scientific Study of Religion* 44(3): 323–48.

Schaffer, Joby, Anand E. Sokhey, and Paul A. Djupe. 2015. "The Religious Economy of Political Tolerance." In *Religion and Political Tolerance in America: Advances in the State of the Art*, edited by Paul A. Djupe, 151–64. Philadelphia: Temple University Press.

Schieman, Scott, and Jong Hyun Jung. 2012. "'Practical Divine Influence': Socioeconomic Status and Belief in the Prosperity Gospel." *Journal for the Scientific Study of Religion* 51(4): 738–56.

Schor, Elana. 2020. "States Differ on Exempting Worship from Coronavirus Closures." Religion News Service, March 24, 2020. https://religionnews.com/2020/03/24/states-differ-on-exempting-worship-from-coronavirus-closures/.

Schwadel, Philip, John D. McCarthy, and Hart M. Nelsen. 2009. "The Continuing Relevance of Family Income for Religious Participation: U.S. White Catholic Church Attendance in the Late 20th Century." *Social Forces* 87(4): 1997–2030.

Seipel, Brooke. 2020. "Louisiana Church Expecting 2,000 at Easter Service Despite Coronavirus: 'Satan and a Virus Will Not Stop Us.'" The Hill, April 10, 2020. https://thehill.com/homenews/news/492277-louisiana-church-expecting-2000-at-easter-service-despite-coronavirus-satan-and.

Seirmarco, Gretchen, Yuva Neria, Beverly Insel, Dasha Kiper, Ali Doruk, Raz Gross, and Brett Litz. 2012. "Religiosity and Mental Health: Changes in Religious Beliefs, Complicated Grief, Posttraumatic Stress Disorder, and Major Depression following the September 11, 2001 Attacks." *Psychology of Religion and Spirituality* 4(1): 10–18.

Sekulow, Jordan. 2020. "The Radical Left Continues to Use the Coronavirus Crisis to Attack Faith and Conservative Values." American Center for Law and Justice, March 31, 2020. https://aclj.org/radical-left/the-radical-left-continues-to-use-the-coronavirus-crisis-to-attack-faith-and-conservative-values.

Selod, Saher. 2015. "Citizenship Denied: The Racialization of Muslim American Men and Women Post-9/11." *Critical Sociology* 41(1): 77–95.

Selod, Saher, and David G. Embrick. 2013. "Racialization and Muslims: Situating the Muslim Experience in Race Scholarship." *Sociology Compass* 7(8): 644–55.

Selyukh, Alina. 2011. "U.S. Researchers Broke Rules in Guatemala Syphilis Study." Reuters, August 30, 2011. https://www.reuters.com/article/us-usa-guatemala-syphilis-idUSTRE77T2J920110830.

Shah, V. Dhavan, Douglas M. Mcleod, Hernando Rojas, Jaeho Cho, Michael W. Wagner, and Lewis A. Friedland. 2017. "Revising the Communication Mediation Model for a New Political Communication Ecology." *Human Communication Research* 43(4): 491–504.

Shariff, Azim F., and Ara Norenzayan. 2007. "God Is Watching You: Priming God Concepts Increases Prosocial Behavior in an Anonymous Economic Game." *Psychological Science* 18(9): 803–9.

Shavers, Vickie L., Pebbles Fagan, Dionne Jones, William M. P. Klein, Josephine Boyington, Carmen Moten, and Edward Rorie. 2012. "The State of Research on Racial/Ethnic Discrimination in the Receipt of Health Care." *American Journal of Public Health* 102(5): 953–66.

Shear, Michael D., and Sarah Mervosh. 2020. "Trump Encourages Protest against Governors Who Have Imposed Virus Restrictions." *The New York Times*, April 17, sec. U.S. https://www.nytimes.com/2020/04/17/us/politics/trump-coronavirus-governors.html.

Shearer, Elisa. 2018. "Social Media Outpaces Print Newspapers in the U.S. as a News Source." Pew Research Center, December 10, 2018. https://www.pewresearch.org/fact-tank/2018/12/10/social-media-outpaces-print-newspapers-in-the-u-s-as-a-news-source/.

Shelton, Jason E., and Ryon J. Cobb. 2018. "Black Reltrad: Measuring Religious Diversity and Commonality among African Americans." *Journal for the Scientific Study of Religion* 56(4): 737–64.

Shelton, Jason E., and Michael O. Emerson. 2012. *Blacks and Whites in Christian America: How Racial Discrimination Shapes Religious Convictions*. New York: New York University Press.

Sheridan, Richard B. 1985. *Doctors and Slaves*. New York: Cambridge University Press.

Sherkat, Darren E., and Derek Lehman. 2018. "Bad Samaritans: Religion and Anti-Immigrant and Anti-Muslim Sentiment in the United States." *Social Science Quarterly* 99(5): 1791–804.

Sherkat, Darren E., Kylan Mattias de Vries, and Stacia Creek. 2010. "Race, Religion, and Opposition to Same-Sex Marriage." *Social Science Quarterly* 91(1): 80–98.

Sherwood, Harriet. 2020. "British Public Turn to Prayer as One in Four Tune In to Religious Services." *The Guardian*, Febuary 14, 2020. https://www.theguardian.com/world/2020/may/03/british-public-turn-to-prayer-as-one-in-four-tune-in-to-religious-services.

Shimron, Yonat. 2020. "John MacArthur Claimed There Is 'No Pandemic': He Was Politicizing Science, Experts Say." Religion News Service, September 1, 2020. https://religionnews.com/2020/09/01/john-macarthur-claimed-there-no-pandemic-he-was-politicizing-the-science/.

Shin, Youjin, Bonnie Berkowitz, and Min Joo Kim. 2020. "How a South Korean Church Helped Fuel the Spread of the Coronavirus." *Washington Post*, March 25, 2020. https://www.washingtonpost.com/graphics/2020/world/coronavirus-south-korea-church/.

Shortle, Allyson F., and Ronald Keith Gaddie. 2015. "Religious Nationalism and Perceptions of Muslims and Islam." *Politics and Religion* 8(3): 435–57.

Sibley, Chris G., and Joseph Bulbulia. 2012. "Faith after an Earthquake: A Longitudinal Study of Religion and Perceived Health before and after the 2011 Christchurch New Zealand Earthquake." *PLOS ONE* 7(12): 1–10.

Singh, Maanvi, Helen Davidson, and Julian Borger. 2020. "Trump Claims to Have Evidence Coronavirus Started in Chinese Lab but Offers No Details." *The Guardian*, April 30, 2020. https://www.theguardian.com/us-news/2020/apr/30/donald-trump-coronavirus-chinese-lab-claim.

Skloot, Rebecca. 2011. *The Immortal Life of Henrietta Lacks*. New York: Broadway Paperbacks.

Smith, Aaron. 2020. "Gun Sales Surge Ahead Of Election Day, FBI Background Checks Show." Forbes. November 3, 2020. https://www.forbes.com/sites/aaronsmith/2020/11/03/gun-sales-surge-ahead-of-election-day-according-to-fbi-background-checks/.

Smith, Bruce W., Kenneth I. Pargament, Curtis Brant, and Joan M. Oliver. 2000. "Noah Revisited: Religious Coping by Church Members and the Impact of the 1993 Midwest Flood." *Journal of Community Psychology* 28(2): 169–86.

Smith, Gregory A. 2021. "About Three-in-Ten U.S. Adults Are Now Religiously Unaffiliated." Pew Research Center, December 14, 2021. https://www.pewforum.org/2021/12/14/about-three-in-ten-u-s-adults-are-now-religiously-unaffiliated/.

Smith, Gregory A., Elizabeth P. Sciupac, Claire Gecewicz, and Conrad Hackett. 2018. "Comparing the RELTRAD and Born-Again/Evangelical Self-Identification Approaches to Measuring American Protestantism." *Journal for the Scientific Study of Religion* 57(4): 830–47.

Smothers, Hannah, Ryan P. Burge, and Paul A. Djupe. 2020. "The Gendered Religious Response to State Action on the Coronavirus Pandemic." *Politics and Gender* 16 (4): 1063–74.

Sobal, Jeff, and Marilyn Jackson-Beeck. 1981. "Newspaper Nonreaders: A National Profile." *Journalism Quarterly* 58(1): 9–28.

Sobieraj, Sarah, and Jeffrey M. Berry. 2011. "From Incivility to Outrage: Political Discourse in Blogs, Talk Radio, and Cable News." *Political Communication* 28(1): 19–41.

Solari-Twadell, Phyllis A., Anne Marie Djupe, and Mary Ann McDermott. 1990. *Parish Nursing: The Developing Practice*. Park Ridge, IL: National Parish Nurse Resource Center.

South Bay United Pentecostal Church v. Gavin Newsom, Denial of Application for Injunctive Relief. May 29, 2020. https://www.law.cornell.edu/supremecourt/text/19A1044.

Southworth, Ann. 2008. *Lawyers of the Right: Professionalizing the Conservative Coalition*. Chicago: University of Chicago Press.

Spitzer, Robert J. 2012. *The Politics of Gun Control*. 5th ed. Boulder, CO: Paradigm.

Starr, Paul. 2020. "When Churches Are Superspreaders." *The American Prospect*, May 27, 2020. https://prospect.org/api/content/1fea747a-9f85-11ea-873b-1244d5f7c7c6/.

Steensland, Brian, Jerry Z. Park, Mark D. Regnerus, Lynn D. Robinson, W. Bradford Wilcox, and Robert D. Woodberry. 2000. "The Measure of American Religion: Toward Improving the State of the Art." *Social Forces* 79(1): 291–318.

Stelter, Brian. 2020. "Dr. Anthony Fauci Says Some Fox Coverage of the Pandemic Is 'Outlandish.'" CNN, September 29, 2020. https://www.cnn.com/2020/09/29/media/anthony-fauci-fox-news-media/index.html.

Stewart, Evan, Penny Edgell, and Jack Delehanty. 2018. "The Politics of Religious Prejudice and Tolerance for Cultural Others." *Sociological Quarterly* 59(1): 17–39.

Strang, Stephen. 2020. *God, Trump, and COVID-19*. Florida: Frontline.

Stratta, Paolo, Cristina Capanna, Ilaria Riccardi, Claudia Carmassi, Armando Piccini, Liliana Dell'Osso, and Alessandro Rossi. 2012. "Suicidal Intention and Negative

Spiritual Coping One Year after the Earthquake of L'Aquila (Italy)." *Journal of Affective Disorders* 136(3): 1227–31.

Stroope, Samuel, Paul Froese, Heather Rackin, and Jack Delehanty. 2020. "Unchurched Christian Nationalism and the 2016 U.S. Presidential Election." *Sociological Forum* 36(2): 405–25.

Stroud, Natalie J. 2011. *Niche News: The Politics of News Choice*. New York: Oxford University Press.

Substance Abuse and Mental Health Services Administration. 2020. "Double Jeopardy: COVID-19 and Behavioral Health Disparities for Black and Latino Communities in the U.S." SAMHSA.gov. Accessed February 21, 2021. https://www.samhsa.gov/sites/default/files/covid19-behavioral-health-disparities-black-latino-communities.pdf.

Suk, Jiyoun, Dhavan V. Shah, Chris Wells, Michael W. Wagner, Lewis A. Friedland, Katherine J. Cramer, Ceri Hughes, and Charles Franklin. 2020. "Do Improving Conditions Harden Partisan Preferences? Communication, Context, and Political Evaluations during Periods of Contention." *International Journal of Public Opinion Research* 32(4): 750–68.

Swami, Viren, Rebecca Coles, Stefan Stieger, Jakob Pietschnig, Adrian Furnham, Sherry Rehim, and Martin Voracek. 2011. "Conspiracist Ideation in Britain and Austria: Evidence of a Monological Belief System and Associations Between Individual Psychological Differences and Real-World and Fictitious Conspiracy Theories." *British Journal of Psychology* 102(3): 443–63.

Swami, Viren, Martin Voracek, Stefan Stieger, Ulrich S. Tran, and Adrian Furnham. 2014. "Analytic Thinking Reduces Belief in Conspiracy Theories." *Cognition* 133(3): 572–85.

Swers, Michele L. 2005. "Connecting Descriptive and Substantive Representation: An Analysis of Sex Differences in Co-sponsorship Activity." *Legislative Studies Quarterly* 30(3): 407–33.

———. 2013. *Women in the Club: Gender and Policy Making in the Senate*. Chicago: University of Chicago Press.

Swire, Briony, Adam J. Berinsky, Stephan Lewandowsky, and Ullrich K. H. Ecker. 2017. "Processing Political Misinformation: Comprehending the Trump Phenomenon." *Royal Society Open Science* 4(3): 1–21.

Tajfel, Henri, and John C. Turner. 1979. "An Integrative Theory of Intergroup Conflict." In *The Social Psychology of Intergroup Relations*, edited by William G Austin and Stephen Worchel, 33–47. Monterey, CA: Brooks/Cole.

Taylor, James B., Sarah A. Gershon, and Adrian D. Pantoja. 2014. "Christian America? Understanding the Link between Churches, Attitudes, and 'Being American' among Latino Immigrants." *Politics and Religion* 7(2): 339–65.

Taylor, Robert J., Linda M. Chatters, Rukmaie Jayakody, and Jeffrey S, Levin. 1996. "Black and White Differences in Religious Participation: A Multi-Sample Comparison." *Journal for the Scientific Study of Religion* 35(2): 403–10.

Thomas, Deja, and Juliana M. Horowitz. 2020. "Support for Black Lives Matter Has Decreased since June but Remains Strong among Black Americans." Pew Research Center, September 16, 2020. https://www.pewresearch.org/fact-tank/2020/09/16

/support-for-black-lives-matter-has-decreased-since-june-but-remains-strong-among-black-americans/.

Thomas, Sue, and Susan Welch. 1991. "The Impact of Gender on Activities and Priorities of State Legislators." *Western Political Quarterly* 44(2): 445–56.

Thomas More Society. 2020. "Pastor John MacArthur Files Declaration against LA County's Repeated Attacks to Shut Down Church." Thomas More Society, August 24, 2020. https://www.thomasmoresociety.org/pastor-john-macarthur-files-declaration-against-la-countys-repeated-attacks-to-shut-down-church/.

Thompkins, Floyd, Peter Goldblum, Tammy Lai, Tristan Hansell, Annanda Barclay, and Lisa M. Brown. 2020. "A Culturally Specific Mental Health and Spirituality Approach for African Americans Facing the COVID-19 Pandemic." *Psychological Trauma: Theory, Research, Practice, and Policy* 12(5): 455–56.

Tocqueville, Alexis de. 1835. "Democracy in America." Vol. 1. Accessed April 12, 2021. http://xroads.virginia.edu/~Hyper/DETOC/toc_indx.html.

———. 1840. "Democracy in America." Vol. 2. Accessed April 12, 2021. http://xroads.virginia.edu/~Hyper/DETOC/toc_indx.html.

Totenberg, Nina. 2021. "Supreme Court Again Leaves State Vaccine Mandate in Place for Health Care Workers." NPR, December 13, 2021. https://www.npr.org/2021/12/13/1063923911/supreme-court-again-leaves-state-vaccine-mandate-in-place-for-healthcare-workers.

Traunmüller, Richard. 2011. "Moral Communities? Religion as a Source of Social Trust in a Multilevel Analysis of 97 German Regions." *European Sociological Review* 27(3): 346–63.

Trump, Donald. 2020a. Interview by Chris Wallace. *Fox News Sunday*, July 19, 2020. https://www.foxnews.com/politics/transcript-fox-news-sunday-interview-with-president-trump.

———. 2020b. "Protecting American Monuments, Memorials and Statues and Combating Recent Criminal Violence." Executive Order 13933, June 26, 2020. https://www.federalregister.gov/documents/2020/07/02/2020-14509/protecting-american-monuments-memorials-and-statues-and-combating-recent-criminal-violence.

Tyler & Bursch, LLP. 2020. "Declaration of Essentiality." Tyler & Bursch, LLP. Accessed December 12, 2020. https://www.tylerbursch.com/religious-petition-to-governor-gavin-newsom.

Uddin, Asma T. 2019. *When Islam Is Not a Religion: Inside America's Fight for Religious Freedom*. New York: Pegasus Books.

Uddin, Asma T., and Andrew R. Lewis. 2020. "When COVID-19 and Religious Freedom Intersect, Political Partisans Rush to Take Sides." *USA Today*, December 11, 2020. https://www.usatoday.com/story/opinion/2020/12/11/partisans-rush-take-sides-when-covid-19-religious-freedom-collide-column/3876908001/.

Uecker, Jeremy E. 2008. "Religious and Spiritual Responses to 9/11: Evidence from the Add Health Study." *Sociological Spectrum* 28(5): 477–509.

Ulbig, Stacy G. 2007. "Gendering Municipal Government: Female Descriptive Representation and Feelings of Political Trust." *Social Science Quarterly* 88(5): 1106–23.

United States v. Ballard 322 U.S. 78 (1944).

USAID. 2020. "The Appointment of Samah Norquist as Chief Advisor for International Religious Freedom to the Administrator of USAID." Press release, July 20, 2020.

https://www.usaid.gov/news-information/press-releases/july-20-2020-appointment-of-samah-norquist-as-chief-advisor.

U.S. Bureau of Labor Statistics. 2021. "Labor Force Statistics from the Current Population Survey: Household Data: Annual Averages: 11; Employed Persons by Detailed Occupation, Race, Sex, and Hispanic or Latino Ethnicity." BLS.gov, last modified January 22, 2021. https://www.bls.gov/cps/cpsaat11.htm.

Uscinski, Joseph E., Adam M. Enders, Casey A. Klofstad, Michelle Seelig, John R. Funchion, Caleb Everett, Stephan Wuchty, et al. 2020. "Why Do People Believe COVID-19 Conspiracy Theories?" *The Harvard Kennedy School (HKS) Misinformation Review* 1:1–12.

Uscinski, Joseph, and Santiago Olivella. 2017. "The Conditional Effect of Conspiracy Thinking on Attitudes toward Climate Change." *Research and Politics* 4(4): 1–9.

Valenzuela, Ali A. 2014. "Tending the Flock: Latino Religious Commitments and Political Preferences." *Political Research Quarterly* 67(4): 930–42.

Vandermaas-Peeler, Alex, Daniel Cox, Maxine Najle, and Molly Fisch-Friedman. 2018. "Wedding Cakes, Same-Sex Marriage, and the Future of LGBT Rights in America." PRRI.org, August 2, 2018. https://www.prri.org/research/wedding-cakes-same-sex-lgbt-marriage/.

Van Prooijen, J. 2016. "Why Education Predicts Decreased Belief in Conspiracy Theories." *Applied Cognitive Psychology* 31(1): 50–58.

Van Prooijen, Jan-Willem, and Karen M. Douglas. 2017. "Conspiracy Theories as Part of History: The Role of Societal Crisis Situations." *Memory Studies* 10(3): 323–33.

Vega, Arturo, and Juanita M. Firestone. 1995. "The Effects of Gender on Congressional Behavior and the Substantive Representation of Women." *Legislative Studies Quarterly* 20(2): 213–22.

Vegter, Abigail, and Kevin R. den Dulk. 2021. "Clinging to Guns and Religion? A Research Note Testing the Role of Protestantism in Shaping Gun Identity in the United States." *Politics and Religion* 14(4): 809–24. https://doi.org/10.1017/S1755048320000528.

Vegter, Abigail, and Margaret Kelley. 2020. "The Protestant Ethic and the Spirit of Gun Ownership." *Journal for the Scientific Study of Religion* 59(3): 526–40.

Verba, Sidney, Kay Lehman Schlozman, and Henry E. Brady. 1995. *Voice and Equality: Civic Voluntarism in American Politics*. Cambridge, MA: Harvard University Press.

Villarreal, Alexandra. 2020. "'You Can't Get Close, yet You Can't Stay Away': Latino Cultural Beliefs Clash with Pandemic Safety." *The Guardian*, August 27, 2020. https://www.theguardian.com/us-news/2020/aug/27/covid-19-latino-family-culture-us.

Wagner, Michael, and Amanda Friesen. 2021. "The Consequences of Denominational Typicality on Individual Political Attitudes." In *New Directions in Religion and Politics*, edited by Brian Calfano. Ann Arbor: University of Michigan Press.

Wald, Kenneth D., Dennis E. Owen, and Samuel S. Hill. 1988. "Churches as Political Communities." *American Political Science Review* 82(2): 531–48.

Walsh, Andrew. 2001. "Religion after 9-11: Good for What Ails Us." *Religion in the News* 4(3). http://www2.trincoll.edu/csrpl/RINVol4No3/revival.htm.

Wang, Hansi Lo. 2018. "Generation Z Is the Most Racially and Ethnically Diverse Yet." NPR, November 15, 2018. https://www.npr.org/2018/11/15/668106376/generation-z-is-the-most-racially-and-ethnically-diverse-yet.

Washington, Harriet A. 2006. *Medical Apartheid: The Dark History of Medical Experimentation on Black Americans from Colonial Times to the Present.* New York: Doubleday.

Wexler, Jay. 2019. *Our Non-Christian Nation: How Atheists, Satanists, Pagans, and Others Are Demanding Their Rightful Place in Public Life.* Palo Alto, CA: Stanford University Press.

Whitehead, Andrew L., and Samuel L. Perry. 2015. "A More Perfect Union? Christian Nationalism and Support for Same-Sex Unions." *Sociological Perspectives* 58(3): 422–40.

———. 2019. "Is a 'Christian America' a More Patriarchal America? Religion, Politics, and Traditionalist Gender Ideology." *Canadian Review of Sociology* 56(2): 151–77.

———. 2020a. "How Culture Wars Delay Herd Immunity: Christian Nationalism and Anti-Vaccine Attitudes." *Socius* 6. https://doi.org/10.1177/2378023120977727.

———. 2020b. *Taking America Back for God: Christian Nationalism in the United States.* New York: Oxford University Press.

Whitehead, Andrew L., Samuel L. Perry, and Joseph O. Baker. 2018. "Make America Christian Again: Christian Nationalism and Voting for Donald Trump in the 2016 Presidential Election." *Sociology of Religion* 79(2): 147–71.

Whitehead, Andrew L., Landon Schnabel, and Samuel L. Perry. 2018. "Gun Control in the Crosshairs: Christian Nationalism and Opposition to Stricter Gun Laws." *Socius* 4:1–13.

Williams, David R. 2012. "Miles to Go Before We Sleep." *Journal of Health and Social Behavior* 53(3): 279–95.

Williams, David R., and Selina A. Mohammed. 2013. "Racism and Health I: Pathways and Scientific Evidence." *American Behavioral Scientist* 57(8): 1152–73.

Williams, Jordan. 2020. "Videos Show Conservative Activists Discussing Limiting Mail-In Voting." The Hill, October 14, 2020. https://thehill.com/homenews/campaign/521054-videos-show-conservative-activists-discussing-limiting-mail-in-voting.

Williamson, Sarah, and Matthew Carnes. 2013. "Partisanship, Christianity, and Women in the Legislature: Determinants of Parental Leave Policy in U.S. States." *Social Science Quarterly* 94(4): 1084–101.

Wilson, Angelia R., and Paul A. Djupe. 2020. "Communicating in Good Faith?" *Politics and Religion* 13(2): 385–414.

Wingfield, Mark. 2020. "MacArthur Asserts 'There Is No Pandemic.'" Baptist News Global, September 3, 2020. https://baptistnews.com/article/macarthur-asserts-there-is-no-pandemic/.

Wittenberg-Cox, Avivah. 2020. "What Do Countries with the Best Coronavirus Responses Have in Common? Women Leaders." *Forbes*, April 13, 2020. https://www.forbes.com/sites/avivahwittenbergcox/2020/04/13/what-do-countries-with-the-best-coronavirus-reponses-have-in-common-women-leaders/.

Wolbrecht, Christina, and David E. Campbell. 2017. "Role Models Revisited: Youth, Novelty, and the Impact of Female Candidates." *Politics, Groups, and Identities* 5(3): 418–34.

Wong, Janelle S. 2015. "The Role of Born-Again Identity on the Political Attitudes of Whites, Blacks, Latinos, and Asian Americans." *Politics and Religion* 8(4): 641–78.

———. 2018a. "The Evangelical Vote and Race in the 2016 Presidential Election." *Journal of Race, Ethnicity, and Politics* 3(1): 81–106.

———. 2018b. *Immigrants, Evangelicals, and Politics in an Era of Demographic Change.* New York: Russell Sage Foundation.

Wood, Daniel. 2020. "As Pandemic Deaths Add Up, Racial Disparities Persist—and in Some Cases Worsen." NPR, September 23, 2020. https://www.npr.org/sections/health-shots/2020/09/23/914427907/as-pandemic-deaths-add-up-racial-disparities-persist-and-in-some-cases-worsen.

Wood, Michael, Karen M. Douglas, and Robbie M. Sutton. 2012. "Dead and Alive: Beliefs in Contradictory Conspiracy Theories." *Social Psychological and Personality Science* 3(6): 767–73.

Woodberry, Robert D. 2006. "The Economic Consequences of Pentecostal Belief." *Society* 44(1): 29–35.

World Health Organization. 2021. "World Conference on Social Determinants of Health." World Health Organization, March 7, 2021. https://www.who.int/sdhconference/background/news/facts/en/.

Wright, James D., and Linda L. Marston. 1975. "The Ownership of the Means of Destruction: Weapons in the United States." *Social Problems* 23(1): 93–107.

Wright, James E., and Cullen C. Merritt. 2020. "Social Equity and COVID-19: The Case of African Americans." *Public Administration Review* 80(5): 820–26.

Yamane, David. 2016. "Awash in a Sea of Faith and Firearms: Rediscovering the Connection between Religion and Gun Ownership in America." *Journal for the Scientific Study of Religion* 55(3): 622–36.

Young, Robert L. 1989. "The Protestant Heritage and the Spirit of Gun Ownership." *Journal for the Scientific Study of Religion* 28(3): 300–309.

Young, Robert L., and Carol Y. Thompson. 1995. "Religious Fundamentalism, Punitiveness, and Firearms Ownership." *Journal of Crime and Justice* 18(2): 81–98.

Yukich, Grace, and Penny Edgell, eds. 2020. *Religion Is Raced: Understanding American Religion in the Twenty-First Century.* New York: New York University Press.

Yurieff, Kaya, and Sara Ashley O'Brien. 2020. "Finding God Online: People Turn to Live-Streaming Religious Services during Coronavirus Pandemic." CNN, March 13, 2020. https://www.cnn.com/2020/03/13/tech/religious-services-livestream/index.html.

Zalis, Shelley. 2020. "In the COVID-19 Era, Female Leaders Are Shining—Here's Why." NBC, June 9, 2020. https://www.nbcnews.com/know-your-value/feature/covid-19-era-female-leaders-are-shining-here-s-why-ncna1227931.

Zapata, Oscar. 2018. "Turning to God in Tough Times? Human versus Material Losses from Climate Disasters in Canada." *Economics of Disasters and Climate Change* 2(3): 259–81.

Zaveri, Mihir, and Johnny Diaz. 2020. "Paula White Says Video About 'Satanic Pregnancies' Was Taken Out of Context." *New York Times*, January 27, 2020. https://www.nytimes.com/2020/01/27/us/politics/paula-white-miscarriage-video.html.

Zimmer, Carl. 2020. "Most New York Coronavirus Cases Came from Europe, Genomes Show." *The New York Times*, April 8, 2020. https://www.nytimes.com/2020/04/08/science/new-york-coronavirus-cases-europe-genomes.html.

Zylstra, Sarah Eekhoff. 2017. "The Life and Times of Redeemer Presbyterian Church." Gospel Coalition, May 22, 2017. https://www.thegospelcoalition.org/article/life-and-times-of-redeemer-presbyterian-church/.

Contributors

Daniel Bennett is Associate Professor of Political Science at John Brown University and Assistant Director for the Center for Faith and Flourishing. He is author of *Defending Faith: The Politics of the Christian Conservative Legal Movement* (Kansas, 2017) and has contributed essays to *Religion and Politics*, *Christianity Today*, and *The Gospel Coalition*, among others.

Kraig Beyerlein is Associate Professor in the Department of Sociology, Director of the Center for the Study of Religion and Society, at the University of Notre Dame, a faculty affiliate at the Center for the Study of Social Movements, a faculty fellow at the Kroc Institute for International Peace Studies, and a faculty fellow at the Institute for Latino Studies. His research and teaching focuses on the intersection of religion and collective action, especially civic engagement and protest activity. Published articles on these and related topics appear in the *American Sociological Review*, *Journal for the Scientific Study of Religion*, *Mobilization*, *Poetics*, *Politics and Religion*, *Social Forces*, *Social Problems*, *Social Science Research*, *Sociological Methods and Research*, and the *Sociology of Religion*.

Cammie Jo Bolin is an Assistant Professor of Political Science at University at Albany, SUNY. Her research interests include identity, participation, and women's leadership in political and religious contexts. With Benjamin Knoll, she is coauthor of *She Preached the Word: Women's Ordination in Modern America* (Oxford University Press, 2018). She holds a B.A. in politics and history from Centre College and a Ph.D. in American government from Georgetown University.

Ryan Burge is an Assistant Professor of Political Science at Eastern Illinois University. He is the author of *The Nones: Where They Came From, Who They Are, and Where They Are Going* as well as *20 Myths about Religion and Politics in America*. He has published over two dozen peer-reviewed articles in a variety of outlets in the social sciences. In addition, he has written editorials for the *New York Times* and the *Wall Street Journal*. His work has appeared in a variety of additional outlets including the *Washington Post*, NPR, NBC News, MSNBC, Fox News, CNN, Vox, C-SPAN, *Christianity Today*, and *Religion News Service*. He is the cofounder and frequent contributor to Religion in Public, a forum for scholars of religion and politics to make their work accessible to a more general audience.

Ryon J. Cobb is Assistant Professor of Sociology at the University of Georgia. His program of research centers on the causes and consequences of racial stratification in the United States. This includes examining how perceived discrimination relates to biological and mortality risk among older adults and assesses whether this relationship varies with one's racial self-classification, with a separate line of work operationalizing the idea that racial identification is a multidimensional social construct. He has published in *Sociology of Religion, Journal for the Scientific Study of Religion, Social Forces*, and *Journal of Immigrant and Minority Health*, among many others.

Melissa Deckman is the Chief Executive Officer of Public Religion Research Institute (PRRI). She is author of *Tea Party Women: Mama Grizzlies, Grassroots Activists and the Changing Face of the American Right* (NYU Press, 2016) and writes about gender, religion, and politics. Her first book *School Board Battles: The Christian Right in Local Politics* (Georgetown University Press, 2005) won the American Political Science Association's Hubert Morken Award for the best book on religion and politics. Her new work focuses on Generation Z's political engagement.

Paul A. Djupe directs the Data for Political Research program at Denison University and is an affiliated scholar with PRRI. He is the book series editor of Religious Engagement in Democratic Politics (Temple University Press) and coeditor of the *Oxford Research Encyclopedia of Politics and Religion* (Oxford, 2020) and *The Evangelical Crackup: The Future of the Evangelical-Republican Coalition* (Temple, 2018). He is the cocreator of and a frequent contributor to religioninpublic.blog and regularly contributes to media coverage of American religion and politics.

Amanda Friesen is Associate Professor of Political Science and Gender, Sexuality, and Women's Studies at the University of Western Ontario and the Canada Research Chair in Political Psychology (Tier 2). She researches and teaches about the intersection of gender, religion, and personality with political engagement, using psychological methods and theory to explore these domains. Her work has appeared in *Political Behavior*, the *International Journal of Public Opinion Research, Politics and the Life Sciences, Social Science Quarterly, Politics and Gender*, and *Politics and Religion*.

Joshua B. Grubbs, Ph.D., is an Assistant Professor of psychology at Bowling Green State University. His work generally focuses on personality, addiction, and religion. He maintains a particular interest in the intersection of personality traits and moral values in predicting controversial behavior.

Contributors

Donald Haider-Markel is Professor of Political Science at the University of Kansas. His research and teaching focuses on the representation of group interests in politics and policy and the dynamics between public opinion, political behavior, and public policy.

Ian Huff is a Senior Research Associate at Public Religion Research Institute. He brings expertise in strategic public opinion research with a focus on elections and issue advocacy. Prior to joining PRRI, he worked for several years as an analyst at the Feldman Group, managing survey research for campaigns for the Senate, House, and governorships, as well as for issue advocacy and labor groups. Before entering the research field, he spent several election cycles working as a campaign field staffer in Virginia and Florida.

Natalie Jackson is the research director at Public Religion Research Institute and has held senior and management positions in media, academia, and nonprofit organizations. Natalie received her Ph.D. in political science from the University of Oklahoma and was a postdoctoral associate at the Duke University Initiative on Survey Methodology. Her work has appeared in the peer-reviewed journals *Electoral Studies* and *Social Science Quarterly*, as well as in several edited volumes.

Robert P. Jones is the President and founder of Public Religion Research Institute (PRRI). He received his Ph.D. in religion from Emory University, an M.Div. from Southwestern Baptist Theological Seminary, and a B.S. in computing science and mathematics from Mississippi College. He is author of *White Too Long: The Legacy of White Supremacy in American Christianity*, which won a 2021 American Book Award, and *The End of White Christian America*, which won the 2019 Grawemeyer Award in Religion. Jones writes regularly on politics, culture, and religion for *The Atlantic* online, NBC Think, and other outlets.

Jason Klocek is Assistant Professor in the School of Politics and International Relations at the University of Nottingham. His work has appeared in the *Journal of Conflict Resolution*, the *Journal for the Social Scientific Study of Religion*, and a number of edited volumes.

Benjamin R. Knoll manages the Survey and Analytics Hub at APQC, the world's foremost authority in benchmarking, best practices, process and performance improvement, and knowledge management. He was previously the John Marshall Harlan Associate Professor of Politics at Centre College in Danville, Kentucky. He earned a Ph.D. in political science from the University of Iowa. With Cammie Jo Bolin, he is the coauthor of *She Preached the Word: Women's Ordination in Modern America* (Oxford University Press, 2018).

Andrew R. Lewis is Associate Professor of Political Science at the University of Cincinnati and a public fellow at PRRI. He is author of *The Rights Turn in Conservative Christian Politics: How Abortion Transformed the Culture Wars* (Cambridge, 2017), and his work has appeared in several social science journals and popular media outlets.

Jianing Li (Ph.D., University of Wisconsin-Madison) is an Assistant Professor in the Department of Communication at the University of South Florida. Her work examines the intersection of mis/disinformation, contentious politics, and social inequality. Her work has appeared in the *Journal of Communication, Human Communication Research, Political Communication, Mass Communication and Society,* and *Social Media + Society.*

Natasha Altema McNeely is Assistant Professor of Political Science at the University of Texas Rio Grande Valley. Her research areas within U.S. government and politics include race and ethnicity, political institutions, political behavior, and voting, campaigns, and elections. She has recently started to examine the political ramifications of Black maternal mortality.

Matthew R. Miles is Professor of Political Science at Brigham Young University, Idaho. He has published over a dozen articles and a book exploring the interaction between individual traits and institutional arrangements. Much of that work focuses on how identities influence political and religious attitudes and behaviors.

Shayla F. Olson is a Ph.D. candidate at the University of Michigan. She studies American political behavior and political communication, with a particular focus on religion and racial attitudes. In her research, she utilizes a combination of text-as-data and experimental methods to analyze racialized political learning within churches and its effect on the racial attitudes of white evangelicals.

Diana Orcés is Assistant Director of Research at Public Religion Research Institute and has held positions in academia and nonprofit organizations. Prior to joining PRRI, she was a research analyst at the American Immigration Council (AIC), Assistant Professor in the Department of Political Science at Oakland University, and a researcher for the Latin American Public Opinion Project (LAPOP). She has published in such journals as the *Annals of the American Academy of Political and Social Science, Latin American Politics and Society, Latin American Research Review,* and *Studies in Comparative International Development.*

Samuel L. Perry is Associate Professor of Sociology and Religious Studies at the University of Oklahoma. His work examines the interplay of power and culture within the empirical contexts of American religion, race relations, politics, and sexuality. He is coauthor of *Taking America Back for God: Christian Nationalism in the United States.*

Jenna Reinbold is Associate Professor of Religion at Colgate University, where she studies contemporary intersections of religion and politics, religion and the culture wars, and religion and human rights. She has published in the *Journal of Church and State* and the *Journal of the American Academy of Religion.* Her recent book, *Seeing the Myth in Human Rights* (University of Pennsylvania, 2017), received an Award for Excellence in the Study of Religion from the American Academy of Religion.

Kelly Rolfes-Haase is an Analyst at the U.S. Government Accountability Office (GAO). Her research areas of expertise include American public policy, policy analysis and evaluation, and the study of identity and politics. She holds a B.A. in anthropology from Rollins College, a joint M.P.P.-M.A. in international affairs and M.A. in American government from Georgetown University, and a Ph.D. in American government from Georgetown University.

Stella M. Rouse is Professor in the Department of Government and Politics and Director of the Center for Democracy and Civic Engagement at the University of Maryland. She is coauthor (with Ashley Ross) of *The Politics of Millennials: Political Beliefs and Policy Preferences of America's Most Diverse Generation* (University of Michigan Press, 2018) and author of *Latinos in the Legislative Process: Interests and Influence* (Cambridge University Press, 2013). She has published articles on Millennials and attitudes about climate change and immigration, the effects of gender on attitudes about COVID-19 among Generation Z, how electoral structures influence minority representation, and the role of religion on ethnoracial political attitudes.

Angel Saavedra Cisneros is Assistant Professor of Political Science at Bowdoin College. His work focuses on the role of ethnic identity in political behavior and psychology. He also looks at how identity and immigration interact across different contexts.

Justin A. Tucker is Director of the Center for Public Policy and Associate Professor of Political Science at California State University, Fullerton. He specializes in research design and analysis, program evaluation, and public policy.

Dilara K. Üsküp is Joint Assistant Professor in Internal Medicine at Charles R. Drew University of Medicine and Science and in Family Medicine at the University of California, Los Angeles. Her research investigates the ways religious and political institutions, attitudes, and ideology interact and shape health behavior to inform public policy. Presently, Dr. Üsküp is a coprincipal investigator of an NIH-funded grant (5T32MH109205-03) increasing the use of technology to deploy preexposure prophylaxis (PrEP) for HIV prevention. Her burgeoning research portfolio includes the areas of politics and theology, cannabis and social equity, and health policy. Dr. Üsküp is a joint doctoral graduate of the University of Chicago's Department of Political Science and the Divinity School.

Abigail Vegter is Assistant Professor of Political Science at Berry College, specializing in American politics, public policy, and research methodology. She maintains an active research agenda focusing on the relationship between religion and gun ownership in the United States, among other things, with publications in *Politics and Religion*, *Journal for the Scientific Study of Religion*, and *Interest Groups and Advocacy*.

Michael W. Wagner is Professor of Journalism and Mass Communication and Director of the Center for Communication at Civic Renewal at the University of Wisconsin–Madison and holds affiliations with the Department of Political Science, the La Follette School of Public Affairs, the Elections Research Center, the Mass Communication Research Center, and the Tommy G. Thompson Center for Public Leadership. He is the founding editor of the Forum section of the journal *Political Communication*. A winner of multiple research, teaching, and service awards, his work focuses on examining how the flow of information in various contexts affects public opinion and political behavior. His research appears in such outlets as *Journal of Communication*, *Annual Review of Political Science*, *Human Communication Research*, and *Politics and Religion*. His most recent book, *Mediated Democracy: Politics, the News and Citizenship in the 21stCentury* (Sage CQ Press) was published in the fall of 2020.

Andrew L. Whitehead is Associate Professor of Sociology at Indiana University–Purdue University Indianapolis and is Codirector of the Association of Religion Data Archives. His work focuses on religious nationalism, politics, sexuality, and childhood disability. He is coauthor of *Taking America Back for God: Christian Nationalism in the United States*.

Angelia R. Wilson is Professor of Politics at the University of Manchester. She has published widely on the intersection of religion, values, and politics in America with five books and several academic journal articles. An experienced political commentator on American politics, Wilson has appeared on BBC News, BBC World Service, *BBC Breakfast*, *Newsround*, and various other international news outlets. As a preacher's daughter from the Bible belt and internationally respected academic, Wilson brings both an authentic and measured voice to the academic analysis of the American Christian Right.

Index

Abbott, Greg, 5
abortion, 85, 102, 123, 124–125, 135, 230
Affordable Care Act (ACA), 63
African Americans. *See* Black Americans
agnostics, 201
Agudath Israel Synagogue, 113–114, 120
AIDS, 130
Alito, Samuel, 116, 119
Alliance Defending Freedom, 100, 102–103, 109, 129. *See also* Christian Legal Movement
American Center for Law and Justice, 103. *See also* Christian Legal Movement
antichrist, 20
Arizona, 137
Armageddon, 25
Asian Americans, 78–79, 81, 83, 87, 89–90, 93–95, 136, 171–173, 176, 180–181, 185–187, 189–190, 193
atheists, 116, 200–201
attendance. *See* services, religious
Australians, 39
authoritarianism, 101

baby boomers, 235
Barr, William, 126
Barrett, Amy Coney, 119, 127
Bauer, Gary, 124

beliefs, religious, 13–14, 87. *See also* prosperity gospel
Beshear, Andy, 103
Bible, 57, 230–231, 241; literal views of, 143, 146, 151–152, 165, 168, 231, 234, 237
Biden, Joe, 80, 107, 125, 137, 242
bike shops, 120
Black Americans, 42, 43, 45, 46, 64, 78–82, 83, 87, 89–90, 93–95, 119, 136, 244; differential effects of COVID-19 on, 69, 171 (*see also* COVID-19, racial disparities of); enslavement of, 73–74; police treatment of, 47, 49, 52, 75; religious affiliation of, 185–187; religious service attendance of, 77, 166–167, 175–177, 217, 219, 221, 224, 228; segregation of, 71, 75, 172; strength of faith and, 180–181, 189–190, 192–195, 212; trust in science and, 179–180 (*see also* trust in science/scientists). *See also* racism
Black church, 76–77, 82, 83–84, 136, 172–173, 187, 240; variability within, 86. *See also* Church of God in Christ
Black Lives Matter (BLM), 42, 122–123, 127, 131, 134–136, 139, 242, 244; public opinion on, 131
bleach, 76
born-again Christians. *See* evangelicals

British, 39
Brown, Khari, 95
Buddhists, 33, 187, 200
Bush, George, 127

California, 61, 103, 109, 117, 129
Calvary Chapel v. Sisolak (2020), 118
Canadians, 39, 212
Catholics, 37–38, 84, 104, 113–115, 118, 124, 148–149, 151, 153, 186–187, 200–201, 207, 213, 217, 219, 221, 228
Centers for Disease Control, 58, 73, 74, 104, 141, 149, 152
China, 6, 32, 64, 66, 124
Christian Coalition, 122
Christian legal movement (CLM), 100–104, 108–110, 120, 129; composition of, 102
Christian nationalism, 43–44, 45, 52, 53, 55, 58–60, 62–67, 101; and authority, 57; defined, 55–56; measures of, 56; and racial differences in effect, 65–66; and racism, 64–65, 242; and science, 57, 60, 241
Christian Right, 122–127, 130–139. *See also* Christian Legal Movement, and specific organizations
Christianity Today, 123
Church of God in Christ (COGIC), 3, 86
Civil Rights Movement, 77, 124
clergy, 3, 17, 77–81, 83–84, 103, 122, 129, 141, 159–160, 228, 232, 234, 240, 243; address of the coronavirus, 88–90, 92–96, 122; encouragement for members to attend in person, 88, 90–91, 95; misperception of, 88; representative role of, 86
collective action, 15, 16, 27, 77; problems, 1, 13, 60
collectivism, 44, 52
Collins, Francis, 3
confirmation bias, 31
congregations (religious), 2, 87–88, 116–118; burden felt by COVID-19 restrictions, 111–121; closure/openness of, 2, 5, 17, 42, 43, 77, 90–91, 104, 138; as essential, 116–118, 128–129, 133; mitigation strategies of, 3, 85, 103, 109, 138; offering remote worship by, 91, 114; partnerships of with public health providers, 85; racial distribution in, 85; reliance on, 16; reopening of, 2, 17; social distancing in, 6,
84, 90; social service provision of, 85. *See also* services, religious
Congress, 207
conservative Christians. *See* evangelicals
conspiracy beliefs, 6, 23, 28, 30–31, 241; determinants of adopting, 29–33; health effects of believing, 40, 76; religious effects on, 28, 30–31, 35–39; role of elites in promoting, 5, 32–33, 76; survey measurement of, 33. *See also* QAnon
conspiracy theories. *See* conspiracy beliefs
contraception, 75, 125
cooperation, 1, 4
Copeland, Kenneth, 14
Coronavirus. *See* COVID-19
Cotton, Tom, 132
COVID-19: as "Chinese Flu," 5, 28–29, 64–66, 76, 83, 127, 135 (*see also* conspiracy beliefs); concern with, 15, 50, 52–53, 77–78, 109, 225; death toll of, xi, 1, 54, 239; disease, description of, 1; hysteria over, 19, 20, 23, 178–179, 230, 232, 235, 236; misinformation about, 28, 32–33, 54, 55, 109, 140, 174 (*see also* conspiracy beliefs); partisan concentration of, 1, 229; perceptions of cases, 141, 147, 153; personal behaviors regarding, 58–59, 127, 130; precautions regarding, 54, 55, 58–59; racial disparities and, 64–65, 69–72, 81, 83, 94; rates of, 2, 5, 13, 32, 54; regional concentration of, 1, 54; stimulus package for, 128; threat from, 16, 20, 22–23, 47, 86–87, 95, 114, 178, 229–230; vaccines for (*see* vaccines); variants of, 4; waves of, 1, 17, 32
creationism, 57
crime, 46, 47
culture wars, 54, 99, 100–101, 103, 109, 121
Cuomo, Andrew, 110

Davis, Kim, 102
Democratic Party, 17, 26, 47, 55, 122, 128, 173, 201–202, 230, 231, 235, 236
denominations, religious, xi
devil, 13, 16, 20, 25, 42
disability, 244
discrimination, 5, 72, 101, 110, 115–120, 124, 126, 129
disgust, 101
distrust. *See* trust
Dobson, James, 124

dogmatism, 34
Dolben Act, 73
Dollar, Creflo, 14

Easter, 226, 233
economy, 62
end times, 21, 25, 27
establishment clause, 112, 120. *See also* First Amendment, religious freedom
ethnoreligious, xi
eugenics, 75
Europe, 239
evangelicals, 15, 35, 43, 44, 47, 50, 52, 114, 116, 118, 179; measurement of, 33, 49; media usage, 142, 147; religious service attendance, 217, 221, 224, 175–176; resistance to government health orders, 43, 99, 101; and sources of pandemic information trust, 141, 149, 151; strength of faith and, 193; support for Trump, 33, 143; theology/beliefs of, 15, 87; and the Trump Administration, 36, 203
Evangelical Advisory Board, 132
Evers, Tony, 61
evil, 14, 16, 20, 25–26, 31
exclusive values, 24–25

faith healing, 15, 24, 30. *See also* prosperity gospel
faith, 243; strength of, 180, 188–189, 192–193, 194. *See also* religiosity
Faith and Freedom Coalition (FFC), 122–124, 127, 128, 130, 133–138
Falwell, Jerry, Jr., 124
Family Research Council (FRC), 122–131, 134–138
Fauci, Dr. Anthony, 140
Fea, John, 124
Federalist Society, 116, 126
Firearm Industry Trade Association, 42
First Amendment, 41, 42, 100–101, 109–110, 112, 128, 229; weaponizing of, 101. *See also* establishment clause, free exercise clause, religious freedom
First Liberty, 100, 103, 110. *See also* Christian Legal Movement
Florida, 220
Floyd, George, 9, 42, 46, 47, 130–131, 135. *See also* Black Lives Matter, protests
Food and Drug Administration (FDA), 32

Fox News, 34, 38, 99, 140, 147, 153–154, 226, 229, 231
Freedom Sunday, 129, 137
free exercise clause, 112–115, 117–120. *See also* religious freedom
fundamentalism, 45
funerals, 3

Galli, Mark, 123
gender, 50, 163, 185, 193, 232; and leadership, 160, 169
Generation X, 232, 235, 236
Generation Z, 235
Georgia, 127, 133, 136
Gohmert, Louie, 137
Google Trends, 47–48
Gorsuch, Neil, 109, 116, 118–120
government health orders, 15, 17, 20, 42, 46, 55, 58, 61–62, 76, 81, 84, 99, 100, 109, 111, 116–117, 123, 126, 128–129, 133, 219–220, 225, 226, 240; attitudes about, 55, 60, 63, 67, 105–106; defiance of, 21, 23–24, 25–26, 42, 43, 84, 88, 92–95, 100, 102–106, 109, 111–112, 117, 129–130, 240. *See also* Christian Legal Movement
Graham, Franklin, 61, 124, 132, 202
guns, 230; background checks for purchasing, 45; ownership of, 48, 205; policy, 47, 56; purchasing of, 41, 43–53; sales of, 41; shops, 41

Hawley, Josh, 137
health, 71–72, 74; maternal, 72, 74–75; social determinants of, 70–72
health care: access to, 5, 69, 72–75, 83; utilization of, 73–74, 76
health orders. *See* government health orders
Hibbs, Jack, 137–138
Hice, Jody, 137
Hindu Americans, 33, 187, 200
Hispanic Americans. *See* Latina/o/x Americans
houses of worship. *See* congregations
housing, 71
Huckabee, Mike, 60, 124
hunting, 44
Hyde Amendment, 125
hydroxychloroquine, 32, 76

ideology, political, 193, 205
immigrants/immigration, 5, 56, 65–66

Inazu, John, 109
incautious behaviors. *See* COVID-19, personal behaviors regarding; COVID-19, precautions regarding
independents, 194
individualism, 15, 26, 44, 52
influenza pandemic, xi
Institutional Review Boards, 74
insurrection (Jan. 6, 2021). *See* January 6th
Insurrection Act, 132
Israel, 124
Italy, 213

Jackson, Jesse, 77
Jakes, T. D., 14
January 6th (2021), 137–138, 242
Jeffress, Robert, 124, 132
Jewish Americans, 3, 33, 113–115, 119, 151, 155, 186, 200, 228
Jim Crow Laws, 74
Johnson, Mike, 137
Johnson Amendment, 125

Kavanaugh, Brett, 116, 119, 120, 127
Kentucky, 102, 103
King, Martin Luther, Jr., 244
Kirk, Charlie, 64, 132
Krugman, Paul, 110

Lacks, Henrietta, 75
Land, Richard, 124
Latina/o/x Americans, 70, 78–79, 81–82, 83–84, 87, 89–95, 136, 171, 176–177, 180–181, 185–187, 189–190, 192–195
leadership, 161–162, 164, 169
Lewis, John, 77
LGBTQ+ Americans, 120, 188
libertarianism, 61, 63
Liberty Counsel, 100, 102. *See also* Christian Legal Movement
Liberty University, 64
lockdowns. *See* government health orders, stay at home orders
Loeffler, Kelly, 137

MacArthur, John, 55, 61, 103, 109
magical thinking, 28, 30–32; and the prosperity gospel, 30. *See also* faith healing
Maine, 129, 141
Mainline Protestants, 44, 147, 151, 186, 217, 219, 221, 228, 234

Manichean thinking, 31–32, 34, 36–39. *See also* evil, dogmatism
March for Life, 125
mask mandate, 17, 55, 60, 117. *See also* government health orders
mask wearing, 3, 225, 239
Massachusetts, 70
Masterpiece Cake Shop v. Colorado Civil Rights Commission, Espinoza v. Montana Department of Revenue, 126
McConnell, Michael J., 117
Meadows, Mark, 124, 137
media: religiosity and consumption of, 143–144. *See also* trust, in the media
Medicaid, 75
medical mistrust. *See* trust, in doctors/health professionals
Medicare, 74
megachurch, 20, 24, 55, 61, 109
Metaxas, Eric, 124
Michigan, 17, 220
Middle Eastern Americans, 193
Millennials, 184, 186–188
Minnesota, 129
Mississippi, 129
mistrust. *See* trust
Moore, Johnnie, 132
Mormons/Latter-day Saints, 151, 187, 200
Multiracial Americans, 193
Murphy, Greg, 127
Muslim Americans, 33, 101, 108, 151, 155, 187, 199–200, 206–208, 242

National Research Act, 74
Native/Indigenous Americans, 171, 193
natural disasters, 212
Neuhaus, Richard J., 240
Nevada, 103, 109, 114, 118, 120
New York, 41, 109, 118, 120, 210–211, 242
New Zealand, 212
9/11, 46, 199, 210–211, 213, 243
non-Christians, xi. *See also* Buddhists, Muslim, Jewish, Hindu Americans, and nones
nones, 33, 37, 149, 151, 185–186, 217, 228, 243
nonreligious. *See* nones
Norplant, 75
Norquist, Samah, 126
North Carolina, 75
NRA (National Rifle Association), 41

Obama, Barack, 46, 127
Obergefel v. Hodges (2015), 102, 126
Ohio, 2, 15, 17
Oklahoma, 220
Oregon, 102
Orthodox Christians, 187
Ossof, Jon, 137
Osteen, Joel, 14, 16, 24

Pacific Islander, 193
pandemic. *See* COVID-19
partisanship, xi, 19, 22–26, 29, 46, 49, 50, 51, 55, 80, 99, 101–102, 104–110, 127, 131, 147, 149–152, 168, 177, 180, 185, 193, 197, 199, 206, 208, 229, 232, 235–236, 240
Paxton, Ken, 41
Peale, Norman Vincent, 19
Pelosi, Nancy, 128
Pence, Mike, 32, 103
Pennsylvania, 137
pentecostals, 24
Perdue, David, 137
Perkins, Tony, 122, 124, 126, 129, 131, 134–135, 137–139
Planned Parenthood, 75, 128, 129, 134
polarization, 53, 60, 67, 100–101, 103–104, 107–110
political institutions, 162–163
Pompeo, Mike, 124, 126
Pope Francis, 114, 202
prayer, 39, 190, 192–193, 211, 213–219, 227, 243
prejudice, 244
presidential election of 2020, xi, 47, 50–52
prisons, 64–66, 75
prosocial behaviors: religion and, 185, 193, 241
prosperity gospel, 13, 87, 91, 95, 109; beliefs of, 13–15, 31, 91; distribution of, 18–19, 26, 34; effects of, 14–15, 16, 22–25; links to other religious attributes, 19, 25; measurement of, 18; and partisanship, 19, 22–24; and race, 25–26, 91, 240, 244; reach of, 14
Protestants, 44, 114–116, 119. *See also evangelicals, Mainline Protestants*
protests, xi, 47, 104, 122–123, 131–135; effects on gun purchasing, 43, 45, 46, 50, 51–53. *See also* Black Lives Matter
PRRI (Public Religion Research Institute), xi, xiii, 28–29, 33y, 101, 116

public health orders. *See* government health orders
Puerto Rico, 75
punitiveness, 45
purity, 5

QAnon, 3

racism, 55, 56, 64–68, 69–73, 83, 135
Reagan, Ronald, 115, 127, 130
Reed, Ralph, 122, 124, 132–133, 136, 137–139
religion, 55; dogmatic, 5; online meetings of (*see* services, religious); and racial minorities, 6; roles of, 4–5, 6
religiosity, 39, 43, 44, 49, 50, 53, 55, 62, 67; racial differences and, 84–85, 95
religious freedom, 23, 25–26, 61, 99–104, 108–110, 112, 114–119, 123, 124–126, 129, 135, 139, 228–229, 237, 241, 242; and discrimination, 101; jurisprudence concerning, 100, 103, 109–110, 111–119; public opinion on, 101, 104–107, 116, 119. *See also* services religious
Religious Freedom Restoration Act (RFRA, 1993), 101
religious institutions. *See* congregations
religious liberty. *See* religious freedom
religious traditions, 19
Reno, R. R., 15
Republican Party, 17, 19, 26, 47, 55, 60, 104, 122, 154, 161, 173, 201–202
research designs, 7
Roman Catholic Diocese of Brooklyn v. Cuomo (2020), 109, 118
Romney, Mitt, 116
Roy, Chip, 137
rural areas, 44

same-sex marriage, 25, 56, 85, 101
Sanger, Margaret, 75, 134
Satan. *See* devil
Scalise, Mike, 127
Schindler, Oskar, 124
Schlapp, Matt, 137
science: denial of, 29–30, 230; relationship with religion of, 3, 30
Second Amendment, 41
services, religious, 77, 111, 114, 163; attendance of, 34, 38–39, 59, 62, 77, 88, 90, 91–92, 95, 168, 187, 191, 211,

services, religious *(continued)*
  213–221, 223–225, 242; cancellation of, 165–166, 176, 213; encouragement to attend in person, 88, 90–91, 95; as spreader events, 42, 43, 55, 61; virtual or online, 77, 91, 99, 111, 114, 211, 213–219, 221–224, 244
Shelter-in-place. *See* stay-at-home orders
Sherbert test, 112–113
silent generation, 235
Sims, J. Marion, 74
slavery, 73–75. *See also* Black Americans, enslavement of
social distancing, 6, 27, 88, 91–92, 95, 130, 135, 177; defiance of, 16. *See also* congregations, social distancing in
social justice, 85
social networks, 4, 16, 27
Solid Rock Church, 5
Soros, George, 136
South Dakota, 220
Spell, Tony, 15
spirituality, 213
Staver, Mat, 103
"stay at home" orders, 17, 41, 47, 86, 117–118, 129, 184, 191, 192–194, 202. *See also* government health orders

Tennessee, 220
Texas, 83
Thanksgiving, 111
Thomas, Clarence, 119
Thomas More Law Center, 100, 103. *See also* Christian Legal Movement
threat, 5, 46, 53, 101–102, 123, 135, 139; elite communicated, 5
Tocqueville, Alexis de, 4–5, 240
tolerance, 101, 198
transgender, 125
travel ban, 64
Trump, Donald J., 19, 21, 29, 41, 80, 83, 102, 107–108, 110, 123–124, 127, 131–139, 202, 226–227, 234, 243; administration of, 21, 29, 32, 103, 124–125, 129; approval of, 38; COVID-19 diagnosis of, 32, 76; and pandemic information, 33, 34, 58, 60, 64, 83, 104, 130, 140, 149, 208, 242; at St. John's Church, 42; support for, 60; 2016 election of, 26
Trump, Donald Jr., 104
trust, 76, 81; in clergy, 77–82, 160, 164, 167; in doctors/health/medical professionals, 70, 72–75, 77–82, 106; in government, 2, 21, 29, 34–35, 38, 72, 76, 83, 141, 151–152; in the media, 29, 55, 60, 99, 142, 152; in others, 2, 16, 21, 24–26, 29, 45, 53; in science/scientists, 29, 43, 55, 78–80, 142, 178–179
Tuskegee Study, 73–74

unaffiliated. *See* nones
unemployment, 184
unrest, civil. *See* protests
unvaccinated population, 4
U.S. Supreme Court, 242

vaccine(s), 4, 63, 67, 70, 76, 82, 239, 240, 241, 242, 243
values, religious, 14, 24–25, 42
victimization, 46
Virginia, 102, 103, 134
voter fraud, 127, 136

Warnock, Raphael, 77, 137
White, Paula, 16
Wiccan, 187
Wisconsin, 61, 141
work, remote, 71
World Health Organization (WHO), 32
worldviews. *See* beliefs, religious, and values, religious
Wuhan, China, 6, 32. *See also* China, conspiracy belief

xenophobia, 63–68

Zoom, 111

www.ingramcontent.com/pod-product-compliance
Lightning Source LLC
Chambersburg PA
CBHW042116300426
44117CB00020B/2968